CLASSICAL TASTE IN AMERICA

1800 – 1840

CLASSICAL TASTE IN AMERICA
1800—1840

Wendy A. Cooper

The Baltimore Museum of Art
Abbeville Press Publishers
New York • London • Paris

This book was copublished by Abbeville Press and The Baltimore Museum of Art in conjunction with the exhibition *Classical Taste in America, 1800–1840,* organized and circulated by the Baltimore Museum:

The Baltimore Museum of Art
Baltimore, Maryland
June 27–September 26, 1993

Mint Museum of Art
Charlotte, North Carolina
November 20, 1993–March 13, 1994

The Museum of Fine Arts, Houston
Houston, Texas
May 1–July 24, 1994

Editor: Walton Rawls   Designer: Monika Keano   Assistant designer: Ronald R. Misiur   Production editor: Alice Gray
Production manager: Simone Rene

Library of Congress Cataloging-in-Publication Data

Cooper, Wendy A.
    Classical taste in America 1800–1840 / Wendy A. Cooper.
        p. cm.
    "The Baltimore Museum of Art, Baltimore, Maryland, June 27–September 26,
1993; Mint Museum of Art, Charlotte, North Carolina, November 20,
1993–March 13, 1994; The Museum of Fine Arts, Houston, Houston, Texas, May
1–July 24, 1994"—T.p. verso.
    Includes bibliographical references and index.
    ISBN 1-55859-385-3
        1. Neoclassicism (Art)—United States—Exhibitions. 2. Art, American—
Exhibitions. 3. Art, Modern—19th century-United States—Exhibitions. I.
Baltimore Museum of Art. II. Mint Museum (Charlotte, N.C.) III. Museum of Fine
Arts, Houston. IV. Title.
    N6510.5.N4C66 1993
    709'73'07475—dc20   93-9784

Author's Note: All measurements cited in picture captions and checklist are overall (height, width, depth), unless otherwise stated.

Front cover/jacket: *Grecian Couch.* See illustration figure 85.   Frontispiece: *Classical Interior.* See illustration figure 79. Title page: *Pier Table* (c. 1830–1840). See illustration figure 102.   Back cover/jacket: Library at "Andalusia." See illustration figure 48.   Spine: See illustration figure 129.   p. 8: Detail, *Curtain Rod* (1833). See illustration figure 135.   pp. 9–12: Detail, *Window Bench* (c. 1808–1810). See illustration figure 84.   p. 13: Detail, *Center Table* (c. 1820–1830). See illustration figure 69.   pp. 15–22: *United States Currency.* See checklist following entry 150.

CONTENTS

Major organizational support for the exhibition
and this publication was provided by
The Henry Luce Foundation, Inc.
National Endowment for the Humanities
National Endowment for the Arts
The Baltimore Sun
Kaufman Americana Foundation

FOREWORD

America's taste for art, learning, interior decoration, fashion, and furnishings in imitation of the ancients was at its most consuming in the early nineteenth century. *Classical Taste in America, 1800–1840* explores the extraordinary extent to which ancient aesthetic forms and intellectual values were embraced by Americans and thus imprinted on the young republic's culture during its early decades.

We are grateful to the Trustees of The Baltimore Museum of Art, under the current leadership of Chairman James S. Riepe, for their unwavering commitment to this ambitious project. The Henry Luce Foundation, Inc., committed major support at the earliest stage of the exhibition's conception, thus lending much-appreciated endorsement to our scholarly effort. We are equally grateful to the National Endowment for the Humanities and to the National Endowment for the Arts for very substantial grants in support of *Classical Taste*. In addition, The Baltimore Sun and the Kaufman Americana Foundation provided important sponsorship assistance. The *Classical Taste* project was also given notable support over four years from two of the Museum's major endowment funds: Maryland National Bank Publications Endowment Fund; and the Alex. Brown & Sons Charitable Foundation Publication Endowment Fund. Supportive contributions came from Mr. Harold Sack; the Elizabeth F. Cheney Foundation; the Museum's Endowment Fund for American Art, made possible by a grant from the children of Jacob and Hilda Blaustein; Mrs. Elaine Wilde; and the Museum's Friends of the American Wing.

Wendy A. Cooper, Curator of Decorative Arts at The Baltimore Museum of Art, dedicated herself to this exhibition and its publication with awesome energy and admirable purpose. We are additionally grateful to Richard L. Bushman for his thoughtful introduction. There is virtually no one on the Museum's staff who has not contributed in a meaningful and substantive way to the realization of this demanding exhibition and its publication. *Classical Taste* exists only because of their outstanding professionalism and committed effort. I also want to acknowledge Richard A. Ransom, Esq., of the Baltimore law firm of Weinberg and Green, whose pro bono legal services were extended to the project on every front.

Finally, I want to express my most sincere personal thanks to our colleagues—Bruce Evans, Director of the Mint Museum of Art in Charlotte, North Carolina, and Peter Marzio, Director of The Museum of Fine Arts, Houston, and every member of their respective staffs—for their commitment and enthusiasm. With their support and participation, it is a pleasure to present *Classical Taste in America, 1800–1840* in our three communities.

Arnold L. Lehman, Director
The Baltimore Museum of Art

PREFACE

To ancient Greece the civilized world has been indebted for more than two thousand years. . . . In Greece, perfection in the fine arts, freedom in government, and virtue in private life, were contemporaneous.

Benjamin Henry Latrobe,
Anniversary Oration, The Society of Artists,
Philadelphia, 1811

During the first four decades of the nineteenth century, America was mesmerized by the classical world. Almost every aspect of American life was affected by a compulsion to emulate classical cultures, whether in architecture, politics, fine arts, education, interior decoration, or dress. So pervasive was this fascination that it produced a huge body of classically inspired artifacts that somehow still seemed distinctively American, despite modern European influences. Complementing these tangible remains of an extraordinary chapter in American taste were influential documents promoting the belief that diligent study of the ancients, the Greeks especially, would reward American society with virtue, morality, and refinement.

America's leaders had understandably turned to ancient political theory for precedents in government, since classical texts had been at the core of American education since the beginnings of this new land. It was a fortunate coincidence that while America was forming a new republic, Europe was actively rediscovering, collecting, and reinterpreting the artifacts of classical antiquity. As had been true throughout the seventeenth and eighteenth centuries, Americans were eager to adopt the most current fashions and styles from abroad. So, in addition to their long-standing assimilation of political ideologies from the ancients, Americans were offered inspiration from the physical remains of antiquity, as reinterpreted by modern Europeans.

Johann Joachim Winckelmann, the great German scholar and leader of the European classical movement, had set the stage for an international classical revival soon after the middle of the eighteenth century. In Rome he produced his most important work, "Reflections on the Imitation of Greek Art in Painting and Sculpture" (1755), which was followed by *The History of Ancient Art* (1764). Winckelmann believed that "There is only one way for the moderns to become great and perhaps unequalled: by imitating the Ancients."[1] His writings nourished several generations of artists and scholars who traveled to Italy to imbibe at the source.

No doubt aware of his continental predecessors, the English artist and engraver Henry Moses expressed the sentiments of numerous contemporaries in 1814 when he wrote, "The study of the unrivalled works of the ancients is essential to the establishment of good taste and correct judgement. . . ." His mentor was Thomas Hope, the eminent collector and designer, "whose knowledge, taste and judgement command the esteem of all who profess and love the fine arts."[2] Like Winckelmann before him, Hope admired the "noble simplicity and calm grandeur" of the finest Greek art.

As noted above, Latrobe believed that the ancient cultures of Greece and Rome, and even Egypt, had provided inspiration for scholars, architects, painters, and sculptors for centuries. The first major revival of classical aesthetics occurred during the Italian Renaissance. At that time, architecture and sculpture were the primary beneficiaries of these classical reinterpretations. The publication of Andrea Palladio's *The Four Books of Architecture* (1571), and the subsequent work of other Renaissance architects created a body of monumental architecture that inspired generations of artists, wealthy gentlemen, and tourists. The discovery of major pieces of classical sculpture encouraged artists to admire and thus model their work after classical interpretations of the human form. Renaissance painters found inspiration in ancient civilizations and drew their subjects from mythology and the lives of the ancients. The creations of Renaissance artists and craftsmen provided an important body of artistic expression that inspired those Americans and Europeans who traveled to Italy in the centuries that followed, and most particularly in the eighteenth and early nineteenth centuries.

The seeds of the next major rekindling of interest in classical art were planted early in the eighteenth century in England and continental Europe. Richard Boyle, Earl of Burlington, became England's principal patron of classical architecture soon after his Grand Tour of 1714–1715. His hero was Palladio and his protégés William Kent and Colin Campbell. For young gentlemen of means, the Grand Tour was expected to foster refined taste as well as to inculcate virtue through exposure to the wonders of Italy and its classical heritage.

One of the most important influences on the classical movement in eighteenth-century Europe was archaeological exploration, beginning with new studies at major sites like Herculaneum in 1738 and Pompeii a decade later. The last quarter of the eighteenth century saw extensive digging at numerous sites in Italy, and this led to the wholesale marketing of classical antiquities in that country and the widespread promotion of classicism. The major collections of sculpture and vases that were subsequently formed in Italy, France, and especially England bear testimony to the depth of interest wealthy travelers took in the remains of antiquity.

In 1733 the Society of the Dilettanti had been founded in England, and while this group of patrons, artists, and architects acquired a reputation for significant imbibing, they were also responsible for the sponsorship of several important publications that precisely illustrated the most significant remains of antiquity, including James Stuart's and Nicholas Revett's *Antiquities of*

Athens, 4 vols. (1762–1816). In addition to publications sponsored by this elite group, numerous other beautifully engraved volumes appeared, including Robert Adam's *Ruins of the Palace of the Emperor Diocletian at Spalatro in Dalmatia* (1764), John Wood's *Ruins of Palmyra* (1753) and *Ruins of Balbec* (1757), and Thomas Major's *Ruins of Paestum* (1768).

Classicism, as expressed in eighteenth- and early nineteenth-century interior decoration, furniture, and furnishings, had two distinct phases, which were manifest in the material productions of both Europe and America. The first phase, early classical style, derived primarily from the Italian travel, the publications, and the work of English architect Robert Adam. While imitation of the ancients in modern architecture was perhaps the most demonstrative and visible expression of the classical movement, the attention to overall interior decorative schemes was a significant outcome.

Acting as both architect and interior designer to the aristocracy of England, Adam coordinated designs for furniture, furnishings, and interior decoration with the architecture. From carpets to wall decoration to ceilings, a new integral harmony was achieved, with designs characterized by their linearity, lightness, and such airy ornament as swags, garlands, and bowknots. The advent of this mode of cohesive interior design began a trend that would be carried to America and expanded upon as the nineteenth century emerged.

The early classical style was first recognized in America just prior to the outbreak of the Revolution, primarily through the importation of goods in the latest style and the arrival of a number of important public objects.[3] Immediately following the Revolution, American artisans embraced this new fashion, and it enjoyed a popularity for more than two decades. The second phase, late classical style, was initiated in France by Napoleon through his architect/designers Charles Percier and Pierre-Leonard Fontaine. Politically as well as artistically, the emperor used the "imitation of the ancients" to promote and strengthen his own position. Because the introduction of this style was closely allied to the Napoleonic Empire, it is sometimes referred to as the Empire style. At the time, it was most often called "Grecian," though "antique," "classical," and "modern" were occasionally used. The term "neoclassicism" was not introduced until the 1880s.

Derived directly from the antique and reinterpreting both Greek and Roman form and ornament, this later phase is generally considered more archaeologically correct, curvilinear, and anthropomorphic than the earlier. Born on the Continent, it was taken to England principally through the efforts of Thomas Hope, a gentleman of means from a major Scottish banking family. Raised in Holland, Hope made his Grand Tour from 1787 to 1795, so he was well versed in antiquity and deeply aware of what had begun to take shape in French decoration and furniture. In 1795, with the Napoleonic Wars impending, he thought it advisable to return to England, and in so doing he carried with him the principles of this current style just emerging in France. Appalled by the taste and fashions of the English, Hope took it upon himself to reform their manner of furnishing and interior decoration. In 1807 he published *Household Furniture and Interior*

Decoration, documenting his furniture designs and the redecoration of his own house on Duchess Street. Like Adam, and Percier and Fontaine before him, Hope focused not only on the creation of individual objects but on the overall interior decorative scheme of rooms.

By the first decade of the nineteenth century this late classical style had begun to appear in America, promoting a vogue that would span nearly four decades and eventually culminate in a national style that defied regionalism. Even after the Revolution and the War of 1812, Americans had continued to look to England, as well as France, for the latest in fashions and refined taste. The leaders in purveying classical taste were the upper-class Americans who traveled abroad in the first decades of the nineteenth century. Eager to absorb as much of the highly regarded European culture as possible, they acquired material possessions and social and intellectual attitudes that enlarged their world and ultimately contributed to the spread of this new fashion in America.

In addition to these gentlemen and women of means, there were a number of native craftsmen who journeyed to Europe to view firsthand the productions so admired by their wealthy clients. Returning with books, prints, sketches, memories, and imported goods for retail, these artisan-entrepreneurs made important contributions to the material and aesthetic heritage of America. Equally significant in this transatlantic infusion of culture and fashion were the prosperous gentlemen and women who emigrated to these shores from France, England, and Germany with a wide assortment of stylish material possessions, not to mention the immigrant artisans who had the talent to capitalize on the fashion demands of resident American patrons.

Anxious to follow European examples, American cultural leaders encouraged the formation of institutions to train artists and nurture the fine arts, hoping to foster virtue and morality in an emerging republic, thus assuring its stability. Academies, athenaeums, special traveling exhibitions, and private collections brought together an impressive array of painting and sculpture, as well as an assortment of antique vases, casts, and fragments from ancient sites. All of this was viewed by Americans with interest, delight, and occasional dismay.

Classically inspired objects produced in America during the early nineteenth century exhibit an inexhaustible variety of ancient forms and motifs. While many of the finest productions relate to English and French designs, instances of direct copying are rare. The distinctiveness of this American classical expression resulted from multifaceted influences on both craftsmen and patrons. Economics, published design sources as well as an individual's visual references, and materials available all influenced the final creation. The most difficult factor to delineate is the role of the client–patron in ultimate design decisions that led to these classically inspired, European-derived, but specifically American expressions.

A significant number of design books, engraved sheets, and periodicals printed abroad were undoubtedly available to Americans. But while it is known that both the Boston Athenaeum and the Athenaeum of Philadelphia had subscriptions to Rudolph Ackermann's *Repository of the Arts,*

Commerce . . ., there are only a dozen or more precise references that source books such as Hope, Ackermann, Smith, and La Mésangère were owned in America. Certainly these volumes were here, or at least they had been examined by patrons and craftsmen abroad. Were these fine craftsmen more likely to have worked from memory and sketches? Were many of these volumes not recorded in the estates of craftsmen because, being simply volumes of illustrations, they were not recognized as significant? Whatever the explanation is, America had a variety of two-dimensional as well as three-dimensional classical design sources to inspire artisans and patrons.

As was true in seventeenth- and eighteenth-century American arts, distinctive regional characteristics in both form and ornament were manifest in these classical expressions. Though this book is not organized by region, characteristics peculiar to various geographic areas are cited and discussed. But accounting for regional taste and preference can be almost as elusive as finding the specific source for many of the designs executed in America. Pervasive throughout the major urban areas is evidence of both French and English influences, often combined in the same object.

Characteristic of classicism, here and abroad, was its rapid evolution into a fashion and taste that was considered to be refined and virtuous. Marketing this taste became a key mercantile activity in Europe, and it did not take long before American merchants and entrepreneurs capitalized on this newest vogue. Changes in style were always seized upon by import merchants and artisans as an economic opportunity, but perhaps more than any other fashion the classical craze pervaded every aspect of material goods, from dresses in the manner of the ancients to pressed glass salts sporting representations of Roman chariots. Rapid developments in transportation and technology were invaluable in spreading this classical taste to that segment of the burgeoning American populace prosperous enough to afford these increasingly symbolic goods.

For a century or more, educated Americans had admired classical heroes, but with their own republic in its infancy the recognition of heroes among their own citizenry became desirable. Virtue and morality were central to preserving the liberty and freedom of this newly created country, so valorous behavior in both men and women was to be recognized and rewarded. However, it was more often the men, war heroes or statesmen, who received the public presentations of monumental pieces of silver and dress swords evoking classical form and ornament.

By 1840 America had begun to shed her blatant dependence on classical precedents and was moving rapidly toward her own native expressions, though still somewhat dependent on European examples. The most demonstrative product that resulted from this evolution was a new national style of upper- and middle-class furniture. Devoid of excessive carving, masses of gilt ornament, and metal mounts, this new style depended upon pure form and highly figured mahogany veneers for its brilliance and appeal.

By the 1840s classical taste had begun to wane, and no longer was every aspect of intellectual and material life veneered with the memory of ancient civilizations. However, the vogue for classical expressions did not cease entirely, for Americans continued to build domestic and public structures with colonnaded porticoes for the next two decades, as well as periodically to borrow from the ancients. In fact, for the past century and a half, classicism has seen numerous revivals, and the enduring quality of Grecian simplicity and grandeur continues to inspire and influence artisans and architects to this day. We can only hope that before the century is over that our leaders will recognize, as the founders of our country so nobly did, that the support of the arts will cultivate morality, virtue, and refinement in our society, and perhaps the glory of Greece will be revived in the cities of America.

Wendy A. Cooper
Curator, Decorative Arts
The Baltimore Museum of Art

INTRODUCTION

POPULAR CULTURE AND POPULAR TASTE IN CLASSICAL AMERICA

During the formative years of American nationhood, classical taste exercised an unprecedented influence on the architecture and decorative arts of the United States. At its peak from 1800 to 1840, classicism affected more objects, reached more deeply into American society, and more profoundly shaped national symbols than any previous international style. Classicism gained strength from the high esteem in which classical culture always had been held. During the Greek Revolution of the 1820s, an American editor reminded his readers that "from the earliest infancy the people of this country have been taught to regard the memory of the ancient Greeks with the highest veneration."[1] Benefiting from this regard, classicism outgrew its initial role as one more in a series of imported fashions and blossomed into a wide-ranging cultural movement.

Classical taste arrived in America just as the nation's leaders, struggling to create a culture worthy of the new republic's place in history, were searching for symbols of unity and strength to unite its disparate parts under the new republican government. Early leaders believed that the United States required a level of civilization to match its achievements in government; the most enlightened Constitution on earth deserved an equally magnificent culture. Classicism met the need.

While this public culture was being formed, American society was expanding at a prodigious rate. The purchase of Louisiana in 1803 doubled the size of the national domain, symbolizing the changes to follow. The population flowed westward into the new territory, highways and canals opening the way; decade after decade, cities more than doubled in size; and new forms of manufacturing immensely increased the national product.

Out of these changes emerged a middle class, a new group of people who were neither aristocrats nor plain workers, but a class between, with more income than ordinary workers and higher cultural ambitions. The middle class comprised a vast market for fashionable goods, from houses with stylish decorations to tablewares, clothing, and furniture. Classical taste was dominant during the emergence of this new class, which helped spread its influence.

The middle class joined with legislators who were planning public buildings, with architects and artisans looking for appealing styles, and eventually with manufacturers in a movement that infused every aspect of the new nation's culture with marks of ancient civilization. The culture of the educated elite in the eighteenth century had become by 1840 the primary stylistic vocabulary of the entire nation.

Classical taste brought with it two important ideals: the promise of perfect beauty and a model of austere patriotism. These ideals elevated classicism above the ranks of previous fashions by giving classical taste a stronger ideological character than its predecessors. Beauty and patriotism were not the only ideals to be found in ancient Greece and Rome, but, to meet their own needs, European writers had extracted these two from the classical past, and Americans adapted them to suit American circumstances.

The promise of perfect beauty was an ideal implicit in the long-standing practice of emulating classical art. For centuries, architects had found inspiration in Greek and especially Roman buildings, treating them as models of ordered beauty. Builders believed that their work continued the classical tradition into modern times, emulating, adapting, elaborating.

In the eighteenth century, this emulation of the classical took a new form. Writers began to think of distinct national civilizations instead of a single, continuing tradition. High civilization flourished for a time in one location and then moved on to another, it was believed, traveling from Egypt to Greece, then to Rome, to Renaissance Italy, and finally to the court of Louis XIV and the present age.[2] Eighteenth-century writers debated the question of which country in the series had reached the zenith of cultural achievement, a relevant question when history was conceived as a series of civilizations succeeding each other. If history was divided into distinct civilizations, the latest generation had to choose the most worthy to emulate.

In the works of European artists and scholars, Greece and Rome vied for supremacy, but by the second decade of the nineteenth century, the artistic superiority of the Greeks was generally acknowledged. "All the most civilized nations of the earth," a writer in an American journal, *The Port Folio*, said in 1814, "unite in considering the Grecian architecture as the standard of excellence; and its forms and proportions, even to the minutest particular, are copied with an exactness that precludes all invention."[3] William Dunlap writing in 1834 opened his summary of the arts in America with the observation that the human is the most perfect of all forms, and "the sculptors of ancient Greece alone attained the knowledge of this form in its perfection, and the power to represent it. . . . We have no standard of beauty, but that which is derived from the country of Homer and Phidias."[4]

Belief in the perfections of Greek art led to the intense study of models from classical antiquity. The importation of the Elgin marbles from the Parthenon and the arrival of the Portland vase, brought from Italy by Sir William Hamilton, were notable cultural events in England because people believed they would learn aesthetic truth from examination of classical objects. The desire to study classical art justified the expense and effort of publishing detailed drawings of classical monuments; the first volume of James Stuart's and Nicholas Revett's *Antiquities of Athens* published in 1762 after eleven years of work, along with a second volume twenty-seven years later, provided readers with a view of correct artistic principles incarnated in ancient buildings. The casts of classical busts that filled the early academies in American cities held similar promise. There observant viewers could absorb the principles of ideal beauty.

In addition to models of beauty, classical civilization was believed to uphold an ideal of austere patriotism. Moderns could look to ancient heroes for inspiration. A writer in the *New England Quarterly Magazine* in 1802 said that "the best ages of Rome afford the purest models of virtue that are anywhere to be met with. Mankind are too apt to lose sight of all that is heroic, magnanimous and public spirited. . . . Left to ourselves, we are apt to sink into effeminacy and apathy." Following that lead, the Latin oration at the 1807 Harvard commencement was on "The Patriotism of the Romans."[5] Moderns could revive flagging patriotism through the study of ancient heroes, giving the arts an important role in the maintenance of public virtue.

These two ideals—the promise of perfect beauty and austere patriotism—accompanied the classical taste to America, and from them Americans fashioned their own ideology of classicism. Some writers have mistakenly suggested that Americans were attracted to classicism because of an affinity with Greek democracy and Roman republicanism.[6] But classical history was too ambiguous about correct taste in government to guide American political principles. Rome reached its highest glory under the emperors rather than during the republic. Greek city-state democracies were too small to be satisfactory models for American democracy, and Sparta, frequently cited for its civic virtue, was governed by an authoritarian regime.[7] Democracy was only occasionally mentioned by authors and artists as a reason for emulating classical civilization.

A more useful lesson to be learned from classical political history was that ruin followed the decline of patriotism. Far from exalting classical republicanism, the frequent depictions of Roman ruins with peasants in the foreground, or animals grazing amid the columns, reminded viewers of the collapse of a once mighty civilization.[8] When Greece and Rome lost sight of the virtues on which greatness was founded, their civilizations crumbled. The lesson to be learned from antiquity was that patriots must labor against tyranny and luxury, or ruin would overtake the nation.

For the most part, Americans did not turn to classical civilization for any kind of political direction. In their comments on classical taste, American writers said little about patriotism and more about beauty. While valuing patriotism, Jefferson, for one, was more interested in finding exemplars of ideal beauty to guide American art and architecture.[9]

Classicism appealed to Americans who were consciously laying the foundations of a new society and culture. They desired beautiful buildings and art in order to join the ranks of the great civilizations. Jefferson said of the national Capitol, which followed classical patterns, "I think that the work when finished will be a desirable and honorable monument of our infant republic, and will bear favorable comparison with the remains of the same kind of the ancient republics of Greece and Rome."[10] Concerned with the dignity of the nation and its honorable place among the civilizations of the world, he was led to classical antiquity for its embodiment of correct taste.

Believing that the nation's culture was on trial, critics rejoiced in every building that displayed good taste. Of the first Bank of the United States, built in Philadelphia in 1798, one critic crowed, "this is the first finished building of any consequence, wherein true taste and knowledge has been displayed."[11] Contemplating his own devotion to architecture, Jefferson said that it "is an enthusiasm of which I am not ashamed, as its object is to improve the taste of my countrymen, to increase their reputation, to reconcile them to the rest of the world, and procure them its praise."[12] He patterned the state capitol at Richmond after a classical temple, hoping to set a standard for the whole nation.[13]

Classical taste blossomed in America after Independence when the United States was first forming its public culture and looking for models to emulate. The destruction by revolution of the traditional order of government created a vacuum in civic life. With the Declaration of Independence, the new nation abandoned monarchy and all its associations. A New York crowd pulled down the statue of George III on Bowling Green; cities changed the names of streets with royal associations; public writs ran in the name of elected governments rather than the king; hereditary titles were forbidden. The old symbols were destroyed and new ones had to be created.[14]

The greatest of the new symbols was the Constitution. As well as establishing a framework of government, the Constitution stood for the union of the states and the bonding of the people, representing their commitment to each other in the common desire to form a government based on popular will. But this single potent document was not enough. The nation needed visible symbols of its unity and strength. In 1839 the commissioners managing the construction of the Ohio state capitol explained to the legislature why the building was worth its high cost. "The architectural monuments of a country cherish national pride and patriotic sentiments, and contribute, in a great degree, to identify the citizen with his country. A state destitute of great public works . . . is not likely to have its institutions cherished and sustained, and its soil defended, with that zeal and tenacity which has always distinguished those regions adorned with monuments of art and architectural magnificence, to which the citizen can, at all times refer, as lasting evidence of the glory of his ancestors."[15]

Classical taste was at its zenith when state capitols like Ohio's were constructed. In every state, classical taste was put to service in creating the symbols of American nationality. The expansion of the nation multiplied the occasions for civic buildings and monuments. While the area of the United States was more than doubling between 1800 and 1840, its population increased more than four times, from 3.9 million to 17 million. That enlarged space, filling with migrating people, brought into existence hundreds of new government units, each one, sooner or later, needing a building. Besides farmhouses and little town centers dotting the land as the nation grew, there were increasing numbers of courthouses and state capitols. Thirteen new states were admitted to the Union between 1790 and 1840, and between 1793 and 1820 alone seventeen new state capitols were constructed.[16] As these new state capitols were erected, the legislatures were not content with unadorned and purely functional structures. The commissioners for the New Hampshire state capitol said in 1814, "it is justly considered derogatory to a respectable and independent State, to suffer the officers of its Government to sit and transact the business of the State in a building mean in its appearance, and destitute of suitable accommodations."[17] Government required buildings worthy of its high functions in a republican society.

Classical taste in capitols first appeared in the style of Robert Adam, the British architect who made his own translation of classical forms in the last third of the eighteenth century. Charles Bulfinch's Massachusetts statehouse in Boston, designed in an Adamesque spirit, was the inspiration for capitols in New Hampshire, Maine, and Vermont, cultural satellites of Boston.[18] After 1810 more direct imitation of Roman and then Greek forms became common. Pennsylvania's capitol was moved to Harrisburg by an act of 1810, and the state erected a building with the major classical elements of American capitols: dome, rotunda, portico, and balanced legislative houses. Occupied in 1821, the Pennsylvania statehouse became a primary model for the next generation. After that date, classical architecture, and more specifically Greek Revival, held the field in the construction of American civic buildings.[19]

Political ideology had little influence on the choice of classical models for state capitols; at most the legislators noted the simplicity of classically based plans.[20] The building committee for the new Connecticut statehouse in New Haven defended Ithiel Town's plan for a rectangular Doric temple with porticoes at each end by saying that it was "proper and necessary to exhibit in our edifices the plain simplicity of our republican institutions."[21]

Rivalry with sister states more than ideological propriety moved the legislators. When the Vermont legislature resolved to erect a new capitol, the report of the building committee in 1833 supported the endeavor by observing that "whilst many of the other States were expending large sums of money in the erection of their public buildings—each endeavoring to surpass the others in the beauty, taste, and elegance of design and workmanship, the State of Vermont would hardly be satisfied with a building that would not compare advantageously in point of convenience and correct taste, with those erected in the neighboring states."[22] The North Carolina building commission wanted a monument of "durability and splendor, that will vie with the proudest specimens of European architecture." By erecting "one of the finest specimens of classic taste," built in accord with "the principles of Architecture, and rules of Architectural taste," they hoped to assert the state's proper place in the world.[23]

The desire for architectural eminence reached into remote rural counties. Citizens who lived in small log houses and were jealous of every penny spent in taxes still supported the construction of handsome courthouses in the classical taste. A visitor to North Carolina observed that the courthouses were "always the most prominent buildings in town and are usually placed in the middle of the main street." Like the state legislators, county leaders competed among themselves for eminence in their public buildings. After the completion of courthouses in Davidson and Guilford counties in North Carolina, a newspaper reported that other counties "stirred by the example of Davidson and Guilford, have entered the lists and are determined to compete with them for the honor of having the finest and most magnificent Court House in the State."[24]

A large part of American public culture emerged out of competition and local vanity. In their desire to outdo their neighbors, ambitious state legislators and county commissioners sponsored and paid for buildings that became symbols of republican government. The instrument of their pride was classical taste. From the grass roots to the national capitol, classical taste and American public culture were inextricably intertwined.[25]

An advocate of public monuments, writing in 1815, touched on another aspect of civic culture in which the classical taste played a part: sculpture. "Let us reflect too," he wrote, "that the arts, by preserving and multiplying the images of the truly great of the nation, and the most impressive memorials of their wisdom and virtue, are powerful instruments of cherishing and animating public spirit and patriotic feeling."[26] By 1815, impressive memorials of "the truly great of the nation" were being preserved in stone, doing their part to keep "patriotic feeling" alive. Before the Revolution, sculpting in stone was virtually unknown in America, and busts of great men were rarely sculpted. After the Revolution sculptors began to receive commissions, many from the builders of state capitols who wanted fitting memorials to adorn the spaces they had created.[27] The sculpture reminded citizens of the country's heroic past, with Washington at the forefront of the patriot band. Scarcely a state capitol failed to find a place for his figure.[28] Jefferson saw to it that the Washington commission from the Virginia legislature went to the French sculptor Jean-Antoine Houdon, reputed to be the best in Europe.[29] North Carolina two decades later commissioned Antonio Canova, Houdon's successor as the best of his time, to do a full-length Washington that became the center of attraction in the capitol building.[30]

Most of this sculpture had a distinctly classical appearance. Nearly every sculptural commission involved the question of classical dress. Should the subject appear in a toga?[31] By the time of the Revolution, classical dress for civic figures was commonplace. Joseph Warren wore a toga into a Boston pulpit when he delivered an oration on the anniversary of the Boston Massacre, and the statue of George III, erected on the Bowling Green in New York City and dedicated in 1770, was clad in a toga.[32] The practice continued unabated into the nineteenth century as the production of sculpture, particularly portraits of eminent figures, grew by leaps and bounds.

The depiction of contemporary figures in ancient cultural forms was sometimes carried too far. Horatio Greenough, the New Englander trained by Danish classical sculptor Bertel Thorwaldsen, went beyond the pale in his depiction of Washington. Commissioned by Congress in 1832, Greenough chose to pattern his figure after Phidias's statue of Zeus, a work known only by its appearance on coins, but considered to be the greatest sculpture of ancient times. Greenough's work presented a gigantic seated Washington, naked to the waist, with right arm raised. When it was finally delivered in 1841, the sight was too much for Americans. The work was removed from the Capitol and eventually installed in the Museum of American History where it now stands as a marvelous curiosity and a reminder that the enthusiasm for classical civilization could become excessive.[33]

Despite failures and objections, togas were conventional for American heroes. Franklin chose to have himself sculpted in a classical gown with a Roman head for the Library Company of Philadelphia. The Italian sculptor Giuseppe Ceracchi produced a number of portrait busts in Roman garb at the end of the eighteenth century. For the North Carolina capitol, Jefferson recommended that Washington be in classical dress: "As to the style or costume, I am sure the artist, and every person of taste in Europe would be for the Roman. . . . Our boots and regimentals have a very puny effect."[34]

Roman clothing was not reserved solely for the founders. By mid-century any notable figure worthy of sculpture could appear bare-chested in Roman fashion or in a toga. John Quincy Adams, John C. Calhoun, Andrew Jackson, and many lesser figures appeared in classical dress. Sometimes the subject wore the toga draped over modern dress, but, in one form or other, this convention became so powerful that a depiction of Daniel Webster without Roman dress came under criticism, as if the Whig champion had not been given his due.[35]

What did these togas mean? Why this incongruous drape of ancient dress over the figures of contemporary Americans? As with all things classical, Roman dress defined the standard of beauty. But dress also invoked ideas about the classical past. The splendors of Greek and Roman civilization cast an aura over familiar public figures draped in togas. Every educated person, and probably many others besides, knew about ancient glories. Greece's prominence was asserted as an uncontested fact in the large public meetings convened to raise money for the Greek revolutionaries. Between 1821, when the revolution broke out, and 1825, the period during which the Greeks held their own against their Ottoman rulers, Americans in city after city were called on to contribute to the Greek cause. The common stock in trade of the orators was the leadership of ancient Greece among all nations of the world. As one speaker said, "Greece the ancient nurse of freedom, science and the arts, wakes from her long trance of death, to the light and splendor of her pristine glory." That enthusiasm for classical virtue must have ennobled modern figures attired in togas, and at least some sculptors must have intended to invest their subjects with value borrowed from the classical past.[36]

Classical history did not exercise the same monopolistic control over the nineteenth-century American imagination that the Bible did over Puritan thought; in early New England modern events and biblical history melded into one.[37] The histories of Greece and Rome lay upon nineteenth-century American events more like the togas draped over modern dress in the sculpted figures. Classical history gave meaning to present events by setting them in the context of antiquity. Americans in togas, the sculpture seemed to say, had virtues like the heroes of the past. American society and government, classical public buildings suggested, had a future that could equal the glories of ancient civilization. The multiplicity of classical allusions in American civic culture revealed the nation's desire to achieve greatness comparable to that of Greece and Rome, under the leadership of men who embodied the virtues of ancient patriots.

The sculpture of leading men and the architecture of public buildings were the primary expressions of civic classicism, a major aspect of the classical movement in America after 1800. But architecture in the classical taste soon spread beyond capitols and courthouses. Classicism first affected nongovernmental buildings with a public character, such as colleges, churches, hotels, and banks, and then went on to store fronts and private houses.[38] The power behind classical taste raised it from a style to a movement, making it widely appealing for many applications.

Classicism eventually touched many vernacular forms, marking a much wider circle of influence of a popular classicism. Even gravestones were affected. Through the colonial period, rural gravestones were largely impervious to the influence of fashion. In country villages throughout New England, where gravestone designs have been closely studied, powerful local traditions governed the evolution of gravestone patterns. Death images and soul effigies were the common designs incised in country stones.[39] The dominance of local traditions ended after 1790, however, when within little more than a decade classical urns replaced the soul effigies of a few years before. Classical influence did not stop a few miles from the coast as earlier imported fashions had done, but penetrated deep inland where local vernacular styles had reigned supreme for generations. The classical movement transformed the work of local craftsmen and the preferences of country people as no fashion before had been able to do. By 1800 virtually every burial ground in New England reflected classical influences, and by 1815 the older traditions had been all but eliminated. The urn and willow were equated with mourning and death.[40]

The spread of classical taste into unlikely areas—fancy needlework is another example—and the formation of popular classicism cannot be attributed solely to the cultural power of the movement. Classical influence diffused also because of a population ready to be instructed in correct taste. In its numbers and influence, this population was unprecedented in American history, made up of people whose fathers and mothers had thought fashion was the business of the gentry alone, but who came to desire refinement for themselves. This newly attuned generation began to look outward for guidance in matters of style, and to recognize a broader standard of taste than the one set by local tradition.

We have come to call the people who comprised this new market for fashion the middle class, and its emergence in the first half of the nineteenth century is a major reason for the unusually wide influence of classical taste. Middle-class people were the ones to bring simplified versions of high-style objects into their houses, immensely enlarging the breadth of classical influence in the population.

The middle class in turn was a product of massive changes in society and the economy during this period. The middle class grew along with cities that were increasing at a prodigious rate.

Between 1800 and 1840 the number of Americans living in towns, defined by the census as concentrations of more than 2500 people, increased from 322,000 to 1,845,000, and the cities supported middling workers in unprecedented numbers.[41] Shopkeepers, managers of industrial firms, professional people, clerks, teachers, and minor government officials, while not claiming to be gentry, adopted ways of living that distanced them from laborers who worked with their hands. These white collar workers provided a huge market for cultural goods like carpets, upholstered furniture, and small decorative items for the parlor. In the East, urban residents on the average spent three times as much as farmers, and much of this went for refinements.[42] This middle class had both the desire and the means to adopt correct taste, which in the first decades of the nineteenth century primarily meant classical taste.

Artisans and manufacturers recognized the possibilities of this new market and expanded production to meet the need. Between 1809 and 1839 manufacturing grew at an average rate of 59 percent in each decade, making inexpensive versions of refined articles available for the expanding market.[43] Housewrights developed efficient methods for constructing houses that were a step beyond the two- and three-room dwellings in which most people lived in 1800. Especially in the towns of New England and New York, carpenters gave these houses classical touches. In New England builders put the gable-end to the front, rather than to the side, and applied pilasters at the corners, evoking the temple form of classical architecture. On other houses, carpenters wrapped an entablature around the top under the eaves and put columns at the door.[44]

Aided by industrialists and well-informed artisans, the middle class in the first half of the nineteenth century created a popular classicism that was nearly as extensive as civic classicism. Civic and popular classicism provided an unprecedented social and cultural context for elite classicism. Never before had a high-end style reached so far into society and culture; never had fashion been democratized as profoundly as was the classical taste.[45] The elite for the first time did not monopolize style.

There had always been an interplay between great public buildings and aristocratic mansions. In America the cupola was a common sign of a courthouse or statehouse, and the gentry borrowed the cupola along with pediments and arches for their own residences. But in democratic America that interplay of cultural forms now extended to common people, at least as far down in the social scale as the middle class. Rather than a class apart, the elite of the new republic were but first among equals.[46] In this sense the classical taste in America was profoundly democratic. From this time on, every stylistic change at the upper levels of society took popular forms that were disseminated among the middle class.

By the middle of the nineteenth-century, styles moved on; the classical taste in architecture gave way to Gothic and Italianate. But in its period of greatest influence, classicism made an impression that could never be erased. When the Colonial Revival began near the end of the nineteenth century, many of the churches and houses that served as models of colonial buildings were not truly colonial but the classicized versions of early architecture. The epitome of colonial New England, the church on the green, was more often than not a Greek Revival building. Statehouses and courthouses moved with the times, but the national Capitol in Washington and the classical statehouses of the early nineteenth century were never replaced as the popular images of republican government.

In the United States, classical taste cannot be dismissed as one more episode in the history of style. Classicism influenced too many tangible aspects of culture from buildings to art forms, pervading the middling as well as the upper levels of society. Far from being a superficial and temporary fashion, classical taste shaped the most prominent symbols of government at a time when the nation was most impressionable. Because the classical movement began when American society, government, and culture were being formed, classical taste in the material culture of the United States came to be identified with America itself.

Richard L. Bushman
Gouverneur Morris Professor of History
Columbia University

One
SOURCES OF INSPIRATION
The European Influence

Mr. Richard Derby . . . has just returned from his tour in Europe, & . . . he is the first who has been a native New England man that has travelled in high style since Mr. Palmer. . . . He was introduced with his lady in due form to their Britannic Majesties. In France he was introduced to Bonaparte, who politely saluted Mrs. Derby, as we hear. . . . In Rome he had the honour of visiting his holiness, who also in his gardens gave his benediction to Mrs. Derby. . . . He tells me that he has brought the Busts, antiques, in Plaster of Paris, with a full sized Appollo Bellvedere, & a Venus de Medicis. What books he had brought I could not learn.[1]

In October of 1803, as Richard Derby returned to his native town of Salem, Massachusetts, the United States was on the brink of major westward expansion. Less than six months earlier, President Thomas Jefferson's ministers to France, James Monroe and Robert R. Livingston, had successfully negotiated the Louisiana Purchase, which doubled the size of the United States. While the country's western interiors would experience unprecedented exploration and growth over the next four decades, Europe, for sophisticated, upper-class Americans, was to remain the center and source of intellectual, cultural, and artistic inspiration. The Derbys' experience was not singular, and the material possessions they returned with proclaimed their enthusiastic espousal of the ideals of classical antiquity as well as the European culture Americans so strongly desired to imitate.

Throughout the eighteenth century, colonial gentlemen traveled to Europe for education, enlightenment, and the opportunity to absorb a cultural and artistic heritage that America did not yet provide. Numerous artists, including Benjamin West, Charles Willson Peale, John Singleton Copley, and Gilbert Stuart, studied abroad, and sometimes stayed abroad, in search of the training and classical sources of inspiration unavailable at home. Following the American Revolution and the establishment of an independent republic, the need for ministers and consuls in European countries increased the constant flow of educated Americans abroad, as venerable statesmen like Franklin, Adams, Jefferson, and Monroe spent time, often accompanied by their families, in the intellectual and political circles of the European capitals.

By the 1790s and early nineteenth century, England and Europe were visually and materially different from what American visitors had experienced earlier in the eighteenth century. While the archaeological sites of Italy and Greece remained much the same, except for the benefits of further excavation, other major centers had begun to reflect dramatically the impact of an aggressive interest in the ideals and physical remains of ancient classical civilizations. Major illustrated publications of these timeworn sites and ruins, growing public and private collections of antiquities, astonishingly different architectural achievements, and a distinctive new vocabulary of furniture and interior decoration, all contributed to create a dramatic new vision that captivated Americans who went abroad.

Pages 24-25

CURTAIN FABRIC

c. 1805

Dudding & Co., England

Glazed chintz

Collection Cora Ginsburg

Several major incentives motivated Americans to travel abroad. The desire to absorb contemporary European culture, both intellectual and aesthetic, ranked high on many travelers' lists, as well as a curiosity to experience "an antiquity without limit," as William Cullen Bryant described it in 1834. Young Nicholas Biddle, as a student at Princeton in 1799–1801, felt that one of the greatest advantages to be gained from traveling abroad was "those moral reflections which naturally present themselves to the mind at the sight of what is great, grand, or magnificent." For Biddle, it was not enough simply to travel and see great sights, one had to "make use of these objects as incitements to virtue and morality" if one were to gain and grow from experiences abroad.[2]

The travel experiences of those Americans with the means to journey abroad during this period benefited much of the country's population both directly and indirectly. Their absorption of modern classicism while in Europe was an important factor in the transferral of this new taste to America. What these travelers brought back with them, both in cultural awareness and material possessions, ultimately left an indelible mark on numerous aspects of American life for several decades. To say that upper-class Americans in the early nineteenth century were "Eurocentric" would not stretch the truth. As in the preceding century, tremendous status was attached to the acquisition of foreign-made goods, but by the early 1800s citizens were encouraged to support America's manufactures if they wished her to prosper. Nevertheless, those who could afford imported goods—ranging from furniture and furnishings to interior architectural elements such as elegantly carved French or Italian marble mantels—cared more about flaunting fashionable classical taste than displaying allegiance to American enterprises.

The first four decades of the nineteenth century witnessed more Americans traveling abroad for a wider variety of reasons than ever before. As Philip Hone, a dedicated diarist (1828–1851) and mayor of New York for one term in 1825, remarked, "All the world is going to Europe."[3] The end of the Napoleonic wars made European travel feasible once again, and after 1815 an amazing number of Americans with diverse reasons were back on the high seas. Many who braved the long voyage went essentially as tourists, in search of cultural and aesthetic inspiration, as well as the latest fashions and newest domestic furnishing styles popular in the international centers of London and Paris. Others went as young students to the great European universities, while artists and writers went for aesthetic and intellectual stimulation and reflection.

Though technological developments in steam engines had shortened the length of a transatlantic voyage, crossings still took about three weeks eastward and five weeks westward, journeys that often were unpleasant and full of risks. Seasickness and discomfort "provoked by the want of comfortable accommodations," made Rembrandt Peale and his colleagues in December 1828 "glad to rise from our sick beds and walk the deck in the grateful beams of the sun."[4] But the positive benefits of a European sojourn assuredly outweighed the negative aspects of going and returning, as evidenced by the many travelers who wrote enthusiastically of their experiences.

EWER

c. 1834

Marked by Baldwin Gardiner
(1791–1869; working, New
York, 1827–1848)

Silver

H. 16⅜ in.

Collection Charles Everett

For some passengers the mortal risk of treacherous gales added to the adventure and thrill of a transatlantic crossing, but most were more concerned that a skillful captain would manage to deliver them safely to port. Indeed, some passengers were so certain their lives had been spared due to the competence of their captain that they commissioned fine pieces of silver as gifts in gratitude. In 1834 a group of American gentlemen, upon their safe return from Liverpool, purchased a silver ewer from the noted New York retailer and silversmith Baldwin Gardiner and had it inscribed, "Presented to Capt. George Maxwell By John Hagan[,] Wm. Oliver[,] Charles Brugier Jr. [,] in behalf of the Passengers on a Voyage on board the Ship Europe Sailed from Liverpool on the 16th March and arrived at New York on the 8th April 1834" (fig. 1). Modeled after a classical form and intended for the service of wine, this functional ewer, elaborately ornamented with grapevines, represented the height of classical taste and fashion.

The statesmen and diplomats who lived and traveled abroad as ministers and consuls were among the first important classical tastemakers of the late eighteenth and early nineteenth centuries. Thomas Jefferson spent more than five years in Europe, from May 1784 to October 1789, and undeniably can be considered the father of classical taste in America (fig. 2). He brought to his diplomatic mission abroad a thorough knowledge of the ancient world, which he had gained through a traditional education at the College of William and Mary and extensive reading in his own library of books on architecture and classical antiquity.

More than a decade earlier, Jefferson had begun construction of his own villa, Monticello. His early study of classical texts had imbued him with the basic ideals and principles that allowed him to become the chief proponent of a new republican classicism. Yet no manner of education, or study of illustrated texts from the eighteenth century, could have affected him as strongly as did the actual experience of visiting the Maison Carrée in 1787, the noted Roman temple from the early Christian period in Nîmes, France. Though Jefferson never journeyed farther into Italy than the northernmost parts around Milan, his response to this most perfect of all antique temples produced a reaction that would reverberate for decades to come. On March 20, 1787, he wrote to his friend Madame de Tesse in Paris: "Here I am, Madam, gazing whole hours at the Maison Quarree, like a lover at his mistress. The stocking weavers and silk spinners around consider me as an hypochondriac Englishman, about to write with a pistol the last chapter of his history."[5]

Jefferson's spirit and philosophy did more than that of any single American of his generation to both initiate and perpetuate the classical style in America. As secretary of state when Washington, the new Federal city, was undergoing major architectural planning, he steered the taste and expression of the country's principal public edifices in the direction of a classical revival style. Once inaugurated as President in 1801, he appointed the British-trained architect Benjamin Henry Latrobe as first surveyor of public buildings. There is no question that President Jefferson was largely responsible for the overall classical taste as evoked by the architecture and sculpture of the new Federal city, as well as the ancient ideals of civic humanism and classical republicanism that were embraced by leading statesmen and educators of his day.

2

THOMAS JEFFERSON
1821
Thomas Sully (1783–1872)
Philadelphia
Oil on canvas
29 x 18 in.
Diplomatic Reception Rooms, Department of State

As America's capital city was taking shape in the 1790s and on into the first decade of the new century, Napoleon's regime was simultaneously changing taste and fashions in Paris under the brilliant and sophisticated leadership of Charles Percier and Pierre F. L. Fontaine, architects and designers to the emperor's court. Among the American ministers in France during this period were James Monroe and his beautiful wife, Elizabeth Kortright Monroe, as well as New York's chancellor, Robert R. Livingston. Both the Monroes and the Livingstons made themselves very much at home during their time in Paris, and the French and Italian purchases they brought back to America bear witness to their delight and satisfaction with this new style inspired by the antique world. The Monroes lived in Paris from 1794 to 1796, and again from early 1803 to 1807, two intensive periods that made them great Francophiles and firmly established their taste for French fashions. Upon their return to the United States in 1807, they shipped home numerous European purchases, including a set of bold, classical armchairs (fig. 3) derived from high-style designs published by Percier and Fontaine, as well as less elaborate chair forms popularly cir-

3

ARMCHAIR
one of four

c. 1800–1810

France

Mahogany

36½ x 23 x 21¼ in.

*James Monroe Museum,
Fredericksburg, Virginia*

culated by Pierre de La Mésangère in his *Collection des Meubles et Objets de Goût*. Although the original upholstery fabric on the Monroe chairs is not known, in 1816, in Washington, Mary Boardman Crowninshield observed ". . . pretty French chairs—mahogany backs and bottoms stuffed, covered with striped rich blue silk."[6]

In the years preceding their move into the President's House, the Monroes created a most fashionable impression among their contemporaries. In December 1815, after young Mary Boardman Crowninshield had dined at the Monroes, she wrote to her mother:

> I think I told you we were to dine at Mrs. Monroe's the day before yesterday. We
> had there the most stylish dinner I have been at. The table wider than we have, and

in the middle a large, perhaps silver, waiter, with images like some Aunt Silsbee has, only more of them, and vases filled with flowers, which made a very showy appearance as the candles were lighted when we went to table. The dishes were silver and set round this waiter.

The plates were handsome china, the forks silver, and so heavy I could hardly lift them to my mouth, dessert knives silver, and spoons very heavy—you would call them clumsy things. Mrs. Monroe is a very elegant woman. She was dressed in a very fine muslin worked in front and lined in pink, and a black velvet turban close and spangled. . . . The drawing-room was handsomely lighted—transparent lamps I call them—three windows, crimson damask curtains, tables, chairs and all the furniture French.[7]

However, the national impact of the Monroes' taste for objects in the French classical style came in 1817 when they moved into the recently rebuilt President's House and embellished it with an extensive quantity of elaborate French furnishings. Among their purchases was a large suite of carved-and-gilt furniture made by the Parisian cabinetmaker Pierre-Antoine Bellangé, a richly fashioned gilt-bronze plateau for the table and numerous pieces of silver, French porcelain vases, handsome silk drapery, and printed French wallpapers.[8] The two craftsmen responsible for carrying out the final decoration of these rooms were the upholsterers Charles Alexandre and René de Perdreauville. Given the Monroes' proclivity for the classical Parisian taste, it is not surprising that the president's "decorators" were both French-born and trained. While there were those who criticized the president for not patronizing American manufacturers, the impact of these extraordinary classical-style European furnishings on all who visited the President's House was significant.

Another impressive French armchair that may have been seen by New York patrons, and perhaps some artisans, was said to be a chair "in which Napoleon Bonaparte had presided as First Consul of the Republic of France" (fig. 4). Given to the New-York Historical Society in 1867, it was "brought from France by Joseph Bonaparte (Comte de Survilliers) given by him to Mr. Lacoste then French Consul at New York. . . ."[9] Still retaining its original red wool upholstery with applied silver tape, this chair bears a striking resemblance to several associated with Napoleon and his palaces. It is also similar to designs No. 311 and No. 318 published by Pierre de La Mésangère in his *Collection des Meubles et Objets de Goût*. An 1804 portrait of

4

ARMCHAIR

c. 1800

France

Painted and gilded wood

38 x 26¼ x 28 in.

The New-York Historical Society, New York, Gift of Louis Borg, 1867.438

5 **opposite**

In the entry hall of Montgomery Place, built c. 1804–1806 for Janet Livingston Montgomery at Annandale-on-the-Hudson, New York, are a number of elegant European furnishings representing the taste of the Livingstons. The French chair, sporting carved dolphins as arm supports, is part of a set purchased in France (c. 1801–1804) by Janet's brother, Robert R. Livingston. The figural candelabra and the porcelain ice pails also reflect the taste for French objects that the Livingstons embraced. The small self-portrait over the chair was painted in Paris by Louis Livingston, the son of Robert. The painting of Andrew Jackson, attributed to Ralph E. W. Earl, was presented to Edward Livingston by the President. Edward Coleman of Philadelphia, whose granddaughter Mary Coleman Livingston married Maturin Livingston Delafield, owned the marble statuary pier table, which he may have purchased in Italy when abroad in 1827.

6

SIDE CHAIR
one of six
c. 1820–1830
New York
Grained and stenciled mahogany veneer
32 x 19 x 17½ in.
The Newark Museum; Gift of Mrs. Van Horn Ely, 1965

Napoleon as first consul by Jean-Auguste-Dominique Ingres shows a closely related chair, and an almost identical chair was once at Malmaison.[10] However, it is impossible to affix a more specific provenance to this chair than that it was brought to America by Joseph Bonaparte probably in 1816. It is tantalizing though to speculate whether or not Thomas and John Constantine, New York cabinetmakers and upholsterers, might have seen this armchair prior to making the chairs and desks for the U.S. Senate chamber in 1818–1819, or the speaker's chair for the Senate of the North Carolina State House in 1823, shown in figure 186.

Robert R. Livingston was appointed minister to Paris by Jefferson in 1801 and held that position until 1804. Before returning to "Clermont," the family's Hudson River estate, the Livingstons traveled leisurely through Europe, arriving home in 1805. Like the Monroes, the Livingstons returned from Paris with numerous French furnishings, including a set of mahogany chairs in a form described by the French as a *chaise gondole* (fig. 5). Other French chairs of this form were also owned in the New York area, so it is not surprising that New York chairmakers were called upon to make their own distinctive variation of this French form inspired by classical precedents (fig. 6).

7

DRESSING TABLE WITH
LOOKING GLASS

c. 1808–1815

France

Mahogany; mirror; marble;
ormolu

53⅞ x 26 x 15 in.

New York State Office of Parks,
Recreation and Historic Preservation,
Clermont State Historic Site

8

COURT TRAIN

c. 1809–1812

France

Silk velvet embroidered in flat
and embossed silver strips and
thread

L. 95 in.

Copyright © 1992 The Metropolitan
Museum of Art, New York; Gift of
Geraldine Shields and Dr. Ida Russel
Shields, 1948 (CI 48.41.1)

While in Paris, Livingston made the acquaintance of young Robert Fulton, a man twenty years his junior and at that time still a bachelor. Fulton, an aspiring painter, had gone to London in 1786 to study with Benjamin West, but by the 1790s his principal attentions were directed to engineering projects, especially in the development of canal systems, and by 1797 he had moved to Paris. Soon after, Fulton became the partner of Livingston in developing a steamboat that would decrease shipping time, and thus increase profits, not only on the Hudson River but eventually the Ohio, the Mississippi, the Potomac, and the James. Back in New York in 1808, Fulton married Livingston's charming young cousin, Harriet. Family history relates that the elegant French dressing table that Harriet owned was a wedding gift from her cousin, Robert (fig. 7). The importation of this handsome piece of French furniture, with its four columnar supports, reveals a strong preference for French furnishings among upper-class Americans, and serves as an important document in the enhancement of classical taste in America through European precedents.[11]

Paris, and particularly the court of Napoleon, was the European center of classical taste for many upper-class American visitors. Women who accompanied their husbands, or fathers, as U.S. ministers often enjoyed the privilege of being presented at court. The sumptuous dresses and richly embroidered court trains made abroad for these ladies rivaled those of their European counterparts. Two extraordinarily handsome trains, one worn by Mrs. Peter Livingston (fig. 8) and another by Mrs. Jonathan Russell, brilliantly portray the extravagant elegance that marked these splendid presentations at court. Made of the most costly cut silk velvet, and then embroidered with either sequins or silver thread and cord, these ensembles echo the sumptuousness of imperial life in Paris during the Napoleonic era.

Another aspect of elegant dressing, both at court and at other prestigious social occasions, included appropriate jewelry to complement one's costume. The new styles of slender, high-waisted dresses with broad low necklines, complemented by hairstyles tightly hugging the head, demanded a bolder, more dramatic fashion in jewelry, quite different from the eighteenth-century vogue for a few pearls or a sprinkling of brilliant diamonds. A greater variety of gemstones was employed in jewelry of this period, but perhaps the most distinctive and innovative development was the introduction of the ensemble known as the *parure.*

Derived from Renaissance precedents, a parure usually consisted of a comb worn on top of the head along with a bandeau in front, a necklace, pendant earrings, and a belt ornament.[12] American ladies acquired elegant parures abroad, and to some extent the fashions at court were transferred to the elite society of major American cities. A few notable American-owned examples survive, including sets worn by Elizabeth Kortright Monroe and one originally owned in the James Dewar Simons family of Charleston, South Carolina (fig. 9). Frequently these ensembles echoed classical themes and used

9

DEMI-PARURE

c. 1820

France or Germany

Iron and cut steel with japanned and gilt decoration

Tiara: 3¼ x 7¼ in.

Necklace: L. 18⅞ in.

Earrings: L. 1⅛ in.

Courtesy The Charleston Museum, Charleston, South Carolina

Italian cameos to express more fully the prevailing fashion for the antique style. The cameos in the Simons family parure are set in cut steel, a type of workmanship that originated in England and was fashionable in Paris by the late 1780s. That upper-class Americans adorned themselves with rich jewels similar to those worn abroad is further substantiated by David Sears's 1818 order for Mrs. Sears of "a diamond ornament for the head—if possible so arranged as to be worn also on the neck. Perhaps the form of a *Star* would answer equally well for either head or neck—a *Crescent* will not suit—Better to have the diamonds of a tolerable size and fewer in number, than a greater number and small—as the latter cannot be reset to advantage."[13]

Mrs. John Quincy Adams was one of the most beautiful and elegantly dressed of American women, who knew well the social importance and use of current European fashion (fig. 10). Born in London to an English mother and an American father, Louisa Catherine Johnson Adams was raised and educated in France and England, prior to her marriage in 1797 to the eldest son of the future President, John Adams.[14] Following their marriage, her husband's diplomatic career took them to Berlin, St. Petersburg, Paris, and London, before the couple returned to America in 1817. Painted in 1816 while John Quincy Adams was United States minister to the Court of St. James's, Mrs.

10

MRS. JOHN QUINCY ADAMS (LOUISA CATHERINE JOHNSON ADAMS)

1816

Charles Robert Leslie (1794–1859), London

Oil on canvas

36½ x 29 in.

Diplomatic Reception Rooms, Department of State

Adams is portrayed in a richly ornamented Empire-style dress in what was one of the most popular colors of the day, "Egyptian earth," a reddish brown hue.[15] Equally fashionable is Mrs. Adams's hairstyle and jewelry. The use of a gem-encrusted comb high on top of her head, along with several ribbonlike bandeaux about the front of the head, and a multistrand bead necklace all conform to current fashions. Her finely embroidered lace drapery and the paisley shawl beneath her right arm complete her ensemble and dramatically echo the costumes of the ancients, as was the contemporary vogue.

By the end of the eighteenth century, styles in ladies' dresses were already changing in America to keep pace with European trends. News of these avant-garde French fashions was readily available, at least to the upper classes, through personal correspondence, popular magazines, fashion plates and fashion dolls, imported goods, and professionals in the trade. The trend toward spare and gauzelike drapery was in imitation of the ancients, as interpreted from vase paintings, carved reliefs, and painted frescoes. The French fashions after the antique spread almost instantly to England, and thus English periodicals such as Rudolph Ackermann's *Repository of the Arts* provided American women with current information on fabrics, accessories, and general fashions. Soon after 1800 these new and daring "Greek" dresses became at once the rage among the younger generation and a source of disapproving comment from their elders.

Young Betsy Patterson, the beautiful, winsome daughter of one of Baltimore's wealthiest citizens, gained notoriety on several counts because of her predilection for things French (fig. 11). First of all in December 1803, against the advice of her family, she married Jerome Bonaparte, the youngest brother of Napoleon Bonaparte, soon to be emperor of France. This marriage took place totally against the wishes of Napoleon, who soon had it annulled. Adding scandal to scandal, the youthful Mrs. Bonaparte proceeded to appear in Baltimore and Washington society in the barest of coverings, much to the dismay of both her friends and detractors. Though never having seen Mrs. Bonaparte, one Washington member of Congress, Simeon Baldwin, reported to his wife:

> Having married a Parissian she assumed the mode of dress in which it is said the Ladies of Paris are cloathed—if that may be called cloathing which leaves half of the body naked & the shape of the rest perfectly visible. . . . Tho' her taste & appearance was condemned by those who saw her, yet such fashions are astonishingly bewitching . . . & we may well reflect on what we shall be when fashion shall remove all barriers from the chastity of women.[16]

The dress in figure 12 was worn by young Miss Patterson; its transparency is apparent, and the overall effect must, indeed, have been bewitching. Some American women went to such lengths to imitate the ancients in fashion that they suffered unhealthy consequences. In 1802 Rosalie Stier Calvert wrote her brother, Charles, about Betsy Cooke, who married Robert Gilmor, Jr., one of the most prominent Baltimore merchants, noting that "it is believed that she will die from a cold she caught at a ball where she wore a Greek dress."[17]

By the end of the second decade of the nineteenth century, the social circles of London and Paris were awash with Americans of status, and their letters and journals reveal the constant whirl of dinners, soirees, and balls that often brought them together far from their native environs. The Gilmors of Baltimore, the Welleses from Boston, and the Ga of New York all convened in Europe, and it was not unusual abroad either close friends or social acquaintances from home.

Like many young Americans of the late eighteenth century, Robert Gilmor, Jr., of Baltimore, had already traveled in Europe as part of his enlightened education from 1799 to 1801. In 1817 when Gilmor went abroad with his second wife, Sarah Reeve Ladson of Charleston, they were warmly welcomed into the elite circles of a cultured and sophisticated society. While in London, Gilmor commissioned Sir Thomas Lawrence, then president of the Royal Academy, to paint portraits of both himself and his wife. Both partners exuded fashion and taste. Five years later, in Baltimore, Thomas Sully painted Mrs. Gilmor as a model of ideal beauty and perfect taste (fig. 13), and, on Robert's instructions, he simply copied her husband's 1818 London likeness by Lawrence (fig. 14).

Mrs. Gilmor's portrait brilliantly displays one of the most current and exotic fashions of the time, a large and exquisitely wrapped

13

MRS. ROBERT GILMOR, JR. (SARAH REEVE LADSON GILMOR)

1823

Thomas Sully (1783–1872), Baltimore

Oil on canvas, original frame

36¼ x 28 in.

The Gibbes Museum of Art / Carolina Art Association, Charleston, South Carolina

14

ROBERT GILMOR, JR.

1823

Thomas Sully (1783–1872),
Philadelphia

Oil on canvas

29⅛ x 24¼ in.

*The Baltimore Museum of Art: Gift of
Albert Hendler, Bernard R. Hendler,
Bernice Hendler Kolodny, and Florence
Hendler Trupp, by exchange
(BMA 1960.43)*

15 below

DRAWING FROM A
SKETCHBOOK

c. 1817–1818

Attributed to Robert Gilmor, Jr.

Watercolor on paper

7 x 9¼ in.

*Maryland Historical Society,
Baltimore; Presented to the Society by
Ellen Gilmor Buchanan (Mrs. Thomas
G. Buchanan)*

16 opposite, top

CENTER TABLE

c. 1810–1820

Probably France

Mahogany, mahogany veneer;
marble; ormolu

30 x 38 in.

The Walters Art Gallery, Baltimore

17 opposite, bottom

ANNULAR LAMP
one of a pair

c. 1790

France

Cut glass; ormolu

H. 32 in.

Stephen Girard Collection, Girard

turban, with colorful drapery flowing from its sides. Numerous portraits of this period attest to the popularity of this fashion, which first came into style just after 1800 following the return of Napoleon's troops from Egypt where this peculiar headdress was worn. Sometimes this fashionable accessory was referred to as a "Mameluke" turban, after the ruling class of warriors who dominated Egypt.[18]

Gilmor's practice when he traveled was not only to keep a journal but to augment it with sketches of both the distinctive natural landscape and notable architecture, as well as interiors. Several of his renderings from this particular European trip present for Americans a rare glimpse of the elegant salons in which the Gilmors were entertained, rooms filled with the most fashionable, classically inspired furniture, and shimmering with the opulence that many upper-class Americans attempted to imitate once back in their own homes. Gilmor's charming watercolor sketch of about 1818 (fig.15) provides a fascinating look at what many upper-class Americans abroad may have experienced. The European setting that the Gilmors observed, with elegant window drapery, large pier glasses, richly framed paintings,

shimmering annular lamps, columnar center table, and musical instruments, was echoed by a similar classical taste embraced by American elite society.

In 1824 the Boston artist Henry Sargent was commissioned to paint a companion picture to his most successful 1821 exhibition painting, *The Dinner Party*.[19] This large and impressive depiction of elite Boston society, titled *The Tea Party* (fig. 61), presents an interesting parallel to Gilmor's European sketch. Indeed, many of the fashionable objects in Sargent's painting may have been imported from France, as they directly reflect current French taste known to upper-class Americans. Sargent's brother-in-law, Samuel Welles, wrote from Paris in 1811: "I have been indefatigably engaged in observing the taste of finishing and furnishing houses in France and in procuring those articles of fashion which can be procured in no other part of the world than Paris."[20] Welles went on to mention that he had obtained, in addition to various furnishings, "Models in wood for the chairs and tabourets" and "drawings of the present fashion of making all articles of furniture," implying that he intended Boston craftsmen to make at least some of his furniture in the French style. However, Welles never returned to Boston, choosing to live the rest of his life in Paris. Hence, it is likely that Henry and Hannah Welles Sargent may have fallen heir to some of the French furnishings Welles sent to Boston.

The marbletop center table in *The Tea Party* closely resembles one that descended in the Sargent family (fig. 16), and possibly Sargent used it as a model for the one he actually painted, though clearly there are some variations. Regardless, he was familiar with this characteristically French form that influenced the taste and preferences of both Boston patrons as well as craftsmen. Several Boston center tables of this form are known, the most superb of which was originally owned by Nathan Appleton. Also of interest is the fact that several of the groups of guests, and their poses, echo drawings by the English artist and engraver Henry Moses in *A series of twenty-nine designs of modern costume, drawn and engraved . . .* (London, 1823), which depicts a number of the rooms in Thomas Hope's Duchess Street mansion.

Gilmor's European sketch shows an extraordinary pair of lamps on the pier table against the rear wall that are similar to a pair of elegant French ones owned in Philadelphia by the French émigré Stephen Girard (fig. 17). While nothing survives to document Girard's purchase of these lamps, they may be the "2 Argand lamps" that were listed together with "1 Organ" and valued at $200 in the 1832 inventory of his "Front Parlour, Up Stairs."[21] Lamps closely related to these are referred to as "Paris lamps" in English trade catalogs of the period, and "Annular French Lamps" in Webster and Parkes's *An Encyclopaedia of Domestic Economy* of *1845*.[22]

Another fashionable lighting device that wealthy Americans must have known from their European travels, and hence adopted for use in their elegant interiors, was the elaborate gilt

18

CANDELABRUM
one of a pair

c. 1804–1820

Signed Rabiat, France

Gilt bronze

H. 35¾ in.

PEDESTAL
one of a pair

c. 1820

Baltimore

White pine with painted and
gilded decoration

H. 36 in.

*The Saint Louis Art Museum: Friends
purchase with funds donated by the
Measuregraph Company in honor of
Henry B. Pflager*

bronze candelabrum. A number of French candelabra with American provenances are known, but perhaps the most interesting are two that have always been used on a pair of painted Baltimore pedestals (fig. 18). Said to have descended through the family of Betsy Patterson Bonaparte, the green-painted pedestals are distinctly the product of at least two Baltimore craftsmen, a cabinetmaker and a decorative painter. The candelabra that have always rested atop these pedestals were probably made in Paris and are signed "Rabiat." The stenciled gilt decoration repeated on all four sides of the pedestals relates to motifs used on other examples of Baltimore painted furniture during the first two decades of the nineteenth century. Massive ormolu candelabra, often in the form of winged female figures that derived from ancient sources, were popular importations during this period. In November 1806 Rosalie Stier Calvert wrote to her father in Antwerp reminding him that: "In my letter I asked you to please send me a pair of candelabra to place on the mantel in the drawing room in the same style as the ones you had here, with bronze figures (those are the nicest I have ever seen). I am sorry, dear Father, to cause you so much trouble, but these are things which have to be chosen by a person of taste."[23] Apparently there were no "lustres or candelabra in Antwerp," so Rosalie wrote back to her father over a year later, in December 1807, that "I will have them sent from London. . . . One of our best friends, Mr. Foster, who is presently embassy secretary, is returning to London. He is a man of taste and someone to whom I can explain exactly what I want as well as at what price."[24]

Classical taste and styles abroad were evidenced in extremely rich European textiles, porcelains, silver, and furniture. Often American travelers purchased such goods either directly in Paris or by special order through agents in America and abroad. Soon after their marriage in 1809, Mr. and Mrs. David Sears of Boston traveled and lived in Europe between 1811 and 1814. Their lifestyle abroad brought them into the most elite court circles and thoroughly acquainted them with current classical taste and the most favored styles. Through their exposure to European culture, their taste inclined strongly toward French fashions. In 1818, when architect Alexander Parris designed an elegant mansion for them on Beacon Street in Boston, they ordered a number of extraordinary objects from Paris. The most unusual piece, and alas one that suffered sorely in transport, was a musical pier table and accompanying clock. On May 12, 1818, Sears wrote to his agent in Paris:

> I am sorry however to say that oweing to negligence in packing the musical pier table is nearly destroyed, the machinery bent & broken and the pipes flattened and twisted into different forms, and the whole loose in the table. . . . The clock and cover came in good order. . . . The table and clock form a beautiful piece of furniture and exactly answer my wishes and had the music been perfect I should have had nothing to desire.[25]

By late 1820 the Searses' house was nearing completion, and the owners were focusing on major aspects of interior decoration. Apparently other Bostonians had procured goods in Paris from an S.V.S. Wilder, Esq., so on December 10th David Sears wrote to Mr. Wilder, requesting him "to purchase curtains & a few ornamental articles for a new house, which I have lately erected. . . ." So that Sears would get exactly what he wanted, he enclosed "patterns of colours & a sketch of the windows for the curtains to be made up, & also the dimensions of the niches for the vases."[26]

Unfortunately Sears did not copy his sketch for the curtains into his letterbook, but he did include the "Memorandum of Mrs. Sears" as follows:

> Two window curtains with cornices, to be made of yellow satin, the colour of the pattern enclosed & sprigged with amaranth with a deep fringe & curtain of white silk instead of muslin— Also to be sent in addition to this two curtains, made in Paris the same quantity of satin and fringe which compose them of the same colour & sprig. Also—Twenty four satins for chairs—backs & seats, without arms, with medallions, shaded with one colour to match curtains—Also two patterns of the same for Sophas. N.B. The frames &c of the chairs & sophas to be made in America—[27]

When the Searses' house was finally completed, these lavish hangings and upholstery fabrics must have made a striking impact upon all who saw them. Charles Russell Codman of Boston was one friend who was impressed enough to remember the Searses' curtains when he wished to purchase new ones for himself in 1824 (fig. 19).

In a letter to Samuel Welles, Esq., in Paris on March 5, 1824, he wrote:

> I am in want of the following articles of furniture for my drawing room
> 2 Window Curtains
> 2 Sofas
> 6 Chairs (Fauteuils)

19

CURTAIN
fragment

c. 1824

France

Silk with wooden mold fringe

Border: W. 3½ in.

Tassel: L. 7 in.

Society for the Preservation of New England Antiquities, Boston; Gift of Dorothy S. F. M. Codman

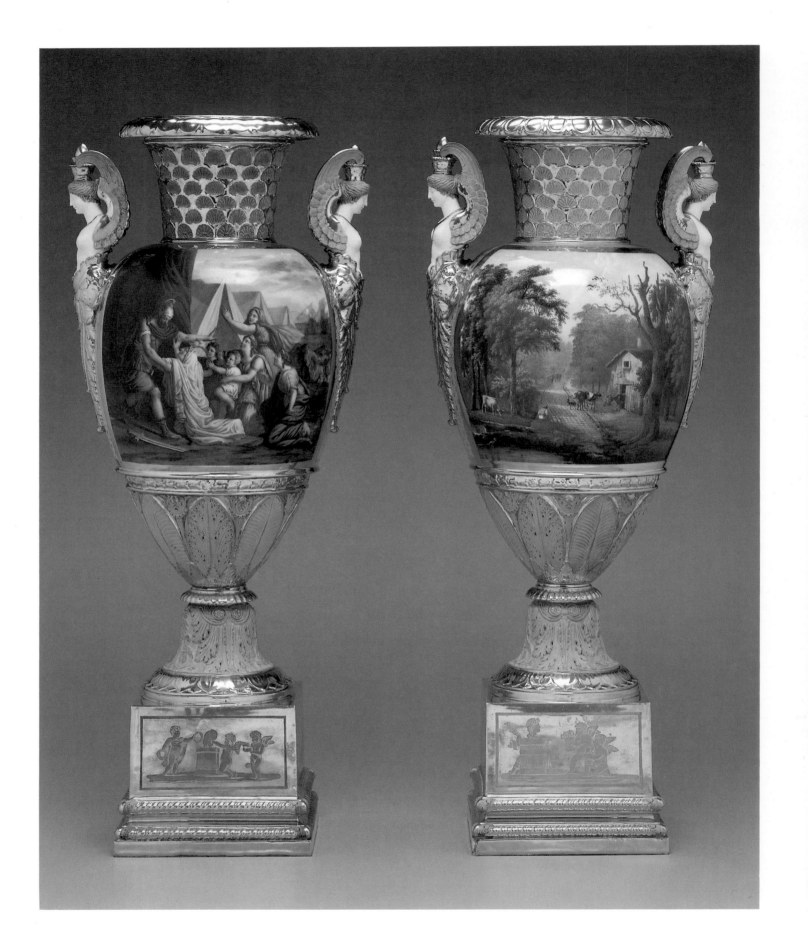

The colors of my carpet are Rose color and yellow and it is not very important which of these colors you select; I think I should prefer the former.

If the Curtains and Chairs are Rose color the fringes and lace and medallions for the chairs and sofas should be of yellow and vice versa—The drapery or inner curtain of white silk. . . .

Mr. Sears imported some time ago, some curtains made of satin and lined which although more expensive I should prefer silk, as I think the latter has a mesquin appearance.

Codman concluded this order by stating, "I wish you to procure these articles to be made for me in the best style—rich but not gaudy."[28] No doubt "in the best style" meant the current classical style preferred in Paris. The French silk curtains purchased by Codman were so highly valued that over time descendants continued to use them, simply reworking the size and form of these brilliant rose and yellow window curtains with their striking floral medallion borders.

Perhaps while in Paris Mr. and Mrs. Sears may have admired the exquisitely mounted and decorated porcelains produced at any number of manufactories within the environs of the city. To the memorandum ordering the silk curtains, Sears added: "Also [send] two large Porcilain vases to place in the niches—The price limited to 500 frances each."[29] Presumably the vases that Sears ordered are the two richly decorated ones that descended to his granddaughter, Clara Endicott Sears, who in 1963 bequeathed to the Museum of Fine Arts, Boston, "the two Sèvres vases bought by the Honorable David Sears, my grandfather, from the possessions of the Empress Josephine of France, the wife of Napoleon the First, at the breaking up of her Chateau Malmaison; these vases were ordered made especially for the Empress Josephine by Napoleon the First" (fig. 20).[30] The association with Malmaison is questionable, and may in part have been perpetuated by an 1886 "Memoir of the Honorable David Sears" that stated he "ornamented the original doorway of his new house in Beacon Street with a pair of beautiful white marble vases saved from the wreck of Malmaison."[31]

Sears's Beacon Street neighbor, Nathan Appleton, also owned a pair of exquisitely painted French porcelain vases, marked by Parisian manufacturer and retailer Marc Schoelcher (fig. 21). Exactly when and

how Appleton acquired these urn-shaped, exquisitely painted vases is not known, though they probably were purchased after his marriage in 1806 and before 1820. Appleton did travel abroad in 1802 and again in 1810, but the second trip took him only to England and Scotland, and not France. Like Sears, Appleton may have ordered his vases through an agent or a friend in Paris. Each vase has two painted scenes, one a pastoral landscape and the other a stormy seascape, per-haps after paintings by Claude-Joseph Vernet. The remaining surface of the vases is gilt, with a shimmering pattern of palmettes and foliate decoration created by a combination of burnished and matte gilding. While the vases are signed "Schoelcher" in overglaze on their bottoms, it is possible that Marc Schoelcher was the retailer and did not actually manufacture them since his factory reportedly was closed by 1810. In 1804 he had opened a salesroom on the Boulevard des Italiens, which became a fashionable venue for sophisticated wares, many of them procured from the numerous local Parisian manufactories.

Americans traveling and buying abroad, as well as ordering from home, provided a ready market for all types of classically inspired French, English, and Chinese export ceramics in the early decades of the nineteenth century. From extensive dinner sets to finely decorated tea sets, many examples with American provenances can be cited.[32] While some clients had the privilege of vis-iting shops abroad and selecting their wares firsthand, others, like Sears, wrote to agents, and still more purchased these symbols of affluence and status from importers in America. Though it is unknown from whom Stephen Girard of Philadelphia acquired his unusually handsome French porcelain tea set in the early years of the century, it represents the highest quality and most fash-ionable taste, with urn-shaped sugar bowl and ewer-form cream pot (fig. 22). Marked by the Parisian partnership of Christophe Dihl and Antoine Guérhard, each piece exhibits a different marbled ground color ornamented with varied gilt decoration. Dihl, the technical and scientific partner in the firm, devoted himself to research in colors and achieved extraordinary success with both color and decoration; hence, his factory was said to rival the finest Sèvres productions. In view of this, it is clear that the variety of color and decoration on Girard's tea set was not a fault but an important mark of Dihl's achievements, and indeed quite innovative as well as fashionable![33] Another European émigré, Rosalie Stier Calvert of Maryland, actually requested a similar set of porcelain when she wrote to her sister in Antwerp in 1807: "I have asked Papa to send me several things; if they haven't been shipped yet, would you buy me four of the prettiest coffee cups you can find—each cup should be of a different <u>color</u>, but of equal size and shape. I want to place them on the mantel, which is the style here."[34]

Whether buying from retail agents at home or abroad, Americans had a wide range of European ceramic tablewares to chose from in the classical taste. Shopping in Paris or London must have been a tantalizing adventure if one was fortunate enough to visit some of the elaborate showrooms retailing wares of refinement and quality. When States Dyckman of New York was in England between 1800 and 1804, attempting to recover his fortune and resolve his financial distress, he visited a number of these establishments, including that of Wedgwood and Byerley. In the fall of 1803, having successfully recouped long-due annuities, he shipped back to New York "11 Trunks of Books and 20 Cases of Various articles," among which was a "Deep blue and white Jasper cameo" tea service bought from Josiah Wedgwood and Thomas Byerley (fig. 23).[35] Dyckman also purchased Coalport porcelain and "richly cut" glass tablewares. The London showrooms of various manufacturers may have been familiar to Americans who read Ackermann's *Repository of the Arts*, since occasionally he illustrated these renowned establishments, as in February 1809 when the showroom of Wedgwood and Byerley was depicted. The classical cameo reliefs applied to the blue jasperware that Dyckman bought must have seemed quite fashionable to him, though some consumers were less enlightened. On April 7, 1805, Byerley noted in the *London Memorandum Book*, "Please do not send any of those designs that have the appearance of immodesty . . . two Angels embracing each other—for I have had them found fault with."[36]

Another fashionable classical commodity that appears to have enjoyed popularity in this country and been imported in some quantity was the French mantel clock. As noted above, David Sears received a clock and cover from his French agent. He was quite pleased with it and felt it looked handsome atop his musical (albeit broken) pier table. "French clocks" are often noted in contemporary inventories of upper-class Americans, and newspaper advertisements of the period also substantiate this vogue. By the early nineteenth century, Stephen Girard owned an elaborate French mantel clock, and when

23

TEAPOT

1803

Wedgwood Manufactory, Staffordshire, England

Jasperware

Teapot and cover   H. 5⅛ in.

Boscobel Restoration Inc., Garrison, New York; On permanent loan from Dyckman House Collection, City of New York Parks and Recreation

Philadelphia silversmith Thomas Fletcher traveled to England and France in 1815, he purchased marble mantel clocks for resale in America.

In 1817 Stephen Van Rensselaer IV of Albany married Harriet Elizabeth Bayard and soon after began to furnish the mansion that architect Philip Hooker had recently built for him and his bride in a most classical and fashionable manner. In addition to classical New York furniture ordered from the French émigré cabinetmaker Charles-Honoré Lannuier, Van Rensselaer embellished the interior with a richly carved statuary marble mantel, atop which he may have placed his French mantel clock with marble columns and ormolu figure of Minerva (fig. 24). In 1813, prior to his marriage, Van Rensselaer traveled to Europe and lived in Paris where he was presented at Napoleon's court and no doubt developed his taste for French styles.[37] The extraordinary marble mantel that once graced the interior of Van Rensselaer's Albany mansion was probably ordered after his return to America. It is an evocative representation of the taste for classical statuary many Americans acquired through exposure abroad to antique sculpture. At about the same time that Hooker was working on the Van Rensselaer house in Albany, Alexander Parris was designing the Sears house in Boston. It is not surprising that these two gentlemen, contemporaries who traveled in France at the same time, both chose to ornament their houses with classical statuary mantels. Sears was directly involved in ordering his mantels, for on November 16, 1819, he wrote to Messrs. Giant Pillans & Co., in Paris: "Gentlemen—The Spartan has arrived with the marble chimney pieces and statues which you were kind enough to have executed for me. I have no doubt that we shall be much pleased with them when we examine them."[38]

The vogue for imported statuary mantels was strong in America during this period, and numerous other examples can be cited, including elaborate ones owned by George W. Bruen of New York, Joseph Bonaparte of "Point Breeze" at Bordentown, New Jersey, and Rosalie Stier Calvert at "Riversdale" in Maryland.[39] Related to these mantels is the marble statuary pier table that Edward Coleman of Lancaster, Pennsylvania, and Philadelphia presumably purchased during his visit to Italy in 1827 (fig. 5), which was probably one of the "tables imported from Rome" noted in his 1841 will and the "1 Marble Table . . . 250." in his room-by-room inventory.[40]

A principal source for the procurement of Italian marbles was Thomas Appleton, American consul at Livorno, Italy, from 1797 until his death in 1840. Since consular officers did not receive a salary, and Appleton was not personally affluent, it was expected that he would make his living as a merchant exporting sundry goods. He actually specialized in the export of works of art, marble statuary, and various ornamental items of classical form. His clients ranged from Boston to North Carolina, and in fact he acted as Jefferson's agent on several occasions. His most constant trade, however, was in the "minor arts," and this included shipments of marble chimney pieces. While often these seemed to be of simple form, there were shipments of quite elaborate ones, exemplified by the "2 white elegant Statuary marble chimnies in 7 Cases" he sent to Thomas Perkins of Boston in 1818, and later in June of the same year, "three cases contg a fine marble Statuary chimney piece," he shipped to David Ware of Philadelphia.[41]

Americans who traveled abroad enjoyed the opulence of tables set with finely wrought silver, including the most fashionable tea and tablewares made in imitation of classical forms. The purchase of English and French silver tablewares by those who could afford them was not uncommon, as evidenced by the numerous foreign pieces with American provenances known today. The importation of new-style forms such as urns and new-fashion teapots provided a major avenue for the transferral of classical style to this country by the last quarter of the eighteenth century. A number of prominent public figures and classical tastesetters, such as President James Monroe, owned impressive French silver.[42] By the early decades of the nineteenth century, specific motifs and ornament were adapted by American silversmiths, at the same time that émigré craftsmen brought with them the latest taste, forms, and fashions.

The documented ownership in Boston, Philadelphia, and New Orleans of French candlesticks demonstrates how imported objects may have provided a source of inspiration for those made by American as well as émigré silversmiths. Both Stephen Girard of Philadelphia and Pierre-Denis de La Ronde of New Orleans owned classical columnar silver candlesticks similar to those produced abroad in brass and gilt bronze (fig. 25).[43] The dramatic Parisian-made, Egyptian-style candlesticks owned by de La Ronde closely resemble a pair, "lacquer'd and bronz'd," illustrated in an English trade catalog of about 1812.[44] The Girard sticks, with bold anthemion leaves encircling their tops, relate to ones made about 1812 in Philadelphia by the partnership of Simon Chaudron and Anthony Rasch. Chaudron had emigrated from Santo Domingo, and Girard is known to have been a client of his, so he may have been familiar with Girard's French sticks purchased in 1805 from Robert P. Branu in Paris. Rasch had come to America in 1804 from Hamburg, Germany, and also may have been well acquainted with classical European styles. The Philadelphia candlesticks combine elements seen on both de La Ronde's and Girard's French candlesticks. Whether Chaudron and Rasch were working from

26

COVERED URN

1819–1838

Marc-Augustin (?) Le Brun, Paris

Silver

H. 12¼ in.

The Baltimore Museum of Art:
Anonymous Gift in Memory of Lydia
Howard DeFord (BMA 1969.24a-b)

EWER

1819–1838

Maker's mark J$_C$A not identified,
Paris

Silver

H. 14 in.

Hampton National Historic Site,
National Park Service, Towson,
Maryland

French or English examples they knew firsthand, or engraved catalogs, is unknown. However, they freely combined motifs to achieve a highly successful expression strongly representative of classical European sources.

A number of impressive and extraordinarily finely wrought pieces of French silver are traditionally said to have been given by General Lafayette to American friends and hosts during his triumphal tour of America in 1824–1825 (fig. 26). Family tradition holds that the elegant silver ewer (right) that descended to Eliza Eichelberger Ridgely of "Hampton," north of Baltimore, was a gift to her father, Nicholas Greenbury Ridgely, from Lafayette. The cast handle in the form of a winged caryatid and the bold band of classical ornament circling the body of the ewer represent the highest-style French silver of the period. The two-handled French urn (left), thought to have been presented to Lydia E. Hollingsworth of Baltimore by Lafayette, provided another equally rich expression of classical ornament for American patrons and craftsmen to absorb and adapt. So crisply and precisely worked are the motifs on the urn that some resemble the finest ormolu mounts used on European and American furniture. The cast classical borders that circle the body of this urn at the top rim, the shoulder, and the base are frequently echoed on the die-rolled borders of American silver of the period. The highly sculptural foliage seen on the base of the body and trailing around the handles is also seen on American-made ewers and other vessels in this highly expressive classical taste.

The unmarked French silver stand holding a covered dish marked by the Philadelphia silversmith Edward Lownes (working 1811–1834) presents another interesting instance of imported European goods (fig. 27). The diminutive stand is laden with finely cast and chased classical ornament: cupids holding doves, floral garlands, partially draped females reclining on dolphins, satyr masks, lyres, and grapevines. The three splayed legs are reminiscent of those on French coffee pots fashioned in the ancient amphora shape. Usually stands like this held glass containers for sweetmeats, jam, or other condiments; the silver covered dish now in this stand may have been a replacement for such a glass container. The inventory of Lownes's estate, taken September 26, 1834, lists a "French sugar bowl" and "French stands," confirming that he imported foreign-made silver probably for resale.[45] Working in a city with patrons who demanded fine and fashionable goods, Lownes was a good businessman and aggressive entrepreneur, knowing that

27

COVERED BOWL IN STAND

1817–1834

Bowl: Edward Lownes
(1792–1834), Philadelphia;
Stand: probably France

Silver

H. 7⁹⁄₁₆ in.

Courtesy Winterthur Museum, Winterthur, Delaware

stylish French silver had a local, if not national, appeal. The quality of this imported silver stand is extremely high, and its classical style must have served as an emblem of taste and refinement for those who could afford to own one.

England, and especially its metropolis, London, provided American travelers with a source of cultural and aesthetic inspiration equally as rich as that found in Paris. The society was lively, and introductions for Americans abounded. For those who might not be familiar with the numerous places of interest, and the variety of museums and private collections, guides were published annually that described everything of interest, often in some detail depending on importance. The fact that American artist Benjamin West was one of the most notable figures in the London art world and president of the Royal Academy gave a number of Americans an instant introduction to specific circles. Numerous American tourists and artists visited his studio where they were exposed to the most current fashions in history painting and portraiture. George Ticknor from Boston "spent half the forenoon in Mr. West's gallery, where he has arranged all the pictures that he still owns."[46]

Among the places that Americans most certainly visited in London were The British Museum, The Royal Academy of Arts at Somerset House, and notable private collections such as those of Thomas Hope, Sir John Soane, and the Marquis of Lansdown. In 1818 *The Picture of London* guidebook devoted eight-and-a-half pages to perhaps the most remarkable collection then under one roof, The British Museum. Established in 1753 by Parliament, the collections already contained by the early nineteenth century Sir William Hamilton's "invaluable collection of fictile or Greek vases," the Townleian collection of antique marbles ("accurately described in a catalogue, sold at the doors"), the Elgin marbles, two of the "finest mummies in Europe," and "many articles of Egyptian antiquities which were acquired from the French by the capitulation of Alexandria in 1802."[47]

At The Royal Academy, a visitor might be fortunate enough not only to visit the galleries and see the collection of casts and models from antique statues but also to attend the annual exhibition that generally opened on the First of May. During the winter season, professors of the Academy read lectures to the students, and guests might procure a ticket of admission from one of the forty academicians or twenty associates. John Flaxman, professor of sculpture, and Sir John Soane, professor of architecture, gave lectures that were no doubt well attended since both gentlemen were held in high esteem.

In 1804 the noted patron, collector, designer, and dilettante Thomas Hope opened his recently renovated and redecorated house on Duchess Street to members of The Royal Academy. Since Benjamin West had been commissioned to paint several canvases for this abode of classical emulation, Americans visiting London must have known of this "museum" and been anxious for admission. Indeed, in the summer of 1830, Rembrandt Peale lamented that "A longer residence in London, and at a more favorable season, would have made me acquainted with many other valuable cabinets, such as those of Mr. Hope, Mr. Baring, etc."[48]

Few contemporary accounts of Hope's showplace survive; however, in 1807 he published his *Household Furniture and Interior Decoration*, which illustrated many of the rooms in the house, along with measured drawings of individual pieces of furniture.[49] To English as well as American visitors, Hope's house must have been a revelation, exhibiting a taste that was close to that of Napoleon and his designers Percier and Fontaine. Indeed, some of the furniture in Hope's Drawing Room was of French manufacture: "The chairs & sofas Parisian, ornamented with lyres etc after the antique."[50] The opening of Hope's Duchess Street house, and his subsequent publication of its interiors and furniture designs, seems to have been the primary tremor in the earth-shaking revolution of taste and fashion in England. It would not be long before the aesthetic and visual effects of these changes would be reflected in America.

The evocative watercolor drawn by Adam Buck in 1813, and now believed to be Buck and his family in their London townhouse, reaffirms the strong classical inspiration that confronted Americans who visited important collections of antiquities in London (fig. 28). Previously

thought to represent Thomas Hope and his family, this important image has been firmly reattributed.[51] Buck was a serious student of vases, and indeed owned a number of those actually shown in the watercolor. In 1811 he proposed a publication of engravings from his own drawings of scenes on Greek vases in British private collections. This was to be issued in ten installments of ten engravings each, but, unfortunately, only the first group seems to have been produced. Buck is perhaps best known for the sentimental engravings copied from his numerous drawings of ladies, often seated in klismos chairs, with children on their laps or at their feet. These popular images were widely distributed, and many made their way to America where they sometimes served as inspiration for ornamental painters (fig. 29). As the vogue for anything in the Grecian or classical taste continued, these simple engravings were transfer-printed onto English earthenwares, such as those in figure 155, which found a ready market among a growing middle class in America.

How strongly were Americans influenced by these new English fashions in the first decade of the nineteenth century, and what types of English furniture did they bring back or import? Judging from surviving material evidence, as well as printed documentation, among the most popular English items imported in the early 1800s were painted chairs, described variously in newspaper advertisements and inventories as "gilt," or "japanned." From Boston to Charleston, English chairs painted with classical landscapes and twining grapevines were owned by some of the most affluent and fashionable families (fig. 30). The Otises and Gores in Boston, the Carrolls and Ridgelys in Baltimore, and the Pinckneys of Charleston, all had sets of delicately fashioned and elegantly painted black-and-gold English chairs. By the end of the second decade, the vogue for fancy painted furniture had been fully embraced by American chairmakers. Easily assembled and cheaply transported, these affordable chairs were a part of many middle- and upper-class households, from Maine to New Orleans.

But what about the high-style klismos chairs that Hope, Ackermann, and La Mésangère illustrated in their respective publications? Were many of these English or Continental examples imported into America? What evidence survives today to indicate that perhaps interiors on this side of the Atlantic might have boasted fashionable, European-made Grecian furniture? When Rosalie Stier Calvert "imported several pieces of furniture from London" in 1807, what was the form and ornament of these pieces?[52] Little is known about the furniture that John Tayloe may have ordered about 1800 to furnish his newly completed mansion in Washington. Just

around the corner from the President's House, this unusual three-story brick mansion was designed by Dr. William Thornton. Surviving today are seven chairs from a larger set (possibly twelve or fourteen) that was originally painted and most probably English in origin. However, the more intriguing object is the klismos chair that has descended in the Tayloe family and may have been part of a larger number that adorned the fashionable drawing room of this most stylish home (fig. 31). With the dramatic curve of its deep tablet top and the unusual circular seat and sabre legs, this chair, made of beech and perhaps originally painted, offers a tantalizing reminder of what might have existed in other American drawing rooms.

In addition to the Tayloe klismos chair, other contemporary visual evidence suggests that a number of Washingtonians may have had sophisticated European klismos chairs. In the portrait of

John Randolph of Roanoke, Virginia, painted by Gilbert Stuart in Washington in 1805, Randolph is seated in a klismos chair with a deeply curved tablet top over which he rests his left arm (fig. 32). Stuart, who painted at least forty-five portraits in Washington between December 1803 and July 1805, broke from his normal convention in the other Washington portraits by placing Randolph in this very classical chair. The only other portrait during that period in which he used a related chair was the image of Mrs. Lawrence Lewis, née Nelly Parke Custis, granddaughter of Martha Washington.[53] Stuart's limited use of this form of chair suggests that perhaps

32

JOHN RANDOLPH

c. 1803–1805

Gilbert Stuart (1755–1828), Washington, D.C.

Oil on canvas

29⅛ x 24⅛ in.

his sitters actually owned chairs of this high-style form and specifically requested to be portrayed in these attitudes. Randolph is known to have been a great Anglophile who visited England almost annually in the latter part of his life. It has been said that "Everything English delighted him and was held up by him as a model," so it is likely that he would have owned the most fashionable Grecian-style chairs from abroad.[54]

Besides the importation of English furniture into America, there are instances of American furniture copied directly from English sources. Thomas Hope's 1807 *Household Furniture and Interior Decoration* appears at least to have inspired numerous American cabinetmakers, but few direct derivations from his designs can be cited. While copies of this important early work were owned in America, few have been enumerated, though it is known that copies were owned in Boston and Philadelphia. In 1819 James Lloyd gave a copy of *Household Furniture* to the Boston Athenaeum, and in Philadelphia both the American Philosophical Society and The Library Company owned Hope. Whether or not Lloyd, a Boston lawyer, had owned the book for long before giving it to the Athenaeum is impossible to determine. Since little is known of the cabinetmakers Thomas Cook and Richard Parkin, either may have come to Philadelphia from England

CLASSICAL TASTE IN AMERICA

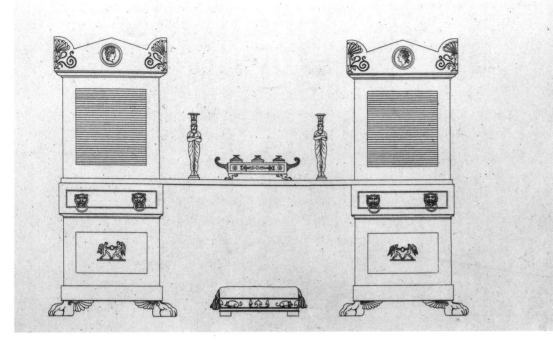

33 opposite

The rich mahogany-veneered sideboard made by the Philadelphia partnership of Thomas Cook and Richard Parkin, c. 1800–1825, was derived from a design by Thomas Hope (fig. 34). Clearly this piece of furniture was meant to support and shelter ornamental as well as useful objects for dining. The Parisian porcelain urns signed "Schoelcher" were originally owned by Nathan Appleton of Boston, and the portrait of *Musidora* by Thomas Sully was exhibited in Baltimore in 1820. The templelike cellarette, attributed to Baltimore cabinetmaker William Camp, was originally owned by John and Eliza Ridgely at "Hampton," and was used to hold spirituous liquors. The classically styled tea set by Samuel Kirk of Baltimore is also directly derived from an English design source, and is thought to have been made for Haslett and Sarah Birckhead McKim about the time of their marriage in 1841.

34

PLATE 11 FROM HOUSEHOLD FURNITURE AND INTERIOR DECORATION
1807
Thomas Hope (1769–1831), London
18½ x 11¹³⁄₁₆ in.

Boston Athenaeum; Gift of James Lloyd, 1819

and perhaps could have seen the publication abroad, or brought a copy with them.[55] At any rate, a sideboard made and labeled during their brief partnership (1820–1825) documents the fact that they must have seen Hope's designs at some time, as the piece almost exactly replicates the "large library or writing-table, flanked with paper presses, or escrutoirs" in plate 11 of *Household Furniture* (figs. 33 & 34).

Whether the patron or the craftsmen decided to make this a sideboard instead of a writing desk is unknown, but several other minor changes were also made, omitting the pediments that "present the shape of ancient Greek house roofs . . . [that] contain the heads of the patron and patroness of science, of Apollo and Minerva."[56] Cook and Parkin omitted the drawers in the mid-sections of the pedestals, but added freestanding columns flanking the tambour slides on the upper sections of the pedestals.[57] That this piece was intended as a sideboard is confirmed by the fact that there are sliding drawers with cutout hand grips (for linens and silverware) behind the tambour doors, and a divided box for bottled liquors that slides out of the lower right pedestal.

Italy, one of the primary sources of classical antiquity, was the ultimate destination for many traveling Americans. However, in 1821 when Eliza Leaycraft Smith of New York traveled abroad with her father, she was thrilled to see Nîmes, "celebrated for its Roman antiquities," but disappointed that they were unable to get to Rome and Naples, and thus she "lost the opportunity of seeing Rome, the great wish of my heart."[58] The physical remains of antiquity were one predominant attraction for numerous American travelers, since many of them had read published accounts of Italy's wonders of antiquity, as well as having seen engraved prints in books and periodicals. William Cullen Bryant expressed the sentiments of most travelers when in 1834 on his first trip abroad he observed: "Everything we saw spoke of the past."[59]

Traveling in Italy afforded the opportunity to visit actual sites, to wander through museums and galleries filled with excavated treasures, and occasionally to make some purchases of either copies, a real classical fragment or vase, or an exceptional mosaic tabletop or statuary marble mantel. Herculaneum, Pompeii, and Paestum were three of the classical sites that attracted Europeans and Americans alike, since they were already well published and had gained a significant reputation. The experience of actually viewing these vestiges of an ancient culture was overwhelming, and some travelers wrote eloquently about their most ethereal thoughts and "the impulse to tread in the footsteps, apparently so recent, of the ancient Pompeiians."[60] Since most visitors proceeding to Pompeii, Herculaneum, and Paestum stayed in Naples en route, they usually availed themselves of the opportunity to visit the local museum that contained thousands of artifacts excavated at those sites. Museum fatigue might well have been a pervasive problem on rainy days like the one Rembrandt Peale spent "examining the antiquities of Herculaneum and Pompeii" in the museum at Naples:

> We commenced with a collection of gold bracelets, chains, ear and finger rings. . . . In the room where those articles are, is a magnificent Cameo, said to be the largest in the world, wrought out of a single piece of agate, about nine or ten inches in diameter. . . . One chamber is filled with a vast variety of articles made of glass, of which substance it was supposed the ancients were ignorant, consisting of plates for window lights. . . . The next room contains about two thousand articles of bronze, many of which were found in temples. . . . Finally, other apartments are filled with an immense, elegant, and varied collection of vases, made of baked clay, of all sizes, and in every imaginable form, ornamented with figures. . . . The walls of two large apartments, on the ground floor, are covered with fresco paintings taken from Pompeii.[61]

The most remarkable ancient Greek site, which awed those fortunate Americans who visited there, was Paestum, about fifty miles from Naples. Largely unknown until the middle of the eighteenth century, Paestum was visited in February 1775 by four adventurous Americans, John Singleton Copley, Mr. and Mrs. Ralph Izard, and a Mr. Archer. By the second decade of the nineteenth century, Paestum gained greater recognition and visitation, and among those who ventured into its malarial environs were young Edward Everett and George Bancroft, from Boston. Bancroft wrote eloquently of the impact of this captivating site:

> We entered and felt the power which a scene like this exercises on the soul. . . . The three public buildings of Paestum which yet stand in glorious ruin, form the most admirable monument of the high minds of its ancient inhabitants . . . the model of ruins [the Temple of Neptune]. It is the most perfect, most picturesque, most beautiful wreck of a temple in the world. . . . The temple has an air of imposing grandeur, which inspires awe into the mind. . . . I repeat this is the ne plus ultra of beautiful ruins.[62]

CLASSICAL TASTE IN AMERICA

While Everett's account of Paestum does not survive, he must have been similarly awed, as years later he commissioned a monumental painting of the ruins at Paestum for his house in Boston. Copying a plate from Thomas Major's *The Ruins of Paestum* (London, 1768), the Boston painter John Ritto Penniman executed this bold panorama in grisaille.[63] For those Americans who never experienced the visual thrill of Paestum, they might have read Henry Pickering's 1822 grandiloquent poem, *The Ruins of Paestum*. Perhaps even more accessible to the nonadventurous were the travel essays written by Nathaniel Parker Willis for the *New York Mirror* in 1833.

For many Americans, Italy possessed a power and seduction that no other country could equal. The center of that lure was Rome, and virtually hundreds of American travelers, artists, and writers have variously expressed their love of this timeworn and modern city over the last few centuries.[64] The attractions were multitudinous, but the summation was often the same. Like many, George Ticknor felt that "Rome is worth all the other cities in the world" and that "One of the greatest pleasures in Rome is certainly going out to see its churches, palaces, and ruins in the evening and by moonlight."[65] The art in the many galleries of the Vatican, the Museum of the Capitoline, the French Academy of the Arts, and the Castel Sant' Angelo, were all attractions not to be missed, by both artists and tourists. For a painter like Rembrandt Peale, the magnificent private palaces, "whose collections of pictures constitute one of the greatest attractions of Rome," were an extraordinary resource of ancient and Renaissance paintings, statues, marbles, and mosaics. For years following his Italian sojourn, Peale drew inspiration from the many masterpieces he had seen. His sensitive portrayal of a modern lady as the Greek poetess Erinna evokes the classical ideals of simplicity and grace (fig. 35). While a portion of this painting is an expression of classicism, there is a Renaissance overtone to the entire mood. Among the varied "souvenirs" that one might bring back from Rome were articles fashioned in mosaic. Fascinated with this intricate production, Peale visited the Studio of Mosaics in a lower apartment of the Vatican. Mosaic tabletops were a particular favorite of American travelers, and as early as 1800 E. H. Derby returned to Salem, Massachusetts, with "Curiosities from Italy he had collected. The marble & inlaid tables, the Bustos, & the Coins & the rich engravings . . . to introduce works of Taste into this Country."[66]

Edward Coleman of Lancaster and Philadelphia visited Europe in 1827. Though he sailed from New York to Liverpool, the remainder of his itinerary is unknown. However, in 1841 he left to his three daughters his "marble mantles and

35

ERINNA, A GREEK POETESS
1845

Rembrandt Peale (1778–1860),
Philadelphia

Oil on canvas

18½ x 15½ in.

*Collection Dorothy McIlvain Scott,
Baltimore: Promised Gift to
The Baltimore Museum of Art (BMA
R.13178)*

tables imported from Rome," suggesting that he may have visited Italy. Just two years before his trip, Coleman had inherited great wealth upon the death of his father, Robert Coleman, the Lancaster iron-master and owner of the Elizabeth Furnace. Before his departure, or immediately upon his return, Edward purchased the grand Philadelphia residence of Joshua Lippincott at 381 Mulberry [Arch] Street: A double-width house built about 1817, its first floor had four sizable rooms: a front and back parlor, a dining room, and a library. In each parlor Coleman had "1 Italian Marble Mantle" valued at $250, with "1 Marble Table . . . 250.00" in the front parlor, and "2 Italian Marble Tables . . . 325.00" in the back parlor.[67]

Since Coleman's two Italian marble tables in the back parlor are listed together, it is likely that they were a pair. While the provenance of the table stamped by Anthony G. Quervelle in figure 36 cannot be documented earlier than the turn of the century, a virtually identical table, though unmarked, descended from Coleman's daughter Harriet through the Livingston and Delafield families.[68] Possibly Coleman saw specimen marble tops like these abroad and either selected the pair himself in Rome or once home determined that he must send to Italy for them. While the Colemans' front parlor appears to have been the music room, the back parlor was no doubt the

36

CENTER TABLE

c. 1827–1830

Anthony Gabriel Quervelle (1789–1856), Philadelphia

Mahogany, mahogany veneers; various marbles; brass

30⅛ x 46¾ in.

The Baltimore Museum of Art: Friends of the American Wing Fund; Decorative Arts Fund; and Purchase with exchange funds from: Gift of Mrs. Edwin O. Anderson, Maplewood, New Jersey; Gift of Elizabeth Baer; Gift of Ellen Howard Bayard; Gift of Harrison T. Beacham; Gift of Col. Louis Beck, Baltimore; Gift of Harry C. Black; Gift of David K. E. Bruce, in Memory of Mrs. Dwight F. Davis, Washington, D.C.; Gift of Mrs. W. W. Crocker; Gift of Mr. and Mrs. Johnson Garrett, Washington, D.C.; Gift of Howard M. Greenbaum, Annapolis, Maryland, in Memory of his Father, Harry Greenbaum; Nelson and Juanita Greif Gutman Collection; Gift of Mr. and Mrs. J. Benjamin Katzner, Baltimore; Gift of Mrs. Albert Lowenthal; Gift of Dr. John L. Peck; Gift of Mr. and Mrs. David Stockwell; Gift of Dr. Richard W. TeLinde, Baltimore; Gift of Mr. and Mrs. Bernard Trupp, Baltimore; Gift of William C. Whitridge, Stevenson, Maryland (BMA 1990.73)

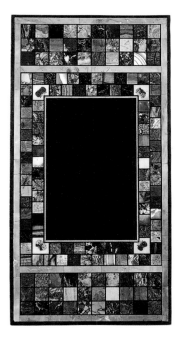

elegant principal salon, and among the furnishings were a pair of rosewood lounges, ten rose-wood chairs, two large mirrors, a glass chandelier, alabaster vases, gilt candelabra, and a gilt cornice with satin window curtains.

Coleman's choice of French émigré cabinetmaker Anthony G. Quervelle as the artisan to fashion his marbletop center tables is not surprising, as Quervelle was among the most eminent makers in Philadelphia at the time.[69] Larger than most center tables, its five scrolled legs with strong paw feet, carved acanthus leaves, grapevines, and rich veneers are characteristic of Quervelle's finest work.[70] The unusual star-shaped stretcher relates to features seen on the facades of Quervelle sideboards and desk and bookcases. The imported cast brass feet are marked by the Birmingham firm of Hamper and Yates, and appear originally to have had a resin coating to preserve the gold-like brilliance of the glittering brass surface. In addition to making fine furniture for wealthy Philadelphians, in 1829 Quervelle, with retailer Lewis Veron acting as agent, sold President Andrew Jackson two center tables and four pier tables for the East Room of the President's House.[71] Less elaborate than the Coleman tables, and having "Blk & Gold Slabs [tops]," President Jackson's "2 Round Tables" cost one hundred dollars each.

Nathan Appleton of Boston was another fashion-conscious American who owned a table with an unusual specimen marble top (fig. 37). Whether his relative, Thomas Appleton, American consul at Livorno, procured this top for him, or it was imported by the Boston cabinetmaker who fashioned the superb base of this distinctive pier table, is unknown. The rectilinear top, composed of

37

PIER TABLE
and view of top

c. 1810–1825

Boston
Mahogany veneer; marble
mosaic; brass
34¼ x 44½ x 20½ in.

Collection Anthony A. P. Stuempfig

approximately 150 squares of different figures and colors of jasper, agate, marble, and other semi-precious stones, has the distinguishing feature of four mosaic butterflies. While these butterflies relate closely to ones on a French mosaic top made at the Manufacture Royale Mosaique by Francesco Belloni,[72] the overall composition and border are similar to a top made in Rome by Giacomo Rafaelli, about 1815.[73] With a cut-brass inlay in the center of the skirt that relates to Appleton's two Grecian couches and two settees, one of which is seen in figure 86, its front paw feet have an unusual drapery swag motif possibly derived from several designs (plates 14, 16, 80) in Thomas Sheraton's *The Cabinet Dictionary* (London, 1803).[74]

When in Italy, some Americans commissioned paintings and sculptures of themselves and their families. The settings they are shown in often proclaim their travel to these ancient and revered

places. Americans who had visited Europe as young people sometimes returned decades later with their wives and children. David Sears and George Ticknor of Boston, as well as Richard Haight of New York, were among these returning travelers. Purportedly for health reasons, Mr. and Mrs. Sears were in Paris the winter of 1829–1830, in Cuba in 1832, and in Italy in 1833–1835. The latter Italian sojourn must have been a memorable one for the family, and their social life probably surpassed that which they might have anticipated in Boston. One contemporary of Sears noted that ". . . his wife and daughters were long remembered as favorites in the cosmopolitan society of the Eternal City, and where he himself was enabled to gratify that intelligent love of art which long before had made him an early friend and patron of the rising genius of the poet-painter Allston."[75]

While in Rome, Sears had an impressive portrait done that depicts him instructing his two sons, David and Frederick, on the art and architecture of Rome (fig. 38). Sears holds a volume in his right hand with "ROMA" on the spine, while an architectural floor plan of the Pantheon is spread on the table before them. In the distant background, through an open window, can be seen a composite view of St. Peter's and presumably the Castel Sant' Angelo. Sears recorded his expenses in a small green-leather notebook he kept while in Rome, noting "Paintings bought at Rome 1834," and farther down the page, "The Travellers—Portraits of self & David & Frederick 200."[76] Unfortunately he did not mention the artist who did this special portrait, but the symbolic cultural message that it projects is clear, with direct allusions to antiquity and the richly furnished surroundings. Sears wished to assure the education and cultivation of taste of his young sons through his own instruction during their stay abroad. This visual statement reinforces the note in the diary of John Quincy Adams on August 12, 1835, that Sears indicated to him that he had been much disappointed in foreign schools for his children and preferred the educational advantages of his own country.[77]

By the 1830s, a number of American sculptors were in residence in Italy, and visits to their studios were requisite for fellow Americans who were students and patrons of the arts. Thomas Crawford had left New York to settle in Rome in 1835, and Horatio Greenough of Boston was working in Florence by 1828. Visits with these artists often resulted in commissions, and such was the case with both David Sears and Mrs. John Jones Schermerhorn, the daughter of Mayor Philip Hone of New York.[78]

In 1838–1839, the English-born artist William J. Hubard painted an evocative portrait of Greenough in his atelier in Florence, surrounded by some of his recent work and his two beloved English greyhounds (fig. 39). Unfortunately, the original painting was damaged in transport, as Hubard wrote to Hiram Powers in Florence on January 20, 1839: "All my pictures that came by Italy were so injured as to be worth nothing. I shall be obliged to copy Greenough's again. The case must have been broken for the contents of Miss G's & my bases were saturated with water and in N.Y. Mr. Coll [?] in repacking thrust the loose articles in by force & all upon the pictures—injuring my pictures and breaking in pieces whatever was by such means perishable."[79]

By the time this image was made, Greenough's reputation was well-established. In January 1839 he wrote to his brother that "A proud and savage concentration is sometime necessary here. . . . I am happy to say this has been my most productive year. No man since Canova has undertaken more."[80]

Greenough's choice of greyhounds as pets introduces an interesting classical allusion. An ancient breed known to have been guardians of the tombs of the pharaohs, greyhounds are also seen in sculpture from the 4th century B.C., further establishing the ancient status of the breed. Greenough's dogs were well known, both abroad and in his native Cambridge, Massachusetts. His favorite, and the one that he chose to sculpt in 1839, was named Arno, after the river that flows through Florence. Arno was "a fine, tall milk-white greyhound," and Greenough wrote that "Everyone is enamoured of him. I gave five dollars for him, and have already received fifty-five dollars worth of pleasure."[81]

HORATIO GREENOUGH

c. 1839

William James Hubard
(1807–1862), Florence

Oil on canvas

36 x 29⅛ in.

Valentine Museum, Richmond,
Virginia

40 below, left

INKSTAND

c. 1838–1847

Obadiah Rich (1809–1888),
Boston

Silver; colorless glass

H. 5⅝ in.

The Fogg Art Museum, Harvard
University, Cambridge, Massachusetts;
Bequest of Mrs. William Norton
Bullard

41 below, right

CHAFING DISH

c. 1838–1847

Attributed to Obadiah Rich
(1809–1888), Boston; Retailed
by Jones, Ball and Poor, Boston
(c. 1838–1847)

Silver

3¼ x 6½ in.

Courtesy Winterthur Museum,
Winterthur, Delaware

With origins in classical antiquity, it is not surprising that greyhounds appear in diverse and varied guises in early nineteenth-century decorative arts: reclining at the foot of a Grecian couch designed by Thomas Hope, engraved on glass tumblers made in Pittsburgh, and cast in silver on inkwells and a chafing dish wrought by the Boston silversmith Obadiah Rich (figs. 40 & 41). While no specific relationship can be discovered between Rich and Greenough, they were both residents of

Cambridge and members of the Boston Athenaeum and surely must have known one another, so it is likely that Rich either used the artist's greyhounds as models or at least knew Greenough's sculpture.

A native of New York, Thomas Crawford was the first American sculptor to establish residence in Rome, and he swiftly expressed his desire for the foundation of a "School of Art" in America. "We have surpassed already the republics of Greece in our political institutions, and I see no reason why we should not attempt to approach their excellence in the Fine Arts, which, as much as any thing else, has secured undying fame to Grecian genius."[82] His marble bust of Mrs. John Jones Schermerhorn (fig. 42) reflects the restrained elegance and ideal beauty that characterized the classical precedents of "Grecian genius" Crawford

and his colleagues so admired. The adoption of classical dress and hairstyle for his sitter draws an even stronger parallel between the world of the moderns and that of the ancients. Crawford transformed the much-beloved daughter of Philip Hone into a Grecian beauty, to be long admired by her family and friends following her premature death at about thirty years of age, in 1840.

Another city that American travelers were likely to pass through in Italy was Livorno, a favorite shopping center and port with "large warehouses, affording great facility for receiving and transmitting goods." According to Rembrandt Peale, Livorno was an advantageous place to purchase marble copies, since "For the convenience of exportation there are several magazines of works in alabaster, executed in Volterra, where the finest alabaster is quarried. I was surprised to find some of these works rivalling the best executed at Florence."[83]

However, Peale's contemporary, James Fenimore Cooper, received an entirely different impression of the copies he found in a Livorno warehouse that sent its goods principally to the English and American markets: "Grosser caricatures were never fabricated: attenuated Nymphs and Venuses, clumsy Herculeses, hobbledehoy Apollos, and grinning Fauns, composed the treasures."[84] Fortunately Cooper was not in the market for copies of classical sculpture.

American visitors to Italy were numerous during the first quarter of the century, but far fewer embarked on more adventurous travel to the exotic countries of Greece, Turkey, and Egypt.

Until the conclusion of the Greek War for Independence in 1828, traveling in Greece was not especially safe, though some enthusiastic Americans did venture there without harm. Young Nicholas Biddle from Philadelphia appears to have been among the first Americans to reach Greece in 1806.[85] Barely twenty years old at the time, Biddle had traveled to Paris in 1804 as an unpaid secretary to General John Armstrong, then minister to France. He later served in the same post for James Monroe in England. Recently graduated from Princeton, Biddle was an avid student and scholar and took every opportunity to travel when he had time off. Even as a student he had recognized the value of travel and the ultimate effect it could have on one's virtue and morality.

By the end of the 1820s and into the 1830s, more American travelers were reaching not only Greece but such little-explored lands as Turkey and even Egypt. Published reports of Napoleon's campaigns in Egypt between 1798 and 1801 did much to stir interest in this exotic land. While the French emperor essentially failed to accomplish his mission in Egypt, one major contribution he did make to his fellow countrymen and numerous others in the following years was the impressive publication, *Description de l'Egypte ou recueil des observations et des recherches qui ont été faites en Egypte pendant l'Expédition de l'Armée Française*. In addition to the more than 55,000 troops Napoleon took to Egypt, he also brought along 150 engineers, scientists, and scholars to study and record both modern and ancient Egypt. Vivant Denon, later to become the first director of the Louvre, was the principal artist and largely responsible for the *Description de l'Egypte*. Published between 1802 and 1829, this series of ten monumental volumes included five devoted to antiquity, three on natural history, two on Egyptian history, and two additional atlases. For those curious readers fortunate enough to review this richly engraved array of the antiquities of Egypt, as well as its modern state, they could only admit to awe at such an accomplished ancient civilization. At least one set of this masterful work was in America by 1838, purchased by The Providence Athenaeum and housed in an appropriately monumental "temple" in the form of a polychromed Egyptian tomb specially designed by John Russell Bartlett.[86]

A number of Americans visited Egypt by the 1830s, including John Lowell, Jr., of Boston; George R. Gliddon, American consul at Cairo, Theodore Allen, and Mr. and Mrs. Richard Haight of New York; and Mendes Cohen of Baltimore. Each of these travelers made a distinct contribution to promoting the vision of Egypt in the period, though some were not widely known until the twentieth century. Lowell left Boston in 1833, visiting England, Belgium, France, and Italy before venturing to Greece and Egypt. In Italy he engaged a Swiss artist, John Gleyre, who traveled with him to record various sites in pencil and watercolor sketches. Unfortunately, Lowell died in Bombay in 1836, after Gleyre had left his employ in Khartoum in 1835. While Gleyre's drawings and watercolors provide an evocative record of the ruins of ancient Egypt as viewed in the 1830s, they were never shown publicly until the mid-twentieth century, and hence were not a contemporary source of influence or inspiration.[87]

CLASSICAL TASTE IN AMERICA

Some of the most fascinating and contemporaneously accessible descriptions of travel in Egypt were the letters of Sarah Rogers Haight, as published in *Letters from the Old World By a Lady of New York* in 1840. The Haights traveled abroad in 1836–1837, and Mrs. Haight wrote prolifically and intelligently about all she did and observed. Her writings are evidence that she was well educated and well read and continued to enlighten herself as she traveled. In Alexandria she noted that they "received at Smyrna a fresh supply of books from London and Paris . . . which, together with our previous provision, gives us a complete travelling library of 100 volumes, all pertinent to the subjects most likely to command our attention in these regions."[88] When she wrote from Thebes, she mentioned that while in Paris she "often pored over the splendid illustrations of Napoleon's great works of Egypt . . . but it was not until I stood in the midst of Carnac's city of ruins that I felt the full force of Denon's remarks when speaking of the temple of Dendera."[89]

Her intelligent observations and detailed descriptions are extraordinary, and must have delighted her compatriots at home who were fortunate enough to read these published letters. Her writings, and the family portrait (fig. 68), indicate that she and her husband were collectors, and more than once she mentions acquiring fragments of objects to add to her "small Egyptian cabinet." When she visited the tombs of the pharaohs in the Valley of the Kings, she was particularly taken with

> the little side chambers of the gallery leading to one of the tombs [where there] are some curious paintings, representing articles of household furniture, ornament, &c. Among which I saw sofas, ottomans, tabourets, and couches, of forms very similar to many now in use. Two large *fauteuils* were of such exquisite form and so richly carved, that I could not consent to leave them behind, but wanted the gentlemen to cut them from the wall and take them away with us.[90]

The impulse to pillage apparently was not beyond this "lady" from New York, as earlier in her journey she had "eagerly seized and appropriated as a trophy . . . [a] once beautiful mini capital" from the Alexandrine Library at Serapium. However, she and her husband did attempt to purchase some significant antiquities, and their "principal object was to obtain one of the beautifully ornamented mummy-cases, with its Pharaoh or pontiff within it untouched."[91] Their time proved "too short to enter upon this contraband speculation" and thus they were obliged to abandon the opportunity of adding a splendid mummy and case to their small Egyptian cabinet.

While the relics and antiquities that the Haights brought back are not known to survive today, many of those that Mendes Cohen collected in Egypt were given by him to the Johns Hopkins University, where they remain today. Cohen's travels in Europe were extensive, taking him additionally to Greece, Turkey, and Russia. However, Egypt's culture and material remains were his greatest passion. In 1832 he wrote of some of the objects he had acquired for his collection, including "a Mummy found at Thebes" and "a Crocodile, which it is too inconvenient to send, and shall therefore hang it up in the Consul's warehouse, so that should any American vessel pass this way and will take it aboard, well and good."[92] While the ultimate fate of Cohen's crocodile is unknown, his modest collection of Egyptian artifacts was the first formed by an American and brought to these shores, where it has been used over the years as a teaching collection.[93]

The Americans who traveled abroad in the first four decades of the nineteenth century returned to America not only with material possessions but with seeds of art and culture from the old world. These seeds varied in species and were planted and nourished in multitudinous places and numerous ways. One fact is clear, however, that had it not been for these American travelers, the richness grafted onto the culture of America during this period would have been considerably less brilliant. The refinement of taste in America began in Europe, and the preference for classical taste came from the many objects, writings, descriptions, and accounts both verbal and written that made their way to Americans anxious to learn of European civilizations past and present. As Rosalie Stier Calvert wrote to her mother in 1804, "We are quite well-informed about what is going on in Europe. I think Americans have a natural relish for knowing everything that is happening in the four corners of the world."[94] Though copying our European counterparts was not new, what we were copying was new, albeit ancient in its inspiration.

The English and European gentlemen, painters, sculptors, and craftsmen who came to America to live and work had a commensurate impact on the cultural and aesthetic life of our country. The knowledge and experience, taste and fashion they acquired in their native lands was rapidly disseminated in America through their work and lifestyles. Those who came in contact with them had the advantage of encountering cultural and material examples they otherwise might never have known. The importance of this immigration is a significant factor in the transferral of classical ideals and their material expressions to American shores.

European émigrés came to America for various reasons, often bringing with them impressive personal possessions, or knowledge thereof, from their former lifestyles. In the 1790s some, like Baron Henri Stier from Antwerp, arrived fleeing the oppression and devastation of the Napoleonic wars.[95] Others, like Joseph Bonaparte, elder brother of Napoleon, came to begin a new life in America after his brother's empire had fallen and the Bonaparte family was forced to leave France. Among those who came were also large numbers of artists and craftsmen. Seeking new opportunities in a rapidly developing country, they saw the probability of success for men and women with talent and knowledge of fashions then current abroad.

Joseph Bonaparte was arguably one of the most significant catalysts in disseminating European culture and artistic knowledge to early nineteenth-century Americans. Soon after his arrival in 1815, he purchased "Point Breeze" in Bordentown, New Jersey, a property of about a thousand acres, where he ensconced himself, his entourage, and his fine and decorative arts collections and library (fig. 43). Though his brother had crowned him king of Spain, in America he was known as the Count de Survilliers, and his friends were some of the most distinguished men in the country.

A generous and gracious host in his elegantly appointed mansion, Bonaparte entertained numerous guests, among whom were "a number of the citizens of Bordentown, and of the country, who, with less pretensions to elegance of dress, were received with a kind hospitality."[96] His ties to Philadelphia were close, as he sometimes lived in the city during the winter season, and among his most intimate friends were Stephen Girard, General Thomas Cadwalader, and Joseph Hopkinson, longtime president of the Pennsylvania Academy of the Fine Arts. From all contemporary reports, "Point Breeze" was a mecca of culture along the Delaware River, and often guests were rowed up to the house in a sixteen-oar barge, reportedly given to the count by Girard.

Although the count's house burned early in 1820, much of the art and elegant furnishings were saved, and a grander edifice was reconstructed and appointed with even more superb art and rich furniture: "It has its grand hall and staircase; its great dining-rooms, art gallery and library; its pillars and marble mantels, covered with sculpture of marvelous workmanship; its statues, busts and paintings of rare merit; its heavy chandeliers, and its hangings and tapestry, fringed with gold and silver."[97] The park surrounding the mansion was "laid out in the style of the Escurial grounds . . . and planted on every knoll with statuary."[98] The Philadelphia artist Thomas Birch captured a glimpse of this sublime setting with its complement of classical statuary, while a local artist,

43

POINT BREEZE, THE ESTATE OF JOSEPH NAPOLEON BONAPARTE AT BORDENTOWN, NEW JERSEY

c. 1817–1820

Attributed to

Charles B. Lawrence (c. 1790– c. 1864), Philadelphia

Oil on canvas

27 x 36½ in.

Photograph © 1992, The Art Institute of Chicago. All Rights Reserved. Through prior acquisition of the Friends of American Art Collection, 1987.170.

Charles B. Lawrence, painted a number of views of the surrounding countryside that visually document the idyllic Claudian landscape Bonaparte created:

> A narrow stream . . . winds down through part of the ground between the mansion and the city. . . . The Count, at great expense and labor, threw a brick arch over the stream and built a long causeway, some twenty feet high. . . . Across the lower end of the lagoon he built an embankment, separating it from the creek. This formed a most picturesque lake, some two hundred yards broad and nearly a half mile long.[99]

The most impressive aspect of Bonaparte's estate, however, was his great art collection, some of which was periodically shown at the annual exhibitions of the Pennsylvania Academy of the Fine Arts. Many of his guests and visitors came especially to view these great and sometimes monumental rarities. Among the artists listed in the exhibition catalogs were such masters as Rubens, Poussin, Rembrandt, Vernet, Teniers, de Heem, and Canaletto. There was also a "Statuary Room" containing antique bronze castings from Pompeii, a *Young Diana and Hound* by Bartolini, a figure of *Ceres* (fig. 55) and *A Female Figure in Roman Dress*, both by Bosio, and several busts of Bonaparte family members by Canova.[100] According to one visitor who had the privilege of viewing the count's summer sleeping apartment

> It consisted of a chamber, dressing and bathing-room, with a small studio, or rather boudoir. The curtains, canopy and furniture were of light blue satin, trimmed with silver. . . . The walls were covered with oil paintings, particularly of young females, with less clothing about them than they or you would have found comfortable in our cold climate, and much less than we found agreeable when the Count, without ceremony, led us before them, and enumerated the beauties of paintings with the air of an accomplished amateur.[101]

Bonaparte journeyed to England for the period 1832 to 1837, returning to "Point Breeze" from 1837 to 1839. In the latter year he returned to England, and finally Florence, where he died in 1844. His estate was left to his grandson, Joseph Lucien Charles Napoleon, who sold "Point Breeze" in 1847, following two spectacular auction sales in 1845 and 1847. These sales were well attended and brought good prices, a testimony to the notoriety of this great classical collection and the popularity of the collector: "The furniture brought fabulous prices, the strife among bidders being the desire to obtain some article that belonged to Joseph Bonaparte, to be cherished as an invaluable relic."[102]

Judging from the 1847 auction catalog, some of the most magnificent furniture was in the "Large Drawing Room" and the "Dining Room."[103] The upholstered mahogany furniture, the rich window hangings, the extraordinary gilt lighting fixtures, and the large gilt pier glasses suggest the taste of a nobleman and document the classical European culture presented in this

wooded landscape along the Delaware. While much of this furniture may have been purchased in Philadelphia following the 1820 fire, several pieces are enumerated as being of French origin, and so may represent pieces rescued from the fire. Two "very rich mahogany Side Tables, supported on Egyptian columns, with black marble top and heavy gilt ornaments, (from France.)" were purchased by the Hopkinson family (fig. 44). As exceptional examples of high-style Egyptian taste in America at that time, they were important pieces of furniture that may have influenced the demands of New York and Philadelphia patrons as they ordered furniture from cabinetmakers such as Charles-Honoré Lannuier, Joseph B. Barry, Michel Bouvier, and Anthony G. Quervelle.

Among the many artists and artisans who came to America over the half century between 1790 and 1840 were architects, sculptors, painters, cabinetmakers, silversmiths, upholsterers, and numerous other tradesmen and women. Their material products provided examples of classical expression that many Americans presumably saw or owned. Some of these émigré artisans became well-established and had prosperous careers, while the ventures of others were short-lived and have left us with but a few tantalizing remains to suggest the bulk of their production. The porcelain manufactory established in New York in 1825 by two Frenchmen, Louis-François Decasse and Nicolas-Louis-Edouard Chanou, had just such a brief life. Chanou had apprenticed at the Sèvres Porcelain Manufactory, so his technical knowledge was invaluable and is reflected in

44

PIER TABLE
c. 1800–1810
France
Mahogany, mahogany veneer; marble; mirror; ormolu
39 x 72 x 23 in.

Philadelphia Museum of Art: Gift of Edward Hopkinson

45

TEA SERVICE

1824–1827

Louis Decasse and Nicolas Louis
Edouard Chanou, New York

Porcelain with gilt decoration

Plate	Diam. 8⁵⁄₁₆ in.
Cream Pitcher	H. 4¼ in.
Teapot	H. 6½ in.
Cup and Saucer	H. 2⅜ in.
Plate	Diam. 7⅜ in.
Sugar Bowl	H. 5⁵⁄₁₆ in.

*Kaufman Americana Foundation,
Norfolk, Virginia*

the few surviving examples from the partners' pottery. The ornately gilt tea set in figure 45 represents the only known marked work of Decasse and Chanou, and is an important statement of the production of this establishment that lasted less than three years. It is interesting that these Frenchmen chose to produce English shapes, which they then ornamented with gilt decoration more akin to Paris porcelains of the period. Perhaps hoping to appeal to a broader segment of consumers by combining English and French characteristics, they selected a bold mark that featured an eagle clutching an olive branch and the emblematic shield of the United States.

Among the various émigré artists and craftsmen seeking work in America were a number of talented Italian sculptors who soon were employed on major projects at the Capitol in Washington, as well as on commissions for private patrons. Giovanni Andrei, Giuseppi and Carlo Franzoni, and Enrico Causici were among those whose work at the Capitol, and in Baltimore, is well known. Employed by émigré architects like Benjamin Henry Latrobe, Maxmillian Godefroy, and Joseph-Jacques Ramée, these sculptors contributed significant classical monuments to major public buildings.

Prior to the advent of the nineteenth century, the arrival of Italian-trained sculptor Giuseppe Ceracchi introduced into America the sculpting of major public figures in the dress and attitude of classical models. Ceracchi had worked with the famous Antonio Canova, executing sculpture for the Pantheon in Rome, and had also spent time sculpting in London and Vienna. An ambitious promoter of himself, according to William Dunlap, Ceracchi came to America with "the design of erecting a monument to Liberty . . . to be one hundred feet in height, of statuary marble, and the cost was estimated at thirty thousand dollars."[104] While his expectations of this great commission and subsequent financial remunerations were not fulfilled, he did leave Americans a legacy of a number of classical portrait busts, in both terracotta and marble, of their political figures. Foremost among those he sculpted, no doubt with the hope of obtaining the major government commission, were Washington, John Jay, Alexander Hamilton, and New York's governor, George Clinton (fig. 46).[105] Early in 1792, soon after he finished sculpting the terracotta bust of Clinton, Ceracchi departed New York for Boston, leaving Clinton with the responsibility for having his bust baked. In this bust, as well as the others

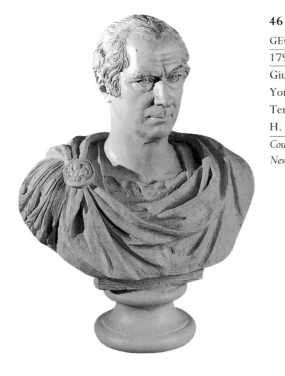

Ceracchi fashioned, the Italian sculptor made an important contribution to the foundation of classical taste in America. Clinton, however, was not terribly concerned about having his bust for all to admire, since more than ten years passed before he fetched it from the estate of the deceased potter, Campbell.[106]

Another tasteful and charming classical expression created by one of this group of Italian sculptors is the bas-relief of Maria Hester Monroe, daughter of President and Mrs. James Monroe (fig. 47). Taken in 1820 by Pietro Cardelli, it was probably completed around the time of Maria's marriage in 1820 to her first cousin Samuel Lawrence Gouverneur. Since Maria and her husband lived with her parents at the President's House for a while after their marriage, this classically inspired bas-relief probably stayed there where it was admired by visitors to the house. Cardelli seems to have arrived in America about 1817, and is chiefly "remembered as leaving two casts from modellings by himself of Mr. & Mrs. [John] Trumbull."[107]

The rich cultural heritage and artistic talent brought to America by European émigrés, combined with the experiences and impressions of Americans who traveled abroad, resulted in an innovative hybridization of classical expressions. Undeniably most of this activity occurred at the upper end of the social and economic scale. However, just as Americans aped Europeans, so the fashions of the wealthy on this side of the Atlantic were copied by others aspiring to similar heights of refinement and fashion. Recognizing the multifaceted influences on the creation of a distinctive American classical expression, we must not lose sight of the numerous European objects and artisans that came to America and in turn inspired the creative genius of our own native artists and craftsmen.

Two

PROPER AMUSEMENTS OF THE VIRTUOUS

Public and Private Collecting

The Pennsylvania Academy of the Fine Arts was barely five years old in 1810 when its president, Joseph Hopkinson, presented the "annual discourse" and referred to the fine arts as "those arts which polish the manners and refine the morals of a people." He discussed the state of art and culture in Europe, and the current problems and dissolution that might cause artists to flee, at the same time rejoicing that this would bring to America's shores "the cultivated intellect, the refined taste and improved genius" of artists from abroad. Hopkinson further recognized a most important opportunity: "this is our peculiar time for transplanting to our western soil, those arts and sciences which have been ripening for ages in Europe. The fruit is offered without the labour of producing it. Let us not reject the precious gift."[1] He continued his lecture by linking morality and the fine arts, and quoted "the elegant and philosophical critic, Lord Kaims," who declared that "a taste in the fine arts and the moral sense go hand in hand."

In 1825, fifteen years after Hopkinson's address and nearly twenty-five years after the founding of the American Academy of the Fine Arts in New York, Gulian Verplank, noted collector and supporter of the academy, addressed the opening of the institution's tenth annual exhibition.[2] He remarked that the academy had been established "in the hope of contributing something towards the cultivation of taste in this country, and the diffusion and improvement of skill in the arts of design." He continued to reflect on the uses and value of the fine arts, adding that "they are fitted . . . by their moral influence upon all classes, to animate patriotism, to raise the genius, and to mend the heart."[3] Verplank concluded his address by quoting that "great and philosophical painter," Sir Joshua Reynolds, who observed: "The labours of the artist may extend themselves imperceptibly into public benefits, and be among the means of bestowing on whole nations refinement of taste; which, if it does not lead directly to purity of manners . . . may, as it is exalted and refined, conclude in Virtue."[4]

Judging from the rhetoric used by those involved with the earliest establishment of collecting institutions in America, the proclaimed purpose was to cultivate and refine the taste of Americans, which would at the same time firmly embue our culture with morality and virtue. By fostering the fine arts and attempting to transplant some of the genius of Europe to America, it was at least professed that Americans would rise to heights of great virtue. However, these institutions were not universally supported, and in 1811 Benjamin Henry Latrobe expressed the concern that "our national prejudices are unfavourable to the fine arts" and that the "real obstacles to the triumph of the fine arts, grow out of the political constitution of society in the United States."[5]

Speaking to The Society of Artists in 1811, Latrobe referred extensively to the modern world's indebtedness to ancient Greece, and most particularly to the fact that "the history of Grecian art refutes the vulgar opinion that the arts are incompatible with liberty."[6] Like others, Latrobe linked the arts and virtue when he stated that "in Greece, perfection in the fine arts, freedom in government, and virtue in private life, were contemporaneous."[7] Latrobe's essential plea for the fine arts, and what they might do for America, came when he postulated that if they "may indeed be pressed into the service of arbitrary power, and—like mercenary troops do their duty well while well paid—yet that their home is in the bosom of a republic; then, indeed, the days of Greece may be revived in the woods of America, and Philadelphia become the Athens of the Western world."[8] Hence, if American society chose to embrace the fine arts, the country might rise to the same heights of taste, morality, and virtue that the ancient civilizations of Greece and Rome were perceived to have done (fig. 48).

Prior to the nineteenth century, there was limited focus in America on collecting and exhibiting the fine arts. While a number of museums and exhibition galleries had been established in the eighteenth century, they were primarily "cabinets of curiosities," and, in the words of the Reverend William Bentley of Salem, were "well accomodated with everything but taste."[9] When visiting Bowen's Museum in Boston in 1803, Bentley not only found a lack of taste but an incredible array of everything from "Rabbits, a Turkey Buzzard, &c." to "The elegant view of Rome borrowed of Dr. Oliver of this Town, & purchased by him from the Gardiner's estate for 9s," which was "beyond praise." Bentley added that while he recognized that "The Busts are ordinary . . . there is real amusement, especially when such places are so rare in our Country."[10] Even Charles Willson Peale's renowned museum, established in Philadelphia in 1784, exhibited curiosities of natural history, including a stuffed swordfish, along with portraits of noted personalities. Thus, the scope of these earlier institutions was much more diverse, with no direct effort to promote fine arts and certainly no concern for refinement of taste.

By 1796, Rembrandt and Raphaelle Peale did attempt to establish a gallery in Baltimore for the exhibition of their work, but it lasted only three years. Not until 1814 did Rembrandt return to Baltimore and erect a building on Holliday Street for another attempt at a gallery and museum. In 1822 Rembrandt's brother Rubens Peale took over the management of the institution until 1830.

In eighteenth-century America there were only a few significant collections of copies of paintings, engravings, and statuary, and since only a small number of people saw them, there was little chance of their cultivating taste or elevating morality. One of the earliest of these belonged to John Smibert, the Scottish émigré painter who worked in Boston between 1728 and 1752. Among his collection of copies of Baroque and Renaissance masters was Titian's *Venus and Cupid* and a cast from the antique of the *Venus de' Medici*.[11] By 1735 he had sold the "Valuable PRINTS, engrav'd by the best Hands, after the finest Pictures in Italy, France, Holland and England," which he had collected in Italy in 1717–1720. Yet when he died in 1752, his inventory still listed "Bustoes and figures in Paris plaster" valued at £ 4.[12] These might well have been the earliest casts in America.

In 1771, twenty-eight-year-old Thomas Jefferson made a list of those "Statues, Paintings &" that he would acquire for an ideal fine arts gallery. Although he never realized this plan, it is not surprising to note that foremost on his list of desirable antique copies were the *Venus de' Medici*, the

Apollo Belvedere, the *Dying Gladiator*, *Antinous*, and the *Farnese Faun*. Even though Jefferson had not yet traveled abroad, his classical studies had taught him the principal sculptural masterworks of antiquity.

Less than fifteen years after Jefferson penned his list, a second *Venus de' Medici* reached the shores of America, brought to Philadelphia in 1784 by the English painter Robert Edge Pine. When Charles Willson Peale founded the Columbianum, or American Academy of Painting, Sculpture, and Architecture in Philadelphia in 1795, he borrowed Pine's *Venus* to open the hall of casts. Admittedly, this was a bold step, exhibiting a nude female sculpture at that date, and for the sake of propriety the lady in question "was kept shut up in a case and only shown to persons who particularly wished to see it; as the manners of the country, at that time, would not tolerate a public exhibition of such a figure."[13] Peale's Columbianum was the first significant attempt at not only the public exhibition of fine arts but also the creation of a school for the study of the human figure.

The emergence of America's academies and athenaeums had begun with great purpose and intent by the first decade of the nineteenth century. As in other areas of culture and the arts, a significant debt is owed to Napoleon for both the initial impetus and subsequent assistance in founding the first fine arts academy in nineteenth-century America. The opening of the Louvre galleries, or Musée Napoleon, in 1801, combined with Napoleon's plundering of Italy's and Egypt's art treasures, resulted in the most extraordinary collection of antique sculpture accessible to the public in Paris. Staggering as the task may now seem, Napoleon's troops hauled overland from Rome more than sixty monumental marble sculptures from the Vatican and Capitoline museums. Private collections were also pillaged in Rome and Florence, and all the booty was carried back to Paris in a grand triumphal procession. Among these spoils were such celebrated antique sculptures as the *Apollo Belvedere*, the *Venus de' Medici*, the *Discobolus*, the *Dying Gladiator*, and the *Laocoön*.[14]

Through the combined efforts of Mayor Edward Livingston of New York and his distinguished brother, Chancellor Robert R. Livingston, then minister to France, the New York Academy of Arts was established in December 1802, and in 1808 renamed the American Academy of Arts (fig. 49). Well acquainted with Napoleon and other influential figures, including Vivant Denon, the chancellor, while residing in Paris, was requested "to procure casts in plaister of the most beautiful pieces of ancient sculpture now collected in the National Museum [the Louvre]."[15] A subscription was circulated in New York to fund the purchase of more casts, and in June 1803 the first shipment of "plaisters" arrived. It included copies of the most celebrated remains of antiquity, among which were the *Pythian Apollo*, the *Apollo Belvedere*, *Venus of the Capitol*, *Laocoön*, *Castor and Pollux*, the *Fighting Gladiator* and the *Grecian Warrior*, *Hermaphrodite*, *Grecian Cupid*, *Ceres*, *Mercury*, *Juno*, *Bacchus*, *Homer*, *Socrates*, *Plato*, and *Demosthenes*. Livingston sent the following instructions for the appropriate presentation of these statues:

48 opposite
Gentlemen like Nicholas Biddle and Joseph Bonaparte embraced the arts of ancient Greece and the classical aesthetic of ideal beauty in their ownership of marble copies of some of the most admired pieces of antique statuary. This marble figure of an Apollino, copied from a statue in the Uffizi Gallery in Florence, was owned by Biddle and is seen in the library of Biddle's country estate, "Andalusia," along the Delaware River north of Philadelphia. Bonaparte also owned a similar figure that adorned the grounds of his estate, "Point Breeze," at Bordentown, New Jersey. In 1833–1834 Biddle commissioned architect Thomas U. Walter to remodel "Andalusia," embellishing it with a grand Greek Revival portico and adding a library with Grecian pediments atop the substantial bookcases.

Mr. John Vanderline is with you to help instruct you & superintend the work—though these statues are viewed by the most delicate women here without a blush, yet the modesty of our country women renders a covering necessary & I beg you that you may begin by preparing one before you suffer them to be exhibited—This is done by getting from the broker [?] a small concave shell or fig leaf which you paint white & hang with a small white pach [sic] thread around the waist. . . . Spectators must be under injunctions not to touch them as the great number of hands that will otherwise slip over them will soon spoil them.[16]

On August 12, 1803, the New York Academy of Arts first opened its doors in an old riding stable on Greenwich Street ironically called the Pantheon. Earlier that year, the academy was already planning additions to its collection of casts, as it requested that the artist John Vanderlyn, then in Paris, go to Italy and procure more casts as well as copies of important paint-

ings. In 1804 both Napoleon and Vivant Denon were elected to honorary membership in the academy, and this gesture resulted in more gifts from the new emperor, including a complete set of Piranesi's twenty-four volumes of engravings. On April 7, 1805, Chancellor Livingston wrote from Paris to Rufus King in New York of this magnanimous gift: "You will find this a very princely present, which will be from its nature I hope not only useful to our young painters and sculptors, but to such other of our fellow citizens as are occupied in works of taste. The architect, the silversmith, the cabinetmaker &c. will find models in their respective professions that cannot fail to impress their taste."[17] These volumes were undoubtedly of value to some New York artists and artisans during the early decades of the nineteenth century, but they were destroyed in a fire in 1839.

Unfortunately, because the academy did not have a dedicated building of its own, over the next two decades its exhibition headquarters moved, and periodically the collections were packed and stored for several years at a time. One has to wonder how much "cultivation of taste" was actually accomplished through an institution as peripatetic as this academy? By 1825 there was a secession of members, and subsequently in 1826 the National Academy of Design was formed, largely under the leadership of New York artists Samuel F. B. Morse, Asher B. Durand, Henry Inman, and William Dunlap. The American Academy of Fine Arts was dissolved in 1841, at which time the National Academy of Design purchased its collection of casts for $400. These, too, were destroyed in a fire in 1905.

Philadelphia and Boston were not far behind New York in forming their respective academies and athenaeums for the moral and cultural enrichment of their local public and the education of young artists. In December 1805, Charles Willson Peale, William Rush, and Joseph Hopkinson drew up a proposal for the establishment of the Pennsylvania Academy of the Fine Arts. This action was undoubtedly precipitated by the gift the previous year of a collection of casts given by Joseph Allen Smith of Charleston, South Carolina. As early as December 1796, Smith had consigned a shipment of works of art to be sent from Italy to Philadelphia expressly "in the hopes that they might possibly be of some service to his countrymen when they should turn their thoughts to the study of Painting & Sculpture."[18] However, the vagaries of the Napoleonic wars led to seizure of the shipment by the French, and only in 1800 was a portion of the collection released. When the casts arrived in 1804 they were temporarily deposited at Peale's Museum, where could be seen "fourteen hundred elegant casts from antique gems . . . [and] many superb casts from the celebrated Statues of Antiquity."[19]

In July 1805 representatives of the new academy asked young Nicholas Biddle, then in Paris, to procure for the institution additional casts, allowing 3300 francs for the objects and their shipment. Biddle's father, William, wrote to his son in Paris in May 1807:

> You may see by the newspaper that the "Pennsylvania Academy of the Fine Arts is now opened in this City." We have built a handsome House in Chestnut between Tenth & Eleventh Streets, & in a very elegant circular room, exhibit to all who pay a quarter of a Dollar, your much admired Casts. The room is fifty feet in Diameter, is handsomely plaistered & finished, the floor is covered with green cloth, and the casts mounted upon neat pedestals have a very good effect. They arrived in excellent preservation, except the Hermaphrodite which was broken.[20]

Nothing is more desirable than a satisfied donor, and by 1809 *The Port Folio* reported that Mr. Smith "was so pleased with this Society, that in a moment of generosity he gave them not only what he had here but some pictures & prints which he has still in Italy."[21] However, it was not until 1812 that the remainder of his collection was released from custody in Italy and shipped to America, though not without mishap. En route, the vessel was captured by a British ship and the cargo confiscated and taken to Halifax. After an eloquent plea from Hopkinson, in July 1813 the twenty-one paintings (and presumably fifty-two prints) were released, sent to Boston where they were reported "thoroughly soaked in sea water," and eventually sent over-

50

39 IMPRESSIONS OF ANTIQUE INTAGLIOS
one tray from a set of 24 forming three cases

c. 1800–1811

Probably the Paoletti brothers, Rome, Italy

Plaster impressions set with gilt paper mounts, fitted into wooden tray lined with blue paper

13 x 8⅛ in. (tray)

Boston Athenaeum; Gift of Samuel Elam, Newport, and the Hon. Richard Sullivan, Boston, 1811

land to Philadelphia. At this point the prints seem to disappear from the record, obviously damaged beyond the devices of contemporary conservation techniques.

In 1807 the Boston Athenaeum was incorporated as "a Repository for productions in these [fine and pleasing] arts," and to "provide for the improvement and refinement of taste in those who aim to be connoisseurs and able to bestow praise and censure with discrimination."[22] While two decades would pass before the Athenaeum erected a three-story building containing a separate room, lit by skylights, for the express purpose of exhibitions of paintings, its collections of sculpture soon began to grow with important gifts from its patrons. In 1817 the architect Solomon Willard presented casts of the ever-popular *Laocoön* and a *Gladiator*, followed in 1821 by plaster models of the Parthenon and St. Paul's Church, Boston. In 1822 Augustus Thorndike presented the institution a gift of eleven "whole-length" casts, eight of which were "full size" figures, and three smaller. This group represented "the most celebrated statues of antiquity," and included an *Apollo Belvedere*, *Laocoön*, *Venus de' Medici*, *Venus of the Capitol*, *Gladiator Borghese*, *The Torso*, *Diana*, and *Hermaphrodite*. The small casts were the *Discobolus*, the *Little Apollo*, and the *Antinous of the Capitol*.[23] In 1824 and 1825 marble busts of Washington by Trentanove and an *Apollo Belvedere* were acquired, making the Athenaeum statuary collection most complete and worthy.

Unlike the academy in New York, whose casts were constantly being packed up and stored away for periods, the Athenaeum's collection was actively used and appreciated by students of art. In fact, among those early students who availed themselves of this resource was young Horatio Greenough. Members were deeply concerned that these examples from the antique be accessible, and in 1827 Chester Harding suggested that "the Institution may place all the Statues in one of the lower rooms of the new building and appropriate the use of it, for certain seasons at least, exclusively to Artists and Amateurs, who may be disposed to reap the advantages which such an arrangement would offer."[24] As Franklin Dexter wrote to the trustees of the Athenaeum in 1833, "The study of the antique is the very alphabet of the art," and clearly in Boston this study was possible and the antique accessible.[25] By 1839 this collection had grown to the extent that a Sculpture Gallery was installed in the same building as the Picture Gallery, and that year the Athenaeum held its first sculpture exhibition.

In addition to the sculpture, paintings, and, of course, books that were acquired by the Athenaeum during the first half of the nineteenth century, the institution also received gifts of a number of important objects copied from antiquity. As early as 1811 they were given a collection of 1500 casts of gems by Samuel Elam of Newport and the Hon. Richard Sullivan of Boston (fig. 50). These casts from the antique, said to have been made by the Paoletti brothers in Rome, filled three cases of eight drawers each. Medals were also popular collector's items, and in 1817 Nathaniel Amory gave "Bronze medallions of the twelve Roman Emperors" and "An Antique Helmet."

By 1831 a copy of the celebrated Portland vase, made in the 1780s by James Tassie in England, was given by Francis Calley Gray (fig. 51). Though the original of this extraordinary object was made of cased glass, probably in Italy by Alexandrians between 27 B.C. and A.D. 14, the Tassie copy in plaster, so unlike the original in material, at least provided a representation for public enlightenment and study. In the 1840 Athenaeum exhibition, there was shown a "Vase, copy of the celebrated Portland," owned by J.J. Dixwell, which might have been one of the more realistic copies made of jasperware in 1790 by Josiah Wedgwood. Two years after the Athenaeum acquired its vase, an image of it appeared as the cover illustration for *The Penny Magazine* . . ., making an additional image of this icon of antiquity known to a wider segment of the population.[26]

In Philadelphia, New York, and Boston, in addition to the athenaeums and academies, a variety of rival entrepreneurs periodically exhibited paintings and sculpture, hoping to attract a curious public and reap appreciable financial rewards. The moral objectives of these ventures were perhaps less pure than those of the infant academies and athenaeums, and their tenure was often shorter than that of institutions serving both artists and patrons. However, these ventures should not be overlooked, for they did provide alternative venues for interested citizens to view both the modern and the antique. One of these institutions, the New England Museum and Gallery of Fine Arts, was described in an advertisement in the Boston Directory of 1821: "It contains a very rich and valuable collection of PAINTINGS from European and American Artists, a handsome collection of STATUARY, in which is a marble Venus by CANOVA, the best work of the kind in this country; together with a great variety of Prints, Medals, & & The Hall is 90 feet by 32, lighted from the top 23 feet high. Open every day,—Admittance 25 cents."[27] Whether the advertised marble Venus was indeed by Canova, or after Canova, is uncertain; however, there were sculptures after Canova exhibited at the Boston Athenaeum in 1839 and 1840. Nathan Appleton had a "Venus after Canova" in the "Entry" of his Beacon Street house, and in 1894 Mrs. Lucius Manlius Sargent gave the Boston Public Library a fine marble Venus after Canova (fig. 52). Another institution that surprisingly was given a Venus at an early date was the Massachusetts Medical College. In 1816 William Sawyer purchased a marble copy of the *Venus de' Medici* at Livorno, and it was soon deposited at the medical college by Dr. John Collins Warren.[28]

While some suggested that if naked human forms were to be exhibited, either the sexes should view them separately or specific parts of the anatomy be appropriately covered, the citizens of Charleston, South Carolina, emphatically expressed their sentiments on the subject in 1797.

51

CAST OF THE PORTLAND VASE

c. 1782

Cast by James Tassie (1735–1799) from the mold made by Giovanni Pichler, England

Plaster

H. 9¾ in.

Boston Athenaeum; Gift of Francis Calley Gray, 1830

Though they favored the formation of a picture gallery in their city, they urged that "all obsenity be banished—let no naked Venus appear, nor wanton Sappho display her wiles. Let the entertainment be the feast of virtue and of taste; not the promoter of lawless passion. . . . Virtuous emotions and interesting thoughts might here be excited and taste improved."[29] Obviously at this early date some Charlestonians saw only immorality in the nudity of antiquity. The objective of the improvement of taste was ever-present in America, and by 1816 the South Carolina Academy of Fine Arts was formed, with a charter finally granted in 1821. However, it survived little more than a decade, and in 1830 expired after several exhibitions and numerous tribulations.

Although collecting, studying, and exhibiting marble copies and plaster casts from the antique was a strong focus for the early fine arts institutions in America, a second equally significant means of improving public taste was through the exhibition of paintings, prints, and other miscellaneous works. Published catalogs from these early exhibitions provide an illuminating look at the wide range of canvases and objects shown.[30] Often there was a conscious blend of works by old masters, or copies thereof, and those by contemporary American artists. Local collectors as well as the sponsoring institutions were often the lenders of many of the paintings, and American artists were encouraged to exhibit whatever current work they wished to. Sometimes the institution would acquire several works by contemporary artists for its permanent collection, or

52

VENUS

19th century

After Antonio Canova
(1757–1852), Italy or England

Marble

68 x 21 x 21 in.

Courtesy the Trustees of the Public Library of the City of Boston, Massachusetts

53

CERES

1809

Adolph Ulrich Wertmüller
(1751–1811), Philadelphia

Oil on canvas

18 x 14⅞ in.

*Westmoreland Museum of Art,
Greensburg, Pennsylvania; Gift of
William A. Coulter Fund, 74.221*

they would be purchased by patrons and later donated.

While seventeenth-century Dutch still lifes and landscapes were popular among collectors and frequently shown at these exhibitions, works by other European old masters, especially Italians, were also favorite exhibition pieces and often religious in subject. Frequently paintings were ascribed to famous old masters such as Rembrandt, Rubens, Raphael, and Domenichino, but in hindsight they seldom were what they claimed to be. On the other hand, good copies of old master paintings, correctly presented, were almost as valued as originals. When Rembrandt Peale traveled to Italy in 1829–1830, he made many copies of important paintings from collections in Florence and Rome. Upon his return to Philadelphia, he exhibited in 1831 his copies at "Sully and Earle's Gallery. In Chestnut opposite the State-House." Among the twenty-seven paintings shown were copies after Raphael's *Madonna della Seggiola*, Guido's *Cleopatra*, Correggio's *Danaë*, and Titian's *Flora*.[31]

Depictions drawn from classical mythology were always popular subjects, and gods, goddesses, and other heroic figures were no exception. In 1811 the Pennsylvania Academy of the Fine Arts staged the first in a long series of annual exhibitions. That year émigré Swedish artist Adolf Ulrich Wertmüller exhibited his *Ceres* (fig. 53) and the more widely noted *Danaë*. Ceres was a safe and popular female figure, as marble statues and plaster casts of the goddess of harvest were commonly imported. By 1816 Joseph Bonaparte had brought *Ceres* by François Bosio, a marble copy after the antique, to "Point Breeze" (fig. 54), and in 1828 a late Hellenistic *Ceres* was given to the Pennsylvania Academy of the Fine Arts, where it reportedly stood by the front entrance under the largest hawthorn tree in America.[32] However, as a female nude, Wertmüller's *Danaë* was more critically reviewed. Completed in Paris in 1787, it represented the epitome of French classical salon painting and was praised by David and others abroad. As early as September 1806, Wertmüller exhibited it in a special room in a house on Filbert Street in Philadelphia. While American patrons were beginning to accept nude marbles and plaster casts from the antique, when confronted with a sensuously and realistically painted female nude their opinions were mixed. Regardless of some critical reviews, *Danaë* was a financial success, reputed to have netted over $800 per year from 1806 to 1810, and sometimes as much as $50 to $75 in a single day.[33]

Like Wertmüller, American artists who worked and traveled abroad were captivated by the classical concept of ideal beauty, and the study of antique sculpture allowed them to master the modeling of the human form. Hence, the depiction of the female nude, as the embodiment of this ideal beauty, provided a tempting challenge to those artists ready to accept it. The more critical question was whether or not the American public could understand and appreciate this realistic depiction of ideal beauty. Two years after Wertmüller's *Danaë* was shown at the academy in Philadelphia, Charles Robert Leslie exhibited a female nude, *Musidora Bathing*, after Benjamin West, at the academy's third annual exhibition. While Leslie's *Musidora* was on exhibition, Thomas Sully began two copies, one of which was presumably the *Musidora* exhibited at Peale's Museum in Baltimore in 1820 (fig. 33). Like the mythological Arethusa from the fifth book of Ovid's *Metamorphoses*, Musidora, the female in James Thomson's *Seasons*, is a girl who is discovered and observed while bathing in a stream. While this female nude does not exhibit the same sensuous nature as that of *Danaë*, she still probably received mixed reviews from the patrons of Philadelphia and Baltimore.

John Vanderlyn was among the first American artists to travel and study abroad extensively at the end of the eighteenth and beginning of the nineteenth century. In Paris between 1796 and 1801, Vanderlyn familiarized himself with the numerous treasures in the Louvre, as well as the current classical taste in grand exhibition paint-

54

CERES

c. 1808

François-Joseph Bosio
(1768–1845), Paris

Marble

42¹¹⁄₁₆ x 16¼ x 12¹³⁄₁₆ in.

Boston Athenaeum; Bequest of Edmund W. Dana

ings. Back in America in 1801, he returned to Europe two years later for almost twelve more years. With an eventual American exhibition in mind, Vanderlyn painted his famed *Ariadne Asleep on the Island of Naxos* in Paris between 1809 and 1811 (fig. 55). By the end of 1811 the work was almost complete and he commented on it: "I think myself it exhibits as much female beauty as I have seen represented in any picture."[34] In 1810 and again in 1812 he exhibited an *Ariadne* at the Paris Salon, perhaps the very one he wrote of in 1811. Sensing that this was a classical and romantic subject America was primed to embrace, Vanderlyn returned to New York in 1815 and shortly thereafter exhibited his monumental nude in the Rotunda, a structure built in City Hall Park to display his *Panorama of Versailles*. For more than a decade this dramatic painting periodically toured in America, including exhibitions in Baltimore (1820), New Orleans (1821), Charleston (1822),

55

ARIADNE ASLEEP ON THE
ISLAND OF NAXOS

1811–1831

John Vanderlyn (1775–1852),
France or America

Oil on canvas

70 x 87½ in.

The New-York Historical Society, New York; Gift of Mrs. Lucy Maria Durand Woodman, 1907.28

56

CAIUS MARIUS AMID THE
RUINS OF CARTHAGE

1832

John Vanderlyn (1775–1852),
New York

Oil on panel

32 x 25⅜ in.

Albany Institute of History and Art, Albany, New York

Savannah (1822), and Boston (1826). In Baltimore, Rembrandt Peale purchased the right to exhibit this commanding masterpiece, noting that the "ladies behaved very handsomely on their Mondays" and that the venue netted over "199 dollars."[35] By 1821 Charlestonians were apparently converted classicists, and the *Charleston Courier* advised that "no man of taste and sensibility, no student of love and beauty, no connoisseur of graceful form should fail to gladden his eyes, to charm his fancy and refresh his imagination with the exquisite performance of Mr. VanDerlyn where the sleeping and unconscious Ariadne is sweetly reclining."[36]

Another mythological subject painting completed by Vanderlyn in Rome, shown at the Paris Exhibition of 1808 and awarded a Gold Medal by Napoleon, was *Caius Marius Amidst the Ruins of Carthage* (fig. 56).[37] Vanderlyn's initial objective in the execution of *Marius* was "to gain a reputation, which is all I am persuaded a real artist should aspire to."[38] An additional objective was the moral message that Vanderlyn hoped this monumental (five by eight feet) history painting would convey: "I thought the man and position combined, was capable of showing in two great instances the instability of human grandeur—a city in ruins and a fallen general. I endeavoured to express in the countenance of Marius the bitterness of disappointed ambitions mixed with the meditation of revenge."[39] Like *Ariadne*, *Caius Marius* also toured for exhibition in America, and when both paintings were shown in Boston in 1826, *Bowen's Boston News-Letter and City Record* reported:

There is not at this time any amusement, nor anything in our City so attracting as the two pictures at the Drawing Room in Cornhill-square. . . . One is Caius Marius. . . . The other is Ariadne. . . . These pictures have given entire satisfaction to every beholder, and it is a question whether the greatest praise has been bestowed upon them by our truly eminent artists Stuart and Allston, or by those great departed critics . . . Napoleon and Jefferson.[40]

The American artists who studied and worked abroad were strongly influenced not only by the classical revival works of Renaissance and Baroque masters but by their European contemporaries. In 1804 Washington Allston was among the first American artists to travel to Rome, where he spent four years painting and studying the work of both old and new masters. By 1805 he was joined by his close friend John Vanderlyn, but they both expressed the feeling that while "Rome is certainly the first place in the world for an artist to pursue his studies. We both regret that there are not a couple more fellow countrymen pursuing the fine arts—as is the case with artists here from other nations who are numerous and less liable to feel the want of society."[41]

While in Rome, Allston painted several landscapes that were not only strongly influenced by the seventeenth-century work of Claude, and more specifically Poussin, but also closely parallel to the work of his German contemporary Joseph Anton Koch. In 1805 Allston completed a major "heroic landscape," *Italian Landscape*, in which rugged nature, the grandeur of classical architec-

57

ITALIAN LANDSCAPE

c. 1805

Washington Allston

(1779–1843), Rome

Oil on canvas

40 x 50¼ in.

Addison Gallery of American Art,
Phillips Academy, Andover,
Massachusetts, All rights reserved

ture, and the rustic simplicity of peasant life all coexist in perfect balance and harmony (fig. 57). In July 1818, in a special exhibition at the Pennsylvania Academy of the Fine Arts, Allston exhibited "8. Landscape and Figures—Morning Scene in Italy 1805"; earlier in May the same year, he had exhibited at the Academy's annual exhibition "20. Landscape—The figures introduced represent Diana and her Nymphs." The picture exhibited in July 1818 may indeed have been the one in figure 57. Living in Boston following his return to America in 1818, Allston consistently exhibited at the Athenaeum's annual exhibitions beginning in 1827. Among the many pictures he showed there were a number of landscapes, including an *Italian Landscape* in 1831, and also one in 1837.

The fashion for idyllic, classical landscapes was often combined with a desire to illustrate mythological tales such as various episodes from Homer's *Odyssey* and Virgil's *Aeneid*. Painters who traveled and trained abroad, both émigré and American-born, were familiar with contemporary works by the great modern masters like Reynolds, West, and Turner, as well as the work of the old masters. The story of Dido and Aeneas going to the hunt, derived from the *Aeneid*, was an appropriately challenging theme for any ambitious artist who wished to cater to the popular taste of American connoisseurs while at the same time demonstrating all his aesthetic skills.

Joshua Shaw was an English-trained painter who arrived in America in 1817 and settled in Philadelphia. His *Dido and Aeneas Going to the Hunt* (fig. 58) embodies all of the spirit of the grand, romantic Claudian-landscape tradition, while at the same time celebrating classical heroes and events. The same subject, painted by the Dutch artist Verkolye, was exhibited at the Boston

58

DIDO AND AENEAS GOING TO THE HUNT

c. 1831

Joshua Shaw (1776–1860), Philadelphia

Oil on canvas

26⅛ x 38½ in.

Munson-Williams-Proctor Institute, Museum of Art, Utica, New York

59

VIEW OF THE COLOSSEUM

1723

Fernando Galli Bibiena
(1657–1743), Italy
Oil on canvas
35⅞ x 60½ in.

Society for the Preservation of New England Antiquities, Boston; Codman House, Lincoln, Massachusetts; Gift of Dorothy S.F.M. Codman

Athenaeum in 1827. Shaw's version enjoyed wide circulation, also being exhibited at the Athenaeum in 1831, the Pennsylvania Academy of the Fine Arts in 1832, and the National Academy of Design in 1835.

Another very desirable subject for modern paintings of the period was found in the romantic and often sublime remains of antiquity. Roman aqueducts standing in partial ruin, the Colosseum in Rome, and the three Doric temples at Paestum were among the principal sites that inspired travelers abroad, be they patrons, artists, or writers. Indeed, as Thomas Cole wrote to his parents in March 1832, "But the things that most affect me, in Rome, are the antiquities. None but those who can see the remains can form an idea of what Ancient Rome was."[42]

In 1827 Nathan Appleton lent fourteen paintings to the Boston Athenaeum's first exhibition, including a picture titled *Ruins*, with no artist named, and one titled *Paestum*, by Thomas Doughty. In that same inaugural exhibition, Alvan Fisher exhibited his *Roman Forum* (after Claude Lorrain), and in the 1834 exhibition Charles Lyman of Boston lent his magnificent and evocative *Remains of the Great Roman Aqueduct* by Thomas Cole. And in 1841 Charles Russell Codman lent his painting of the *Colosseum* (1723) by Fernando DeGalli Bibiena for exhibition at the Athenaeum (fig. 59).[43] When Thomas Cole visited Paestum in 1832, he wrote:

> . . . we came within sight of the temples of Paestum, just as first beams of the sun were breaking upon them . . . as it has done for two thousand years! but how the accompanying scene has changed. Once they stood in the midst a city—now in a desert and they look around on the desolation like beings who had been wrought by wrong beyond the power of suffering more and with unchanging countenances calmly enduring all.[44]

While viewing these impressive ruins, Cole made some sketches, and later related to William
Dunlap that he had "painted, since my return, a view of those magnificent temples, for Miss
Douglass. The commission was given in Rome" (fig. 60).[45] This diminutive, evocative view that
Miss Douglass commissioned from Cole was exhibited at the National Academy of Design in
1833. When Cole died in New York in 1848, his close friend William Cullen Bryant delivered a
laudatory funeral oration to members of the academy in which he made reference to Cole's jour-
ney to Paestum, noting that he saw "the grandest and most perfect remains of the architecture of
Greece, standing . . . and painted a view of them for an American lady."[46]

Periodically in most major American cities there were special exhibitions featuring monumental
or important pictures that traveled from city to city for public showings. Buildings and rooms
suitable for these venues varied, and while some entrepreneurs maintained rooms specifically for
this purpose, occasionally artists used their own painting rooms for special exhibitions. Often
financial gain was the primary motive for these traveling venues, and certainly Rembrandt Peale's
Court of Death must have been among the most lucrative, bringing in nearly $9,000 in thirteen
months of showing in various cities.[47] Another very popular picture was Washington Allston's
Dead Man Restored to Life by Touching the Bones of the Prophet Elisha. Henry Sargent's paintings of *The
Dinner Party* and *The Tea Party* (fig. 61), commissioned as exhibition pictures in 1821 and 1824 by
David L. Brown of Boston, were widely exhibited, in Boston, Salem, New York, Philadelphia,
and Montreal.[48] Brown, an entrepreneurial type who also had a drawing school in Boston, must
have found traveling these paintings for exhibition financially successful. At the time, they were
greatly admired for their reality and the fidelity with which every figure and object was painted.

The elegant image of Boston society that these paintings revealed must have attracted both those who were part of it and those who aspired to such heights of taste and refinement.

In 1813 the Baltimore artist Francis Guy advertised an exhibition of just twelve paintings, "At the Old Exchange." Apparently distressed with his lack of success in Philadelphia exhibitions, Guy registered a plea to "the gods who fill the grand saloon in the academy of fine arts, Philadelphia" to come to Baltimore, "where they would assuredly find real, not pretended, patrons of paintings." He cited the "temple now erecting by Mr. Peale," and was confident that "this infant Herculean city will become the Athens of America."[49] His hopes were high, and almost as a challenge to Latrobe's desire that "Philadelphia become the Athens of America," Guy espoused the same dream for Baltimore. Certainly these architects and artists had some self-interest in promoting the arts, but the conviction with which they made their claims suggests that they truly believed that America would become a stronger and more virtuous society if its citizens were exposed to, and embraced, the fine arts.

In addition to paintings, in the early nineteenth century engraved prints provided another, more financially affordable, source of inspiration and exposure to classical art and architecture, as well as old master paintings. Theodore Lyman of Boston owned a series of prints after Raphael's famous frescoes that adorned the Vatican's papal apartments known as the Camera della

62

THE SCHOOL OF ATHENS

1780–1800

Giovanni Joannes Volpato
(1733–1803) after Raphael
(1483–1520), Italy

Engraving on paper, original
frame

22¾ x 30¼ in. (sight)

*Society for the Preservation of New
England Antiquities, Boston; Harrison
Gray Otis House, Boston; Gift of the
children of Arthur and Susan Cabot
Lyman*

Segnatura. Painted for Pope Julius II, these paintings encompass the theme of the whole realm of human knowledge, portraying Theology, Philosophy, Law, and Poetry. Raphael's portrayal of *The School of Athens* (fig. 62) features Plato and Aristotle, the leaders of the two rival schools of Greek philosophy, as central figures in a grand arcaded Renaissance hall, surrounded by figures skillfully grouped around the other principal philosophers of the classical world. This brilliant composition captures in one overarching framework the entire spectrum of Greek philosophers so well-known to educated young men like Lyman. Following his graduation from Harvard in 1810, Lyman traveled abroad, making important contacts and acquiring a valuable library. Quite possibly he purchased his prints while traveling in Europe.

Sometimes artists in America resorted to copying engraved prints if original oil paintings, or good copies of them, were unavailable. In 1812, the Reverend William Bentley visited Rev. N. Fisher "to see a painting in Imitation of Claude Lorrain's Temple of Apollo, from an engraving by Wootton."[50] Like Fisher, Neapolitan-born émigré artist Michel Felice Corné also copied an engraving of a painting by Claude Lorrain, *The Mill* (1648), for his *Italian Classical Landscape* in 1805 (fig. 63). Corné arrived in Salem, Massachusetts, in 1800 and executed a wide-ranging body of often rather naive work prior to his move to Newport in 1822. Perhaps his most ambitious project was the wall murals depicting the Bay of Naples in Sullivan Dorr's Benefit Street house in Providence. Not only did Corné copy Lorrain's *The Mill*, but his Salem pupil George

63

ITALIAN CLASSICAL LAND-
SCAPE

1805

Michel Felice Corné
(1752–1832), possibly Boston
Oil on panel
35¼ x 59⅛ in. (sight)
Society for the Preservation of New England Antiquities, Boston; Harrison Gray Otis House, Boston; Gift of Sumner Appleton Weld

64

FIELDING LUCAS, JR.

1808

Thomas Sully (1783–1872),
Philadelphia

Oil on canvas

29 x 24 in.

*The Baltimore Museum of Art: Group
of Friends Purchase Fund (BMA
1935.29.1)*

Ropes also made an identical image in 1806, noting on the back of the canvas that his painting was "From a picture at the Pamphili Palace in Rome."[51]

While fine arts academies and public exhibitions emerged quite early in the nineteenth century, the phenomenon of private collecting was slower to gather momentum. Writing from New York in 1814, Samuel F. B. Morse lamented to his wife that "A fine painting or a marble statue is very rare in the houses of the rich in this city. . . . individuals who would not pay fifty pounds for either, expend double that sum to vie with a neighbor in a piece of furniture."[52] In Morse's opinion, the priorities and taste of the well-to-do upper classes were not yet refined enough to include the fine arts in their domestic interiors. However, by 1827, when Morse addressed the National Academy of Design, he was able to cite a dozen New York painting collectors of note. Amongst those he included were Colonel William Gracie, Philip Hone, and the Messrs. Stevens, who had aboard their steamboat *Albany* twelve impressive paintings, including "BUONAPARTE *crossing the Alps*, copy from David. [by] C. B. Lawrence" and "Ariadne. [by] J. Vanderlyn."[53] Obviously the objectives of the academies had begun to be accomplished, and a taste for fine arts had taken root in America and was beginning to flourish.

The situation in Boston seems to have been similar, and by 1831 an English traveler observed, "A taste for the fine arts is not, at the same time, limited to the public exhibition-room." This same gentleman went on to comment further on his Boston visit:

> At one gentleman's house especially, in Beacon Street . . . I saw several marble statues and sculptures of remarkable beauty . . . a finely executed copy of Canova's Hebe, a Sleeping Nymph, a Genius of Silence, and a Dancing Nymph: and of the latter, a superb mantel-piece of the same material, brought from Italy, adorned by female figures of surpassing elegance, and perfected in a style of superior workmanship that could scarcely be exceeded.[54]

Henry Tudor's observations of "marble statues and sculptures" in private homes in Boston may seem surprising, but the fact is that many of the elite, including David Sears, George Ticknor, Thomas H. Perkins, and Nathan Appleton, had "statuary" in their homes. In fact, the home Tudor described might well have been that of David Sears, as his Beacon Street house had an elegant carved statuary mantel. Nathan Appleton's listing of his "Works of Art" (n.d.) included a "Marble Statuette of Cicero" in the Library, a "Bronze Statue of Demosthenes" in the Drawing Room, and a "Cupid in Marble by Gibson," and "Venus after Canova" in the "Entry."[55]

A virtually unknown Boston-area collector who owned a large number of marbles, plaster casts, paintings, and engravings at his death in 1829 was Barney Smith of Milton.[56] Among the marble statuary in his home, the former Governor Hutchinson house, were two handsome groups of "Bacchus and Ariadne" and "Apollo and Daphne." He also owned a "Minerva," a "Washington," and a "Laocoon," in addition to a large number of plaster casts and small-scale sculptures, including a "Demostines," a "figure of Hercules," a "Venus en torso," and a "female figure bearing a lamp."[57]

When Thomas Sully painted Baltimore merchant and publisher Fielding Lucas in 1808, he depicted Lucas with his right hand resting on a copy of the head of Laocoön from the well-known ancient sculpture that both Sully and Lucas may have known from a cast in the Pennsylvania Academy of the Fine Arts (fig. 64).[58] Whether Lucas ever owned a copy of Laocoön is not indicated in his estate inventory, so perhaps Sully's allusion to this important antique sculpture was merely meant to suggest Lucas's aesthetic taste and refinement.

The vogue for small-scale marbles and plasters in American domestic settings of this period has not been fully recognized, but surviving objects and written documentation support its popularity. Vito Vite, an Italian entrepreneur, apparently marketed in major eastern cities "Elegant, Superior, and tasteful Mantel Ornaments" imported from his manufactory in Italy. In November 1825, he advertised for sale in Boston an extensive assortment of marbles that included "a superb Plato [plateau], ornamented with a group of the three Graces; two Temples of the Vestals; Dancing Figures, Vases, &.; Washington crowned by Victory."[59] While the entire "superb Plato" no longer survives, Charles Russell Codman did own a set of marble urns and vases for a plateau that had as part of it a group of Three Graces (fig. 118). Perhaps Codman purchased the one that Vite advertised, as his ledgers indicate that he paid Vito Vite $85 for a purchase in December 1825.[60]

Two eloquent marble heads representing *Mercury* (fig. 65) and *Ganymede* were originally owned by Mayor Theodore Lyman of Boston, and may have been purchased soon after he moved to Gore Place in Waltham, Massachusetts, in 1835.[61] Finely modeled from antique precedents, these are the type of marble bust that could be procured through agents like Thomas Appleton in Livorno, Italy. In 1807, when Rosalie Stier Calvert of Riversdale desired "two plaster casts for our north drawing room," she appealed to her sister, since "Papa writes that

65

GANYMEDE

c. 1835

Possibly Italy

Marble

21 x 12½ x 10⅛ in.

Courtesy Museum of Fine Arts, Boston.
Gift of Mrs. Henry Lyman

they are all too indecent, but [people] have changed on that subject here. I should like to have one of the Apollo Belvedere and my husband says he must have the Venus de Medici sent too. . . . At all events, if the statues are such that I cannot put them in the drawing room, I shall put them in my husband's study."[62] Apparently Rosalie was pleased when "the charming statues" arrived in "perfect order," though she noted with a certain coyness, "The Olympian victor is a little too *deshabille*, but what beautiful lines and expression!"[63]

While the collecting of Greek and Roman vases had been popular among the elite in England since the late eighteenth century, the extent of vase collecting in America was limited. However, surviving physical evidence, as well as written and visual, suggests that some enterprising acquisitors had small collections of vases. Robert Gilmor, Jr., was well-known for his extensive painting collection and his modern sculpture collection, but his antiquities are less well-documented. In the 1823 annual exhibition at The Peale Museum in Baltimore, he exhibited "An Etruscan Vase . . . being at least 2700 years old."[64] A second and more evocative statement of Gilmor's interest in vases can be seen in the very private image of the elder Gilmor in his study, steadied by his cane, with a red-figure ewer perched inside a similar kylix in the left foreground (fig. 66). Did Gilmor purchase these ancient treasures on one of his sojourns abroad, or were they acquired through an agent? Did he have more than just these two specimens? His household inventory does not reveal any answers to these questions, but a further examination of Gilmor papers and journals may eventually lead to greater knowledge of his interest in antiquities.

A number of Etruscan vases reached these shores through the kind auspices of Lucien Bonaparte and the generosity of his brother, Joseph Bonaparte. In 1828, Lucien, the Prince de Canino, excavated a cache of Greek vases in the Etruscan graves of Vulci, on his estate in Italy. Soon after this discovery, he published *Museum étrusque de Lucien Bonaparte Prince de Canino, Fouilles de 1828 a 1829, Vases peints avec inscriptions* (Viterbo, 1829–1830). Shortly thereafter, he sent his brother Joseph a number of vases, presumably with instructions to present at least one of them to the American Philosophical Society, of which both Lucien and Joseph were elected members (fig. 67). In May 1833, Joseph sent his good friend General Thomas Cadwalader a magnificent black-figure amphora, no doubt one of the vases originally found by Lucien. In a letter that announced the forthcoming delivery of this gift, Joseph Bonaparte wrote from London to Cadwalader, "I hope to spend the winter with you in Philadelphia, in the meantime, I beg you to accept an Etruscan vase that my brother Lucien has replaced here."[65] Apparently at the same time, Bonaparte sent a stamnos to his friend the noted Philadelphia physician Dr. Nathaniel Chapman. In 1836 he presented to the American Philosophical Society a kylix described as "an Etruscan cup, very antique, found on the estate of Lucien Bonaparte, Prince of Canino, in the researches made in 1828–29 in that district. . . . This donation was accompanied by the '*Museum Etrusque* of Lucien Bonaparte,' containing a description of nearly two thousand articles found in the same locality."[66]

As Morse noted, there were in New York by the 1830s a number of significant painting collections, among which was that assembled by Luman Reed. In addition to his paintings, Reed also

67

ATTIC RED-FIGURE STAMNOS
c. 490 B.C.
Attributed to the Kleophrades Painter
Reddish-brown earthenware
H. 13³⁄₁₆ in.
Philadelphia Museum of Art, on loan to the University Museum of Archaeology and Anthropology, University of Pennsylvania, Philadelphia

ATTIC RED-FIGURE KYLIX
replacement stem and foot
c. 470 B.C.
Attributed to the Penthesilea Painter
Reddish-brown earthenware
H. 3¾ in.
The University Museum of Archaeology and Anthropology, University of Pennsylvania, Philadelphia; Gift of American Philosophical Society

ATTIC BLACK-FIGURE NECK AMPHORA
c. 530 B.C.
Possibly the Antimenes Painter, Athens
Reddish-brown earthenware
H. 21¼ in.
Private Collection on loan to The Walters Art Gallery, Baltimore, Maryland

had collections of engravings, shells, and minerals, and three cork models of the great temples at Paestum sent to him from Naples by his son-in-law, Theodore Allen. Allen also sent Reed a box containing "*Miniature facsimiles* of Greek, Egyptian, and Etruscan vases," noting that these were not sent "as toys, though I fear they may be at first deemed mere gewgaws, but as specimens . . . whose scale give a [illeg.] & exact idea of ancient vases than can be formed from seeing engravings of them."[67]

Another New York traveler and connoisseur, whose adventures already have been cited, was Richard Haight, whose wife described their travels to Europe and Egypt in *Letters from the Old World by a Lady of New York* (1840). A marvelously detailed and descriptive depiction of the Haight family in their New York home was painted in the 1840s, presumably after the publication of Mrs. Haight's book (fig. 68). This gouache tells us everything that the Haights want us to know about their cultured existence. In addition to a happy family, they have a fine library, a sculpture of the *Three Graces* (probably after Canova), a well-appointed greenhouse, and most importantly, a collection of vases appropriately displayed across the top of the library bookcases. To heighten this picture of domestic and cultural virtue, the artist has shown the family perusing a map of Italy, as Mrs. Haight holds a book, probably her own publication, and they all review their journey and European experiences. Since it is known that the Haights did purchase antiquities when they were in Egypt, they may have obtained the vases when in Italy, where a ready market for things of this type existed. The sculpture in the niche might also have been selected by them in Rome. Like other affluent Americans raising families in the 1830s, the Haights made certain that their children were exposed to the arts, history, and material remains of the ancients, with the hope that this might refine their taste and cultivate morality and virtue in this future generation of Americans.

Just as Americans had looked to ancient Greece and Rome for models on which to base the government of their new republic, they simultaneously looked to ancient cultures, as well as modern European culture, for models in the fine arts. Rhetoric of the American literati conveyed a belief that if their new government was to prosper, virtue and morality must flourish. They believed (or at least professed) that knowledge and appreciation of the arts would assure stability. Additionally, refinement and cultivation of taste would also follow if modern European culture were absorbed. During the first four decades of the nineteenth century ample opportunities existed for many literate Americans, even if they did not travel abroad, to gain knowledge of the arts of both ancient Greece and Rome, as well as modern Europe. At the same time, many Americans were calling for the establishment of their own national arts tradition, not only in the fine arts but also in literature. The encouragement and support of American artists provided by the early academies and athenaeums fostered such growth, while at the same time enriching and refining America's classical taste.

68 opposite

RICHARD K. HAIGHT FAMILY

c. 1848

Attributed to Nicolino Calyo
(1799–1884), New York

Gouache on paper

20 x 15 in.

Museum of the City of New York, New York; Bequest of Elizabeth Cushing Iselin, 74.97.2

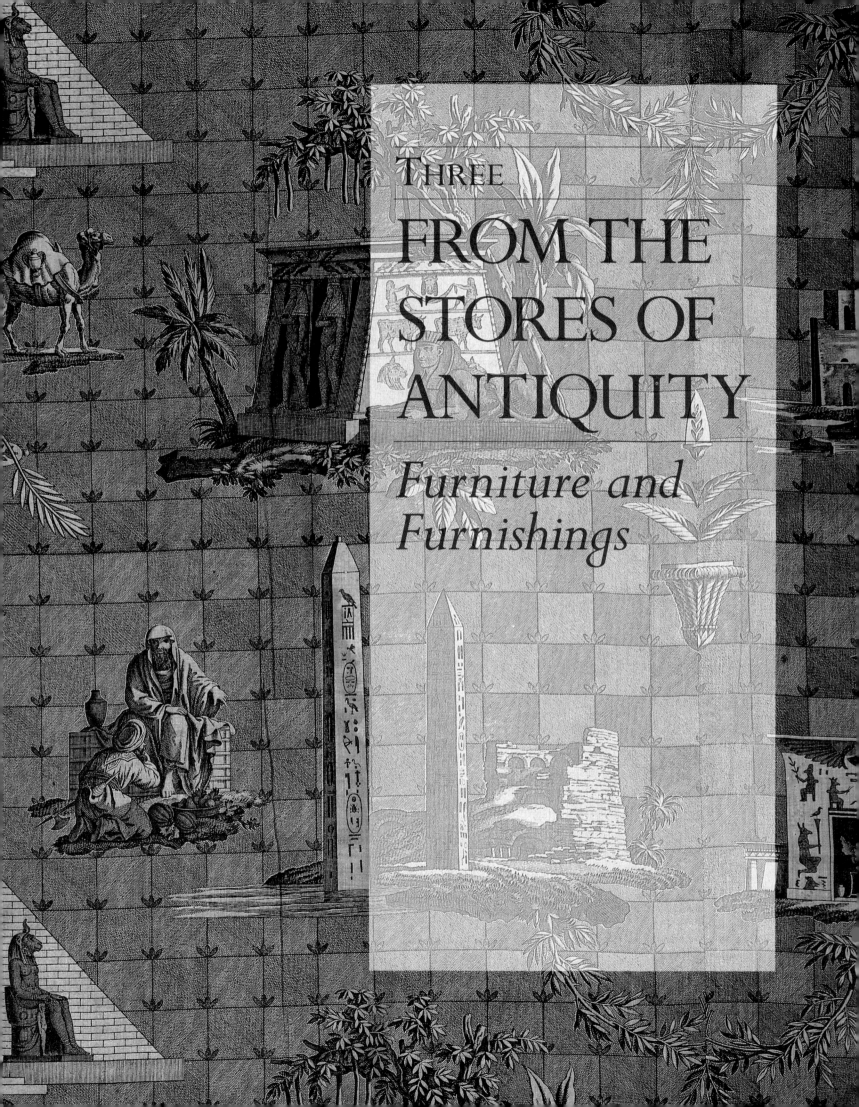

THREE

FROM THE STORES OF ANTIQUITY

Furniture and Furnishings

When Thomas Hope arrived in England in 1795, he instantly felt a "tacit acknowledgement of our [England's] inferiority in the arts of elegance and taste."[1] This unabashed recognition that taste was different in England resulted from Hope's familiarity with the current manifestations of classicism in France. His extensive travels and education on the Continent had also acquainted him with the marvels of antiquity in Italy and Greece. As a connoisseur, patron of the arts, and gentleman of taste, Hope was determined to bring English taste into line with the most fashionable and elegant styles popular in Europe.

In 1804 Thomas Hope introduced a totally new style of furniture and interior decoration to England through the refurbishing of his Duchess Street house. To formally announce his intent, he invited the members of The Royal Academy of Arts to view his house by issuing them tickets of admission in February 1804. He further promoted this "deviation from the prevailing style of furniture" with the publication of *Household Furniture and Interior Decoration* in 1807, detailing the interior and furniture designs introduced in this impressive house. In so doing, he acknowledged his debt to the French, and most especially his admiration for his acquaintance Charles Percier, "who, having professionally devoted his career to the study of the antique *chef-d'oeuvres* in Italy, now devotes the latter portion of his life to the superintendence of modern objects of elegance and decoration in France."[2] Indeed Hope more than admired Percier, he literally copied a number of his designs, which were published in his *Recueil de Décorations intérieures . . .* (Paris, 1801, 1812).

Most importantly, Hope reinforced and fostered the spread of this new, more archaeologically derived classical taste that had been introduced to Europe by Napoleon through his principal architects and decorators, Charles Percier and Pierre-François-Leonard, as well as painters like Jacques-Louis David. He also directly recognized his admiration of the ancients when he remarked on the "trophies, terms, caryatids, griffins, chimeras, scenic masks" that "once gave to every piece of Grecian and Roman furniture so much grace, variety, movement, expression, and physiognomy."[3] He attributed his sources of inspiration for such elegance directly to "those productions of Nature herself," and "those monuments of antiquity which shew the mode in which the forms of nature may be most happily adapted to the various exigencies of art."[4] Following the sixty plates comprising his *Household Furniture and Interior Decoration*, he appended a "list of the different works, either representing actual remains of antiquity, or modern compositions in the antique style, which have been of most use to me in my attempt to animate the different pieces of furniture here described, and to give each a peculiar countenance and character, a pleasing outline, and an appropriate meaning."[5] Hope was an important link in a chain reaction that had begun on the Continent, and it was not long before the ripples were felt across the Atlantic in the infant American republic.

Even before Hope's Duchess Street House was ready for the first invited guests, the English designer Thomas Sheraton, a principal progenitor of the earlier light and linear classical style, recognized the imminent changes coming about in furniture and interior decoration. In *The*

Cabinet Dictionary (London, 1803), Sheraton referred to French innovations, having seen "some of the latest specimens of French chairs, some of which we have been favoured with a view of, that they follow the antique taste, and introduce into their arms and legs, various heads of animals."[6] This new "antique taste" was already well developed in France. Assuming that Sheraton wished to be as stylish as possible, he introduced into his *Dictionary* a number of "Grecian" forms, including chairs with "cross fronts" (curule), a dining table, and a Grecian couch, squab, and sofa. In defining the term "Grecian" he used it "to signify anything executed or shaped in imitation of the Greeks. Many writers have celebrated the praises of this people, as having left to posterity, models of sculpture and architecture, much superior to any nation. Particularly the Grecian Architecture has always excelled every other attempt; and has been, therefore, the generally allowed example of fine buildings, and the best taste in architecture."[7]

Throughout the second half of the eighteenth century various books carefully delineating classical architecture were available to architects. Many of these publications were owned in America by individuals or private library societies. Among the books detailing architectural monuments of antiquity that most likely would have been referred to were the numerous works by Piranesi, Stuart and Revett's *The Antiquities of Athens*, vols. 1 and 2, and Thomas Major's *Ruins of Paestum*. While architects and patrons had ample sources, cabinetmakers, chairmakers, upholsterers, and silversmiths, prior to 1800, had few books that specifically and accurately depicted antique objects. Certainly they could avail themselves of the architectural source books, view the specimens from antiquity then in The British Museum, or perhaps visit private collections. Additionally, they might have been aware of two publications by the architect Charles Heathcote Tatham: *Etchings . . .* (1799) and *Designs for Ornamental Plate, Many of which have been executed in silver, from Original Drawings* (1806).

The refinement of taste in early nineteenth-century America may have begun with the fine arts, but almost simultaneously it extended to architecture, interior decoration, furniture, and various other furnishings. As Joseph Hopkinson stated in his 1810 address to members of the Pennsylvania Academy of the Fine Arts, "it [fine arts] is equally required in selecting and disposing the internal decorations and furniture; which are sometimes, even in houses of the most fashionable, most ridiculous and shocking." Like Hope, Hopkinson perceived a lack of taste and elegance, and he believed that "the mechanics . . . employed in these services, have the most indispensable occasion for cultivating their talents, and improving their taste; especially while their employers are resolved not to do so." Just as in the fine arts, Hopkinson believed that the necessary improvement in interior decoration and furniture would come "from the stores of antiquity." He was quite correct when he observed that "It may surprise some to learn that most of the ornaments introduced to the persons and houses of the wealthy and the gay, under the irresistible recommendation of being 'new fashions,' are really some thousands years old; purloined from the relics of former ages. . . . How various! how inexhaustible! is the profit and pleasure to be derived from the studies of antiquity."[8] The sources of inspiration that defined this new style for American mechanics and their patrons were indeed inexhaustible, and the profit and pleasure

would be equally so. Already Americans had a century and more of experience in borrowing ideas and designs from abroad, and the primary difference at the outset of the nineteenth century was, as Hopkinson noted, that the reservoir of images and ideas was virtually limitless. Consequently, Americans did borrow profusely not only from antiquity but also from their contemporaries, and most especially from the French and the English (fig. 69).

During the first four decades of the nineteenth century, these sources of inspiration ranged from actual imported objects and émigré craftsmen who brought both images in their minds as well as sketches and printed design plates and books, to an ever-growing number of popular periodicals illustrating the latest taste in fashions, furniture, and interior decoration. In addition, the publication of price books in London, which prompted a similar practice in urban areas of America, also promoted this new style. Perhaps the most remarkable fact is that only occasionally were these American interpretations so direct as to suggest total plagiarism.

Even today, with current scholarship rapidly increasing, the most difficult question to answer is specifically what sources were actually owned by American patrons and craftsmen. Published catalogs of private library societies, acquisition books, and an occasional inventory or auction reference continue to add to this body of knowledge. However, this search is still frustrating, as one is reminded that the appraisers of Duncan Phyfe's estate in 1854 simply noted that in the "open garret" were "1 lot Cabinet Maker's Books & Drawings .50."[9] Tracking the specific ownership of these important design sources in America is an ongoing pursuit. However, still a relatively unknown factor is the extent to which mechanics such as cabinetmakers, upholsterers, silversmiths, and others in trades associated with interior decoration owned and actively used such printed sources. In addition to the derivation of American designs from English and French printed sources, the recognition of actual imported objects serving as models must also be strongly acknowledged. Finally, the cross-pollination accomplished through immigrant mechanics who came to America with knowledge of the most fashionable European taste and styles should not be overlooked.

What did Americans choose to borrow from antiquity via their English and European contemporaries? First and foremost they borrowed specific forms derived directly from "the stores of antiquity"; and secondly, but of equal importance, they borrowed vast quantities of ornament that they adapted and applied to modern western objects. The principal forms that were borrowed, such as the klismos and curule forms, ewers, vases, urns, and others, continued to be copied over time and space in a wide range of different variations, determined sometimes by regionalism, and sometimes by economics.

The most ubiquitous of these forms can be seen in what the ancient Greeks called a *klismos* chair, which in the eighteenth and nineteenth centuries was known as either a "scroll back" or "Grecian" chair. The French began to adapt this form in the 1790s, and by 1802 *The London Chair-Makers'*

69   opposite
While Americans borrowed a limitless number of forms and quantity of ornament from the ancients, most of what was created on this side of the Atlantic exhibited an unmistakable American aesthetic. Shown in the interior of a parlor from Waterloo Row, a group of Baltimore townhouses designed by Robert Mills in 1818, is some of the most distinctive American furniture in the new Grecian style. While the klismos form of the chair, the Grecian-cross base of the table, and the tripod base of the lamp stand echo Greek and Roman precedents, the painted decoration is purely a Baltimore interpretation. The lamp stand and center table (c.1820–1830), with an imported scagliola top featuring a painted scene of ancient ruins, were originally owned in the Wilson family of Baltimore. The dramatically shaped klismos chair is one from a set owned by Arunah Abell of Baltimore, and the tablet top of each of the surviving twelve chairs has a different motif derived from ancient designs published by Thomas Sheraton.

70

SIDE CHAIR

1810–1820

Attributed to Duncan Phyfe
(1768–1856), New York

Mahogany, mahogany veneer

32½ x 18½ x 18¾ in.

Collection Mr. and Mrs. George M.
Kaufman

and Carvers' Book of Prices included "Scroll-Back" chairs, as well as "Tablet-Top" chairs, with the option of "Laying back the front of the tops to the front sweep of the back legs." The same publication offered the option of "Grecian front legs" that were more deeply "sweep'd" than a regular leg. Hope's *Household Furniture and Interior Decoration* illustrated a large number of tablet-top chairs with Grecian front legs, as well as a side view of a typical scroll-back side chair in plate XL. As early as 1805, the English designer George Smith engraved drawings of "Parlour Chairs" similar to the scroll back chairs being shown in the London price books. When Smith published these designs in his *A Collection of Designs for Household Furniture* (London, 1808), he noted that the seats of these chairs might be "French stuffed, and finished in red morocco leather, on the border of which may be printed a Grecian ornament in black; over the heads of tacks may be put a molding of brass, or of dyed wood in imitation of ebony."[10]

The earliest documented American manifestation of the scroll back chair seems to have been made in New York by 1807. In that year, cabinetmaker Duncan Phyfe billed William Bayard of New York for a total of thirty-two "Mahogany Chairs"; ten side chairs and two armchairs owned by Bayard and believed to be among those recorded on the bill are now in the collection of the Winterthur Museum.[11] These scroll back chairs have double cross bannisters in their backs and reeded front Grecian (saber) legs. They represent one of many variations on this popular form of

71

SIDE CHAIR

1810–1820

New York

Mahogany

33³⁄₁₆ x 18¼ x 15 in.

Museum of the City of New York, New York; Bequest of Mrs. Miles Whiting 71.120.12a

new style chair derived from Grecian models often seen on antique grave stele and vases. Other versions of New York scroll back chairs substituted either lyres, harps, eagles, or foliate cornucopias for the cross bannisters (figs. 70 & 71). Additional embellishments included "Preparing the front legs for lion's paws"—a suitable Roman treatment—and a variety of carved motifs ornamenting the crest rail, ranging from cornucopias to bound fasces or wheat, tied with a bowknot.[12]

The scroll back chair, produced with variations in the front legs, carved crests, and backs, may have been the most popular New York chair of the first quarter of the nineteenth century, and it was produced by numerous chairmakers and carvers listed in the city's directories during the first few decades of the nineteenth century. The armchair in figure 72, while related to

72

ARMCHAIR

1810–1820

Attributed to Duncan Phyfe
(1768–1856), New York

Mahogany

33⅛ x 20⅛ x 16¾ in.

Private Collection

the Bayard ones, exhibits differences in the carving of the crest rail, the turned front legs, the carved and turned arm supports, and the seat frame, which is upholstered half-over a reeded rail. All of these variations reflect the choices that a client had to make, which in turn determined the total cost of the final product. As noted, the New York price books, patterned on London ones, defined specific costs for variations in detail.

One of the most innovative early nineteenth-century interpretations of the klismos, or scroll back, chair was produced and patented in Boston by chairmaker Samuel Gragg. The son of a New Hampshire wheelwright, Gragg was a windsor chairmaker and familiar with the technique of bending wood, and the various types of wood most suitable for this purpose. Having arrived in Boston from New Hampshire around 1800, Gragg may have seen imported scroll back chairs, or known of the London price books that noted scroll backs, as well as the rates for bending "Grecian Cross" bannisters in chairs. He was also probably well aware of the numerous high-style painted chairs currently being imported from England. Hence, he was perfectly in fashion when he patented his "elastic chair" in August 1808, and advertised the following May that he sold "Patent CHAIRS and SETTEES, with elastic backs and bottoms, made in a new, elegant and superior style, of the best materials."[13] While it is unlikely that Gragg was aware of the parallel production in Brussels of chairmaker Jean-Joseph Chapuis, it is almost certain that he recognized the imminent popularity of this new taste for the antique, and this is precisely what he responded to with his "new, elegant and superior style" chairs and settees.[14] The side chairs that Gragg produced using his "patented" bending technique ranged from those with a continuous rear stile and side seat rail with a separate turned front leg, to the most evocative form employing a continuous piece of bentwood from the scroll of the top of the stile through the sweep of the Grecian front legs (fig. 73). In addition, Gragg produced chairs with great scrolled arms made of a single piece of wood bent in a 180-degree curve; an extraordinary feat as well as a magnificent result. Unfortunately though, the durability of this particular design had its limitations, and these armchairs have not survived in great numbers. While the delicate and sensitively painted surfaces of Gragg's chairs evoked classical overtones through the utilization of motifs such as peacock feathers, acanthus leaves, and honeysuckle, much of this decoration has not so well survived the ravages of time.[15]

Judging from seventeenth- and eighteenth-century American furniture, it is not surprising that strong regional preferences and distinctions continued through the classical period in the first four decades of the nineteenth century. One notable observation is that the deep, curved "tablet-top" form often seen in both French and English sources was more popular in Boston, Philadelphia, and Baltimore than in New York where it is less frequently found. Furthermore, the form and ornament of the tablet-top chairs produced in Boston, is quite distinct

73

SIDE CHAIR

1808–1815

Samuel Gragg (1772–1855), Boston

Painted ash and hickory

34⅛ x 18 x 20 in.

Courtesy Museum of Fine Arts, Boston. Charles Hitchcock Tyler Residuary Fund

from that preferred by patrons and mechanics in Philadelphia and Baltimore. What determined these differences, and were these choices signifying conscious tendencies toward French or English preferences? Or were they the product of patrons and chairmakers exercising a combination of choices that resulted in a form that became a regional expression? Did the presence of a larger number of émigré French patrons and craftsmen in Philadelphia result in a stronger tendency toward French styles? With as much information as the past few decades have yielded in the study of American arts and culture, it is still difficult to give definite answers to these multifaceted questions.

The Philadelphia side chair in figure 74, which descended in the Hare family of Philadelphia, is among the most high-style interpretations of the Greek klismos form, and evidences all the richness and elegance of the finest imported examples.[16] Yet it has a distinctiveness that belies its American, and specifically Philadelphian, manufacture, though the inlaid brass ornament is seen on English furniture and may have been imported from England. However, the strong rectilinear quality of these chairs suggests more of a French inspiration, while the bold tablet-top is both English and French in derivation. The continuous curve of the rear stiles straight down into the rear legs, marking a separateness from the horizontal seat rails, seems to be more specifically a French convention, whereas the square, tapering legs with slight outward curve are seen on both English and French examples.

The tablet-top above two horizontal splats of the chair in figure 74 distinctly echoes an important set of Philadelphia painted chairs (fig. 78, right), as well as the 1809 design by the English-trained architect Benjamin Henry Latrobe for painted chairs for the oval drawing room of the President's House (fig. 75). Working directly with the fashionable and elegant first lady, Dolley Madison (fig. 76), Latrobe commissioned Baltimore chairmakers Hugh and John Finlay to execute this set of thirty-six chairs, two sofas, and four settees.[17] Could Latrobe's avant-garde designs for the Madisons have influenced patrons and makers in Philadelphia? It is possible that the President's furniture may have been one of several factors affecting this region's preferences. The boxlike wooden slip seat frame (fig. 74) that rests on top of the rails is also indicative of a type preferred by Philadelphians (or their upholsterers), and its flat and linear quality initially derives from French sources. The cut-brass inlaid ornament across the tablet and front seat rail is set in a veneer of highly figured rosewood, while ebony is used with the stars and anthemions. The brass stars on the stiles conceal the pins that secure the horizontal back rails. In James Barron's *Modern and Elegant Designs of Cabinet and Upholstery Furniture* (London, 1814), a plate at the back shows twenty-nine designs for stars, anthemions, scroll-ended stringing, etc., that can be purchased either "In Brass" or "In Hard Wood."

The very fashionable Boston Grecian chair in figure 77 presents a dramatic contrast to the linear form of the Philadelphia example. The rounded ends of the tablet-top, the deeply curved rear stiles that continue onto and along the top of the seat rail, the drapery carved splat with scrolled anthemion decoration, and the molded rear stiles and front legs, all combine for an effect of flow-

74

SIDE CHAIR
one of a pair

c. 1815–1825

Philadelphia

Mahogany rosewood, ebony; brass

33¼ x 19 x 23⅛ in.

Collection Mr. and Mrs. George M. Kaufman

75

DRAWINGS FOR A CHAIR FOR
THE PRESIDENT'S HOUSE

c. 1809

Benjamin Henry Latrobe
(1764–1820), Baltimore

Watercolor on paper

5¼ x 5⅛ in. (each)

Maryland Historical Society, Baltimore

76

DOLLEY MADISON

c. 1817

Bass Otis (1764–1861),
Washington, D.C.

Oil on canvas

29 x 24 in.

*Courtesy The New-York Historical
Society, New York, Gift of Thomas J.
Bryan, 1867.308*

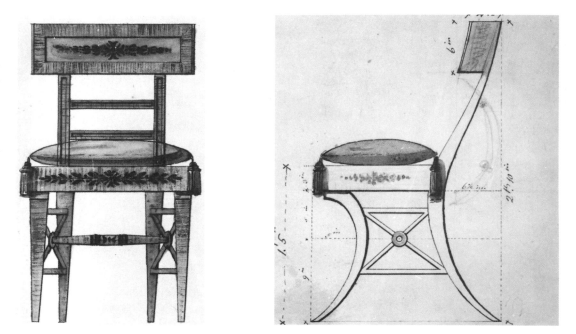

ing, curvilinear continuity. Instead of inlaid brass ornament, the surface decoration is carved and integral with the overall form. This chair is as distinctly a Boston product as the one in figure 74 is a Philadelphia example. While designs for chairs with tablet-tops like this Boston example were published in 1802 in Pierre de La Mésangère's *Collection des Meubles et Objets de Goût*, it appears that Boston chairmakers were more directly influenced by English design sources. By 1819 the Boston Athenaeum was given a copy of Thomas Hope's *Household Furniture and Interior Decoration*.

Both the Boston Athenaeum and the Athenaeum of Philadelphia had subscriptions to Rudolph Ackermann's monthly publication *Repository of the Arts* (London, 1809–1828).

While Boston chairmakers produced a wide variety of Grecian chairs, including scroll back types, specific characteristics appear consistently to define Boston classical chairs.[18] The deeply curved rear stiles seen on this chair echo the very fashionable seating furniture drawn by English artist Henry Moses for his *A Series of Twenty-nine Designs of Modern Costume* (London, 1823). Inexpensive and prolific engravings, often after drawings by Adam Buck, also frequently illustrated Grecian klismos chairs with similarly curved backs, and were popular prints sold in Boston. An informative aspect of this particular chair is that when acquired, with its mate, they both retained their original stuffing and black horsehair upholstery edged in red Moroccan leather. In contrast to the angular wooden edge of the seat frame on the Philadelphia chair, the use of leather edging on the Boston chair similarly accents the sewn, square edge outlining the sides of the seat.

The most dramatic, classically inspired klismos chairs made in America are the high-style painted examples produced in Baltimore and Philadelphia. A comparison of two chairs from these cities evokes a visual impression similar to that seen in the Philadelphia and Boston examples above (fig. 78). Circumstantial evidence suggests that the Philadelphia chair (on right) was designed by Benjamin Henry Latrobe in 1808 for William Waln, and may have been a precedent for Latrobe's 1809 President's House design.[19] The overall form of these early painted chairs is closely related to the mahogany and rosewood, brass-inlaid Philadelphia chair in figure 74, and may have been the precedent that defined this regional form, along with Latrobe's design for the Madisons' chairs. The chairs are part of a suite of furniture whose surviving pieces include a window seat (fig. 83), a pair of card tables, a backless sofa or chaise longue, a pier table, and sixteen side chairs. The design and decoration of this suite reflects the knowledge and understanding on the part of the designer of some of the most avant-garde sources of the period, including publications by Sheraton, Hope, Smith, Flaxman, and Percier and Fontaine. Certainly Latrobe's background and talent suggest that he was probably the designer, and thus responsible for introducing to Philadelphia the first demonstrably Grecian interpretations of American furniture. The archaeo-

CLASSICAL TASTE IN AMERICA

logically derived decorations painted in strong reds, black, ochre, and gilt echo the sources drawn by men like Thomas Sheraton, James Stuart and Nicholas Revett, and Charles Heathcote Tatham.

The Baltimore painted side chair in figure 78 (left) presents a very different interpretation of the Grecian form. The deeply curved back joining the top of the seat rail, the powerful outward curve of the rear legs, and the turned and tapered front legs contrast dramatically with the Philadelphia example. The trapezoidal seats and rectilinear tablet-tops with related decoration drawn from Thomas Sheraton's *The Cabinet-Maker and Upholsterer's Drawing-Book* (London, 1791–1793) are their only common denominator. Both construction features and painted techniques indicate different makers and decorators. Most important though, the Baltimore example is the high-style precedent of a regional form that was adapted and reproduced in large quantities for both local and export trade through the 1820s and 1830s. The eleven surviving chairs from this set, made originally for Arunah S. Abell's house "Woodburne," exhibit such fantastic creatures on their tablet-tops as unicorns, griffins, sphinxes, and swans. The various other classical motifs are commonly derived from antiquity and include palmettes with drapery on the front legs, anthemions and winged thunderbolts on the side rails, bound fasces on the front rail, and an eagle standard with a laurel wreath and torches at its center on the stay rail of the back. The strong yellow, green, and black decoration chosen for the Baltimore chair are also dramatically different from the colors of the Philadelphia suite. Possibly these chairs were conceived as part of a total scheme of interior decoration, as is thought to be the case with the Philadelphia painted suite of furniture that probably adorned William Waln's house on Chestnut Street.

Both of these extraordinary painted chairs exhibit the "knowledge of the classic designs of Grecian workmanship" that George Smith referred to in *A Collection of Ornamental Designs, after the Manner of the Antique, Compos'd for the Use of Architects, Ornamental Painters* . . . (London, 1812), when he stated: "In the Grecian works of art, every attention was evidently given to produce a flowing and correct outline; and so to arrange the parts in masses, that the whole should appear clear and distinct: their compositions being neither overloaded nor deficient, but each part relieving another: and it is this happy relief, this rejection of little parts, that gives to their works so chaste and pleasing an effect."[20]

Another significant form borrowed from antiquity, and translated both abroad and in America in numerous variations, was the curule, or "Grecian cross," form. An early adaptation of this device has already been cited in the crossed bannisters of the scroll back armchair noted above (fig. 72), possibly derived from forms defined in the 1802 London *Book of Prices*. A wide variety of seating forms employed the "Grecian cross," ranging from window seats, tabourets or stools, chairs, settees, and sofas. Thomas Sheraton illustrated a "Parlour Chair" in plate 31 of *The Cabinet Dictionary* that had a curule or cross front perched upon paw feet, and two elaborate "Drawing Chairs" in plate 47 with curule front and back legs. Hope's publication of 1807 illus-

78 *opposite*

SIDE CHAIR
one of original set of twelve

c. 1820–1830

Baltimore
Painted maple and cherry with polychrome, stenciled, and free-hand gilt decoration; cane
33⅞ x 20⅛ x 24³⁄₁₆ in.

The Baltimore Museum of Art: The George C. Jenkins and Decorative Arts Funds (BMA 1972.46.1)

SIDE CHAIR

c. 1808–1810

Philadelphia
Painted white oak, yellow poplar, and white pine; cane
34¼ x 17¹¹⁄₁₆ x 20¹¹⁄₁₆ in.

Kaufman Americana Foundation, Norfolk, Virginia

trated an armchair in plate XX "after the manner of the ancient curule chairs," and in plate XXIX he showed two "folding stools" presumably modeled after Roman seating forms that Napoleon also copied for his military furniture. By 1808 the *Supplement to the London Chair-Makers and Carvers Book of Prices for Workmanship* illustrated "Grecian Cross fronts" (p. 22 and pl. 3). George Smith depicted three "Drawing Room X Seats" in plate 53 of his 1808 publication, and Ackermann called similar forms tabourets and window seats. Hence, there appears to have been as much variation in the terminology as there was in the interpretation of the basic curule form.

In America the patrons and cabinetmakers of New York quickly adapted this form to a number of very sophisticated seating pieces in the first two decades of the nineteenth century. In Boston by the 1820s and 1830s it was popularly used for stools. Perhaps the rarest of these forms is the side chair, similar to that shown by Sheraton in 1803, with the Grecian cross front atop paw feet and having backward splayed rear legs with paw feet (fig. 79, far right). Originally owned in the Mays family of Philadelphia, this chair is closely related to a sketch attributed to Duncan Phyfe that the late Charles F. Montgomery believed probably accompanied a letter from Phyfe to Charles N. Bancker of Philadelphia about 1815. In January 1816 Phyfe billed Bancker for a quantity of mahogany furniture, so presumably Bancker had made his decision based upon the two sketches Phyfe sent prior to receiving the order.[21] A more frequently seen New York variation on this Grecian-cross-front chair utilizes the curule form as the side supports of the chair, as seen in the suite of side chairs, armchairs, and sofa made for Thomas Cornell Pearsall now in the collections of The Metropolitan Museum of Art.

The logical adaptation of this Grecian-cross-front form for a larger piece of seating furniture is seen in a number of settees and sofas. The effect produced by the overall design of the settee in figure 79 (left) is most harmonious since the back legs echo the curule form of the front supports.[22] The graceful outward curve of the front of the arms is reminiscent of the scroll-back klismos chair, and the carved ornament of drapery swags, tassels, and fasces bound with bowknots emphasizes the unity of both the classical form and ornament of this settee. Another variation on this form is found in larger sofas, like the ones made originally for Thomas Cornell Pearsall and James Brinkerhoff, where two slightly narrower Grecian-cross fronts are employed.[23] In these pieces a beautiful and continuous line is created from the top scroll of the front arm support, curving through the center of the cross (ornamented with a cast-brass lion's head) and down to the brass paw foot.

Stools, or tabourets, were illustrated with great variation in both French and English design sources, and hence became increasingly popular in America in the early nineteenth century. New York chairmakers and patrons embraced this form with the same enthusiasm that they showed for Grecian cross-front chairs, settees, and sofas. The New York stool in figure 80 is related to contemporary French and English designs, but the source it most closely resembles is a bronze example of "Antique Seats from Originals at Rome" drawn by Charles Heathcote

79   opposite

The ancient curule form is featured in this tasteful classical interior with a diminutive New York settee on the left and a Grecian-cross-front side chair on the right, attributed to Duncan Phyfe. The New York scroll-back side chair seen through the arch has front paw feet and an unusual harp back. The meticulously drawn floral watercolors on vellum hanging above the settee were executed by French artist Antoine-Ferdinand Redouté (1756–1809). Flanking the doorway are a pair of American sconces with carved and gilded eagles. The lyre-based work table to the left of the doorway was made in Boston, c. 1810–1825.

80

FOOT STOOL

c. 1810–1815

New York

Mahogany

17¾ x 19 x 16 in.

Collection Peter G. Terian

Tatham and illustrated in his *Etchings* . . . (London, 1806). Tatham made an allowance for creature comfort by placing on this bronze seat a cushion of "red Cloth" with great tassels at the corners. While a stool identical to this example in The Mabel Brady Garvan Collection at Yale University has been attributed to Salem, Massachusetts, on the basis of the carved leafage on the legs, the close parallel to other New York carving and production suggests manufacture in that urban center.

Inventory listings for this period contain frequent references to footstools, stools, tabourets, and ottomans. Robert Gilmor, Jr.'s, 1848 inventory listed "2 Small painted Ottomans @ .75" in the Large Dining Room, and "2 Ottomans @ 4." in the Front Drawing Room. Luman Reed of New York also had "2 pr Ottomans . . . 6." in his Picture Gallery, and "2 Taborettes" in the Drawing Room and "1 pair of taborettes" in the Parlor, each pair valued at $20.[24] In Boston, Nathan Appleton owned a pair of "X" form stools similar to ones illustrated by Thomas Hope (plate XII, no. 3).[25] An 1880s photograph of the interior of Samuel Welles's house on Summer Street in Boston shows several cross-form tabourets that may have been made in Boston based on small-scale models of French furniture sent from Paris to the Welles family.[26]

By the 1820s and 1830s the popularity of relatively plain, veneered footstools increased tremendously. Duncan Phyfe included a pair of handsome veneered footstools in the suite of furniture that he made for New York lawyer Samuel A. Foot.[27] A number of the document-ed examples appear to have been made in Boston. The footstool in figure 81 is representative of this type of functional yet classically derived form. With the label of Hancock, Holden and Adams Furniture Warehouse, 37 Cornhill, Boston, affixed to the bottom of this footstool, it can be dated precisely to the time of this brief part-nership, 1836–1837. Sometimes these footstools were fashioned in more elaborate forms, featuring pierced anthemions and scrolled, carved leafage.[28] By 1840 when John Hall, the English-born archi-tect living in Baltimore, published *The Cabinet Makers Assistant*, he illustrated two plates (33 and 34), each with six elaborate designs, for fashionable footstools.

81

FOOT STOOL

1836–1837

Hancock, Holden & Adams, Boston

Mahogany veneer

15½ x 20³⁄₁₆ x 15¾ in.

Collection Mr. and Mrs. Stuart P. Feld

By the early nineteenth century new fashions in domestic architecture created a need for different forms of furniture, and elegant houses often required window seats for recesses. Hence, a variety of different forms of window seats were designed and produced, sometimes related to the curule form, or more closely following Grecian precedents. While few surviving examples of imported window seats are known, one has to wonder whether or not the charming youth in Bass Otis's 1825 *Portrait of a Seated Boy* is posed atop an English prototype or an American adaptation (fig. 82). This sophisticated cross-form seat is closely related to one illustrated by Ackermann in *The Repository of Arts* in January 1809, and described as having "a very good effect executed in bronze, with the rosettes, fillets, and other ornaments of the frame in mat gold. It might be covered with green velvet, with stripes of rose colour."[29] Since Otis provided such a detailed rendering of the seat, one suspects that he was copying an extant object; the following year he included a portion of an almost identical seat in his portrait of *Margaret Heberton Newkirk and Child*, suggesting that in fact he was working with an existing model. A window seat closely related to both the Ackermann plate and the Otis illustration was owned by Stephen Van Rensselaer IV of Albany.[30]

Elegantly decorated on both sides, the Baltimore stool, or chaise longue, in figure 83 might have been used in a window recess, or perhaps out in the middle of a drawing room or gallery, as George Smith's backless "Ottoman for Gallery" suggests. This particular "stool" appears similar to the form described in *The London Chair-Makers' and Carvers' Book of Prices* for 1808 as one "with bolster scrolls at each end." These forms ranged in size from five feet to six-and-a-half feet, and may have been made en suite with other seating forms like Grecian couches and chairs. Indeed, several Baltimore Grecian couches with almost identical decoration are known, as well as other related stools with similar decoration.[31] The "bolster scroll ends" echo those on the window seats discussed above, and the short, saberlike legs are an adaptation of the

dramatically curved Grecian legs described in the price books. Robert Gilmor, Jr.'s inventory noted "2 Painted Chintz covered Window seats" in his "Large Dining Room," and they may have been decorated in a related manner with rosewood graining and free-hand gilding.

The gilt decorative motifs on this stool are adapted from classical sources and are indicative of the painted designs seen on many examples of painted Baltimore furniture. As a burgeoning port city with growing resources and wealth in the early nineteenth century, Baltimore attracted foreign-trained craftsmen well equipped to satisfy the desire of elite patrons for the latest fashions from abroad. John and Hugh Finlay, Irish-trained ornamental painters, became the leading craftsmen for fancy painted furniture in Baltimore, and thus established a vogue in that city that was carried on by numerous others at varying economic levels. This stool, as well as related examples, is most likely the work of these talented artisans.

A very different form of window seat, closely derived from "French bed" designs, was made en suite with the painted Philadelphia Grecian side chair in figure 78, and may have been intended for the three recesses of the drawing room in William Waln's Chestnut Street house designed by Benjamin Henry Latrobe (fig. 84). The fact that the rear legs are simpler, and the back of the seat is undecorated, supports its specific function as a window seat designed to be placed against a wall. Like the chairs and other forms in this suite, its overall surface is painted with a strong red ground and then completely ornamented with classical gilt motifs. The more angular and stylized motifs on the legs and ends of the seat derive from Egyptian palmettes, and were also employed by English and French designers. The use of the applied gessoed-and-gilded molding beneath the seat rails and skirts on all the pieces in the suite suggests a woven fringe that sometimes was actually used on English and French furniture. This window seat, along with the rest of the suite, represents some of the most archaeologically correct and classically sophisticated American furniture

82 opposite

PORTRAIT OF A SEATED BOY

1825

Bass Otis (1764–1861), probably Pennsylvania

Oil on canvas

20¼ x 14¾ in.

Westmoreland Museum of Art, Greensburg, Pennsylvania; Gift of William A. Coulter Fund, 60.91

83 below

STOOL (OR WINDOW BENCH)

c. 1820–1840

Attributed to John Finlay (1777–1851) and/or Hugh Finlay (1781–1831), Baltimore

Cherry and walnut painted to simulate rosewood

24 x 72 x 21 in.

Collection Mr. and Mrs. George M. Kaufman

84

WINDOW BENCH

c. 1808–1810

Philadelphia or Baltimore

Painted and gilded wood; brass; cane

20⅞ x 52⁷⁄₁₆ x 16¹¹⁄₁₆ in.

Collection Mr. and Mrs. George M. Kaufman

of the first decade of the nineteenth century. The fact that Latrobe designed a residence, planned the interior wall decoration, and then presumably created furniture en suite for the room, reflects a major change in the approach to household decoration in America; a change that recognizes the upper-class French and English practices that began in the second half of the eighteenth century and were more widely adopted by the early nineteenth century.

Among the most stylish forms that any drawing room or parlor could be adorned with in the first decades of the nineteenth century was a Grecian couch. In contrast to a sofa that had ends of equal height, a couch was typically characterized by one end's being higher than the other, with a bolster fitted into the curve of the higher end. Thomas Sheraton illustrated three related "Grecian" forms in *The Cabinet Dictionary,* which included a couch (pl. 49), a squab (pl. 50), and a sofa (pl. 73). Precisely how he intended the couch and squab to differ he failed to explain, simply defining squab as "a kind of seat," and the couch as "from *coucher,* French, to lie down on a place of repose." Interestingly, George Smith seemed to prefer the term "chaise longue" and did not use "Grecian couch" in his 1808 publication. Throughout the first half of the nineteenth century, the couch experienced many manifestations, from exceedingly high style to the less ornamented, veneered expressions drawn by John Hall in *The Cabinet-Makers Assistant* (Baltimore, 1840).

The New York couch in figure 85 presents an example of the richly carved, gessoed-and-gilded surfaces that well-to-do New York patrons seemed to prefer. The fruit-filled carved cornucopias, supported by strong, hairy paw feet, offer a contrast in surface treatments between highly burnished gilt and *vert antique*, in imitation of ancient bronze. The convex seat rail with ebonized ground and delicately detailed gilt-stenciled decoration supplies a third surface variation. The foliate carved and gilded curvilinear ends continue the visual movement and reflective quality of the cornucopia upward to the outward scrolled arms. The twisted gilt rope edging across the back crestrail, terminating in a bold, gilt rosette, repeats the gilt decoration and unifies this shimmering tour de force of form and ornament. Fragments of what is believed was the original deep coral silk covering were found under later upholstery, indicating that when new this Grecian couch made a significant statement as a most expensive and stylish example of New York seating furniture of its time.[32]

American regional interpretations of the Grecian couch form varied tremendously, and while wealthy New York patrons preferred richly carved and gilded surfaces and stenciled decoration, elite Bostonians chose different, but equally sophisticated, ornamental details. In 1817–1819, when Nathan Appleton built his second house on Beacon Street in Boston, just two doors away from the house David Sears was then constructing, he ordered the richest Boston furniture that was available.[33] His front parlor displayed four Grecian couches, judging from photographs taken in the 1880s, a large pair and a shorter pair (fig. 86).[34] While it is rare for pairs of couches to have survived together, the production and use of pairs was not unusual. Restrained yet rich, Appleton's couches exhibit the finest Boston craftsmanship in the use of rosewood veneer and rosewood graining, cut brass inlay, brass stringing, and stamped brass mounts. Upholstered with a loose, buttoned cushion, and having a slightly convex upholstered foot, this couch resembles several designed by Hope (pl. XXVIII), though he placed a crouching greyhound at the foot of one of his couches "after the manner of similar animals on Gothic sarcophagi."

85

GRECIAN COUCH
c. 1815–1825
New York
Ebonized wood with stenciled, gilded, and *vert* decoration
33⅞ x 89½ x 25¼ in.

The Baltimore Museum of Art: Gift of Cornelia Machen Geddes, Sacramento, California (BMA 1991.147)

86

GRECIAN COUCH
one of a pair

c. 1818–1830

Boston

Rosewood with rosewood
graining; brass

34⅞ x 70¼ x 23¾ in.

*Courtesy Museum of Fine Arts, Boston.
Gift of a Friend of the Department, the
William N. Banks Foundation, the
Seminarians, Dr. and Mrs. J. Wallace
McMeel, and Anon*

Appleton's sophisticated taste might well have been fostered by his knowledge of European styles gained on several trips abroad prior to the decoration of his second house. In 1802, at age twenty-two, he traveled to England, Holland, and France, where he visited numerous manufactories, including the Gobelins manufactory of tapestry and the national manufactory of porcelain at Sèvres, as well as the Musée Napoleon filled with the emperor's spoils of antiquity plundered from Italy. In 1810 he took his wife on a sojourn in England and Scotland for her health, so once again he was exposed to the most fashionable English taste for classical furniture and interior decoration. Appleton was attuned to European taste and styles, so it is not surprising that he (or Mrs. Appleton) chose an exquisitely printed English glazed-cotton fabric for slipcovering their couches. The survival of the back portion of a cover for one of the larger couches (fig. 87) documents the use of fancy slipcovers on high-style furniture. At the same time it shows how a fabric was chosen that echoed the bold anthemion motifs of the cut-brass inlay across the front rail that presumably would have been obscured by the slipcover. The original vibrancy of the rich blue and the highly polished glaze are preserved in a small sample of the fabric that appears never to have been used, or at least washed. In April 1823, the Boston cabinetmaking firm of Isaac Vose & Son advertised recently "received by the London Packet . . . rich ell wide London Chintz, with high glazed colored linings."[35] Possibly the cabinetmaker who fashioned Appleton's couches may also have provided the elegant slipcovers.

Among the highly sophisticated pieces of furniture with which Nathan Appleton adorned his house at 39 Beacon Street were an extraordinary pair of Boston rosewood-veneered and gilded pedestals, or candelabra (fig. 118). This form was relatively rare in classical American furni-

ture, but very familiar to English and Continental patrons. Hope, Smith, and Ackermann all illustrated designs for candelabra, and in November 1815 the latter stated that the form was "suitable to the support of an argand lamp, or the globe for a gas-light."[36] While today we generally think of candelabra as holders for multiple candles, the early nineteenth-century definition generally referred to the pedestal that held the candleholder as a candelabra. The eminent English cabinetmaker George Bullock designed some noteworthy candelabra, and it is possible that Appleton knew of such designs or had actually seen the form in use on his sojourns abroad.

In 1826, Peter and Michael Angelo Nicholson discussed "Roman Furniture" in *The Practical Cabinetmaker, Upholsterer, and Complete Decorator* and remarked that "The most splendid article of furniture used by the Romans were their Candelabra."[37] While one period definition indicated that a candelabra was intended to hold a lighting apparatus, in Henry Sargent's *The Tea Party* we see candelabra in the corners of the room with large urns atop them, and the candles are in holders placed on brackets on the walls. Statuary, or various antique vessels such as ewers, might also have adorned the tops of these very Roman forms. Indeed, Hope does illustrate "candelabra, or stands" holding various silver forms.

In the Nicholsons' discussion of "Roman Furniture," they described other forms including tables that

> were generally sustained by a pillar, some having a low pedestal, others with a base supported by three, and sometimes four short turned legs, or ornamented with the paws of animals. In the decoration of Roman furniture, chimerical figures were

87

SLIPCOVER FOR GRECIAN COUCH

c. 1818–1830

Boston, fabric made by Richard Ovey, London

Glazed chintz

46½ x 27 in.

Society for the Preservation of New England Antiquities, Boston; Gift of William Sumner Appleton

CENTER TABLE

c. 1825

New York

Rosewood veneer with gilt and verte decoration; scagliola; brass

29 x 36 in.

Museum of the City of New York, New York; Gift of Mrs. Egerton L. Winthrop, 36.160

used in very great abundance; garlands and festoons were also employed occasionally. In point of taste, the Roman furniture was stiff, and often too much overcharged with ornament; it wanted the fine-flowing outline, simplicity, and chastity of Greek furniture.[38]

Based on this description, the so-called "pillar and claw" tables defined in London price books as early as 1796, and often cited in nineteenth-century American inventories, were thought to derive from Roman rather than Greek precedents. Card tables, pembroke or breakfast tables, dining tables, and center tables were all variously referred to as "pillar and claw" if they had a central pedestal supported by three or four paw feet. Perhaps one of the most literal, and "overcharged with ornament," interpretations of this pillar and claw (or paw) form is the New York center table made for merchant Stephen Whitney in the first quarter of the nineteenth century (fig. 88). Related to a small group of New York card and center tables,[39] this example is richly embellished with every manner of ornament from cut-brass inlay, carved and gilded as well as *vert antique* surfaces, stenciled decorations, rich veneers, and a painted scagliola top depicting the classical myth of Mettius Curtius.[40] Each element of this table, from the painted top to the fluted central column with acanthus foliage around its base to the tripod, paw-footed base bespeaks classical form and ornament. The cut-brass inlay and incredibly intricate gilt stencil decoration is indicative of the most expensive New York workmanship. The overall form of a central columnar support with painted top and tripod base is seen in other less elaborate New York examples and represents a specific regional preference.

Significant evidence survives to support the observation that some wealthy American patrons adopted the European penchant for furnishing and decorating their principal rooms in a totally

coordinated manner, as Hope promoted through the example set by his Duchess Street house. Extant suites of expensive furniture ordered for specific houses suggest possibly quite elaborate schemes of decoration, as have already been documented for gentlemen like William Waln of Philadelphia and John Wickham of Richmond. Stephen Van Rensselaer IV of Albany, a man with both taste and resources, traveled abroad in 1813, was presented at Napoleon's court, and purchased rich *objets d'art* in Paris.[41] Just four years after his return to America, he commissioned Albany architect Philip Hooker to build a mansion in the latest classical style on Broadway in Albany. Van Rensselaer imported lavish accoutrements for his house (fig. 24), along with at least six pieces of the most high-style New York classical furniture made by the Parisian-trained cabinetmaker Charles-Honoré Lannuier.[42]

While this furniture survives as extraordinary evidence of his personal taste and wealth, there are still many unanswered questions

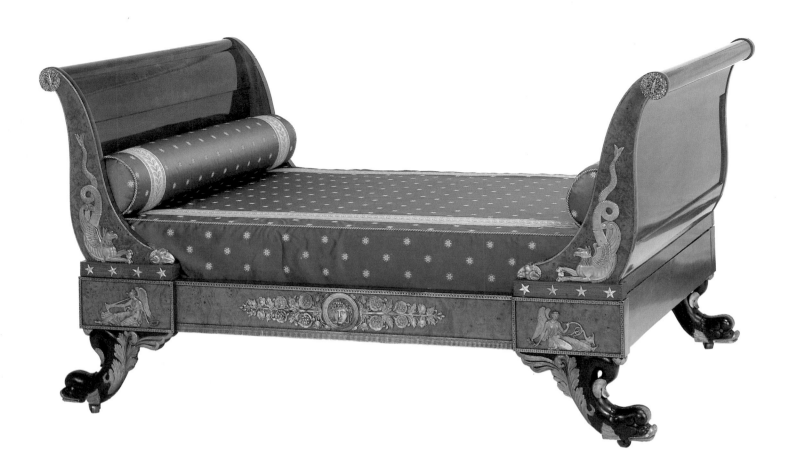

with regard to why Van Rensselaer chose Lannuier, who determined the forms selected, and what role Lannuier may have played in the overall decorative scheme for the rooms in this new mansion. Van Rensselaer's card tables and pier table are not unique in Lannuier's repertoire, but the magnificent French bedstead (fig. 89) stands out as one of his most ambitious productions. The combination of specially chosen exotic veneers, four beautifully carved and patinated dolphin feet, the most superior gilt-bronze mounts, and cut-brass inlay combine to evoke a visual extravaganza in the bedchamber more elaborate than any other American bed known. French beds, those intended to have one long side placed against the wall, were not unknown in America. In fact, a labeled Lannuier French bedstead with what is believed to be its original crown survives today (fig. 90). Made originally for Mrs. Isaac Bell (1791–1871) of New York, this bedstead is more in the English tradition than the French style evidenced in the Van Rensselaer example.

During Monroe's occupancy of the President's House, accounts for 1819 indicate that a number of "crown beds" were set up and hung with rich fabrics and trimmings. While the term "French bed" might also refer to a four-post bedstead with hangings in the French style,[43] beds meant to be placed in alcoves or simply against the wall were known to Americans from Monticello in the late eighteenth century to the 1833 broadside published by Joseph Meeks & Sons of New York (fig. 168).

89

BEDSTEAD

c. 1817

Charles-Honoré Lannuier
(1779–1819), New York

Mahogany and satinwood with painted and gilded decoration; ormolu

45½ x 85½ x 60 in.

Albany Institute of History and Art, Albany, New York; Gift of Mrs. William Dexter

This bedchamber in the Bartow-
Pell Mansion Museum, in the
Bronx, New York, c. 1836–
1842, is dominated by the superb
French bedstead made by French
émigré cabinetmaker Charles-
Honoré Lannuier and what is
believed to be its original crown
made for Mrs. Isaac Bell of New
York about 1810–1819. Closely
related to designs in Pierre de La
Méssangère's *Collection des Meubles
et Objets de Goût,* the crown on
this bedstead, with its mahogany
veneer, gilt, and cast ormolu
ornaments, provides the canopy
from which elaborate silk hangings are supported. The hangings
on French crown beds were
always intended to completely
enclose the occupant, providing
the same kind of privacy and pro-
tection from drafts that a fully
hung four-post bed would have
afforded.

The most challenging question is exactly how Stephen Van Rensselaer's French bedstead was hung. Did Lannuier make a "crown" (like the one he fashioned for the Bell bed) or other type of wall-mounted ornament from which to suspend elegant silk hangings? It is likely that Van Rensselaer had seen beds like this in France, and possibly in America, as contemporary descriptions indicate Joseph Bonaparte had some impressively draped beds at "Point Breeze." If Lannuier received Pierre de La Mésangère's annually published plates of *Collection des Meubles et Objets de Goût* from his brother Nicholas in Paris, then he (or his upholsterer) had numerous examples from which to choose a drapery treatment. Did Lannuier coordinate these hangings, or did he turn the project over to an upholsterer in New York, or Albany, once the bedstead was completed? The answers to all of these important questions have yet to be discovered. Published design sources of the period provided ample choices, and imported fabrics were available along with elaborate tapes, fringes, and tassels.[44] As more and more surviving evidence, both material and written, is accumulated, a fuller picture of this aspect of household furniture and interior decoration in America will emerge.

As has already been demonstrated, Americans freely borrowed forms, design elements, and ornament drawn from both ancient and modern civilizations and recombined them into fashion-able expressions for stylish interiors. In many instances forms were directly borrowed and vari-ously adapted either in toto or as a part of the whole. Just as there was a fascination with Greek and Roman antiquity, there prevailed a similar interest in the culture and physical remains of ancient Egypt, a civilization "more ancient than Antiquity."[45] This interest was most dramatically inspired by Napoleon's 1798 campaigns in Egypt, and fostered by the resulting publications, *Voyage dans la Basse et la Haute Egypte (1802)* and *Description de l'Egypte* (1809–1828) by Baron Vivant Denon.

Recent scholarly research documents a significant number of instances in which American cabi-netmakers borrowed Egyptian forms and ornament from their Italian, French, and English con-temporaries.[46] Published period sources, for both architecture and furniture, delineated Egyptian form and ornament, and these were absorbed and adapted to varying degrees in America. As early as 1808, Benjamin Henry Latrobe proposed a design for an interior in the Library of Congress in the Egyptian style. While it was not until the 1830s that several noted Americans traveled extensively in Egypt, visits in European cities provided limited exposure to aspects of Egyptian culture.

Travelers to London might have seen Thomas Hope's Egyptian Room in his Duchess Street man-sion, or perhaps the dramatic facade and interior of Egyptian Hall on Piccadilly. By the end of the first decade of the nineteenth century, the monuments of Egypt might have enclosed one at night if one's bedhangings were fashioned from the Parisian-made copperplate-printed toile first manu-factured about 1808 by Jean-Baptiste Huet (fig. 91). Huet derived the bold and exotic images printed on linen textile from engravings by Pagelet and Berthault after Cassas.[47]

As early as 1810, the Dublin-born Philadelphia cabinetmaker Joseph B. Barry advertised in the *Aurora General Advertiser* that he had for sale "a variety of the newest and most fashionable Cabinet Furniture, superbly finished in the rich Egyptian and Gothic style," among which were "3 pair Eliptic Bureaus, Columns and Egyptian Figures."[48] Barry appears to have been among the first American cabinetmakers to seize upon this Egyptian taste and incorporate it into his design vocabulary. In January 1812 he advertised that he had "lately returned from Europe [and] during his stay in London and Paris, He made some selections of the Most Fashionable and Elegant Articles." Whether he acquired a copy of George Smith's 1808 *A Collection of Designs for Household Furniture* in London, or possibly Smith's 1812 publication of *A Collection of Ornamental Designs, after the Manner of the Antique*, is unknown, but he must have been familiar with Smith's "Design for a Sideboard" (pl. 92) when in 1813 he fashioned the sideboard in figure 92.[49] Smith noted with reference to his sideboard design that "the Egyptian style is proper for Dining Rooms [but] there is no better kind of work calculated to produce a grand effect, so far as relates to furniture than what is usually called Gothic." Indeed, Barry combined both

91 top

TOILE FRAGMENT: LES MONUMENTS DE L'EGYPTE
detail

c. 1808

Designed by Jean-Baptiste Huet (1745–1811), Jouy, France

Roller-printed cotton

57¼ x 72 in.

The Baltimore Museum of Art: Gift of Dena S. Katzenberg, Baltimore (BMA 1984.158)

92 bottom

SIDEBOARD

1813

Joseph B. Barry (c. 1760–1838, working 1810–1822), Philadelphia

Mahogany; brass

51¼ x 82¼ x 24¾ in.

Private Collection

93

SIDEBOARD AND KNIFE BOXES
1810–1815

Attributed to Joseph B. Barry (c. 1760–1838, working 1810–1822), Philadelphia

Mahogany; brass

67¼ x 87⅝ x 25¾ in.

Courtesy Winterthur Museum, Winterthur, Delaware

Gothic and Egyptian styles in the 1813 sideboard he signed, but a related one that he presumably made for Rebecca or Rachel Gratz about the same time was conceived in a more boldly Egyptian style (fig. 93). This sideboard's reeded columns with massive paw feet relate closely to Smith's 1808 design in the Egyptian style, and the accompanying knife boxes echo this design, being flanked by similar columns with paw feet.[50]

In 1817–1819, when Nathan Appleton built his second mansion on Beacon Street in Boston, he chose a design for a fireplace surround from William Pollock's *Modern Finishings for Rooms* (London, 1811) in the style of an Egyptian pylon facade with a Greek key motif ornamenting the sides. Though Boston interior decoration and furniture designs of this period exhibit limited Egyptian inspiration, one popular form stands out as also modeled after the Egyptian pylon. The card table (fig. 94) labeled by the noted Boston cabinetmaking firm Isaac Vose and Son has a pylon-shaped pedestal that unmistakably echoes the ends of this architectural form peculiar to ancient Egypt. Produced probably by a number of Boston cabinetmakers who offered variations in elements of carving and design, this form of card table is a distinct regional expression closely related to pedestal-end sideboards from Philadelphia or Baltimore, which also echo the Egyptian pylon form.[51]

CARD TABLE

1819–1824

Isaac Vose (1767–1823) and Isaac Vose, Jr. (1794–1872), Boston

Mahogany, mahogany veneer

29⅛ x 32½ x 18 in.

The Saint Louis Art Museum: Gift of Mrs. Daniel K. Catlin

The Egyptian taste was savored and expressed in several other media besides furniture in the first quarter of the nineteenth century in America. A large porcelain dessert service, owned in Boston possibly by the Sargent family, exhibits an amusing vocabulary of pseudo-Egyptian hieroglyphics (fig. 95). Manufactured at the Crown Derby factory in Derby, England, probably in the Duesbury-Kean period, 1795–1810, the almost whimsical ornamentation on this service was inspired by illustrations of actual inscriptions published at the time. The large number of surviving pieces and the unusual variety of specialized forms in this service suggest that it must have been not only costly but intended for a fashionable, well-to-do household.

While American silver in the Egyptian taste was not widely produced in the nineteenth century, forms, motifs, and ornament that referenced Egyptian sources did appear during the first quarter of the century. Though diminutive and thus easily overlooked, the die-stamped sugar tongs with female herms looking like a cross between Egyptian and Grecian maidens are a handsome representation of this exotic style (fig. 96). Marked by a New York and Charleston partnership in association between 1815 and 1828, these fashionable utilitarian objects make a sophisticated statement of taste already seen in other media owned and used in American households. Whether these technologically advanced utilitarian tongs were made in New York by Maltby Pelletreau, or imported from England or France, is undetermined at this time, but the statement of style they make remains the same regardless. Related to a variety of other media from statuary marble man-

tels to carved-and-gilded pier table supports, these tongs demonstrate the pervasive aspect of classical ornament on objects owned in America in the early nineteenth century.

Among some of the most demonstrative and evocative Egyptian-inspired furniture forms made in America are a related group of side and armchairs produced in New York (fig. 97).[52] Doubtless derived from ancient Egyptian models like those discovered at Thebes and illustrated by Denon in *Description de l'Egypte*, these chairs are among the most anthropomorphic examples known, having four paw feet all facing forward as if ready to break into a powerful stride at any moment. They may derive more directly from the two "Drawing room Chairs" (pl. 56) illustrated by George Smith in his 1808 *Collection of Designs*. In addition to the Egyptian-style legs and paw feet on one of Smith's chairs in particular, there are also other Egyptian motifs on both of the chairs, including winged discs.

ARMCHAIR

c. 1815–1825

New York

Ebonized and gilded maple

38 x 26½ x 27¾ in.

Courtesy Winterthur Museum, Winterthur, Delaware

These high-style New York chairs all exhibit a variety of surface ornament, ranging from ebonized surfaces with some carved and gilded ornament to the most elaborate type of New York gilt-stenciling, as seen on the illustrated example. The commanding presence and thronelike stance of these chairs bespeaks their original ancient purpose, as well as marks their contemporary symbolic function as seats for esteemed merchants and revered members of the household and community. While there is no provenance associated with the armchair illustrated, the New York merchant Stephen Whitney owned a pair of related ones with front paw feet, ebonizing, and carved and gilded ornament.[53]

By the 1820s there was a virtual "mummy mania" in America, as the exhibition of recently arrived Egyptian mummies came into vogue. This particular phenomenon was triggered in 1823 by the arrival in Boston of a mummy and accompanying sarcophagus from Thebes. The Massachusetts General Hospital was the lucky recipient, and not too long after, "Padihershef," as the mummy was called, went on exhibition at Mr. Doggett's Repository of Arts in Market Street. By the fall of 1823, officials decided to tour the mummy, and Doggett and Company became the entrepreneurial exhibitors. By late fall Padihershef was exhibited in New York, along with a six-page handout with four illustrations and an essay on "the unparalleled magnificence and sublimity" of ancient Egypt.[54] This venture did not meet with tremendous financial success, as the influx of more mummies from Egypt diluted the draw, and by 1824 the *American Statesman* reported the arrival of "TWO MUMMIES, fresh from Thebes. At this rate, the flesh of mummy will be as cheap as that of dogs. The market is already glutted; a few more of these Egyptian carcasses, with a mermaid or two, and the stock of our museums will be as cheap as candidates for the presidency."[55]

There can be little doubt that the craze for mummies in America by the end of the first quarter of the nineteenth century must have heightened the impulse among some patrons and mechanics to feature motifs drawn from Egyptian culture. Sphinxes provided a totally alien and exotic image and can be found on a number of imported objects, as well as several extraordinary special commissions. A French or English marbletop center table with four gilt sphinx feet and an accompanying set of chairs with sphinxes perched atop the front legs have a history of early nineteenth-century ownership in Baltimore.[56] A variety of French and English forms employed sphinxes as supporting members on such objects as beds (La Mésangère, 1804, pl. 128), pot cupboards, and jardinieres (Smith, 1808, pls. 130 & 143).

The fact that the Egyptian taste might have been particularly fancied in the dining room, as George Smith promoted, is further supported by the survival of two impressive New York cellarettes with sphinx supports (fig. 98).[57] Again we find in these monumentally posed objects an interesting integration of Egyptian and Roman form and motif. Winged paw feet support a platform on which two sphinxes perch, supporting in turn a container in the form of an ancient Roman sarcophagus, now intended to hold wine or liquor bottles. The irony of employing the classical sarcophagus form as an object to hold alcoholic substances has been

98

CELLARETTE

c. 1810–1820

New York

Rosewood and mahogany veneer
with ebonized and gilded decoration; brass

30¹⁄₁₆ x 34⁷⁄₁₆ x 21⁷⁄₁₆ in.

Yale University Art Gallery; The
Mabel Brady Garvan Collection

noted in recent scholarship on this particular cellarette.[58] Indeed, the sarcophagus form appears to have been among the most popular models for cellarettes, along with colonnaded temple-forms such as the one in figure 33 that was made for John Ridgely presumably by William Camp, cabinetmaker of Baltimore. The New York cellarette traditionally has been said to have been owned by Stephen Ball Munn, a wealthy New York dry-goods merchant, who moved into a fine Broadway mansion in the mid-1810s. As a neighbor of Stephen Whitney's, possibly Munn became aware of the taste made fashionable by the exploration of Egyptian culture.

Related in style and spirit, and equally monumental in form, is the silver vase presented to Hugh Maxwell by the merchants of New York, as "A Testimony of the high sense entertained of Your Integrity, Ability, Firmness and Perseverance in the Discharge of Your Duty as DISTRICT ATTORNEY of the City and County of NEW YORK" (fig. 99).[59] Though this silver vase is marked with the stamp of Baldwin Gardiner, a New York retailer and brother of Sidney Gardiner (d. 1827), it was fashioned in the Philadelphia shop of Thomas Fletcher. A letter dated August 28, 1828, from Baldwin Gardiner to Fletcher, provides revealing information:

99

VASE

1829

Presented to District Attorney
Hugh Maxwell, Esq.
Marked by Baldwin Gardiner
(1791–1869; working in New
York 1827–1848), made by
Thomas Fletcher (1787–1866),
Philadelphia
Silver
24 x 20¹/₁₆ x 17¼ in.

*Courtesy The New-York Historical
Society, New York, On permanent
loan from the New York Law Institute,
L.1959.5*

Dear Sir: I have been applied to, to make a *Splendid Vase* & a *pair of Pitchers*, intended to be presented by the Citizens of New York to Mr.[Hugh] Maxwell (the District Att[orne]y) as a token of their respect and approbation of his course of prosecuting the late conspiracy cases, so called—The price to be paid for the *Vase & Pitchers*, from $800 to $1000. These are the particulars.

If you are disposed to make them, and in such a way as will answer my just expectations of profit, I shall be glad to have you undertake . . . them—and I am ready to say I shall be satisfied *with a very small profit*; the more so to enable you to bestow the greater pains in *their elegant execution*, for I shall look as much to the honor of [the] thing, as to the profit. Of course, I shall expect to have my name stamped upon the bottom. . . .

Please let me [know] how soon I may expect your drawings.[60]

Standing a little over two feet high, this special commission combines the Roman tripod candelabra base with Egyptian sphinxes, all topped by a vase the form of which was derived from the famous Warwick vase. Just five years before (1824–1825), Thomas Fletcher and Sidney Gardiner had made the extraordinary pair of vases presented to De Witt Clinton in recognition of his role in building the Erie Canal.[61] Fletcher might have seen firsthand the Warwick vase in the conservatory at Warwick Castle on his European sojourn in 1815. Even if he had not seen the original, he did visit the London showrooms of the silversmiths to His Majesty George IV, Rundell, Bridge and Rundell, where he saw "cases filled with goods of the most costly kind, a fine vase copied from one in the possession of the Earl of Warwick at Warwick Castle which was dug from the ruins of Herculaneum. [It] is beautifully made—it is oval, about ⅔ the size of that made for Hull [the Hull urn is 28 inches tall]."[62] This impressive English silver copy of the ancient vase may have inspired not only the De Witt Clinton vases but the Maxwell one as well. Designs for silver by Charles Percier, as well as by Charles Heathcote Tatham, employed sphinx supports, and Fletcher may have also seen abroad candelabra centerpieces with sphinx supports like one made in 1805 by Philip Cornman for the Earl of Selkirk.[63] However, the question that still remains is who decided on the sphinx motifs for this major commission, and why was an Egyptian style, combined with Roman, selected? Was this the preference of New York patrons or the Philadelphia silversmith who designed the piece? The fact that Egyptian sphinxes were chosen for this major presentation piece of silver suggests that the Egyptian style enjoyed a greater height of popularity than has previously been acknowledged in the American fascination with various ancient cultures.

Were New York patrons and mechanics more taken with sphinxes than their colleagues in other parts of the country? Did William Croghan, a wealthy Pittsburgh entrepreneur, specifically request that his rosewood-grained and gilt suite of New York furniture in the mid-1830s have Egyptian motifs integrated into the overall decorative scheme? Two Grecian couches and six side chairs survive from this set, and all of the chairs have cast-brass sphinx ornaments on their splats. In the mid-1830s Croghan built a fine mansion that he called "Picnic House," and presumably this fashionable New York rush-seated furniture (which would have had cushions) was intended for the principal parlors (fig. 100). Today two rooms, a double parlor, survive in the Cathedral of Learning at the University of Pittsburgh.[64] The interior architectural decoration of these rooms is bold and impressive, combining Greek, Roman, and Egyptian forms and motifs, with the fireplace surround and overmantel subtly echoing the Egyptian pylon form. Without contemporary evidence, one can only speculate about the owner's consciousness of using sphinx mounts and the pylon form in a fashionable Graeco-Roman parlor.

The manifestation of Egyptian forms and motifs in early nineteenth-century architecture was limited. However, by the late 1830s there appeared a rather significant Egyptian architectural expression in Philadelphia "At the warehouse on South Second Street previously occupied, but still owned, by Jas. B. Barry." A contemporary insurance survey notes that "the 'former Bulk window'. . . was replaced with '2 large cased posts & 3 folding sash front doors,' the facade was

100 opposite
The bold Grecian style of the interior woodwork of "Picnic House," built in Pittsburgh in the mid-1830s by William Croghan, suggests designs published by architects like Asher Benjamin and Minard Lafever. The pylon shape of the fireplace surround is derived from ancient Egyptian precedents, and perhaps it was no coincidence that the painted and grained suite of New York furniture (including two Grecian couches and several side chairs) that Croghan ordered for "Picnic" was ornamented with brass mounts depicting Egyptian sphinxes.

decorated with '4 large square boxed opened Egyptian Columns—each crowned by a large Carved Human Bust, Square Capt. The whole surmounted by a plain Egyptian entablature and cornice.'"[65] Richard Parkin was the current tenant, and soon after the renovation he advertised at the "Egyptian Hall," 134 South Second Street. Presumably Parkin was responsible for both the concept of remodeling the facade and the financial investment. Whether he was familiar with William Bullock's Egyptian Hall on Piccadilly in London is unknown, though he may have seen Ackermann's 1815 illustration of it in *The Repository*.[66] Regardless of his source of inspiration, it was an enterprising move to undertake the renovation of the building's facade in the hope that its bold and exotic features would attract fashion-conscious clientele.

The most monumental and impressive pseudo-Egyptian object designed and made prior to 1840 in America was the "temple for tomes," or elephant folio cabinet, constructed in 1838 to hold, among other folio volumes, the Providence Athenaeum's set of the *Description de l'Egypte*.[67] Designed by John Russell Bartlett, an avid Egyptologist, the case's ornament, and probably even its overall form, derived from images published in the volumes themselves.[68] When completed, the cabinet occupied a central position in the Athenaeum's main reading room, until it was moved to the lower level in 1851.

Although in 1809 the English publisher Rudolph Ackermann referred to "the barbarous Egyptian style," as opposed to "the classic elegance which characterized the most polished ages of Greece and Rome," there is clear evidence that American patrons were undaunted by such barbarism and continued to choose Egyptian forms and motifs, often combining them with the more favored Graeco-Roman style.

While forms such as the klismos and curule were borrowed from antiquity, perhaps the most pervasive pillaging occurred in the use of ancient motifs and the numerous ways in which they were combined as both form and ornament. From the Renaissance onward, publications by architects and designers recorded these vast stores of antiquity, and thus many visual images were readily available to Europeans and Americans alike. Though Americans often followed a basic European formula, like any cultural expression objects took on a distinctive quality in the actual execution. Different regions exhibited preferences for specific interpretations, and to an extent similar preferences can be observed in regional proclivities for certain motifs and ornaments. However, a multitude of classical motifs such as lyres, cornucopias, swans, dolphins, eagles, ser-pents, griffins, caryatids, and columns were used throughout America, and while regional prefer-ences prevailed, freedom of choice meant that there was little exclusivity. The derivation and meaning of the primary motifs used can be found principally in classical mythology and other aspects of the culture, most especially architecture. The extent to which American patrons and mechanics recognized meaning is a more difficult question, although among those educated in the classics, even through English translations, it is likely there was a reasonably high level of under-standing. Judging from the abundance and availability of classical statuary, especially images of

102

PIER TABLE

c. 1830–1840

New York

Ebonized, gilded, and stenciled
wood; marble; mirror

38 x 44 x 18 in.

Kaufman Americana Foundation,
Norfolk, Virginia

Apollo, Venus, and Ceres, Americans may well have recognized and understood many of the attributes popularly associated with these mythological gods and goddesses.

The use of swans, lyres, dolphins, and cornucopias, often seen in combination, is easily understood since all were frequently portrayed attributes of Apollo, Venus, Neptune, and Ceres. The myth relating that the swan sings before its own death links it to Apollo, while swans also pull the chariot of Venus, associating these elegant creatures with love. As a patron of music, Apollo is frequently depicted holding a lyre. Venus, born out of the sea and carried to land on a scallop shell, often has a dolphin associated with her, similar to the one nestled at her feet in the *Venus de' Medici*. And Ceres, goddess of agriculture and the fruits of the earth, frequently appears with a cornucopia symbolizing plentitude.

Some of the earliest French Empire designs employing swan motifs occur in furniture drawn by Percier and Fontaine and executed for the Empress Josephine, whose device was a black swan.[69] It is entirely possible that John or Hugh Finlay, the Irish-born ornamental painters working in Baltimore by 1800–1801, were familiar with these designs either through firsthand observation or knowledge of printed designs. Hugh Finlay traveled to England and Europe in 1810, and in December the same year he advertised that he had in his shop on Gay Street "a number of Drawings, from furniture in the first houses in Paris and London, which enable them to make the most approved articles in their line. . . . N.B. Any articles not easily procured here may be obtained through the medium of H. Finlay, who will remain in Europe several months."[70]

In October 1832 John Ridgely of "Hampton" was billed $327 by John Finlay for a suite of painted and gilt furniture that included fourteen chairs, a pier table, a center table, and "1 Sofa with Gilt swans & Chimera legs without Damask for covering" (fig. 101). The sofa was the single most expensive piece, costing $80 without the fabric covering, which was specified as damask and was probably either a woven silk damask or wool with a stamped damask pattern.[71] With ends in the form of swans, the design of Ridgely's sofa is related to plate no. 285 published by La Mésangère in *Collection des Meubles et Objets de Goût* in 1808; an almost identical design was copied by Ackermann in his *Repository* in 1811. George Smith also showed very similar elegant, rectilinear sofas with graceful swan arms for a "State Drawing Room" (pl. 152) in his 1808 *A Collection of Designs*. Whether it was Finlay, or Ridgely, who suggested the use of these fashionable swan motifs is unknown, but there is evidence that either might have fostered the idea. A bound volume with La Mésangère plates nos. 619–690 (missing 627, 633, 634, 640, 646) has descended in the Ridgely family, suggesting that Eliza or John Ridgely may also have owned earlier designs. Surviving today is Ridgely's copy of Smith's 1826 publication, so possibly he owned the 1808 design book as well. The chairs from this suite (fig. 101) are related to other Baltimore Grecian chairs of this period with gilt decorative motifs of scrolled foliage and bold anthemions.[72] However, they have a distinctive lyre-shaped splat decorated with a pair of gilt swans that echo a design drawn by Thomas Hope.

In a similarly bold expression, a New York cabinetmaker designed a pier table with a swan-lyre as the principal motif (fig. 102). Thomas Hope had used a related convention in plate 54 of *Household Furniture and Interior Decoration* for the end of a small dressing table he described as "ornamented with the bird of Venus." Owned originally by Judge Hugh Halsey (1794–1858) of Bridgehampton, New York, this table exhibits the most sophisticated features of late classical New York ornament.[73] The sculptural quality of the carved and gilded swan-lyre is echoed in other aspects of the table's decorative elements, such as the robust paw feet with *vert antique* decoration, the carved and gilded cornucopia brackets, and the carved and gilded Corinthian capitals surmounting the black marble columns. Related cornucopia brackets of this distinctive New York type are seen on the Grecian couch in figure 85. The use of black marble (also called "Egyptian" marble in the period) for the columns and the top commanded a higher price than the more common white marble. The stenciled fruit, floral, and leaf motifs are

103 clockwise

TEA AND COFFEE SERVICE

1818–1819

Anthony Rasch and Company
(working 1807–1809,
1813–1819, 1820), Philadelphia

Silver

Teapot	H. 9⅞ in.
Waste bowl	H. 6¼ in.
Coffee pot	H. 11⅛ in.
Cream pitcher	H. 9¼ in.
Sugar bowl	H. 8⅛ in.

North Carolina Museum of Art,
Raleigh; Gift of Mr. and Mrs. Charles
Lee Smith, Jr., in honor of Dr. Robert
Lee Hunter

typical of the gold- and bronze-powdered stenciling seen in some of the finest New York workmanship of this period. Of exceptional quality is the trompe l'oeil foliage and the fan decoration on the lower shelf. The overall form, as well as the carved and decorative stenciling on this table, is closely related to that found on a desk and bookcase attributed to John Meeks.[74]

The swan motif afforded both designers and craftsmen a multitude of opportunities for decorative exploitation. In 1802, Percier and Fontaine illustrated a vase with swan handles in plate 34 of their *Recueil*. In the same plate they also showed a ewer with an arching caryatid figural handle. In 1818–1819 the Bavarian-born silversmith Anthony Rasch was commissioned by the State of North Carolina to make an elegant silver tea and coffee service.[75] Presented to Udney Maria Blakely "In grateful remembrance of the gallantry" of her late father, this five-piece service exhibits some of the most stylish form and ornament of the time (fig. 103). The covered sugar

bowl with sweeping swan handles and the cream pot with winged caryatid handle literally echo the designs of Percier and Fontaine's plate 34.

Born in Passau, Bavaria, Rasch is thought to have trained as a silversmith, perhaps in Hamburg, Germany, before coming to America in 1804. Whether or not he ever saw Percier and Fontaine's designs is unknown, but assuredly he had seen something that inspired him to create these classically derived French-style vessels. With its graceful handles and broad circular rim, the sugar bowl echoes the ancient kylix shape, and the cream pot, though small, echoes the form of a larger ewer. The three cast eagle finials, and the eaglelike spouts further reiterate motifs drawn from antiquity that were popular sources for silversmiths in the early nineteenth century.

A distinctive interpretation of early classical form and ornament, probably drawn directly from a contemporary source, is seen in the six-piece tea and coffee service made for the

104

TEA AND COFFEE SERVICE
1841
Samuel Kirk (1793–1872), Baltimore
Silver, parcel gilt; ivory or bone
Coffee pot   H. 14⅜ in.; Teapot H. 9⅜ in. (upper right); Sugar Bowl   H. 7 in.
National Museum of American History, Smithsonian Institution; Gift of Mrs. William Duncan McKim
Teapot   H. 9½ in. (upper left); Cream pitcher   H. 8¼ in.; Waste bowl   H. 6⅛ in.
Maryland Historical Society, Baltimore; Gift of Mrs. William Duncan McKim

105

ARGAND LAMP

c. 1810–1815

Probably England, labeled and retailed by Lewis Veron (1793–1853), Philadelphia

Brass, bronze; glass; marble

H. 24⅛ in.

Dallas Museum of Art; The Faith P. and Charles L. Bybee Collection, gift of Faith P. Bybee

McKim family of Baltimore by Samuel Kirk (fig. 104).[76] Believed to have been made for Haslett McKim (1812–1891) around the time of his marriage to Sarah Birckhead in 1841, the three pots echo the shape of common Greek and Roman terracotta lamps, while the open waste bowl and covered sugar exhibit the kylix form also seen in Rasch's covered sugar bowl with swan handles. At first it might appear that Kirk drew inspiration for this set from George Smith's 1808 *Collection of Designs for Household Furniture*, as a number of plates (especially no. 141) illustrate the related forms and motifs. However, the recent discovery of Kirk's exact design source introduces a little known volume that may have been used by other American artisans.[77] Kirk's own copy of L. N. Cottingham's *The Smith and Founder's Director containing a Series of Drawings & Patterns for Ornamental Iron and Brasswork* (London, 1823) is now in the Kirk archives in the Library of the Maryland Historical Society, and contains pencil sketches adapting some of the printed designs for antique lamps into tea and coffee pots. Plates sixty-one and sixty-five in particular appear to have provided the direct inspiration for this very unusual tea and coffee set in the antique style.

Another type of useful yet decorative object sporting swans in a different medium is the richly fashioned two-light Argand lamp in figure 105. Retailed and labeled by "Lewis Veron & Co Philadelphia," this lamp was doubtless imported by Veron from a Birmingham, England, manufacturer who probably affixed Veron's label prior to shipment. Related to both Thomas Fletcher and Sidney Gardiner by marriage, Veron was part of a well-established network of Philadelphia mechanics and retailers.[78] Veron not only imported goods for resale, but he also acted as agent for various Philadelphia artisans. In 1829 he sold furniture made by cabinetmaker Anthony G. Quervelle to Andrew Jackson for the President's House.

The central design feature on the base of the lamp is the cast-brass and gilt swan, nestled in grasses and appropriately flanked by a stand of cattails. The expense and rich patina of this lamp is seen in the variety of materials and surface treatments that both reflect light and add contrast to the overall concept. The oil font is appropriately urn-shaped and patinated to appear as antique bronze, and ornamented with a contrasting wreath of gilt grape leaves. Other cast-brass elements are also gilt, from the pine cone finial on the font to the foliate scrolls on the arms and the leafage pendants beneath the burners, heightening the overall reflective capacity of the lamp. The primary reflective parts are the cut-glass prisms suspended from the pressed-glass rings around the burners and above the swan. Based on a design invented and patented in 1780 by the Frenchman Armée Argand, these lamps burned with less smoke and greater light and heat than candles or simple wick lamps.[79]

Lyres, traditionally associated with Apollo as patron of music and god of the sun, hence keeper of time, have always been suitable for use on clocks. Some of the handsomest lyre-form clocks were produced in France in the late-eighteenth and early nineteenth centuries. Hence, it is not surprising to find American clockmakers fashioning the cases of wall clocks in the form of a lyre (fig. 106). While wall clocks with lyre-shaped midsections to their cases are rare, they merely represent a more costly version of the "improved timepiece" patented by Simon Willard of Roxbury, Massachusetts, in 1802. Commonly referred to today as banjo clocks, in

106

WALL CLOCK

c. 1825–1835

Aaron Willard (1757–1844),
Boston

Gilt wood; brass; églomisé panels

H. 38½ in.

Private Collection

the early nineteenth century this reference was unknown, nor is it clear exactly how the more costly lyre-shape clocks were referred to. The overall gilt surface of the Aaron Willard improved timepiece in figure 106 marks it as probably one of the most costly types of wall clock. The additional carving on the case, the cost of the gold leaf, and the larger reverse-painted glass in the throat of the clock all add to the basic cost. While a number of related lyre-shaped timepieces by Willard and his contemporaries are known, the majority have mahogany cases with, occasionally, the front carved leafage in gilt.

The snub-nosed dolphins that pulled the scallop shell of Venus across the seas are variously seen in classical mosaics and on Minoan pottery. Whatever the source of this fantastic creature of the deep, it quickly became one of the favorite motifs of American patrons and mechanics in the early nineteenth century. More commonly found in French sources than English, dolphins were much

PIER TABLE

c. 1825–1830

Attributed to Anthony Gabriel
Quervelle (1789–1856),
Philadelphia

Mahogany and mahogany veneer
with gilt and *vert* decoration;
mirror

44 x 50 x 24 in.

Private Collection

loved in New York and Philadelphia, and rarely seen in New England furniture. The bold and sculptural form of these serpentine creatures made their use as supporting members in various furniture forms a natural expression. The textured surface of their bodies, with scales that when wet might shimmer and catch reflected light, made them additionally appealing to receive the varied surface treatments that included mixed layers of green tones mottled with gold- and bronze-powdered paints, as well as gesso and gold leaf. As feet on New York beds and pier tables, or as side rails and arm-supports on chairs as well as sofas, they create a visually strong statement. The dramatic dolphin-ended sofas made in New York and Philadelphia are among the most scintillating pieces of early nineteenth-century American seating furniture, and a distinctly American expression.

Perhaps the boldest use of dolphins in American furniture is seen in the pair of sculptural pier tables made in Philadelphia and attributed to French émigré cabinetmaker Anthony G. Quervelle. These tables are said to have been owned originally by Henry Middleton Rutledge, who with his wife, Septima Sexta Middleton, left South Carolina and moved to Nashville, Tennessee, in 1816 (figs. 107 & 108). The grand height and scale of these tables, combined with their strong three-dimensional quality, suggest that they were made for a monumentally proportioned interior. The bodies of the dolphins are echoed by the carved foliage that curves away from the rear pilasters of the table. The scrolled cornucopia brackets beneath the front skirt continue the curvilinear theme, which is echoed by the deeply shaped lower shelf. The massive paw feet and foliate ornament that support the entire ensemble complete this image of sculptural strength. This pair of pier tables was originally made en suite with a center table that had three dolphin supports and identical paw feet.[80]

Over time, as these pieces were separated, their original surfaces were variously treated, and mistreated. After a great deal of technical and documentary research, the pier table in figure 107 has had its surface carefully restored, correctly using multiple layers of several shades of green, bronze-powdered paint, and numerous layers of tinted shellac.[81] While the overall surface effect might at first seem startling to our twentieth-century aesthetic, one has to imagine the more subtle light of Argand lamps and candles by which it would have been seen in the first half of the nineteenth century.

Card tables with lyre-shaped pedestals were popular in Philadelphia as well as Boston, but only rarely are these lyres formed from fantastic creatures like swans, serpents, or dolphins.

108

PIER TABLE
detail

c. 1825–1830

Attributed to Anthony Gabriel Quervelle (1789–1856), Philadelphia
Mahogany and mahogany veneer with gilt and *vert* decoration; mirror
43¹⁵⁄₁₆ x 50⅛ x 23¹⁵⁄₁₆ in.

Courtesy Winterthur Museum, Winterthur, Delaware

However, presumably a specific request from patron Stephen Girard led to the fashioning by Philadelphia cabinetmaker Henry Connelly of a pair of card tables with lyre-shaped dolphin pedestals (fig. 109). Associated with a bill, "To one pair Card Tables . . . $90," from Connelly to Girard dated October 27, 1817, it is thought that these tables may have been a wedding present to Girard's niece, Henriette, who married General Henri Lallemand on October 27, 1817.[82] However, why they have descended with numerous other articles owned by Girard himself remains a puzzle. The costly use of rayed veneers on the inside surface of the top, combined with the brass paw-foot casters, contributed to the high cost of these most extraordinary tables.

The sinuous forms of dolphins also lend themselves to the ornamentation of elaborate, gilt-frame looking glasses, or mirrors, sometimes in combination with other mythological sea creatures such as hippocampi, or sea horses. Although by the end of the first quarter of the nineteenth century there were numerous carvers and gilders listed in the city directories of the major urban centers, it

109

CARD TABLE

1817

Henry Connelly (1770–1826),
Philadelphia

Mahogany

30 x 36⅛ x 19½ in.

*Stephen Girard Collection, Girard
College, Philadelphia*

is still difficult to ascertain the national origin of some of these frames since often American makers also sold quantities of imported frames. Even the assurance of the use of an American wood is not always positive identification since in the early nineteenth century American woods were being exported for use by English craftsmen.[83] The distinctive sculptural nature of the looking glass in figure 110 suggests an American origin, and most likely a specific New York or Philadelphia maker.[84] Both carved dolphins, rapaciously devouring the cornucopias, remind us of Philadelphia dolphins and at the same time the preponderant use of cornucopias and carved fruit baskets on New York furniture. The beehive amidst sheaves of wheat that tops the entire composition further echoes the theme of abundance and plenty that seems an appropriate assemblage of ornaments for a rapidly growing nation with tremendous resources and abundant talent. Though this particular mirror has no specific provenance, its creative combination of classical elements does not repeat conventional English or European designs, which further suggests an American origin.

110

LOOKING GLASS

c. 1835–1845

New York

Gilded pine; mirror

42 x 37½ in.

Private Collection

When James Rundlet of Portsmouth, New Hampshire, built his mansion house in 1807–1808, he purchased an elaborate pair of girandole mirrors, each of which was surmounted by a sea horse having a mottled-green painted finish (fig. 111). Extremely delicate, yet of commanding presence, these circular mirrors with convex glasses, were most probably English imports. With scrolled sconces, or girandoles, attached to these mirrors, they are related to a design published by George Smith in his 1808 *Collection of Designs for Household Furniture*. Smith noted that:

> In apartments where an extensive view offers itself, these Glasses become an elegant and useful ornament, reflecting objects in beautiful perspective on their convex surfaces; the frames, at the same time they form an elegant decoration on the walls, are calculated to support lights. . . . in general, they will admit of being executed in bronze and gold, but will be far more elegant if executed wholly in gold.[85]

111

GIRANDOLE MIRROR
one of a pair

c. 1805–1815

Probably London

Gilded pine; mirror; glass; brass

41 x 25¼ x 3⅛

Society for the Preservation of New England Antiquities, Boston; Rundlet-May House, Portsmouth, New Hampshire; Gift of Ralph May

Rundlet's mirrors were predominantly gilt, and he used them in a manner similar to that suggested by Smith. They hung at opposite ends of his front parlor, which was papered with elegant "Peach Damask" wallpaper and a "Paris Flock Border" and approximately twenty feet in length. "Reflecting objects in beautiful perspective on their convex surfaces," these glasses represented the most expensive and fashionable taste of the period.

Perhaps the most appropriate object for the dolphin motif to adorn is the utilitarian fish slice, or server. While this form is commonly seen in English silver of this period, marked American fish slices are rare.[86] This ancient sea creature, said to be the king of fish and thus an attribute of Neptune's, was translated onto a silver server for fish by the Philadelphia silversmith Lewis Quandale (fig. 112). Adequately pierced to outline the dolphin as well as allow for the drainage of any liquids the fish may have been cooked in, this amusing creature with its tail totally curled over upon itself represents another evocative visual manifestation of classical imagery carried into the everyday life of upper-class Americans.

The abundant use of animal motifs gleaned from the stores of ancient ornament appears on many different forms of high-style silver made in America. Often drawn directly from modern

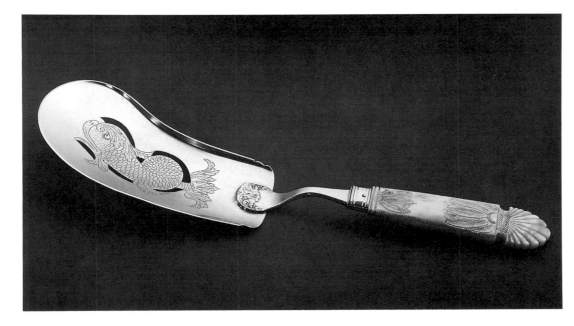

European sources, which were inspired by classical or Renaissance precedents, these useful objects symbolized an American consciousness of classical forms and motifs, while evoking the affluence of their owners and their knowledge of the latest European taste and fashion. Among the most elegant and aesthetically commanding objects are the sauceboats made by Anthony Rasch in Philadelphia between his arrival in 1809 and his departure for New Orleans in 1820 (fig. 113). Like the tea set Rasch made in 1818–1819 (fig. 103), these sauceboats were directly inspired by contemporary French silver designs. The manner in which the sinuous snake becomes

COVERED EWER

1807–1811

Jean Simon Chaudron
(1758–1846), Philadelphia

Silver

H. 16¼ in.

Collection Peter A. Feld

not simply ornament but also the form of the handle, and the small creatures with wings and paw feet that actually form the feet supporting the plinth, is masterful. The ornate ram's head spout, with applied anthemion scrolls on the body of the sauceboat beneath, and the corresponding applied leafage under the handle, bespeak the finest quality of workmanship by a craftsman familiar with Continental, and perhaps Parisian, goldsmithing.

From the first decade of the nineteenth century, the popularity of the classical ewer form began to grow, and over the next four decades it became one of the most abundantly produced utilitarian silver forms. Originally conceived for true classical usage as wine ewers, in the twentieth century they are more generally associated with the service of water. One of the most purely classical examples was marked by Simon Chaudron of Philadelphia (fig. 114). This large and stunning covered ewer is amply ornamented with scrolled foliate motifs, anthemions, and acanthus leafage, with a dramatically arched handle outlined with a sinuous and scaly snake, and a cast-and-applied ram's head mask at the base of the handle. Related in overall form and ornamentation to plates 49 and 52 of Thomas Hope's 1807 *Household Furniture and Interior Decoration*, the spout and domed base follow closely Percier and Fontaine's plate 34 in *Recueil*.

115

COVERED EWER

1812–1820

Thomas Fletcher (1787–1866)
and Sidney Gardiner (d. 1827),
Philadelphia

Silver

H. 16 in.

*Courtesy Winterthur Museum,
Winterthur, Delaware*

Though this extraordinarily classical European form bears the mark of Chaudron, it is likely that it was made by a younger journeyman in his shop, perhaps Anthony Rasch. Born in 1758 in the Champagne district of France, Chaudron was trained in Switzerland as a watchmaker and emigrated to Santo Domingo in 1784, and presumably by 1794 to Philadelphia. Listed as a watchmaker and jeweler by 1799 in Philadelphia, Chaudron was never listed as a silversmith through 1819, when he moved with his family to Demopolis, Alabama. In 1809 he entered into partnership with Anthony Rasch, though it is possible that prior to that time Rasch may have been working as a journeyman in Chaudron's shop and would have had the skill and firsthand knowledge of French designs to execute a ewer of this sophistication. With the large number of French émigré craftsmen who flocked to New York and Philadelphia during the Napoleonic wars, it is also possible that there were others in Chaudron's shop capable of executing this type of production.

Less pure in terms of classical form, yet more varied with respect to the number of creatures cavorting about as both ornament and form, is the silver covered ewer fashioned by the noted Philadelphia partnership of Thomas Fletcher and Sidney Gardiner (fig. 115). From the dolphin finial to the dog's head and snake handle to the four paw feet supporting the plinth, this bulbous ewer strongly speaks of classical allusions. The employment of snakes as handles on ewers, as well

116

SET OF THREE ARGAND
LAMPS

c. 1827–1848

Messenger and Son, Birmingham,
England, retailed by Baldwin
Gardiner (1791–1869; working
in New York, 1827–1848)

Parcel gilt; bronze; glass

H. 25 in.

*The Baltimore Museum of Art: Bequest
of Ellen Howard Bayard (BMA
1939.203a–c)*

as on other vessels from which spirituous liquors might be consumed (see fig. 202), is doubtless a subtle allusion to the evil that might come from an excessive indulgence in such spirits. The quality of workmanship, as well as the sophistication of this ewer's design, aptly define the knowledge of the maker as well as the competence of the shop. Fletcher and Gardiner were keenly competitive entrepreneurs, and Fletcher's 1815 sojourn abroad no doubt familiarized him with numerous objects fashioned in the latest taste. In addition to purchasing goods for resale, and visiting various foreign manufactories to observe methods of production, Fletcher also bought pattern books, and in Paris purchased a "Catalogue of Antiques" for $1.50, a "Sketch Book" for $3, "Engravings" for $50, and "Models" for $165.[87] The models must have been casts of antique artifacts and no doubt were the "great variety of antique models from which to compose the ornaments of their work" that General Winfield Scott referred to in a letter of 1821.[88] By 1820, Fletcher and Gardiner employed approximately twenty workers and were well apprised of current fashion and taste abroad. Their surviving silver indicates that they were definitely following contemporary sources, whether from printed books or actual examples they had viewed firsthand.

Lighting apparatus, especially Argand lamps that necessarily had a font, or vessel, to hold the fuel, provided a perfect arena for the employment of classical forms such as ewers, urns, amphoras, and the rhyton, an ancient drinking vessel. While most of these objects were imported from English manufacturers in Birmingham and Manchester, many of them had labels affixed that named the American importer or retailer. Argand lamps could be purchased in sets of three, or pairs of just two single-armed lamps. The elaborate set marked inside the base, "Messenger and Son," retailed by Baldwin Gardiner of New York, brother of silversmith Sidney Gardiner of Philadelphia, is a lavish example that combines numerous antique forms with a variety of ornament (fig. 116). The Roman tripod bases and columnar shafts are topped by imposing ewers and an amphora-shaped urn that serve as reservoirs for the fuel. A vast panoply of cast-and-gilt foliate ornament adorns the surface, incorporating animal motifs of birds and snakes. The effect of ornament applied over the form is heightened by the contrast between the patinated surface of the basic form and the fire-gilt surface of the ornament. When seen at night in the light given off by these lamps, the shimmering quality of the fire-gilt ornament must have been impressive, signaling the owner's refined classical taste and ample pocketbook.

Whether English manufacturers and American consumers were aware of the mythological and iconographic significance of the boar's head rhyton is doubtful, but they did no doubt associate it with classical cultures, and, hence, it became a likely candidate for adaptive use. Rhytons were illustrated on ancient vases, and drawings of vases owned by Sir William Hamilton could have provided this visual source for designers and manufacturers.[89] While to date the author has not seen any rhyton Argand lamps marked by American retailers, the pair in figure 117 has a long history of ownership in the Adams family of Quincy, Massachusetts. Like John Adams's "household gods," these icons of antiquity provided visible evidence of one's cultivated taste and desire to own objects of the latest fashion.

117

PAIR OF ARGAND LAMPS

c. 1825–1840

Possibly Thomas Messenger (and Sons), Birmingham, England

Bronze

H. 9½ in.

Adams National Historic Site, National Park Service, Quincy, Massachusetts

118 opposite

In the second-floor drawing room of the house built for Harrison Gray Otis of Boston in 1796 are an array of American, English, and Italian furniture and furnishings. The rosewood-veneered pier table and pedestal, or candelabrum, were made in Boston for Nathan Appleton probably about 1817–1820. The painted English armchair is from a large suite originally owned by Mr. Otis. The richly ornamented girandole mirror, one of a pair, is probably English and was purchased by James Rundlet for his new house in Portsmouth, New Hampshire, about 1807. The alabaster sculpture of the three graces and the accompanying urns were presumably part of a larger group forming a plateau for a dining table owned by Charles Russell Codman of Boston.

The singular most important part of an eighteenth- and early nineteenth-century craftsman's education was a thorough grounding in the classical orders of ancient architecture and the corresponding principles of classical proportion. Hence the basic recognition that architecture might serve as the foundation for all interior constructions, and without such essential knowledge an artisan's ability to create an object with correct balance and proportion was severely limited. In his 1803 *The Cabinetmaker's Dictionary*, Thomas Sheraton devoted eighteen pages to the subject of the "column, in architecture . . . the principal part of the whole order of any building."[90] He discussed each of the five orders (Tuscan, Ionic, Doric, Corinthian, and Composite), giving historical references to how the ancients used them, while illustrating each with detailed annotations on proportion and perspective. Assuming that most cabinetmakers and journeymen were likely to have a strong background in such knowledge, it is not surprising that there exists a direct correlation between architecture and furniture, as well as many other useful objects in different media.

While an enormous quantity of form and ornament employed by early nineteenth-century craftsmen was drawn from three-dimensional objects surviving from antiquity, an equally large proportion was inspired by architecture and its integral forms and ornamental motifs. Among the forms most commonly used by cabinetmakers were columns, employed both as actual structural elements of support and ornamental screens. However, American craftsmen took great liberties in their varied use of columns, and rarely did they define an order meticulously. Center tables, pier tables, and card tables were the most popular candidates on which columnar supports were employed. The use of one central columnar support (fig. 88) as well as that of three perimeter columnar supports (fig. 16) has already been illustrated. Sheraton defined the term "Pillar, or column, in architecture . . . but in cabinet making, it is generally used to signify the posts which support the tester of a bed; and a single massy one on which the top of claw tables rest."[91]

The most restrained use of columnar supports in American pier tables is seen in the high-style tables made in Boston during the second decade of the nineteenth century. Firms like Isaac Vose & Son, Vose and Coates, and Archibald and Emmons produced some of the most elegant tables, utilizing extraordinary quality mahogany and rosewood veneers combined with a wide variety of stamped-brass banding and cast mounts. Closely related to French examples of the period, these pieces commanded significant prices. The Boston wine merchant and importer John Davis Williams paid Vose and Coates $280 in 1818 for "2 Mahogany Pier Tables with marble tops."[92] The documentation has not survived for the pair of rosewood-veneered pier tables that Nathan Appleton purchased at about the same time for his new mansion on Beacon Street, but conceivably they were even more costly due to the use of rosewood instead of mahogany veneer (fig. 118). Designed particularly for the front and rear parlors of Appleton's bow-fronted abode, the marble top of one of the tables is slightly curved to fit the concave surface of the front wall between the windows. George Ticknor's columnar work table is another example of this refined Boston statement highly derivative of French designs and taste (fig. 209).

119

CARD TABLE

c. 1805–1820

Attributed to Duncan Phyfe
(1768–1856), New York

Mahogany, satinwood; brass

31 x 37⅛ x 20 in.

Collection Peter G. Terian

A sophisticated variation on the central-pillar card table was one with a cluster of carved pillars, or columns. One of a pair, the New York example in figure 119 descended from the merchant Thomas Cornell Pearsall (1768–1820). Made originally for Pearsall's city mansion, "Belmont," the tables were part of a large suite of furniture ordered from the shop of Duncan Phyfe. The other surviving pieces from the suite include twelve side chairs and two armchairs with "Grecian cross" legs, a sofa with a double "Grecian cross" front, and a pair of curule foot stools, now in the collection of The Metropolitan Museum of Art.[93] The double elliptical top, exquisitely carved columns, Grecian legs with carved leafage, and brass paw feet with casters, made this pair of tables some of the most costly card tables produced by Phyfe. Pearsall married Frances Buchanan in 1799, so presumably they purchased these tables during the first decade of their marriage while they were furnishing "Belmont," which was located at 57th Street and the East River.

One of the boldest and most architectonic furniture forms introduced into America in the first two decades of the nineteenth century was the *secrétaire à abattant*, or fall-front desk. Distinctly derived from French and German design sources, this monumental form was interpreted differently in the major urban style centers. The one ordered by David Sears of Boston, presumably for his new mansion on Beacon Street built between 1818 and 1822, was a specially conceived desk clearly designed for use by a busy merchant and entrepreneur (fig. 120). The client's desire for additional filing and storage space resulted in an exceedingly wide desk having paneled doors on each end that open to reveal twenty-four pigeonholes, two drawers, and six rows of small brass knobs, the function of which remains a mystery. Hence, the need to relieve the facade resulted in paired columns flanking the central section. The entire facade was beautifully ornamented with the most highly patterned mahogany veneers available. In a typically chaste Boston manner, the columns are plain with the exception of cast-and-gilded brass capitals and bases. The overall impression of this desk suggests an Egyptian expression, with the capitals resembling lotus leaves. While *secrétaires à abattant* from other urban areas always employed flanking columns, this example is the only one known to use the device of paired columns.

On a much different scale from center tables, pier tables, card tables, and *secrétaires à abattant* is the elegant and architectonic sinumbra lamp made by Messenger and Sons, Birmingham, England, and imported and marked by New York retailer Baldwin Gardiner (fig. 121).[94] With a central shaft in the form of a bronzed column with gilt Corinthian capital and applied gilt mounts ringing the circular base and marking the corners of the plinth, this lamp exemplifies the height of fashion and style available in urban American centers. Sinumbra lamps, patented in 1820 by an Englishman, Mr. Parker, employed the same principle as an Argand lamp yet utilized a circular,

120

SECRETAIRE A ABATTANT

c. 1820–1825

Boston

Mahogany, mahogany veneer; marble; ormolu, brass

57¼ x 52⅜ x 19¹/₁₆ in.

Photograph © 1992; The Art Institute of Chicago. All Rights Reserved. Gift of the Antiquarian Society through Lena Turnbull Gilbert Fund, 1983.30

slightly ovoid font that completely eliminated any shadow. These lamps were popular abroad and in America during the 1820s and 1830s, and English trade catalogs of the period illustrate a large selection of pedestal bases for both sinumbra and "Isis" lamps. According to Webster and Parkes's *An Encyclopaedia of Domestic Economy* (1845):

> The last improvement upon the French lamp appears to be what has been generally called by the manufacturers the *Isis lamp*, fig. 130, and which is now most generally seen in the shops. In this the external appearance of the reservoir is reduced to a mere brass bead, and the ground glass distributor being brought quite to the front, no shadow is projected, and this part appears as perfect as this lamp can be. They are now frequently used as table lamps, and are manufactured in an almost infinite variety of patterns, of various prices and degrees of ornament and elegance, of brass, bronze, or part porcelain and part brass.[95]

121

SINUMBRA LAMP

1827–1848

Thomas Messenger and Sons, Birmingham, England, retailed by Baldwin Gardiner (1791–1869; working in New York, 1827–1848), New York

Brass, iron; glass

H. 27¼ in.

Courtesy Winterthur Museum, Winterthur, Delaware

The elaborately ornamented cut glass shade on this lamp is original, and the shape is typical of that found on both sinumbra and Isis lamps.

Caryatids, draped female figures used as supporting columns, were first seen in classical architecture on the Erectheion in Athens (1409–1406 B.C.), and at Delphi. Later employed at Hadrian's Villa at Tivoli, near Rome, they became primary motifs in Roman architecture.[96] Like columns, caryatids were a popular form borrowed from antiquity from the Renaissance on through the nineteenth century. In Europe they were employed as supporting members on a wide variety of tables, as well as masterful pieces of silver. Emigré artisans, primarily from France, brought with them a working knowledge of designs and actual objects that employed caryatid forms, many of which were winged caryatids. Percier and Fontaine, La Mésangère, and Thomas Hope all liberally utilized caryatids both as functional form and ornament.

Perhaps the purest representations of classical caryatids on an American-made piece of furniture are those on the statuesque pier table

CLASSICAL TASTE IN AMERICA

labeled by Charles-Honoré Lannuier, the Parisian-trained cabinetmaker who emigrated to New York in 1803 (fig. 122). The cast-lead-and-gilded female figures are draped and posed in a manner similar to the maidens on the Erectheion, with Ionic scrolls atop their heads. Unknown is the name of the style-conscious patron who commissioned this table, but possibly the decision to use this most classically derived caryatid was determined by the patron, as these exact figures do not appear on any other documented Lannuier, or New York, furniture. Not unreasonable is the question whether or not Lannuier might have ordered these maidens from abroad. While no firm documentation exists to support the theory that he was importing parts, this possibility should be considered for further investigation.

Images of classical Grecian caryatids were assuredly available in America if a patron or artisan had access to a variety of printed sources delineating ancient architecture. A fascinating image illustrating a piece of probable New York furniture incorporating a caryatid is the portrait of young William Paterson Van Rensselaer, Jr., (1835–1854) by Francesco Anelli (fig. 123). Exhibited in 1847 at the Albany Gallery of Fine Arts, this painting was listed as no. 131, entitled "Portrait of a Child, as Cupid by F. Anelli" owned by William Paterson Van Rensselaer, Sr. The Grecian couch, or chaise longue, that the young Cupid is shown reclining on might well have been a piece of furniture made in New York City, or at least an artist's rendition inspired by pieces he had seen in

122

PIER TABLE

1805–1819

Charles-Honoré Lannuier
(1779–1819), New York

Rosewood veneer, mahogany;
ormolu; cast and gilt lead caryatid
figures; marble

36 x 50¼ x 22½ in.

All rights reserved, The Metropolitan Museum of Art, New York; Rogers Fund, 1953 (1953.181a,b)

patrons' houses. William, Sr., had married Eliza Bayard Rogers of New York in May of 1833. In that same year the couple commissioned Philip Hooker to design for them a fashionable townhouse at 6 Elk Street in Albany. This sweetly evocative painting makes one ponder the nature of furnishings the stylish young couple acquired for their new house. Or did Anelli simply "invent" the couch with sculptured caryatid end support using inspirations from furniture he had known abroad?[97]

Among other objects on which caryatids were frequently employed were lighting devices. In 1806 the English designer Charles Heathcote Tatham illustrated a caryatid holding "A Branch Light, designed & executed in Bronze, at Rome, in the Year 1796" in his *Designs for Ornamental Plate* (pl. 13). A year later, Hope's designs also showed a similar candelabrum. The cast-brass caryatid that supports the font for a solar lamp in figure 124 clearly relates to Tatham's candelabrum, as well as those larger figures seen on imported marble statuary mantels and impressive pier tables. While the font on this particular example is marked "Cornelius & Co./Philad./Patent/April 1st, 1845.," it is possible that Cornelius imported these cast figures from an English manufacturer. Caryatids such as these were employed on lamps at least by the 1820s.[98] In Webster and Parkes's *An Encyclopaedia of Domestic Economy* they illustrated an annular lamp with round shade similar to Tatham's caryatid candelabrum.[99]

123 opposite

"PORTRAIT OF A CHILD, AS CUPID," WILLIAM PATERSON VAN RENSSELAER, JR.

c. 1837

Francesco Anelli (c. 1805– c. 1878), Albany, New York; Frame by B. G. Whitman, New York, 1837

Oil on canvas; original frame 40¼ x 50¼ in.

Albany Institute of History and Art, Albany, New York; Gift of Justine Bayard Erving, niece of the subject, 1951.3.8

124

SOLAR LAMP

1843–1849

Cornelius and Co. (working c. 1840–1851), Philadelphia

Brass; marble; glass

H. 30½ in.

Private Collection

More frequently seen on high-style New York furniture of the second decade of the nineteenth century are carved, gilded, and painted winged caryatids. While there is a distinct variation in these figures, a number of pier tables and pairs of card tables are documented to the shop of Lannuier. The most stunning pair of Lannuier pier tables, recently rediscovered, are two that appear to have been purchased from Lannuier between 1816 and his death in 1819 by a French émigré, Armand de Balbi (1778–1838?) (fig. 125). Both tables are stamped "H.LANNUIER/

125

PIER TABLE

1816–1819

Charles-Honoré Lannuier
(1779–1819), New York

Mahogany; marble; ormolu,
brass; mirror

35 x 47¼ x 19⁹⁄₁₆ in.

Collection Peter G. Terian

NEW-YORK," and one bears in addition a printed label used by Lannuier between 1816 and 1819, as well as the stamp "JACOB." Both of these tables were found in France, as they were presumably shipped to de Balbi's daughter in 1839 following his death in New York.[100] It is reported that de Balbi came to New York when he was twenty-four, about 1802, so it is possible that he knew Lannuier through French alliances and friends. Much of Lannuier's furniture appears to have been directly inspired by design plates from La Mésangère, and these particular tables bear a striking similarity to the "Glace de Toilette" illustrated in plate no. 254 published in 1807. In addition, perhaps, to receiving designs from Paris, Lannuier no doubt imported the finest ormolu mounts. Whether or not the die-stamped brass banding with which he so frequently ornamented his furniture was imported is unknown, since he possibly could have been making that in his own shop or purchasing it from a local artisan. There is no question that the parlor in which these sophisticated and fashionable pier tables were displayed must have been among the most admired in New York.

Lannuier and other New York cabinetmakers also used winged female figures as supports on card tables, armchairs, and ottomans or settees. Several of these labeled and attributed pieces were owned by prominent New Yorkers, but they were not the only ones who desired and had access

126

ARMCHAIR
one of a pair

1810–1819

Attributed to Charles-Honoré
Lannuier (1779–1819), New
York

Mahogany with gilt decoration;
ormolu

35½ x 22 x 20½ in.

*Maryland Historical Society,
Baltimore; Bequest of J. B. Noel Wyatt*

to these extraordinary American manifestations of classical taste.[101] Patrons in other major urban areas also owned caryatid furniture by Lannuier, among whom were James Bosley (1779–1843) of Baltimore and John Wickham (1763–1839) of Richmond. The surviving pieces of Bosley's attributed Lannuier suite include a pair of card tables, a pair of armchairs (fig. 126) and five matching side chairs, and a pair of settees, or ottomans.[102] Bosley's estate inventory for his Fayette Street house in Baltimore listed in the front parlor a large set of furniture covered in yellow damask that included two sofas, twelve mahogany chairs, two lounges, two ottomans, and four rout tables.[103] As a prosperous Baltimore merchant, Bosley most likely had contacts in New York and may have specially commissioned this suite.

In 1812 Richmond lawyer John Wickham commissioned the architect Alexander Parris to design an elegant new town house.[104] The extraordinary painted interior wall decorations in this

house, combined with surviving furniture, and Wickham's 1839 room-by-room inventory, provide convincing evidence of elegant classical taste in this emerging southern city. While Wickham's inventory included four card tables on the first floor, there is little doubt that the "2 Card tables . . . 50.00" noted "In the drawing room A" must have referred to his labeled Lannuier winged caryatid pair (fig. 127). While one of the other two card tables listed was described as mahogany, both were only valued at $10 each.[105] Recently returned to the Wickham house, this rosewood-veneered pair of card tables, like Bosley's, may possibly have been en suite with the two sofas and covers, sixteen chairs and covers, and one pier table, also enumerated in the same room.

Still unknown, however, is the manner in which Wickham procured his elegant pair of card tables. Originally from Southhold, New York, on the north fork of Long Island, perhaps he had some contacts in New York and may have directly commissioned these special tables. On the other hand, Richmond newspaper advertisements during the first two decades of the nineteenth century document the importation of expensive New York furniture. Adjectives used to describe much of this furniture proclaim it to be "in the latest, most elegant and fashionable style," "of the newest fashions," and even "Of a new and fashionable pattern." Some of these ads indicate the New York makers or merchants who made or shipped the goods, while others seem to be speculative auction goods, and occasionally pieces "of first rate workmanship, and materials, and made for customers, and not intended to have been sold."[106]

In addition to cabinetmakers, other American and émigré artisans adapted European precedents employing winged caryatids to their productions. Just prior to Anthony Rasch's ornamenting a silver cream pitcher with a caryatid handle (fig. 103), Dr. Henry Mead of New York made an undecorated porcelain amphora-shaped vase with winged figural handles (fig. 128). Copying current French precedents similar to the vases purchased by David Sears in 1820 (fig. 20), Mead's successful production of porcelain in America was the first such instance since the short-lived eighteenth-century Philadelphia manufactory of Gousse Bonnin and George A. Morris (working 1770–1772). J. Leander Bishop's *A History of American Manufactures* (1866) recorded that in 1819 "The manufacture of Porcelain, of fine quality, from domestic materials, was commenced in New York, by Dr. H. Mead."

While little is known about Mead's manufactory, in October 1819 he announced in the *New York Commercial Advertiser* that "A Manufactory has, on a small scale, been commenced, and some first rate workmen imported from France."[107] By hiring French artisans, Mead was assured that at least in taste and fashion, if not in quantity and economics, he could match the European competition. It is particularly significant not only that he was using American materials but that his initial production catered to the classical taste most Americans were desirous of embracing. In 1819 when he submitted examples of his work to the New-York Historical Society, *Niles' Weekly Register* (February 27, 1819) reported that "their forms, their composition, their enamelling and everything gave universal satisfaction."[108]

128

VASE

1816

Dr. Henry Mead, New York

Soft-paste porcelain

H. 13³⁄₁₆ in.

Philadelphia Museum of Art:
Exchanged with Franklin Institute

129 opposite

PAIR OF VASES

1833–1838

Tucker and Hemphill or Joseph
Hemphill, Philadelphia

Porcelain with painted and gilded
decoration; ormolu

H. 22 in.

Philadelphia Museum of Art,
Purchased: The Baugh-Barber Fund,
the Thomas Skelton Harrison Fund,
the Elizabeth Wandell Smith Fund,
Funds given in memory of Sophie E.
Pennebaker, and Funds contributed by
the Barra Foundation, Mrs. Henry W.
Breyer, Mr. and Mrs. M. Todd Cooke,
the Dietrich Americana Foundation,
Mr. and Mrs. Anthony N. B. Garvan,
the Philadelphia Savings Fund Society,
and Andrew M. Rouse
(1984–160–1,2)

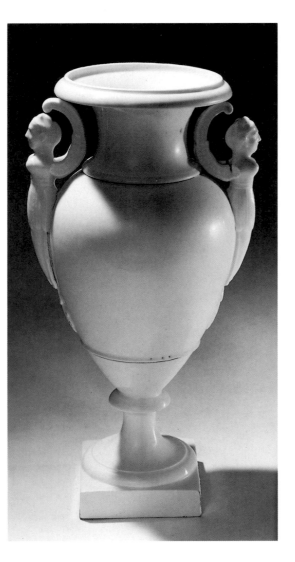

When William Ellis Tucker established his porcelain manufactory in Philadelphia in 1826, among the forms he produced were amphora-shaped vases similar to Mead's earlier examples.[109] Definitely in competition with French ones produced specifically for the American public, Tucker's production included not only vases with porcelain caryatid handles but ones with cast gilt-bronze handles (fig. 129).[110] This particular pair has winged griffin handles that may have been cast by the Philadelphia manufactory of Charles Cornelius.[111] Of monumental size, and proudly ornamented with views of the recently completed Philadelphia Waterworks, it has been suggested that these may have been made to display the Tucker Manufactory's accomplishments at one of the Franklin Institute's annual exhibitions. Tucker's manufactory is a prime example of how ingenious American artisans and businessmen met the challenge presented by European competition and at the same time assisted in the transfer of European classical taste to eager American consumers.

Related to the two-handled vases, or urns, that French and American porcelain manufacturers produced were a small number of large blown-glass, two-handled vases equally reminiscent of classical forms. Thought to be presentation pieces celebrating important dates or events (e.g., births or marriages), these colorless glass vases appear to be a hybrid of antique vase forms; the body derives from the krater while the great loop handles relate more to those seen on the kylix. The ribbed or gadrooned ornament on the one in figure 130 suggests similar ribbed decoration on Roman vases. Most of these vases have hollow knop stems that contain English or American coins; the coin in the illustrated example is an American silver eagle quarter minted between 1834 and 1840. Since two pieces that descended in the family of New England glassmaker Thomas Cains have coins in their stems and relate to these vases, these examples are usually attributed to the major New England glass works, either Cains's Phoenix Glass Works, the Boston and Sandwich Glass Works, or the New England Glass Company.[112]

The covered silver presentation vase made by the brief Boston partnership of Jesse Churchill (1773–1819) and Daniel Treadwell (working 1813–1816) exhibits another form that American

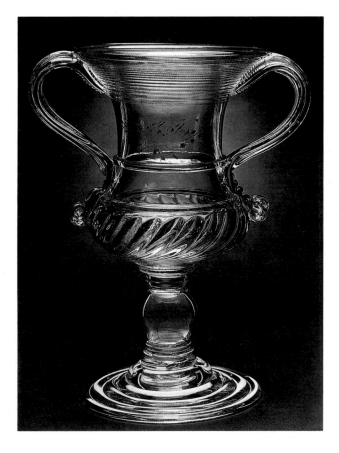

130

TWO-HANDLED VASE

1834–1840

Attributed to Phoenix Glass
Works (1819/1820–1870),
South Boston, Massachusetts
Free-blown glass; 1834–1840
silver eagle quarter
H. 11¾ in.

*Los Angeles County Museum of Art;
Purchased with Funds provided by the
Michael J. Connell Foundation*

artisans adapted from antique precedents (fig. 131). Exactly what models the designer of this vase might have seen is unknown, but the overall form, division of parts, ornamentation, and animal-head handles relate to a series of Roman vases, several "from Piranesi," illustrated by Henry Moses in 1814.[113] While the Boston version is much simplified and undoubtedly more diminutive than the antique models, the innovative use of eagle's head handles, instead of satyr mask, ram's head, or snake's head, shows American adaptability while essentially maintaining the classical style. Churchill and Treadwell used identical eagle's head handles on a wine cooler presented to Commodore Oliver Hazard Perry for his victory on Lake Erie, September 10, 1813.[114]

When this vase was presented to Thaddeus Mason Harris in 1816, in recognition of his service as first grand chaplain of the Grand Lodge of Massachusetts, it was given in a beautifully fashioned mahogany-veneered case. Outlined in ebony and accented with gilt-brass paw feet and great shell handles on the sides, the box is lined with two layers of blue-green and green paper. Since Jesse Churchill's younger brother, Lemuel, was a cabinetmaker, it is thought that he probably supplied this handsome veneered box. Aspects of the box, specifically the reeded engaged corner columns, are related to a work table inscribed in chalk "Churchill" on the bottom.[115]

While foliate ornament was a primary component of the rococo style of the eighteenth century, it had its origins in antiquity, and thus these ancient foliate motifs were heavily revived in the first half of the nineteenth century. The most ubiquitous of these motifs were the acanthus and anthemion leaves. Both of these plant forms were often used in classical architecture, with the acanthus being a primary part of the Corinthian and Composite orders. The acanthus derived from a Mediterranean species, *Acanthus spinosus*, that also looked like thistle, parsley, or poppy leaves.[116] The anthemion was thought by some to be based on the flower of the acanthus, but probably it more generally resembles the flower and leaf of the honeysuckle.[117]

American artisans knew these motifs well, and employed them readily. Whether their knowledge came from viewing drawings after antique objects, or modern productions that drew upon classical models, has yet to be discovered. Carvers and gilders, and silversmiths in particular, provide us with the most voluminous body of this type of classical ornament. The covered tureen with four matching sauce tureens that David Sears of Boston purchased from Anthony Rasch in Philadelphia boldly exhibits a well-executed assemblage of leafage combined with paw feet and dramatic masks (fig. 132). All of the foliate elements on this remarkable service can be found in

131

COVERED VASE WITH
PRESENTATION BOX

1816

Presented to the Reverend and
Right Worshipful Brother
Thaddeus Mason Harris
Jesse Churchill (1773–1819) and·
Daniel Treadwell (working
1805–1816), Boston
Vase: silver; Box: mahogany;
ormolu; blue paper lining
Vase: H. 14½ in.; Box: H. 17¾
in.

Collection Mr. and Mrs. Stuart P. Feld

drawings after the antique, especially by Tatham, Percier and Fontaine, or Henry Moses. Worthy of note is the fact that the very plate (34) from Percier and Fontaine's *Recueil* that detailed two forms related to Rasch's tea set made for the State of North Carolina (fig. 103) also illustrated a covered tureen with lid and finial similar to the Sears pieces. The fantastic masks that cover the junctures of the handles on the body of the tureens are not only related to ones seen in *Recueil* but also to several illustrated by Hope (pl. 57), which he described as the "Different heads of the Indian or bearded Bacchus."

Exactly why and when Sears purchased these tureens in Philadelphia is still speculative. As has been noted, after the Boston firm of Churchill and Treadwell ceased about 1816, no silversmiths remained in Boston who were capable of fashioning silver of this quality.[118] Since Sears traveled to

132

COVERED TUREEN AND FOUR
MATCHING SAUCE TUREENS

c. 1820

Anthony Rasch and Company
(working 1807–1809,
1813–1819, 1820), Philadelphia
Silver

Covered tureen: H. 12 in.

Collection of the Sears Family

Sauce tureens: H. 9¾ in.

Collection Mr. and Mrs. Stuart P. Feld

Philadelphia on occasion and is known to have stayed with the Cadwaladers while there, he might personally have selected or discussed this commission with Rasch. Between 1813 and 1818 Rasch traded as Anthony Rasch and Company, and in 1818 entered a short-lived partnership with George Willig, Jr. By September of 1819 that venture succumbed to financial distress, and by January 1820 Rasch advertised a newly established silver manufactory in New Orleans. Presumably Sears purchased his silver service of tureens between 1813 and 1818, in anticipation of moving into his new mansion on Beacon Street.

Anthemion leaves appeared everywhere, on every conceivable medium and on almost every type of object. Used extensively abroad and in America, they might be termed the leitmotif of the period. From the floor to the tabletop to the ceiling, this ubiquitous ornament proclaimed the refined classical taste of the owner whether molded on stoneware spittoons, die-stamped on silver flatware, or cast in brass encircling the perimeter of a magnificent chandelier. Interior decoration was not fashionable unless anthemion leaves were integral. The Nicholas Biddle family, of

133

FLATWARE

1830–1840

Thomas Fletcher (1787–1866),
Philadelphia

Silver

Fish slice:	L. 14⅜ in.
Serving spoon:	L. 14⅜ in.
Soup spoon:	L. 8¹⁵⁄₁₆ in.
Fork:	L. 7¾ in.
Fork:	L. 6⅞ in.
Dessert spoon:	L. 7⅜ in.
Teaspoon:	L. 6¹⁄₁₆ in.

Collection Mr. James Biddle

"Andalusia" on the Delaware River, owned silver flatware made by Thomas Fletcher of Philadelphia with bold anthemions stamped on both the front and back of each handle (fig. 133). Even the bookcases of Biddle's library, designed by Thomas U. Walter in 1834–1836, were topped with grand anthemions (fig. 48).

In 1817 George Hyde Clarke of Albany bought a tract of land at the north end of Lake Otsego (near Cooperstown) and almost immediately began "Hyde Hall," a large country house designed by Albany architect Philip Hooker.[119] The first phase of construction was a modest "cottage," but the second phase was of monumental size with a parlor and dining room that rivaled the scale of English country houses. By the time the second portion was nearing completion in 1831–1833, Clarke and his wife, the former Anne Cary Cooper (widow of James Fenimore Cooper's brother, Richard), began to furnish these major entertaining rooms (fig. 134).[120] With coved ceilings seventeen-and-a-half feet high, and two enormous triple windows in both the drawing room and dining room, just hanging the windows was a challenge. Albany draper Peter Morange was employed to supply the fabric, fringes, and all the cornice rods and hanging equipage for this textile tour de force. Among the "10 Prs Gilt Rods" and numerous "Ornaments" that he supplied were probably the carved and gilded anthemion ornament and rod in figure 135. While much of the furniture came from the Albany partnership of Meads and Alvord, other miscellaneous fur-

nishings were ordered from New York City, including mirrors, lamps, a "rich gilt clock with music," and "one porcelain Dinning and dessr Service, rich bouquet and yellow border," purchased from Baldwin Gardiner in 1833.[121]

Among the numerous purchases from Gardiner's "FURNISHING WAREHOUSE" at 149 Broadway, New York, were three cast-brass chandeliers, two for the dining room and one for the drawing room. While Gardiner no doubt imported these, one of the burners on the drawing room chandelier is marked "B.GARDINER/N.YORK" (fig. 136).[122] Perhaps the primary decorative motif in the drawing room was that of anthemions, for this magnificent cast-brass lighting device is circled with anthemions. With four Argand-type burners and four candleholders, this chandelier was altered to burn alcohol when originally purchased. Gardiner's November 1833 bill to Clarke lists all three lighting fixtures, including "alteration of d[itt]o for alcohol burners . . . 8.00." The drawing room chandelier, "1 Centre Gilt 4 lt Lamp" cost $165, and the "1 Set hangings for d[itt]o . . . compt." was $50; the "1 Cut glass dish for Chandelier" was billed at $15 two months later. On the same date that the chandeliers were billed, Gardiner listed charges for "1 Barrell Alcohol," and the following month he billed "1 doz ex. Chimnies" at $3.[123] Particularly interesting is the combination of four burners and four candleholders, presumably so that if one's alcohol supply was depleted light would still be provided by the candles.

Classical Greek and Roman antiquities exhibit a profusion of floral ornament, often including foliate scrolls with blossoms, massive garlands, and openwork baskets overflowing with fruit or flowers. Sometimes carried on the heads of maidens or seen topping columns, such a basket illustrated by Hope in plate 52 was referred to as a "flower basket." While the French and English were producing openwork baskets of porcelain, silver, and silverplate by the last quarter of the eighteenth century, they did not become popular in America until about the second decade of the nineteenth century.

Silver examples were commonly called cake baskets in America, and they exhibit a variety of forms and employ several technological processes, including die-stamping, casting, raising, and drawing. The exceedingly chaste example in figure 137 was marked by New York silversmith Frederick Marquand (working 1830–1838). The cast floral feet and handles contrast dramatically with the restrained die-stamped banding encircling the rim, midsection, and base.[124] The drawn and woven wire resembles imported English silver and Sheffield plated baskets. Since Marquand was listed in New York directories between 1830 and 1838 as a jeweler and importer, the question arises as to whether or not he actually made this basket, commissioned it from a New York or Philadelphia silversmith, or imported it. Acquired in Natchez, Mississippi, this basket had a long history of ownership in the Williams family of that city.

At the Franklin Institute's 1825 Annual Exhibition for the Products of National Industry, silversmith Harvey Lewis exhibited among his entries a waiter, a pitcher, and a cake basket.[125] Since a number of baskets marked by this extraordinary maker are known, it is impossible to determine whether the one in figure 138 may have been his 1825 entry.[126] However, it vividly portrays "the most beautiful and otherwise remarkable specimens" that Lewis wrought.[127] The intri-

137

CAKE BASKET

1830–1838

Frederick Marquand and
Company (working 1830–1838),
New York

Silver

W. 16½ in.

*The Baltimore Museum of Art:
Decorative Arts Fund (BMA 1988.6)*

138

CAKE BASKET

1813–1825

Harvey Lewis (working
1813–1825), Philadelphia

Silver

Diam. 10⅛ in.

Private Collection

cately cast and pierced foliate band that circles this basket closely resembles examples drawn from antiquity. Since Lewis was not only a founding stockholder of Philadelphia's Athenaeum but a manager of The Apprentices Library Company of Philadelphia (incorporated 1821), he had access to a large range of printed source material. While not identical to a specific example, this foliate scroll border resembles several illustrated in Henry Moses's *A Collection of Vases, Altars, Paterae, Tripods, Candelabra, Sarcophagi, &c.* (London, 1814). Elaborate scrolled motifs such as this were so popular and appealing that Moses even used one to frame the title page of his publication. Lewis's adaptation from the antique is an exemplary representation of the ingenuity evidenced by American artisans as they reinterpreted classicism.

Thomas Fletcher, who was also actively involved with the founding of the Franklin Institute and served as its first treasurer and later as vice-president, was equally adept at integrating floral and foliate motifs into his classical silver for domestic use. The beautifully designed sauceboat with tray (one of a pair—possibly a set of four originally) in figure 139 shows Fletcher's ingenious use of foliate ornament as he employs a pendant bud for the handle. The bold three-dimensional quality of this sculptural handle contrasts with the flatter, more restrained, die-stamped banding and chased leafage on the underside of the sauceboat. The overall form of the body of the sauceboat recalls classical terracotta oil lamps with incurved handles and protruded spouts. Probably

139

SAUCEBOAT ON STAND
from a set of four

c. 1825–1835

Thomas Fletcher (1787–1866), Philadelphia

Silver

Sauceboat: H. 8¾ in.; Stand: L. 10¹⁵⁄₁₆ in.

Collection Elizabeth Feld

"GRECIAN-SHAPE" PITCHER
on left

1827–1838

Tucker Factory (1827–1838),
Philadelphia
Porcelain with polychrome and
gilt decoration
H. 8½ in.

*The Baltimore Museum of Art:
Purchase with exchange funds from The
Mary Frick Jacobs Collection (BMA
1992.121)*

"VASE-SHAPE" PITCHER
on right

1827–1838

Tucker Factory (1827–1838),
Philadelphia
Porcelain with blue and gilt deco-
ration
H. 9 in.

*The Baltimore Museum of Art:
Purchase with exchange funds from
Bequest of Elizabeth Arens and
Adelaide Arens Morawetz, from the
Estate of Henry Arens; Bequest of Ellen
Howard Bayard; Nelson and Juanita
Greif Gutman Collection; and The
Mary Frick Jacobs Collection (BMA
1992.120)*

made by Fletcher's shop in the 1830s, following the death of his longtime partner Sidney Gardiner in 1827, the more naturalistic aspect of this design foreshadows a move toward the rococo in American silver of the mid-nineteenth century. Interestingly, these sauceboats were made for Mark Wentworth Pierce and his wife Margaret Sparhawk, of Portsmouth, New Hampshire, and bear the crest from the Pierce coat of arms. Still unexplained is why these afflu-ent Portsmouth natives chose Fletcher as the maker of some of their choicest classical silver.[128] Fletcher was born in New Hampshire and began his business in Boston, so it is possible that he still maintained contacts in New England; or perhaps a Boston retailer was marketing his silver or taking special orders from clients, as was the case with his New Orleans trade.

In addition to monumental vases with figural handles, numerous utilitarian wares were made by the Tucker China Manufactory in Philadelphia. Pitchers appear to be among the first forms man-ufactured, and judging from the surviving numbers they must have been good sellers during the duration of the firm's existence from 1827 to 1838 (fig. 140). Many of Tucker's wares, including the pitchers, were ornamented with a variety of floral and foliate designs echoing French prece-dents that reflected motifs reminiscent of classical ornament. Of the two pattern books that Tucker composed, one defined shapes of wares and the other ornamentation.[129] Tucker assigned names to certain shapes (sometimes seemingly without reason): the pitcher on the left in figure 140 was called the "Grecian shape" while the one on the right was called the "Vase shape."[130]

In 1830 the Franklin Institute praised Tucker's production, noting that "the forms are generally chaste, and copied from the best models."[131] William Ellis Tucker knew well the French and

141

PAIR OF SPILL VASES

1827–1838

One vase made in Paris and decorated at the Tucker Factory (1827–1838), Philadelphia; the other made and decorated at the Tucker Factory, Philadelphia

Porcelain with green and gilt decoration

H. 6¾ in.

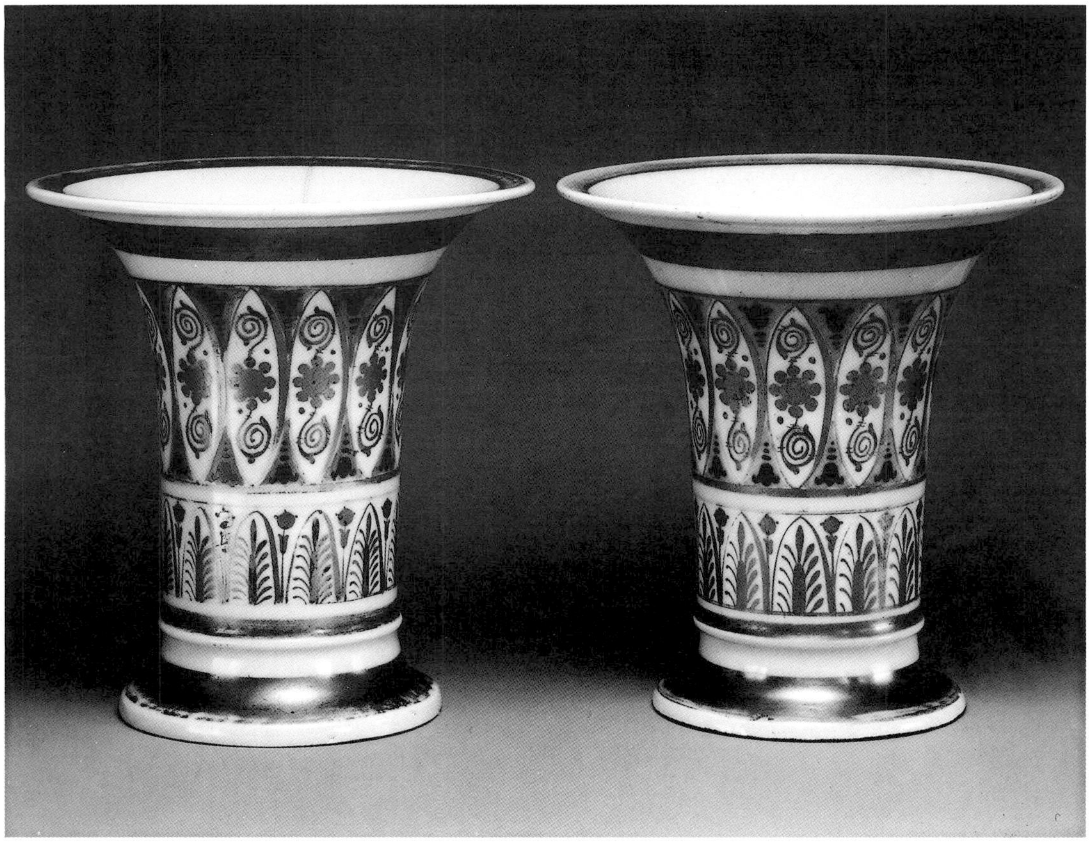

English products he was competing with, since he had begun his career working in his father's china store, selling imported products between 1816 and 1823. In fact, Tucker continued to import and decorate foreign china in addition to producing his own, which was deemed "second only in point of perfection to those of France," comparing favorably "in color, surface, and gilding with the French."[132]

The recently discovered spill vases in figure 141 present interesting evidence that indeed Tucker continued to decorate imported wares, as well as produce and decorate those of his own manufacture. The shape and ornamentation of these vases is almost identical to drawings nos. 63 and 64 in his *Pattern Book I.*[133] However, while the decoration on both appears to be by the same hand, the bodies of the vases are definitely different in the composition of the porcelain.[134] With broad flaring rims and gilt foliate decoration, these vases, though diminutive, are reminiscent of the tall, flaring flower baskets drawn from antiquity.

In the preceding discussion numerous objects have been reviewed that have varying types of classical ornament. Carved, gilt, painted, and stenciled were the predominant types, along with an assortment of cast, chased, and stamped ornament. The brass ornaments, whether cast or stamped, so frequently used on furniture were either fire-gilt or coated with clear or tinted shel-

142

MRS. JOHN FREDERICK LEWIS
(ELIZA MOWER LEWIS)

1827

Jacob Eichholtz (1776–1842),
Philadelphia

Oil on canvas

36 x 28½ in.

*Courtesy Pennsylvania Academy of The
Fine Arts, Philadelphia. Gift of Mrs.
John Frederick Lewis (The John
Frederick Lewis Memorial Collection)*

lac to enhance and protect their shimmering, goldlike finishes. This ornamentation was an important and integral part of household furniture and interior decoration during this period, and often denoted economic status as well as fashionable classical taste. Lovely Eliza Mower Lewis (1788–1865), painted by Jacob Eichholtz in 1827, gently rests her arm on a stylish marbletop pier table with Ionic columnar supports topped by a wreath and lyre ornament, either stenciled or cast in brass (fig. 142).[135]

Most of this cast- and stamped-brass ornament was imported from either England or France, though some of the stamped brass may have been produced in America.[136] A number of English hardware catalogs from this period survive to document the enormous variety of parts and patterns that were available to general retailers, cabinetmakers, upholsterers, and others. One of the most extraordinary catalogs to survive was issued by Thomas Potts (working 1829–1833) of Birmingham, England, and it has actual samples of the stamped brass wares sewn inside the front cover (fig. 143). Backplates for furniture pulls, several sizes of paw feet for clocks and small boxes, and fancy escutcheon ornaments are a few of the pieces actually shown. Inside the catalog Potts, like his competitors, illustrated an even wider assortment of furniture and drapery hardware, including commode handles, shells and rings for drawers, and drawer knobs with ornamental roses. Some of the more elaborate and costly ornaments, like the curtain pole or cornice ends, were composed of numerous stamped pieces strung together on a rod (fig. 144). As was customary in these catalogs, each illustration is annotated with the item's number and price.

Another fascinating body of cast- and stamped-brass ornament, never used but apparently ordered by the Boston cabinetmaker Henry Kellam Hancock (working 1816–1840), brother of the more well-known William Hancock (working 1820–1838), survives today (fig. 145).[137] Discovered in the possession of a Hancock descendant, in a nineteenth-century wicker trunk, these brasses were still wrapped in their original blue paper with inscriptions on the outside. On the top of the trunk was an 1850s Boston newspaper with an ad for the closing of Hancock's shop.[138] Whether all of these were imported, either from France or England, or some possibly made in America, is as yet undetermined. Many of the cast pieces appear to be fire gilt, while the stamped-brass ones have a lacquer finish. Though most of the pieces are ornamental, a large number were also functional, such as candlearms and candle sockets and various mechanical devices for dining tables, desks, table tops, and drawers. The ornamental mounts exhibit the full range of classical vocabulary from foliate motifs to swans to putti and other figural forms, both male and female. Given the large quantity of mounts that Hancock had in stock, perhaps he supplied his brothers, William and John, with hardware he imported during the 1820s and 1830s.

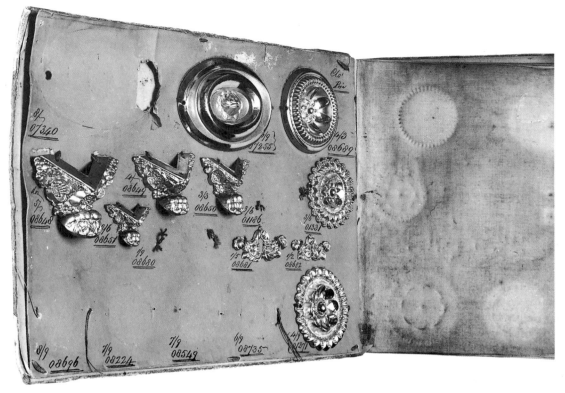

143

TRADE CATALOG: DESIGNS
FOR CURTAIN PINS, CURTAIN
POLES, DRAWER HANDLES,
KNOB CUPBOARD TURNS,
BED CAPS, CLOAK PINS,
DOORKNOBS, ETC.

1829–1833

Thomas Potts (working
1829–1833), Birmingham,
England
Paper; leather; fabric; brass
6½ x 10 in.

*Museum of Art, Rhode Island School of
Design, Providence; Gift of Samuel H.
Tingley, 49.088*

144

PAIR OF CURTAIN-ROD
ORNAMENTS
from a set of four, one disassembled

c. 1825–1835

England
Stamped brass
H. 11¼ in.

*Dallas Museum of Art, The Faith P.
and Charles L. Bybee Collection*

An important element of classical taste in American homes was not only the furniture but also the furnishings, which included wall decoration or coverings, window hangings, upholstery, lighting devices, and floor-coverings. As promoted in both France and England by designers like Percier and Fontaine, and Hope, more than in any other previous period the early nineteenth century embraced the concept of a coordinated scheme of interior decoration. Imported as well as domestically produced textiles, carpets, and wallpapers were integral expressions of the total impression presented by a tasteful and fashionable interior.

Great emphasis was placed on supporting American manufacturers, which must have been problematic when foreign products were sometimes more affordable. But American entrepreneurs were well aware that to prosper and survive they had to compete in a difficult market. Their advertisements often boasted that their goods were warranted as good as, if not better than, foreign ones. As Ebenezer Clough, a Boston wallpaper manufacturer, added to his billhead in 1800, "Americans, Encourage the Manufactories of your Country, if you wish for its prosperity."[139]

Many American wallpaper manufacturers imported papers as well as making their own on this side of the Atlantic. Given the extraordinary variety of foreign and American papers that survive today from the period, along with written documentation of orders for papers, the walls of many of our ancestors' houses must have presented an incredibly brilliant and evocative background for their richly veneered and ornamented furniture and furnishings.

In December 1814, Messrs. Virchaux & Co. of Philadelphia submitted a number of designs "of their own invention" that they intended to execute "at their Manufactory of Paper Hangings."[140] Presumably they submitted these unique designs for copyright, since they seem to have deposited them with a district court. While Virchaux is known also to have imported papers, one of his border designs—"Top border for number forty one"—was especially patriotic in nature, as well as classical in style (fig. 146). Virchaux described his border on a small printed paper that was submitted with the sample: "Composed of horizontal garland of green leaves, with a red altea flower in the center and bud, on the top an arch ornamented with pearls, palms, and rosettes, and an eagle with extended wings in gold color on a purple ground. The same stars as those on the paper number forty one, are repeated between the arch and the garland."[141] This handsome and colorful border should have had great appeal to upper-class Americans anxious to express their belief in the republic, as well as their endorsement of classical taste. Virchaux's design carefully incorporated floral and foliate motifs, all surmounted by great eagles with outspread wings. Whether or not his paper "number forty one" and border "number forty two" were actually manufactured is unknown, but if so they should have been bestsellers among his Philadelphia patrons.

146

"PAPER HANGING 42"

1814

Virchaux and Company, Philadelphia

Polychrome printed wallpaper

11½ x 28½ in.

Prints and Photographs Division, Library of Congress

FOUR

MACHINES INTRODUCE MUSES TO THE MASSES

The Popular Dissemination

There is nothing more remarkable connected with the history of the United States, than the immense rapidity with which some of the present towns, cities, and villages have started up from countries that were literally howling wilderness but a few years ago. This phenomenon has been constantly occurring in the vast country to the westward of the Ohio River, but has by no means been confined exclusively to the western States; for in some of the middle States, particularly that of New York, the rapid growth of numerous towns and settlements has been truly astonishing. From a long list of names might be selected Utica, Ithaca, Rochester, and Buffalo, as amongst the most conspicuous in this respect.[1]

By the 1830s a rapidly growing population, combined with the movement westward to burgeoning urban centers in the Ohio and Mississippi River valleys, began to create an increased demand for fashionable material goods. Along with this demand came major technological developments both in America and abroad that resulted in the possibility of manufacturing greater quantities of less costly goods; hence "machines introduced muses to the masses."[2] New avenues of transportation through which to distribute these goods were also a significant factor as canals and steamboat routes expanded in the 1820s and 1830s. Capitalism and competition became the bywords in this quickly changing country, as western centers of production competed with more established, yet ever changing, East Coast centers. The marketing and distribution of goods became tremendously competitive, as manufacturers lured consumers with promises that "Orders from any part of the continent will be attended to with punctuality and despatch."[3]

Between 1800 and 1840 the population of the United States more than trebled, rising from 5.3 million inhabitants to just over 17 million. While there was considerable growth in East Coast urban areas, the rise in population in nonurban areas and smaller towns was also significant, especially following the opening of various canals in the 1820s. Population growth in rural areas between 1800 and 1840 represented an average of 96 percent of the total population increase in the country.[4] The emergence and growth of western cities and towns was an important factor in considering venues for the spread of taste through mass-produced goods. Middle-sized cities like Pittsburgh, Albany, Cincinnati, and New Orleans, ranging in population from 20,000 to 50,000 in 1830, became significant consumer and distribution centers. Combined with meeting the needs of a high nonurban population, there developed an enormous market for more moderately priced goods that would convey the owner's status as a person of taste and refinement. The level of knowledge of, or interest in, the ancient classical world among the literate western population is difficult to assess. However, the visual as well as verbal imagery that surrounded a significant percentage of the entire United States population most certainly must have had an impact on their aesthetic sensibilities, if not their intellect.

Whether in cityscape, townscape, or rural landscape, America boasted numerous architectural references to both Roman and Greek classical monuments by the 1830s. From Virginia's State

CLASSICAL TASTE IN AMERICA

Capitol, designed by Jefferson after the Maison Carrée (1789), to Latrobe's Bank of Pennsylvania (1800), to William Strickland's Second Bank of the United States (1824), and Thomas U. Walter's Girard College Founder's Hall (1833), a vast range of public and private structures emerged in America. As if searching for an identity with these classical cultures, architects and patrons embraced the pillars and porticoes of the ancient world as if they were natural parents. From bridges and bathhouses to the technological innovations of pumping stations and water-works, images and allusions to the classical world proliferated. Even in rural western towns, where the principal public edifice was either the bank or the courthouse, the chaste classical style was almost always the approved design. Even asylums, almshouses, and cemetery entrances did not escape the passion of benefactors and town fathers for "a chaste imitation of Grecian Architecture, in its simplest and least expensive form."[5] Comparable to the visual proliferation of columns and porticoes was the growing number of new or renamed towns boasting Greek or Roman names like Athens, Demopolis, Aurora, and Troy.

In addition to the abundant architectural references derived from classical antiquity, an ever-expanding body of printed material also brought classical history, literature, and numerous visual images to a broad and increasingly literate population. Ultimately, the effect of this flourishing amount of printed material made reading a necessity of life everywhere in America.[6] Daily and weekly newspapers, along with weekly and monthly magazines, provided the primary vehicle for transmitting knowledge to all literate segments of the population. This knowledge ranged from local news to literary presentations, as well as information from distant and exotic climes, reporting on everything from archaeological excavations to the latest fash-ions. In 1810, Philadelphia boasted nine daily papers, "as well as several meritorious periodical publications, embellished with very beautiful engravings, of extensive circulation."[7] The enor-mous body of magazines came and went, with some lasting only an issue or two, while others continued successfully for years.[8] Occasionally the names, like *Minerva*, *Portico*, and *The Parthenon*, even suggested classical imagery. In 1824 one observant muse wrote in *The Cincinnati Literary Gazette*

> This is the Age of Magazines—
> Even skeptics must confess it:
> Where is the town of much renown
> That has not one to bless it?[9]

The information presented in this vast array of printed material varied greatly, but hardly any issue of most magazines appeared without some classical references. Like many of its contempo-rary publications, *The Port Folio*, printed in Philadelphia between 1801 and 1827, often referred to the ancient world as well as the contemporary world. In November 1809 its weekly "Court of Fashion" column issue spoke of "the capricious goddess" and her view that "The Roman mantle, in orange, scarlet, or blue Georgian cloth, edged with a narrow gold tape, is a very graceful and convenient defence against the night air." Volume twelve, in 1814, contained "Thoughts of a

Hermit . . . on Architecture," which noted that "All the most civilized nations of the earth unite in considering the Grecian architecture as the standard of excellence." Another column in *The Port Folio* was entitled "Classical Literature," and in a specific issue "Latin Comedy" was discussed.

By the 1830s a number of cheaper periodicals diffusing "useful knowledge" emerged, and it was these that reached a larger readership composed primarily of the middle- and upper-middle-class American public. Among the most influential of these magazines were, perhaps, the two American editions of *The Penny Magazine*, issued every Saturday in New York and Boston by the Society for the Diffusion of Useful Knowledge in London. This fascinating and informative periodical was always well-illustrated and carried stories as well as images on a diversity of modern and ancient subjects, including Egyptian antiquities at The British Museum, the story of Laocoön as told by Virgil, the Elgin Marbles, the Temples of Paestum, and extracts from a play by the Greek tragedian Aeschylus. Other publications were also illustrated, and frequently the frontispieces of not only *The Penny Magazine* but others, like *The Analectic Magazine*, *The Family Magazine*, and *The Lady's Book* (published by L.A. Godey & Co., Athenian Buildings, Philadelphia), bore illustrations of classical icons or fanciful scenes comprising numerous classical allusions.

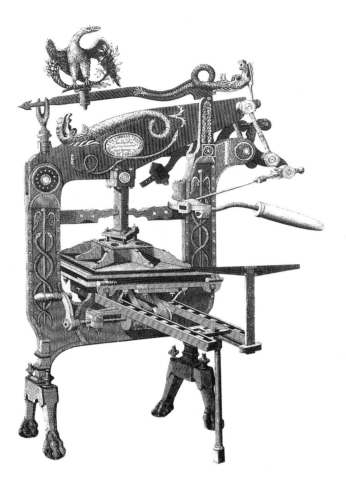

147

COLUMBIAN PRINTING PRESS LABELED "PHILADELPHIA 1813"

Abraham Rees, The Cyclopaedia. Philadelphia (1810–1824)

10⅜ x 8¼ in.

Courtesy The Winterthur Library: Printed Book and Periodical Collection

The vast volume of printing in the United States during the first four decades of the nineteenth century ranks high among the numerous changes that occurred in society during this period. The impact on the culture of America due to the dissemination of information was significant. This was a major avenue for communicating knowledge of the ancient world to many, especially those who had not the advantage of a classical education. Hence, it is not surprising that the most acclaimed printing press invented in America during this period was boldly embellished with classical imagery (fig. 147). Designed and made in Philadelphia by George Clymer in 1812–1813, it was aptly named the Columbian Press and introduced to the printers of Europe by 1817. Praised for its extraordinary "beauty, durability, and power, as well as facility of pull,"[10] this press was made entirely of cast and wrought iron. It was deemed superior to previous English inventions because "So slight a degree of strength is necessary to print a royal sheet on this press, at one pull, that it completely removes from the printing business the long standing reproach of presswork being destructive of health and life."[11]

Though not specifically designed for public purview, this "machine" was skillfully and beautifully ornamented. The press was crowned by a counterpoise lever (fig. 148) that had a sliding

weight fashioned as an eagle (a symbol of power and authority recalling the emblem on the standards of Roman legions) grasping in its claws an olive branch and a cornucopia; one end of this lever terminated in an arrow, while the opposite end was a fantastic scrolled dolphin. The frame of the press was appropriately flanked with two caducei, an attribute of Mercury, messenger of the gods, who was also credited with the invention of the alphabet. Most likely Clymer's national pride, coupled with an appropriate association with the superiority of classical cultures, resulted in this evocative design, all supported on four massive, classically inspired paw feet.

Technological developments in the printing process were central to the popularization and commercialization of classical taste in America. While the printed word was important, this process was not limited to paper only. The cheap replication of images on a variety of useful material goods resulted in the introduction of a broad range of utilitarian as well as decorative objects for the home displaying classical imagery. It is not surprising that by the 1830s that famed icon of antiquity, the Warwick vase, found its way into the drawers and closets of the American home. Reproduced abroad in both silver and porcelain, and in America in silver, in 1832 it appeared on the cover of the Boston edition of *The Penny Magazine*, and three years later was adapted in silver as a presentation vase from the citizens of Boston to Daniel Webster (fig. 201). After that time, for Bostonians at least, it appears to have lost its English association and become "The Webster Vase," as depicted on "Palmer's Odoriferous Compound or American Sweet Bag, Approved and Patronized By The American Public" (fig. 149). A sweet bag was a "small bag or sachet filled with a scented or aromatic substance, used for perfuming the air, clothes, etc."[12] Perhaps only in America could this well-known marble vase, made in the 2nd century A.D. and measuring over eight feet across, be reduced to a mere few inches and printed on perishable silk. Mr. Palmer, an entrepreneurial Boston druggist/chemist, recognized the appeal this image would have to a prosperous populace anxious for fashionable goods in the classical taste.[13]

148

COUNTERPOISE LEVER FROM
A COLUMBIAN PRINTING
PRESS

c. 1813

Probably Philadelphia

Cast iron

20 x 50¾ in.

Collection Allan L. Daniel

149

PALMER'S ODORIFEROUS
COMPOUND OR AMERICAN
SWEET BAG

c. 1835–1840

Massachusetts

Silk

2¾ x 3½ in.

*Courtesy, Essex Institute, Salem,
Massachusetts*

Perhaps the most widely circulated material commodity in early nineteenth-century America was coinage, and it is not surprising that these die-stamped pieces of copper, silver, and gold bore references to classical iconography. With the national mint established in Philadelphia by 1792, Liberty, America's goddess, and the eagle, its classical symbol of authority, were the images chosen for the obverse and reverse of the earliest coins (fig. 150). It may be no coincidence that the eagle on Clymer's Columbian press seems to be a descendant of the one stamped on the silver dollar minted in 1795, while the Liberty figure on the same coin resembles "a buxom Roman maiden . . . with a Roman dignity that recalls some massive marble bust of Minerva or Dea Roma, goddess of Rome."[14] Though the selection of images of Liberty and the eagle for the two sides of dimes, half-dollars, dollars, and five-dollar pieces did not change during the first four decades of the century, there were subtle changes in the depiction of these images over time. For example, by 1817 Liberty's cap was discarded as she was transformed into a young Venus with a coronet encircling her head. In 1836 new coinage was conceived, visually expressing a bold departure from that of the preceding three decades. Thomas Sully was responsible for the sketch of a seated Liberty figure for the obverse, while Titian Peale drew the flying eagle on the reverse. Though the seated Liberty suggests a direct source in the so-called Fates carved in the east pediment of the Parthenon in 435 B.C., the eagle seems to derive wholly from nature.

Military accoutrements worn and used by American militia companies in the first half of the nineteenth century afforded another public arena through which all citizenry were exposed to classically inspired objects like helmets and broadswords. Since most militia units never saw battle, and military training was a secondary pastime, the principal public venues for displaying these symbols of authority were in parades, balls, and varied celebrations for visiting dignitaries.[15] A fascination with ancient military equipage was first evidenced with Percier and Fontaine's 1802 design for Napoleon in *Receuil, "Salle exécutre au Château de Malmaison et details des*

150

UNITED STATES CURRENCY

1795-1840

1795 Dollar,

Silver   Diam. 1⁹⁄₁₆ in.

1809 Half Dollar,

Silver   Diam. 1¼ in.

1817 Cent,

Copper   Diam. 1⅛ in.

1840 Dollar,

Silver   Diam. 1⁹⁄₁₆ in.

Collection of The American
Numismatic Society, New York

Trophées qui la décorant," which was framed by a series of eight ancient helmets superimposed on accompanying broadswords. In 1839 *The Family Magazine* published three sequential articles that discussed in detail "Ancient Armour," illustrating shields, helmets, and body armor while citing passages from classical literature. The dragoon-style helmet worn by the 5th Regiment Cavalry of New Milford, Connecticut, appears to have been used originally by a New York state unit and later "refurbished" by the Connecticut regiment, adding the comb, cap plate, artillery button, and painted decoration (fig. 151). The short sword made by N. P. Ames, of Springfield, Massachusetts, for the United States Army Artillery was modeled after a French example of the same period (fig. 152). Both the French and American swords derive their form and ornament from early Roman broadswords.

151 top

MILITIA HELMET

c. 1820–1840

Donald Fairchild, New Milford, Connecticut

Leather; tin; paper

H. 11 in.

Courtesy Winterthur Museum, Winterthur, Delaware; Gift of Mrs. Alfred C. Harrison

152 opposite

SHORT SWORD AND
SCABBARD

c. 1833

N. P. Ames, Springfield,
Massachusetts

Steel; brass; leather scabbard

L. 25 in.

*Old Sturbridge Village, Sturbridge,
Massachusetts*

153

COVERED BANDBOX

c. 1830

United States

Block-printed paper on cardboard, newspaper lining

13 x 17¼ x 14 in.

*Cooper-Hewitt Museum, National
Museum of Design, Smithsonian
Institution; Gift of Eleanor and Sarah
Hewitt, 1913-17-8a,b*

Another eminently affordable item that many upper- and middle-class Americans owned and traveled with was a bandbox, called thus since its original function was to hold gentlemen's linen neckbands and lace bands. Especially popular in America by the 1820s and 1830s, these round or oval lightweight cardboard boxes were used for storing and transporting all manner of apparel. Colorful, useful, and highly fashionable, these decorative boxes also supplied an element of status for middle-class Americans. With prices so low as to range from 2 cents each to sometimes about $1.12 for a "nest" of boxes, the ornament on these boxes was a stylish symbol of taste transmitted to the middle classes.[16] Covered with wallpapers, as well as papers printed specifically for bandboxes, they presented images almost as wide-ranging as their sizes, colors, and prices. Some boxes depicted architectural fantasy, while others showed recent architectural accomplishments like the New York Merchant's Exchange and the Capitol in Washington, D.C. The new advances in transportation embodied in railroads and canals were also a prime subject, appropriately praising American progress. The bandbox shown in figure 153 presents classical transportation at its finest, with winged griffins vigorously pulling a maiden's chariot as they push aside an ancient vase obstructing their path. While this paper was probably printed in America specifically for use on bandboxes, its source of inspiration may have been a wallpaper frieze entitled "Griffons" issued in 1814 by the Parisian manufactory of Jacquemart and Benard.[17] If one could not afford griffins on one's pier table, then griffins on a bandbox may have been the next best way of displaying one's taste for decoration in the classical mode.

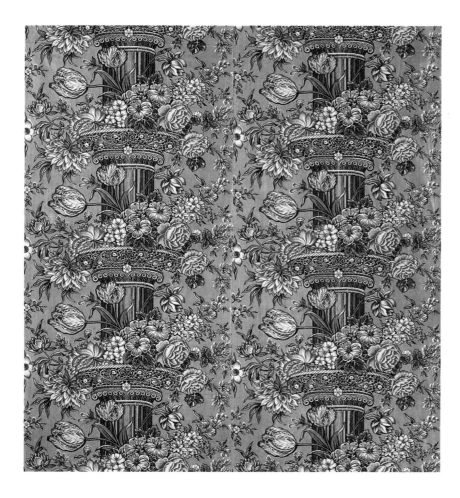

154

PILLAR PRINT
fragment

c. 1830–1835

England

Cotton chintz

82 x 50 in.

*Old Sturbridge Village, Sturbridge,
Massachusetts*

Even if you could not afford Composite (Roman), Corinthian, Ionic, Doric, or Tuscan capitals on your abode, you could at least have them on your window hangings or bed curtains. Between 1825 and 1835 a style of roller-printed and glazed fabrics, then referred to as "architectural" and now known as pillar prints, was produced in England and prodigiously consumed by an eager American public (fig. 154). By the mid-1820s, machine-printing textile technology in England began to advance rapidly, obviously driven by an economic force spurred by the growth of new commercial markets at home and abroad. Employing a number of engraved or etched copper rollers, these printing machines could carry out multicolor printing using new mineral dyes in a single application. Hence, these vertically oriented prints exhibited great and gaudy exuberance as they overflowed with floral and foliate motifs as well as scrolls, fluted columns, and baskets of flowers. In bolder and brighter terms they echoed an earlier period of architectural block-printed fabrics popular in England between about 1798 and 1810; however, it was these later pillar prints that found an eager and newly affluent audience in America.

Another area in which the English found a growing American market was that of ceramics. Owning and displaying a delicately potted and handsomely decorated English earthenware tea set was an ideal many Americans could now afford. The yellow-glazed tea set with transfer-printed maternal domestic scenes exemplifies a type of status symbol with classical overtones that graced many American parlors (fig. 155). Though unmarked, this set may have been made in Staffordshire at any number of productive potteries, or at a pottery in the northeastern counties like that of Robert Maling at Newcastle, established in 1817. The sweetly portrayed scenes of mother and child are typical of numerous prints inspired by Adam Buck's drawings and exported to America (fig. 29). Not only do these scenes applaud maternal virtues, like teaching your child to write and play the piano or harp, but they also endorse classically inspired furniture forms like Grecian couches, scroll back chairs with Grecian legs, and lyre-form music stands. It is especially amusing that instead of a simple cart to cavort in, the lucky child depicted on the covered sugar bowl seems to have a Roman chariot for his plaything. An interesting survival of the technological side of this repetitive transfer-printing on ceramics is an engraved copper plate with repeated mother and child designs (inspired by Buck) that descended in the Maling family of potters.[18] By the mid-1820s, the total "dollar value of imported English earthenwares ranged from twelve to

thirteen times the [total] value of porcelain imported from England, France, and China combined."[19]

The English ceramic market played on American pride in recent developments and architectural accomplishments as Staffordshire potters transferred engraved American views to their pottery for export. This was a clever way of assuring commercial success in producing affordable and desirable goods for the American consumer's rapacious appetite. In 1829 when the stock of the late John and Richard Riley of Burslem, Staffordshire, was offered for sale, the *Staffordshire Advertiser* remarked on the "most excellent assortment of dark blue, printed, painted and other descriptions of earthenware, suited for the American markets, in which market the deceased carried on extensive dealings."[20]

Numerous other Staffordshire potters also shared this rich American market. In John Ward's 1843 *The Borough of Stoke-upon-Trent*, Samuel Alcock of Burslem was described as "largely engaged in the export trade to America," and Enoch Wood & Sons of the same town was "reckoned the largest exporters of that article from Staffordshire to the United States of America." An 1833 Factory Report recorded that 1100 people were employed at Wood's pottery, so the production as well as exportation was indeed considerable.[21] By 1842, a group of thirty-eight New York dealers deemed the wares of Staffordshire potters so cheap that they were "within the means of the poorest."[22]

155

TEA SERVICE

c. 1790–1810

England

Transfer-printed earthenware

Teapot	H. 5⅞ in.
Sugar Bowl	H. 5⅞ in.
Cream Pot	H. 6 in.
Tea Bowl and Saucer	H. 2½ in.

Old Sturbridge Village, Sturbridge, Massachusetts

156

PLATE
*with view of Water Works,
Philadelphia*

c. 1820–1840

Ralph Stevenson (working
1805–1840) and Williams,
Cobridge, England
Transfer-printed earthenware
Diam. 10 in.

*The Baltimore Museum of Art: Bequest
of George C. Jenkins (BMA
1930.65.51)*

COVERED SAUCE TUREEN,
STAND, AND LADLE
*with views of the bank of Savannah
and the Insane Hospital, Boston*

1814–1830

J. and W. Ridgway (working
1814–1830), Hanley, England
Transfer-printed earthenware
H. 7¼ in.

*The Baltimore Museum of Art: Bequest
of George C. Jenkins (BMA
1930.65.199,.200)*

Staffordshire potters worked hard at developing trade relationships with American dealers since this market represented an important and lucrative part of their business. A good example of the marketing efforts of major entrepreneurial pottery owners is demonstrated by the fact that in 1822 John Ridgway, like other contemporaries of his, visited the United States. He traveled to Boston, New York, Philadelphia, and Baltimore, making connections with dealers, taking orders, showing patterns, and commissioning American views. In Boston he spent three hours touring the city searching for the best views, and in Baltimore he surveyed the public buildings seeking the most suitable for sketching. The fact that close to a hundred American views on Staffordshire pottery productions have been recorded is testimony not only to the potter's ingenuity but, as well, to the affordability and popularity of their wares (fig. 156). While most of the production depicting American cities focused attention on the major East Coast centers, recognition of ample markets in Western centers is evidenced by views of Pittsburgh, Louisville, and Cincinnati. The platter illustrated in figure 157 shows the prosperous city of Pittsburgh from across the Allegheny River. By 1832 the city and its environs boasted a population of close to 20,000, along with 270 manufacturing establishments, including eleven iron founderies, two glass houses, six rolling mills and nail factories.[23]

American pottery manufacturers were not to be daunted by strong English competition. On August 1, 1829, the editor of *Niles' Weekly Register* noted with smug American pride that "The manufacture of a very superior ware called 'flint stone ware' is extensively carried on by

Mr. Henderson at Jersey City, opposite New York. It is equal to the best English and Scotch stone ware, and will be supplied in quantities at 33⅓ pc less than like foreign articles will cost, if imported."[24] Later the same year, following an exhibition at the American Institute in New York, the editor again noted that Henderson's stoneware pitchers "are from classical models, and very elegant." The same account alluded to Henderson's "flint ware pitchers on the model of those found in the ruins of Herculaneum," a conclusion that may have been based on the fact that Henderson's most expensive pitcher (and the only one given a pattern name) was called "Herculaneum," and priced at $13.50 per dozen in his 1830 "List of Prices" (fig. 158).[25] Ironically, not only was Henderson attempting to undercut English prices, but at least in the instance of his Herculaneum pitcher he was directly copying a pitcher produced contemporaneously by William Ridgway. Though the English molded stoneware pitchers of this identical form that survive are unmarked, the first pattern book of William Ridgway and Company, containing 196 patterns, illustrated an identical pitcher as No.1 (fig. 159).[26] Ornamented with foliate scrolls, satyr masks, trailing grapevines, and a figural handle depicting Pan, this reasonably priced stoneware pitcher brought a touch of antiquity to American tabletops.[27] Utilizing a much cheaper material than silver, it replicated a form that previously only the well to do could afford, like the French ewer (fig. 26) and the Philadelphia cream pot with caryatid handles (fig. 103).

157

PLATTER
with view of Pittsburgh

1829–1836

James and Ralph Clews (working c. 1819–1836), Cobridge, England

Transfer-printed earthenware

L. 19⅞ in.

The Carnegie Museum of Art; AODA Discretionary Fund, 82.49

American technological developments in the manufacture of pressed glass represent an important contribution to the glassmaking industry, resulting in the production of affordable, yet fashionable, goods. Like the profusion of cheap English ceramics offered for middle-class consumption, American pressed glass articles also introduced classical iconography to parlors and dining rooms. By 1825–1826 the first known patents were issued to glass manufacturers in Pittsburgh and Massachusetts for pressed glass furniture knobs. A few years later utilitarian tablewares were being produced, and by the 1830s a wide range of forms and patterns were available at reasonable prices. In 1829 the Englishman John Boardman visited the annual fair of the American Institute in New York, and observed that "The most novel article was the pressed glass,

159

UNMARKED WILLIAM
RIDGWAY STONEWARE JUG,
SHOWN WITH DESIGN NO. 1
IN FACTORY DESIGN BOOK
early 1830s

*Courtesy Geoffrey A. Godden, Sussex,
England*

which was far superior, both in design and execution to anything of the kind I have ever seen in either London or elsewhere. The merit of its invention is due to the Americans, and it is likely to prove one of great national importance."[28]

Indeed this invention *was* of "great national importance," and it had a major impact on the commercialization of glass in America as well as abroad. It was not long before the English, French, and Belgians, and later the Bohemians and Scandinavians, adopted this revolutionary American technology. Made to imitate and compete with more expensive domestic and imported cut glass wares, pressed glass articles ranged from small cup plates and salts to more monumental compotes, covered caskets, and candlesticks. Cup plates and salts provided the cheapest and widest assortment of classical forms and motifs (fig. 160), with eagles, anthemions, scrolls, cornucopias, paw feet, and even the proverbial classical maiden drawn in a chariot. Available in colorless glass, or in various colors or combinations of colorless and colored, these evocative salts found their way to a multitude of American tables. By 1840 in Philadelphia, one dozen salts sold for one dollar, an indication of their extreme affordability.[29] The importance of salt in everyday food consumption has a long tradition, so it is not surprising that in the early nineteenth century it was thought "almost an indispensable necessary, so insipid would be most kinds of food without it."[30] Though today few salts survive with their original covers, during certain times of the year and in very humid climates covered salts were almost a necessity (fig. 161).

More expensive and ambitious forms of pressed glass tablewares were also produced, which continued to promote classical forms and motifs. The Roman candelabrum form, so highly praised by Peter and Michael Angelo Nicholson in 1826–1827, is echoed in the pressed bases with vesti-

160 left

SALT DISH

c. 1830–1840

Probably Boston and Sandwich Glass Company (1825–1888), Massachusetts

Opaque powder blue pressed glass

H. 1¾ in.

The Baltimore Museum of Art: Purchased with exchange funds from the Bequest of Edward Snyder (BMA 1993.1)

161 right

COVERED SALT DISH

c. 1820–1830

Probably Boston and Sandwich Glass Company (1825–1888), Massachusetts

Colorless pressed glass

H. 3⅛ in.

The Baltimore Museum of Art: Decorative Arts Fund (BMA 1989.333)

gial paw feet used for an elegant compote and a statuesque candlestick (fig. 162). The bowl of the compote is ornamented with a rich foliate scroll motif similar to those drawn directly from antiquity by Charles Heathcote Tatham, and numerous other designers who were copying Roman precedents. The candlestick is formed not only of pressed parts, but the globular mid-section is blown and finished with the addition of tooled and pattern-molded elements. An important factor in the economics of this mass-production was the interchangeability of parts, as can be seen in the bases of the compote and candlestick. Another ancient form introduced to tabletops in pressed glass was the sarcophagus, or covered casket, which might have been used as a butter tub or container for condiments (fig. 162). Previously this form might have been found in the dining rooms of the well to do in the guise of a lead-lined wine cooler, or cellarette. But thanks to technology and American ingenuity, by the 1830s a broader segment of the population could have sarcophagi as dining equipage also, though this time on the tabletop instead of under the sideboard.

In addition to candlesticks, lighting devices of numerous types comprised a significant portion of glass production in nineteenth-century America. Several New England glasshouses advertised "Grecian lamps," along with "antique and transparent lamps, etc. . . . for domestic supply, and exportation to the West Indies and So. America."[31] The New England Glass Company is known to have produced a large and varied quantity of annular lamps, as well as plain and cut shades and chimneys for them. Combining both pressed and blown techniques, the pair of lamps in figure 163 has blown fonts attached to a square pressed base in the form of a pillar with fluted corners surmounted by crouching lions and ornamented with flower baskets on each side. The diminutive astral lamp in figure 164 has a blown and blown-molded, baluster-shaped shaft

162 above

COMPOTE

c. 1835–1850

New England

Colorless pressed glass

H. 5⅝ in.

The Corning Museum of Glass,
Corning, New York; Gift of Louise S.
Esterly

CANDLESTICK

c. 1830–1835

New England

Colorless pressed glass

H. 8¹³⁄₁₆ in.

The Corning Museum of Glass,
Corning, New York; Gift of Louise S.
Esterly

COVERED CASKET WITH
TRAY

c. 1830–1840

Midwest

Colorless pressed glass

H. 5 in.

The Corning Museum of Glass,
Corning, New York

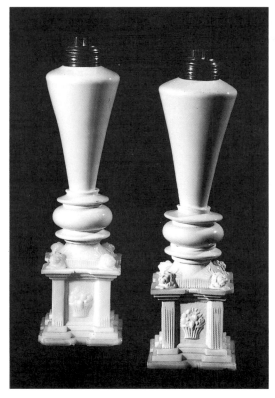

of deep amethyst glass, surmounted by a ground and richly cut shade. The cylindrical metal fitting above the glass base bears a rectangular label that reads "N.E. GLASS Co. BOSTON."

Glass manufactories flourished throughout the United States, from East Coast centers to the Midwest, making available locally a vast array of utilitarian goods. Not only pressed wares but blown and blown-molded wares were fashioned in classical forms or with motifs drawn from the proverbial stores of antiquity. Echoing the ancient two-handled urn, the diminutive blown glass vase in figure 165 is the more affordable answer to the monumental example with a coin in its knop shown in figure 130. The maker of this "half-sized" two-handled vase, probably made in a New England glasshouse, may have been familiar with the work of Thomas Cains at the South Boston Flint Glass Works, or his later Phoenix Glass Works.

The single most popular and prodigiously manufactured glass product was the blown-molded figured flask of the second quarter of the nineteenth century. Produced in huge quantities by numerous American bottle glasshouses, these variously ornamented utilitarian flasks were relatively cheap items. Testimony to the huge numbers of flasks produced by some houses is an 1825 advertisement of the Philadelphia glass manufacturer T. W. Dyott who offered for sale "3000 gross Washington and Eagle pint Flasks; 3000 gross Lafayette and Eagle pint flasks; 3000 gross Dyott and Franklin pint flasks; 2000 gross Ship Franklin and Agricultural pint Flasks; 5000 gross assorted Eagle pint flasks; 4000 gross eagle, cornucopia and etc., half pints."[32] Presumably Dyott was wholesaling these flasks to druggists and wine merchants across the country, who would have filled them and labeled them for resale.[33] In 1823 the Hartford apothecary Frederick Bull informed his public that "the Flasks and Bottles are now full of the following, viz.

165

TWO-HANDLED VASE

c. 1820–1840

Probably New England

Colorless blown glass

H. 5 in.

Old Sturbridge Village, Sturbridge, Massachusetts

Madeira wines . . . Also COGNIAC BRANDY, which has been a voyage to India; Old Jamaica Spirit, from London: Holland Gin, Metheglin fresh leghorn oil, etc.etc."[34]

Blown-molded flasks were ornamented with a vast variety of commemorative motifs as well as ornamental designs popularizing national themes and classical iconography: political heroes from Washington to Jackson, technological accomplishments like the development of numerous railroads, international celebrities such as Lafayette, and monuments marking significant victories. The flask in figure 166 was made at the Baltimore Glass Works and on one side depicts General Washington, America's first great hero and "Cincinnatus" figure of farmer turned venerable general, and on the other side the Battle Monument in Baltimore "erected in 1815 . . . an elegant pillar of beautiful marble, raised to commemorate the gallantry and patriotism of those citizens who fell in defence of the city."[35]

By the 1820s and 1830s, one of the most prominent as well as utilitarian features in the parlor of a prosperous household was a cast-iron stove, or fireplace. In many houses this primary source of

FLASK
with portrait of Washington on one side, the Battle Monument of Baltimore, on the other

c. 1825–1840

Baltimore Glass Works
(1800–1890), Baltimore

Light-green blown-molded glass

H. 7⅛ in.

The Corning Museum of Glass, Corning, New York

heat was also an important symbol of taste as well as economic assertion. A wide range of form and ornament in iron stoves existed for the consumer to choose from, including two-column and four column stoves, and an innovative one invented in Philadelphia called "Pierpont's Doric Fireplace." In 1820 the Lehigh Coal Company sent Dr. Eliphalet Nott, president of Union College near Albany, a quantity of anthracite coal with the request that he build a stove that would burn this hard coal. A noted inventor and authority on the combustion of fuels, Nott produced in 1826 what he called a "Saracenic Stove," but it was not entirely safe or successful. However, by 1832 he perfected and patented a cast-iron stove, lined with firebrick, that safely burned anthracite coal. Appropriately dubbed Nott's Patent stove,

it was produced at Nott's factory in Albany, run by his two sons, and at several other companies that he licensed to manufacture it. By 1830 the country's supply of timber was beginning to dwindle, and wood was $15 per ton, while anthracite coal was $10 per ton.[36] Hence, Nott's patent stove represented an important economic development in cost-saving for home heating during the second quarter of the nineteenth century. When Nott began production of these innovative stoves in 1832, the consumer could choose between a Gothic design or one with classical motifs; large stoves cost $60 while small ones were $38.[37] The stove in figure 167 descended in the Nott family and represents one of the most highly ornamented, and probably most expensive, cast-iron stoves produced in this period. Laden with classical motifs from winged griffins and urns to swags and classical scenes suggesting love themes, this stove must have been the epitome of taste in a parlor of the 1830s. With architectural pretentions suggesting a hierarchy of parts expressed by columns, a balustrade, and even a central pair of windows glazed with isinglass and illuminated from behind by the fire, this stove was not only useful but highly decorative. Commercial entrepreneurs knew how to capitalize on the consumer's desire for useful articles ornamented in the classical taste even when they fashioned such utilitarian items as stoves and fireplaces.

The aggressive growth and development of American technology and manufactures during the 1820s and 1830s evolved not only because of a growing demand for affordable goods, but also because of U.S. tariffs and the closing of ports to foreign goods. While a ready consumer market had a great deal to do with the success of American manufactures during this period, the exces-

167

BASE-BURNING STOVE

c. 1832

H. Nott and Company, Albany,
New York

Cast iron; isinglass

59 x 29 x 19 in.

New York State Museum, Albany

sive importation of foreign goods in the teens had resulted in major distress among many artisans by 1820, and hence an outcry for help. In 1866 J. Leander Bishop wrote of the "unchecked importation of foreign goods" as he chronicled the year 1819 in *A History of American Manufactures from 1608 to 1860*. He further lamented that "Importations having been for several years, and still continuing greatly in excess of the exportations . . . the balance had to be paid principally in solid money."[38]

Before the end of the second decade of the nineteenth century, organizations had been formed in many cities to encourage and promote American manufacturing. Some of these societies also initiated annual fairs or exhibitions to foster and reward innovative and exceptional American craftsmanship. The Franklin Institute in Philadelphia, the American Institute in New York, and the New England Society for the Promotion of Manufactures and the Mechanic Arts in Boston were among the organizations that encouraged excellence in American manufactures. As early as December 31, 1816, an address was presented to the American Society for the Encouragement of Domestic Manufactures, "To the People of The United States," which drew parallels with antiquity as it waved a banner for America. The Committee that composed this address maintained that "The fictions and fables of antiquity are realized in the short annals of our country":

> Like the young Hercules, it strangled in its cradle the destroying serpents and would prove equal to every labour. But foreign manufactures, like the garment poisoned by the Hydra's blood, threatens our dissolution; our funeral pile is lighted; but the mighty hand will interpose, and rescue us from death to immortality. And if it be asked who has that power? we say it is The *People!*[39]

Innovative American technologies continued to challenge European production as America began to compete fiercely with European imports. Bishop recorded for the year 1825, "Pittsburg glass undersold the imported in Eastern cities, and received the premium of the Franklin Institute in the last year, over numerous specimens."[40] To some extent, by the 1830s many Americans did begin to meet the challenge to "disdain the fashions of foreign climes; . . . let your dress be national; let your ornaments be of your country's fabric, and exercise your independent taste in suiting the array of your toilet to your own climate and your own seasons."[41] However, the impulse to follow European fashion was so strong it could not be entirely broken.

A new vogue in fashionable furniture for the upper middle classes emerged by the 1830s, and in time it became virtually a national style. However, as with other American productions, this style also owed a debt to foreign designs, including those of both continental and English sources. Joseph Meeks & Sons' innovative advertisement of 1833 illustrated forty-four designs, a large percentage of which were cribbed from George Smith's *Cabinet Maker and Upholsterer's Guide* (London, 1826) (fig. 168).[42] Similarly, those designs that employed broad, veneered surfaces with scrolled

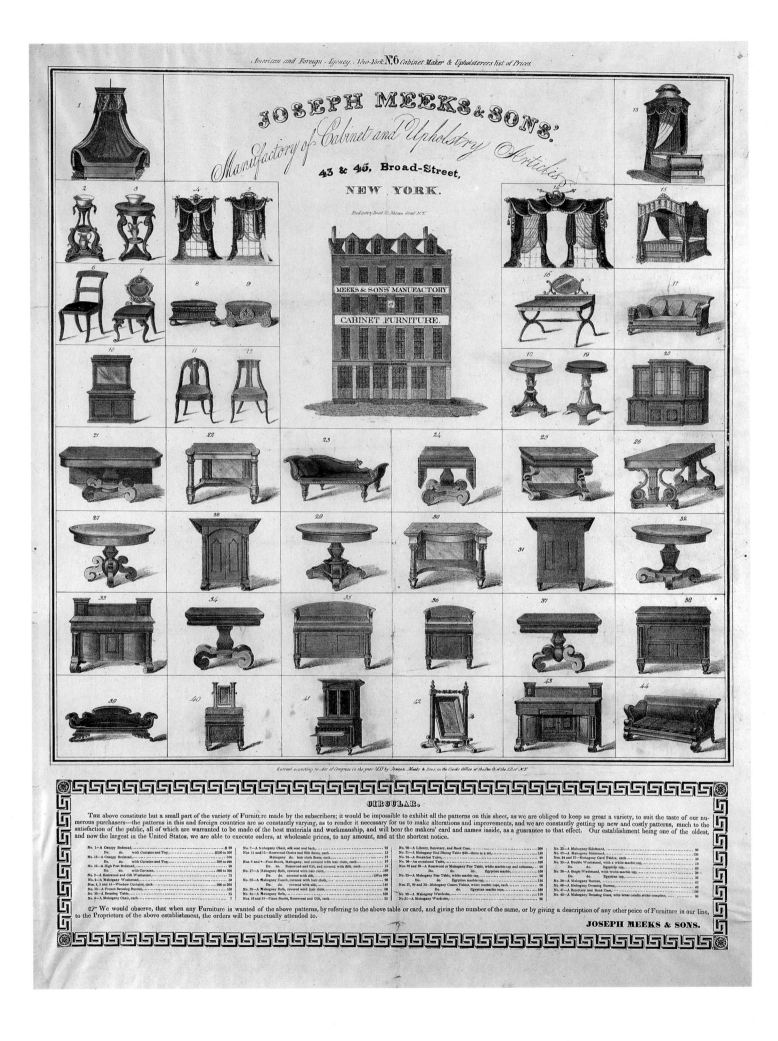

169 opposite

DESK AND BOOKCASE
c. 1825–1835

Attributed to John Meads
(1777–1859) and William
Alvord, Albany, New York
(working together c.1824-1835,
partners 1827-1835)
Mahogany, mahogany and rosewood veneers; brass, ormolu;
glass
89¼ x 50½ x 27½ in.

*The Baltimore Museum of Art: Young
Friends of the American Wing Fund*
(BMA 1989.616)

supports or feet and freestanding or engaged pillars seemed to derive from German, or central European, as well as French sources. The increased immigration of German artisans in the 1830s no doubt also contributed to the transferal of aspects of popular German "Biedermeier" fashions to America.[43] For over a decade or more, highly figured veneers became the hallmark of this new fashion in American furniture, and thus it is not surprising that in 1832 there were over ten mahogany yards in New York.[44] In 1867 the Philadelphia upholsterer George Henkels wrote in his *Household Economy* that Santo Domingo produced the finest mahogany, which was "formerly used for panels in wardrobes and headboards of bedsteads and fronts of bureau drawers." However, he also lamented that "the best wood has been cut off," and after "the depletion of the wood on this island, Cuba mahogany was the best to be had."[45]

Meeks was not the only East Coast cabinetmaking establishment aggressively marketing highly figured veneered furniture, as numerous others produced all forms of furniture in this style with varying degrees of elaboration, sophistication, and expense. Even virtuosos like Duncan Phyfe fashioned this popular style of furniture in the 1830s. In Albany, New York, one of Phyfe's and Meeks's chief competitors was John Meads. An English immigrant who came to New York City in 1792, he completed his apprenticeship there with his English master Samuel Miller, and by 1802 he had relocated in Albany.[46] In 1827 he entered into partnership with young William Alvord, and together they supplied both the elite and upper middle class with finely fashioned, elaborately veneered furniture. Meads and Alvord supplied much of the furniture to George Hyde Clarke for "Hyde Hall," as well as to clients such as Governor De Witt Clinton, Solomon Van Rensselaer, and Erastus Corning I.

The superior desk and bookcase in figure 169 was originally owned by either James Vanderpoel or his younger brother John Vanderpoel, as it is stamped twice with a "VP" brand, and descended through the family. James, a successful lawyer, moved from Kinderhook, New York, to Albany in 1831 as a circuit judge and member of the state assembly. Hence, it is possible that about that time he might have ordered a handsome desk and bookcase for his Albany residence. Related to other furniture made by Meads and Alvord, this piece may represent some of their finest work. The use of a variety of richly patterned mahogany and rosewood veneers, stamped brass moldings, inlaid brass stringing, and ornately carved muntins in the glazed doors represent time and money expended in the fabrication of this desk and bookcase. The unusual brasses are original and identical to brasses on other Albany and documented Meads pieces. The ebonized ball feet with central stamped-brass banding echo a Boston characteristic reinforcing Meads's tendency occasionally to integrate New England detailing into his work. The overall form of this piece is related to ones made in New York City, and slightly reminiscent of the "Secretary and Book Case" that Meeks illustrated on his advertisement.

By 1840, John Hall, an enterprising English émigré architect who was first listed in Baltimore directories in 1835, had published *The Cabinet Makers Assistant embracing the most modern style of*

170 right

THE CABINET MAKERS
ASSISTANT

1840

John Hall, Baltimore. Printed by
J. Murphy

5½ x 9¼ in.

Courtesy The Winterthur Library:
Printed Book and Periodical Collection

171 below

MAN SEATED, "MR. WING"

c. 1840

New England

Watercolor and gouache on paper

17¹/₁₆ x 14½

Courtesy Museum of Fine Arts, Boston.
M. and M. Karolik Collection of
American Watercolors and Drawings,
1800–1875

Cabinet Furniture . . . for the use of practical men (fig. 170).[47] Not only did Hall produce the first American cabinetmakers' design book, but it appropriately featured the first widespread national expression in sophisticated American furniture. As he so truthfully stated in his preface, "the style of the United States is blended with European taste, and a graceful outline and simplicity of parts are depicted in all objects." As usual, American artisans seemed to be borrowing from abroad, applying their own interpretations or changes, and coming up with a distinctively American product. Like Thomas Hope and his followers almost two decades earlier, Meeks promoted in this new national style gracefulness, harmony of parts, and simplicity of outline, all attributes revered by the moderns in the furniture of the ancients.

Meeks's advertising broadside and Hall's publication are just two of the numerous indications that the popularization of this new national style would soon approach monumental proportions. Along with new technologies that led to faster production of larger quantities of veneer came new and more expansive marketing and merchandizing techniques. The transportation revolution that began to occur in the 1820s with the establishment of numerous canals, a rapidly growing number of steamboats servicing major inland cities via riverways, and the already well-established coastwise shipping trade made the sale and distribution of this furniture so widespread that it reached not only to the Mississippi River Valley but to the West Indies and even South America.

The gentleman depicted in the revealing watercolor in figure 171, thought to be a Mr. Wing, is proudly posed with his modern-style center table, side chair, and desk and bookcase with three bold scroll supports. While it is impossible to determine the regional origin of this fashionable furniture, no doubt it is in the latest vogue and reflects the influences of the work of Meeks and Hall. Of particular interest is the amount of fabric evident in this interior. The covering on the table, the drapery on the left, the brilliant blue on the writing surface of the desk, and the green fabric that lines the inside of the bookcase doors all combine to make a statement of prosperity and refinement. The gentleman's ample library and his current involvement with open book and paper on the table all proclaim his cultivated nature.

While furniture in this late classical or Grecian style can be found in many regions of America, unless it is specifically labeled it is often difficult to determine its place of manufacture. The introduction of this new style in America heralded the demise of regional expressions in American classical furniture. Surviving material evidence supports the export of furniture sold by John Meeks and Sons, as well as other makers, to Mississippi River towns such as Natchez. The center table in figure 172 is identical to Meeks's illustration number 27 on his 1833 broad-

172

CENTER TABLE

1830–1845

Joseph W. Meeks and Sons, New York

Mahogany veneer; "Egyptian" marble

29⅛ x 36½ in.

Melrose, Natchez National Historical Park, National Park Service, Natchez, Mississippi

side, and was presumably purchased by the McMurrans of Natchez about the time of their marriage in the early 1830s. The price of this table with a white marble top as listed on the broadside was $80, but for an additional $20 one could have an "Egyptian marbletop."[48] Meeks noted at the bottom of his broadside that "The above constitute but a small part of the variety of Furniture made by the subscribers. . . . We are constantly getting up new and costly patterns much to the satisfaction of the public."[49] In 1845 the McMurrans built "Melrose," a fine plantation house on the outskirts of Natchez, and moved this table, along with other furnishings, to their new residence.

Another example of this bold yet sophisticated style, which was found, and thus probably owned, near Natchez, is the graceful curvilinear pier table in figure 173. While this particular form of pier table does not appear on the Meeks broadside, it does bear most of its original paper label identifying it as a product of the Meeks manufactory. The exuberance of the curves that completely define the form of this table, from its deeply shaped top, scrolled supports, and almost whimsical scrolled feet, mark it as a distinctive American product. As in the case of the center table from neighboring "Melrose," the purchaser of this table also preferred the more costly black Egyptian marble.

Indicative of the vast variety of innovative forms produced in this new "style of the United States" is the music stand in the form of a lyre in figure 214. Unlabeled and without any specific provenance, it is difficult to determine from outward appearances in what region of the country this useful form was produced. Found in the Baltimore area, possibly it was made in New York or Philadelphia and shipped for retailing to Baltimore. The presence of poplar as a secondary wood suggests a mid-Atlantic origin. The fact that it is not like any of the forms shown by either Meeks or Hall, nor any known to date from newspaper or city directory advertisements, bears testimony to "so great a variety . . . of new and costly patterns" alluded to by Meeks.

What were the essential furnishings of an upper- or upper-middle-class parlor that gave it the appropriate expression of taste, refinement, and fashionable ambience? By the 1820s and 1830s, one of the primary pieces of furniture in any parlor was the center table, which usually functioned as a focus for family activities, particularly reading, and hence it held the central source of light in the room, usually an astral or sinumbra lamp with a large glass shade. The anonymous young man painted by John Bradley in the late 1830s (fig. 174) is posed beside a marbletop center table holding his book, with a handsome astral or sinumbra lamp beside him on the table. The central pedestal of the table echoes the current national style promoted by numerous artisans like Meeks, while the lamp resembles those types imported and sold by Baldwin Gardiner at his "Furnishing Warehouse" at 149 Broadway, New York (fig. 121). In 1845, Webster's *An Encyclopaedia of Domestic Economy* discussed "The last improvement upon the French lamp . . . the *Isis* lamp . . . now frequently used as table lamps . . . manufactured in an almost infinite variety of patterns, of various prices and degrees of ornament and elegance, of brass, bronze, or part

porcelain and part brass." Gardiner advertised that he was "an importer of Lamps and Chandeliers" and that he also had on hand "an extensive variety of Miscellaneous House Furnishing Articles."[50]

The noted miniature artist Eliza Goodridge from Worcester, Massachusetts, painted two portraits of Mary MacCarty Stiles Newcomb in the 1830s that more fully reveal these key priorities of domestic perfection (fig. 175). Miss Newcomb's parlor not only had a center table cluttered

with books and the necessary lamp but other furnishings, including the proverbial scroll sofa and a set of simple, scroll-back fancy chairs. The ever-popular scroll sofa, like center tables, lamps, and books, was often included in portraits of upper-middle-class folks, suggesting that it also was an important symbol of taste and status. The young man in figure 176 has been portrayed with all of the appropriate symbols of refinement, taste, and fashion: a grand fluted column in the background, a handsome veneered scroll sofa—replete with stamped brass ornament on the bolster—and a group of books indicating his literary and scholarly pursuits.

The competition among American cabinetmakers, chairmakers, looking glass makers, and clock-makers whose products were geared to the upper middle classes was fierce from the 1820s to the 1840s. Evident in their advertisements is this chal-

176

YOUNG MAN ON SCROLL
SOFA

c. 1840

Attributed to Joseph Whiting
Stock (1815–1855), New
England

Oil on canvas

54 x 40 in.

Private Collection

lenge to capture as large a segment of this economically advantageous market as possible. The various lures that they used to attract a clientele focused on economics, service, and the ability to dispatch goods to distant places. Reasonable prices or the lowest cash prices, punctuality, fidelity, and promptness, and a willingness to ship anywhere on the continent were frequent pledges seen in period advertisements. Establishments ranged from those extremely specialized in the type of goods offered to literally the "warehouse" or "wareroom" that carried all forms, prices, and styles of furniture. In some instances certain makers, or brokers, openly appealed to specific segments of the market. For instance, when Alexander Kinnan and States Mead of New York became partners in 1823, their label stated that they had "a superior and complete assortment of elegant and highly finished Furniture" on hand. They further noted that "Southern gentlemen and others are respectfully invited to call and examine for themselves." The labeled chest of drawers with dressing glass made during their partnership (1823–1830) is a handsome representation of the type of furniture that utilized very high quality mahogany veneers and was ornamented with ebonizing and gold-powdered stencil decoration (fig. 177). It is unknown whether they were producing every part of a chest like this, since ebonized and stenciled columns, turned feet, scroll supports, and looking glass frames might have been purchased from more specialized makers. On the other hand, they may have had a decorator within their shop whose task was limited to those functions. Until the specific organization and make-up of nineteenth-century cabinet shops is more fully explored, answers to these questions will be speculative.

177

CHEST OF DRAWERS WITH
LOOKING GLASS

1823

Alexander P. W. Kinnan and
States M. Mead, New York
Mahogany with gilt stenciling
63 x 36 x 25 in.

Collection Joseph O. Matthews

Although looking glasses are by their very nature fragile, the large number of makers listed in the 1830s in New York City indicates that there must have been a considerable export trade in this commodity. In 1832, John H. Williams, who had worked at 315 Pearl Street since 1812, stated that he was a "Manufacturer of Looking Glasses in every variety of size and style, Particular attention paid to packing orders for the country, by the quantity or single Glass, which will be put at the very lowest market prices."[51] Williams was most likely selling at both retail and wholesale prices. Glasses like the one in figure 178, probably made in the 1830s, might have been purchased with reverse-painted glasses in the upper section or, perhaps at a lower price, with plain mirrored glass. With competition at its peak, lures such as "newest patterns," "best quality," and "lowest Factory prices"

178

PIER GLASS

c. 1825

John H. Williams, New York
Pine with gilt decoration; mirror
54 x 28 in.

Museum of the City of New York, New York; Anonymous Gift in memory of Margaret D. Stearns, 89.89

were attractive enticements to many customers. The fashionable cornucopias ornamenting the corners of this looking glass make it a particularly appealing example.

Occasionally specialized craftsmen also became entrepreneurial importers, offering elegant European objects for the home in addition to the domestic wares they manufactured themselves. In April 1823, Isaac Vose and Son, Boston cabinetmakers, "received by the London Packet, a large and elegant assortment of Lamps," which they advertised along with fabrics, fringes, laces, cornices, brass ornaments, and "every material suitable for the decoration of Drawing Rooms, and other apartments. . . ."[52] In 1819 Thomas Palmer was listed as a carver and gilder in the Baltimore directory, and by 1835–1836 he was operating a "Looking Glass & Fancy Hardware Store." Palmer sold not only imported "French and German Looking glass Plates" (presumably in frames of his own manufacture) but also imported goods such as lighting devices and mantel clocks. His trade advertisement provides an illuminating visual statement of the type of goods he offered, which his successors, Cariss & Schultz, must have continued to purvey, calling their establishment a "furnishing store" by 1845 (fig. 179).

Increased affluence among a larger segment of the public meant that more American households could afford to decorate their homes with domestic and imported luxury goods like wallpapers, curtains with trimmings and elegant cornice rods, carpets, fancy upholstered or slip-covered fur-

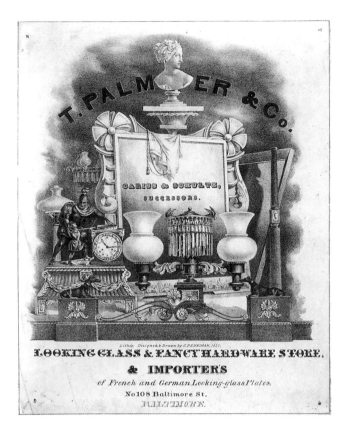

niture, elegant lighting devices, and rich china and glass tablewares. In addition, improved manufacturing techniques and keen competition reduced prices. The development of furniture and furnishing warehouses offered a wide assortment of goods and foreshadowed the innovative department stores of the latter part of the century. Enterprising cabinetmakers, chairmakers, and upholsterers continued the eighteenth-century tradition of essentially offering almost complete interior decoration services. A number of extensive "Upholstery Furnishing Rooms" existed in major urban areas and serviced both tradesmen and private patrons, increasing the distribution of fashionable goods.

An enterprising Boston artisan and entrepreneur, William Hancock, opened his Furniture and Upholstery Warehouse on Market Street in 1820. By the end of the decade, Hancock's business had grown and at the peak of his prosperity his warehouse occupied Nos. 37–53 Cornhill (Market) Street.[53] He advertised a variety of furnishings, including "spring seat rocking chairs" that were not only technologically innovative but also praised for their recuperative powers.[54] As the younger brother of cabinet- and chairmaker Henry Kellam Hancock, it is possible that he looked to his elder brother for the frames for seating furniture he was upholstering and selling.[55] A bill dated May 19, 1829, from Hancock's "Furniture and Upholstery Warehouse" indicates that he was not only selling rocking chairs, but it also listed "16 Grecian chairs."[56] In 1828 William Hancock was awarded a premium at the Franklin Institute exhibition as "the maker of the best chairs."

Perhaps as a result of William Hancock's acclaim in Philadelphia at the exhibition, his younger brother John opened "Upholstery Furnishing Rooms" in that city in 1830.[57] Using the same illustration of a Grecian couch on his advertisements and labels that his brother used in Boston (which was also copied by numerous other advertisers across the country), he stated that he kept "all kinds of Upholstery Goods, and attend[ed] personally to every branch of the Business." Hancock appears to have imported from his brother's manufactory in Boston most of the unupholstered furniture frames that he offered for sale, including "a great variety of splendid Spring Seat Rocking Chairs, Which, for ease and comfort, cannot be surpassed." The chair illustrated in figure 180, labeled by Hancock, is one of the typical Boston rockers that was fitted with a spring seat and then upholstered with the customer's choice of fabric. These chairs were made in a variety of woods, with mahogany and walnut being the most costly. Ones made of maple were usually grained to simulate curled maple or rosewood, like the one in figure 180, and a customer might choose the covering from a large selection of fabrics including plush, haircloth, leather, worsted damask, or moreen.

Depending on the fabric used, a finished rose-wood-grained rocking chair might cost between $10 and $15, while a mahogany one upholstered in haircloth cost $17.[58] Often these chairs added a rich and brilliant presence to a room, as the colors of the various fabrics offered ranged from crimson, yellow, and salmon plush, to blue or maroon leather, or green and crimson morocco. Additional trimmings included different color combinations of flat and raised gimp and brass nails.

When John Hancock died in 1835, his upholstery business may have been the largest in Philadelphia, employing thirteen workers and occupying a four-story, 31-by-43-foot brick warehouse, which also housed his shop, or workrooms. The appraisers of Hancock's estate compiled an eighteen-page inventory of his warehouse stock that today provides an illuminating picture of the volume and variety of his business.[59] In addition to upholstered and unupholstered seating furniture, among the numerous goods and supplies that Hancock had on hand were venetian blinds, mattresses, stamped brass ornaments, fringes, silk and worsted tassels, and quantities of cornice and curtain fittings and fixtures. The Hancocks' activities in both Boston and Philadelphia provide important indications of the growing prosperity in America that fostered the growth of major mercantile ventures to meet the demand of those affluent enough to decorate their homes in a rich and tasteful style.

American ingenuity and industry led to another distinctively national product that was to have great appeal to the masses because of its efficiency, affordability, and fashionable appearance with classical overtones. The development of a sizable shelf clock industry in northwestern Connecticut between 1815 and 1845 was the result largely of the creative genius of clockmaker Eli Terry, Jr. Between 1815 and 1845 Terry received eight patents for brass- and wooden-wheeled clocks, and numerous other makers in the area took advantage of his inventiveness by copying these various improvements along with those of their own devising. By 1835, a total of

180

ROCKING CHAIR

1829–1835

William Hancock, Boston, retailed by John Hancock and Company, Philadelphia

Maple with gilt decoration

41 x 24 x 27 in.

Courtesy Winterthur Museum, Winterthur, Delaware

nearly 100,000 wood and brass clocks were made in the towns of Plymouth, Bristol, and Farmington, Connecticut, employing "many women . . . chiefly in making and painting the dial-plates."[60] With success based largely on mass production and interchangeability of parts, there was strong competition among these Connecticut clockmakers during this period to increase production, decrease costs, and maximize profits. The market for these clocks was already growing by 1819, and in that year it was reported that in Bristol, Connecticut, there was one manufactory that produced about 2000 brass clocks annually. A number of other factories made large quantities of wooden clocks each year that were "almost all sent abroad for a market, and principally to the southern and western states."[61]

In 1836, Eli Terry's company, in responding to a request from merchants in Ohio for clocks, enumerated six different types of clocks available and ranging in price from $4.50 to $16, noting that "For cash we make a liberal discount."[62] But artisans in the western territories also saw the opportunity to capitalize on this lucrative market, and some advertised their clocks "Warranted superior to any bought from the Eastern States."[63] Makers like Phineas Deming of Vienna Township, Trumbull County, Ohio, produced timepieces virtually identical to those exported by Terry and his contemporaries, presumably at competitive prices (fig. 181). With a one day, thirty-hour wooden movement housed in a case almost identical to many Connecticut models, Deming participated in a market that must have held some tight competition. While it is most likely that these clockmakers were little interested in cultivating "classical taste" in their patrons, they nevertheless supplied their public with numerous forms and decorative motifs that echoed the columns, scrolls, carved paw feet, cornucopias, eagles, and other images associated with the stores of antiquity. By 1840, many prosperous households probably could afford, if they did not already have, a fashionable shelf clock.

181

SHELF CLOCK

c. 1820

Phineas Deming (b. c. 1755), Vienna, Ohio

Tiger maple, poplar; painted and gilded wooden dial; églomisé panel

30¾ x 17½ x 5 in.

Collection Walter and Kathryn Sandel

Perhaps the largest enterprise during this period was that of the manufacture and shipment of "fancy furniture," particularly chairs and settees. While most sizable cities and towns had a number of chair manufactories, the concentration of large producers who specifically advertised that they sold "chairs in pieces for exportation" or had "Knockdowns fit for the Southern Market" seemed to be in and around the mid-Atlantic cities of New York, Philadelphia, and Baltimore (fig. 182). Albany was another center for chair manufacturing in the 1820s and 1830s, primarily due to the opening of the Erie Canal and the developing market north and west of the upper

Hudson River. Just as the clockmaking industry burgeoned in western Connecticut due in part to the widespread availability of water power, so a lucrative chair industry also evolved in Hitchcocks-ville (Riverton) under the impetus of Lambert Hitchcock (fig. 183). Manufactories in Pittsburgh and Cincinnati emerged in competition with eastern sources and frequently advertised that they warranted their work "equal to any manufactured west of the mountains, and not inferior to any made east."[64] Makers who advertised in their respective city directories repeatedly used the same small illustrations that seemed to be generic printers' cuts from New York to Cincinnati.

A few illustrations showing the facades of fancy chair manufactories are known from trade advertisements and period watercolors, drawings, or engravings. However, the most illuminating depiction and surviving documentary evidence of an early nineteenth-century fancy chairmaker is that of David Alling of Newark, New Jersey (fig. 184). Not only do two extraordinary paintings of the exterior of his establishment exist, but, in addition, eleven volumes of business and estate

182

SIDE CHAIR **right**
one of six

c. 1820–1830

Baltimore

Ebonized wood with gilt stencil decoration; ormolu

33¼ x 18 x 23 in.

The Baltimore Museum of Art: Gift of Florence Hendler Trupp, Baltimore (BMA 1977.33.5)

SIDE CHAIR **left**

c. 1820–1840

Pennsylvania

Ebonized tulip poplar and hickory with painted and gilded decoration

35⅛ x 18⁷⁄₁₆ x 22 in.

Collection Milton E. Flower

183

SIDE CHAIR

c. 1832–1843

Hitchcock, Alford & Co.,
Hitchcocksville, Connecticut

Painted and stenciled maple; cane

34 x 17 x 15½ in.

The Hitchcock Museum, Riverton,
Connecticut

records spanning the years 1801 to 1857 provide ample documentation of an extensive local and export trade.[65] Alling's trade to southern markets began in 1819 when he shipped 144 ornamented fancy chairs to New Orleans to be sold on commission there and in Natchez. By the decade between 1826 and 1835, three-fourths of Alling's production was being marketed in the South and to Latin America. More than 17,000 chairs were sent to southern ports in that ten-year period, with Natchez, New Orleans, and Mobile receiving almost two-thirds of the 148 shipments listed.[66] It is notable that the average unit price of chairs shipped southward at this time dropped from $2.90 to $1.73, most likely to compete with manufacturers in other eastern cities as well as those emerging in places like Pittsburgh and Cincinnati.[67]

Alling, along with numerous other competitors, was responsible for bringing fashionable seating furniture to the upper and middle classes of the Mississippi River Valley. Presumably soon after her marriage in 1823, Martha Eliza Stevens Edgar Paschall was painted by an unknown artist in elegant attire, seated on one of two fancy chairs, atop either a woven carpet or a painted floor-cloth (fig. 185). She had grown up in Kaskaskia, Illinois, on the Mississippi River southeast of St. Louis, and married General John Edgar in 1823. Edgar had been granted a tract of land in Kaskaskia because of his distinguished service in the American Revolution, and in time he became one of the richest men in the Northwestern territory and the largest private landowner.[68] Although by 1830 Kaskaskia only had a population of 1,000, its location on the Mississippi, with easy access to St. Louis, Natchez, and New Orleans, assured upwardly mobile folks like the Edgars of being able to procure stylish clothes and furnishings directly from eastern centers. Martha Eliza's fancy chairs resemble those described in Albany, New York, advertisements as

184

THE HOUSE AND SHOP OF DAVID ALLING, NEWARK, NEW JERSEY

c. 1835

United States

Oil on canvas

18¼ x 26½ in.

The New Jersey Historical Society, Trenton; Gift of Mrs. Clarence W. Alling (1928.5)

"ballback," and are often associated with New York area manufactories. In the early 1820s, Albany chairmakers like John Bussey and Gerrit Visscher advertised "Curled Maple, Gilt—Grecian, Frettbacks, Schrollbacks, Slatbacks, and Ballback Chairs, with Cane and Rush Bottoms."[69]

A combination of competition and ambition spurred the growth of furniture manufacturing in southern and western centers, as well as in less major urban areas in the East. Stylistic influence from Baltimore fancy chairmakers must certainly have inspired the producer of the Grecian side chair in figure 182 (left). Though at first glance this plank-seated, tablet-top, painted chair appears naive in comparison to its city cousin (fig. 182, right), upon closer examination it is a truly sophisticated interpretation of the more costly urban model. Though the seat is wood, it is subtly contoured and painted to appear as if lightly stuffed and upholstered with leather, having a convincing finishing touch of painted, trompe l'oeil brass tacks outlining the edge of the plank seat. The views of commodious houses painted on each tablet top of the four surviving side chairs in this set at first appear fictional, but closer study of the individualistic delineation of each suggests that they were probably known residences. This precedent does exist in an earlier set of Baltimore painted chairs (c. 1800–1805) that have country houses of wealthy Baltimoreans depicted on the front of each tablet.[70]

In addition to the mass production and exportation of more affordable furniture with classical overtones, special commissions for wealthy private patrons, or for major public buildings such as state capitols, provided a major means of disseminating classical taste to southern and western regions. In 1819 Thomas Constantine, cabinetmaker of New York City, billed the United States Capitol for forty-eight chairs and forty-eight desks for the Senate chamber. Inspired by a design from Thomas Hope's 1807 *Household Furniture and Interior Decoration* (pl. 59), the U.S. Capitol chairs were seen and admired by numerous senators as well as visitors to the Senate chamber. Hence, it is not surprising that in 1823, William Nichols, the architect in charge of the renovation and enlargement of the North Carolina State House at Raleigh, also chose the Constantine brothers to provide the new draperies, canopy, and speaker's chair for the remodeled Senate chamber (fig. 186).[71] The bill, dated July 19, 1823, to the State of North Carolina "per Wm Nichols Esqr," was from John Constantine, upholsterer and brother of Thomas, the cabinetmaker. Constantine charged $1650 "To furnishing draperie of crimson **Damask** and ornaments complete for 6 windows, and canopy & chair for the Speaker of Senate chamber in the Capitol." An additional $100 was also billed "To Expenses, coming on from New York to put up d[itt]o."[72] While the rear legs, seat frame, and deeply swept rear stiles with reeded, quarter-round fan motif on top of the seat rail follow closely both Hope's design and Constantine's chairs for the U.S. Capitol, the scroll back top, great scroll arms, and front turned legs differ. Whether it was Nichols's idea to vary the design or Constantine who suggested that these variations would be more fashionable is speculative. The great scroll arms are reminiscent of those seen on Samuel Gragg's patent "elastic" chairs, as well as those used by Duncan Phyfe and others.[73] Originally decorative brasses ornamented the seat rail, the scroll arm terminations, and the side scrolls of

185 opposite

MARTHA ELIZA STEVENS
EDGAR PASCHALL

c. 1823

United States

Oil on canvas

52¼ x 40⅛ in. (frame)

© 1992 National Gallery of Art, Washington, D.C.; Gift of Mary Paschall Young Doty and Katharine Campbell Young Keck

186

SPEAKER'S ARMCHAIR
from the Senate Chamber of the
North Carolina State House

c. 1820

John and Thomas Constantine,
New York

Mahogany; replacement brass
casters

35 x 25 x 24 in.

North Carolina Division of Archives
and History

the crest rail, but alas these have long been missing. Nichols contracted with Constantine only for this most important chair and its furnishings; all of the other legislative furniture was commissioned from Cornelius J. Tooker, a Fayetteville, North Carolina, cabinetmaker.[74] The economics of buying locally made furniture figured into this decision, but it is a significant statement that the principal and most classically derived piece of furniture in this southern state house was ordered from New York, and it arrived in a capital city devoid of all but overland transportation.

When the North Carolina State House remodeling was completed by 1824, it was among the most impressive classical public edifices in the southern states. In addition to the pseudo-porticoes of engaged Ionic columns projecting from the long east and west fronts, there was a massive domed rotunda that surmounted the central section in which was displayed the marble statue of George Washington commissioned from Antonio Canova in 1820 and installed in the State House in 1821 (fig. 190). This enormous white Carrara marble masterpiece depicting Washington in the garb of a Roman general caused numerous critical comments, and one traveler from Pennsylvania thought it "rather an obscene thing, and in my opinion a disparagement of the person, and fine feelings of the immortal Washington."[75] Others however thought it a monument "of liberality and taste."[76] One can only imagine the reaction of North Carolina planters upon viewing the great American general and Cincinnatus, half naked, with tablet and pen in hand.

Those gentry and visitors who viewed the Senate chamber were most impressed with not only the speaker's chair but also the accompanying hangings by Constantine. In 1824 Mrs. Anne Royall was overwhelmed by the legislative halls "hung round with the richest damask silk . . . a brilliant red, of the most costly texture, with gold fringe and tassels . . . round the windows and chairs of both Houses." Two years later in 1826, Pamela Savage admired "the window curtains of crimson damask silk which cost 100. dollars a piece, over each window is a gilt eagle holding the looped curtain in his beak."[77] Sadly the State House burned to the ground in June 1831, irreparably damaging the Canova sculpture. Miraculously, the speaker's chair, though somewhat damaged, was the only significant piece of furniture saved, a major tribute to its tasteful classical style.[78]

The exportation of objects made in the East had a distinct impact on the transferal of fashionable classical taste to objects made in western regions. In addition, the migration westward of craftsmen trained in eastern centers may also have been a significant factor in this dissemination of taste, but that is more difficult to document. Equally important is the 1830 production of *The Pittsburgh Cabinet Makers' Book of Prices*, which shows a close relationship to *The Philadelphia Cabinet and Chair Makers' Union Book of Prices* for 1828. Three closely related sideboards, all labeled or signed by Pittsburgh (area) makers and produced in the 1830s, or early 1840s, demonstrate the direct influence of Philadelphia styles and workmanship on this rapidly developing Allegheny Valley center.[79] While all three sideboards are of similar form and ornament, the proportions, as well as the carved elements on each, vary considerably and reinforce the fact that they came from three distinct shops. The sideboard in figure 187 is stamped four times "Wm ALEXANDER," who was listed in Pittsburgh directories from 1837 to 1844 as a cabinetmaker and pianoforte maker in Sharpsburg, a suburb of Pittsburgh. While little is known about Alexander, he may have trained in Philadelphia and moved to Sharpsburg following his apprenticeship. Philadelphia directories do not list any likely William Alexanders who may have worked in the cabinetmaking trade. The overall form of this sideboard follows the description for "a Pedestal Sideboard" listed in *The Pittsburgh Cabinetmakers' Book of Prices* for 1830, excepting that the elaborate carved features are not listed in the price book. Of the three Pittsburgh sideboards, the Alexander one seems to have the most accomplished carving, with the fruit baskets flanked by scrolls that top the pedestal particularly neatly executed. Alexander's extraordinary use of veneers in convex fan and lozenge shaped patterns, and the carved scrolls with lotus and

SIDEBOARD

1837–1844

William Alexander, Sharpsburg,
Pennsylvania

Mahogany, mahogany veneer;
marble; mirror

57¾ x 75¼ x 26¼ in.

Collection David Conrad Hislop

grapevine ornament, relate closely to documented pieces of furniture by the Philadelphia cabinetmaker Anthony G. Quervelle. With three documented Pittsburgh examples all exhibiting quite different details, it is unlikely that these pieces, or parts of them, were Philadelphia products. Most probably the enterprising mechanics of Pittsburgh were aggressively matching the Philadelphia competition, and doing so at lower prices, judging from a comparative analysis of the two price books previously cited.

As all the above evidence indicates, living in the interior portions of the United States in the 1820s and 1830s certainly did not mean living an unfashionable and spare lifestyle if one was prosperous enough to afford otherwise. Steamboats and canals greatly expanded the commercial and consumer opportunities for the middle as well as the upper classes. In 1832, Nashville, Tennessee, located on the Cumberland River, had a population of 5,566, and was "a flourishing town . . . accessible to steamboat navigation" with "all the features of a commercial depot, having numerous stores, a branch of the U.S. bank, and two other banks."[80] The captivating group portrait of Ephraim Hubbard Foster, his wife, and their five children confirms that life in Nashville by the mid-1820s could be exceedingly stylish and tasteful (fig. 188). Foster, born in Kentucky, was a lawyer by training, but he had military experience under Jackson at the Battle of New Orleans and political experience briefly as a state senator. The Fosters' fancy gilt chairs, their red draperies with fringe, and fashionable garb, including young Jane Ellen's extraordinary plumed

188

EPHRAIM HUBBARD FOSTER
FAMILY

c. 1825

Ralph Eleaser Whiteside Earl
(1788–1838), Tennessee
Oil on mattress ticking; original
frame
53³⁄₁₆ x 70¹⁄₁₆ in.

*Cheekwood, Tennessee Botanical
Gardens and Fine Arts Center, Inc.,
Nashville; Gift of Mrs. Josephus
Daniels (69.2)*

turban, all denote a stylish life of classical harmony and domestic virtue. The original gilt frame, with its deep cove molding, turned baluster ornamentation, and carved shells in the corners, might have come from an Eastern looking glass and picture-frame maker.

By the 1820s and 1830s many visual manifestations of form and ornament derived from classical sources had permeated the American consumer's world. Depending upon your economic means, there were ample opportunities to embellish your home with this fashionable classical taste. For those prosperous enough to afford it, classicism was a fashion and a style. Intellectually the connections that literate Americans drew between a pressed glass salt with Aurora drawn in a chariot and the classical world are difficult to assess. Perhaps there was no conscious cerebral connection, but then maybe that was not the objective. Collectively these forms and images represented a symbolic ideal and awareness of the ancient past, and to the aesthetic aspects of daily life they afforded a refinement and beauty that would have been sorely missed had there been no American admiration for the remains of antiquity.

FIVE

AMERICAN HEROES: CLASSICAL STYLE

Public and Domestic Virtue

The Italian Renaissance revived the classical concept of civic humanism, as well as a renewed interest in the human attributes of virtue and morality as reflected in the writings of ancient Greek and Roman authors. Seventeenth- and eighteenth-century Europe espoused these classical values, but perhaps nowhere were they more sincerely studied and embraced than in eighteenth-century America. The "quest for virtue" was particularly prominent in the writings of colonial Americans, as their classical educations prepared them for the establishment of the new republic. *The New Jersey Magazine* announced in 1787: "Now it is virtue alone, that qualifies a man for the discharge of . . . important offices. . . . It is virtue, that gives him a true taste of glory, that inspires him with zeal for his country, and with proper motives to serve it to the utmost of his power. . . . The end of all study, therefore, is to make men virtuous."[1]

Virtue was held to be a necessary and positive result of education in eighteenth-century America, and the classics were read to inspire "noble patterns of behavior."[2] In his July 4th oration in 1783, Doctor Joseph Warren of Massachusetts proclaimed "That Virtue is the true principle of republican governments [and] has been sufficiently proved by the ablest writers on the subject."[3] Heralded was classical republicanism, the sacrifice of private interests for the good of all mankind. This concept of classical virtue that eighteenth-century Americans espoused, the virtue of the Romans, "had flowed from the citizen's participation in politics; government had been the source of his civic consciousness and public spiritedness."[4] In his *Farewell Address*, George Washington recognized "that virtue or morality is a necessary spring of popular government."[5]

Educated Americans of the eighteenth century, those who were to become the founders of the nation, looked to the ancients for illustrious models, whether of virtue, morality, or civic humanism. They found their models in Roman generals, emperors, and senators. However, once the Revolution was over and it was clear that a new country was emerging, it was no longer enough just to honor and worship classical heroes, America needed "symbols of stability," living inspiration, and tangible examples of virtue. Though they studied the ancients, revered them, and hoped to learn from them, at the same time they desperately needed their own "illustrious heroes" to honor. While they read and admired classical literature, they craved a native American literature of their own. In 1805 a youthful valedictorian at the University of Pennsylvania Commencement aptly spoke, saying, "Heroes of Greece and Rome, I hail you in my country's name, here offer to you the incense arising from that noble flame which your illustrious examples have enkindled in our country."[6]

Almost immediately following the Treaty of Paris in 1783, American leaders recognized this need for illustrious models of virtuous behavior if this infant nation was to survive. The creation of classical-style American heroes resulted in numerous rhetorical and visual displays that brought to the public eye classically inspired products. The first and most significant hero to ascend "to the Temple of Honour through the Temple of Virtue" was our own American Cincinnatus, General George Washington. The purpose of creating American heroes for a new

189

TOILE FRAGMENT: THE
APOTHEOSIS OF FRANKLIN
AND WASHINGTON

c. 1785

England

Copperplate-printed cotton

95 x 56⅝ in.

Private Collection

and diverse nation was twofold: to recognize past deeds performed for the good of all men, and, thus, to promote virtuous behavior and inspire future good works by others. Long before the death of General Washington, which unleashed a torrent of oratorical eulogies and memorial art, the farmer turned general, then President, was elevated to the status of a classical hero and godlike figure.

European engravers and fabric manufacturers saw a ready market among upper-class Americans for commemorative articles immortalizing the country's new "classicized" heroes. By 1785 copperplate-printed toiles were being offered by merchants, and the visual message was saturated with appropriate classical imagery. "The Apotheosis of Franklin and Washington" (fig. 189) created a new mythology; the esteemed general was depicted with sword in one hand and reins in the other, driving a chariot drawn by leopards. The youthful America, seen for the first time as a Greek goddess, was seated behind him holding a caduceus and a shield announcing "American Independence."[7] Mounted troops and native Americans blowing trumpets surround the chariot, and symbols of battle are clustered about the "Liberty Tree." Franklin is led to the Temple of Fame by Athena, goddess of war, holding a shield with thirteen stars emblazoned on it. He holds one end of a banner proclaiming "Where Liberty Dwells there is My Country," as a classically draped figure of Liberty grasps the other end. The message could not be clearer, America was beginning to amass her own gallery of classicized heroes.

The theory that the creation of "role models" at this time resulted from a conscious effort on the part of men like Thomas Jefferson, who "set out systematically to create a pantheon of American

LAFAYETTE AND MISS HAY-
WOOD VIEWING CANOVA'S
STATUE OF GENERAL GEORGE
WASHINGTON

c. 1831–1841

Albert Newsam (1809–1864),
Philadelphia, after Joseph
Weisman and Emanuel Gottlieb
Leutze (1816–1868), published
by Peter S. Duval (1831–1879).
Frame manufactured by the
Philadelphia partnership of James
Horton and Josiah A. Waller, c.
1841
Lithograph; original frame
30 x 24 in.

*North Carolina Division of Archives
and History*

heroes," has been advanced by noted historians.[8] Indeed Jefferson was instrumental in the commissions for two of the most significant sculptures of George Washington, the one by Houdon, for the Virginia State Capitol (1785–1789), and that of Canova, for the North Carolina State Capitol (1821–1824) (fig. 190). However, by 1810 Joseph Hopkinson of Philadelphia called for a proper monument to the *pater patriae* and lamented that

> Washington lies neglected. Not a stone tells the stranger where the hero is laid. No proud column declares that his country is grateful. . . . The stranger who, in days to come, shall visit our shore, will exclaim, show me the statue of your WASHINGTON, that I may contemplate the majestic form that encompassed his mighty soul; that I may gaze upon those features once lighted with every virtue; and learn to love virtue as I behold them.[9]

In imitation of the classical tradition of erecting monuments to honor celebrated heroes, on January 6, 1810, the Maryland State Legislature authorized a lottery to raise funds to construct a monument to Washington in Baltimore. By February 1813 a competition was announced, and on July 4, 1815, the cornerstone was laid for a monument designed by Robert Mills, a young South Carolina architect who trained with Benjamin H. Latrobe. By 1825 a column 165 feet 4

inches high was completed, and in 1829 a 14-foot statue of Washington by Italian émigré sculptor Enrico Causici was placed atop the column. Mills's final design contribution to the monument, the cast-iron tripods and fence surrounding the base, was completed by the late 1830s.[10]

Though the Washington Monument in Baltimore was the first permanent structure to honor the father of our country, there had been a series of temporary triumphal arches erected along the route taken by Washington when he made a celebratory tour of the major eastern cities following his inauguration in 1789. While illustrations survive depicting several of these arches, ones that bore a closer relationship to classical Roman precedents were the triumphal arches constructed for the 1824 visit of General Lafayette. Though French, General Lafayette played a role in the American Revolution that made him an American hero. His tour of the United States from August 1824 to September

1825 immortalized him in the eyes of all Americans. In Philadelphia alone, thirteen arches were erected, all designed by William Strickland, the noted American architect of such admired classical structures as the Second Bank of the United States, and his apprentice draftsman, Samuel Honeyman Kneass (fig. 191).

As the most fashionable and avant-garde city in America, Philadelphia put on a splendid display for Lafayette, and "sought not only to imitate but to surpass the triumphs of ancient Rome."[11] However, the wooden arch constructed on Fourth Street was not the most monumental (fig. 192). The grand procession for Lafayette in Philadelphia reached its zenith at Independence

191

WILLIAM STRICKLAND

1829

John Neagle (1796–1865), Philadelphia

Oil on canvas

30 x 25 in.

Yale University Art Gallery; The Mabel Brady Garvan Collection

Hall, where the most elaborate arch was erected, one specifically modeled on the Arch of Lucius Septimius Severus in Rome. Forty-five-feet high, thirty-five-feet wide, and covered with canvas painted in imitation of stone, this construction was crowned with wooden figures of Justice and Wisdom, having "all the beauty and lightness of drapery, of the Grecian school," carved by sculptor William Rush, and Philadelphia's coat of arms painted by Thomas Sully.[12] Strickland's role in this celebration was not limited to classical architectural arches and their

192

TRIUMPHAL ARCH IN HONOR OF LAFAYETTE

1824

Samuel Honeyman Kneass (1806–1858), Philadelphia

Watercolor and ink on paper

21¾ x 30⅝ in.

Courtesy Independence National Historical Park Collection, Philadelphia

193

COVERED URN

1812–1813

Presented to Captain Isaac Hull

Thomas Fletcher (1787–1866)

and Sidney Gardiner (d. 1827),

Philadelphia

Silver

28¼ x 21 x 12½ in.

Collection Hull P. Fulweiler

construction. In addition, he composed a triumphal march entitled "Come Honor the Brave!" that was published by George E. Blake, a Philadelphia music merchant, with an illustration of his most monumental "Grand civic Arch erecting in Chestnut street opposite the State house."

Following the immortalization of our country's founders, the next major opportunity to recognize virtuous acts was the War of 1812. Those exceptional naval officers who performed admirably were honored with parades, orations, and presentations of elaborate pieces of silver. Their valorous deeds were heralded with the hope that they might stir someone else to perform with "distinguished gallantry and conduct. . . in eminent service . . . to his Country." Among the first of this period to be cited and given a major piece of "plate" modeled after classical forms was Captain Isaac Hull, commander of the frigate *Constitution*. Barely two months after war was declared, America won the first major naval victory when within less than half an hour the guns of the *Constitution* had completely toppled all three masts of the British frigate *Guerrière*, leaving her a total wreck. This early victory was applauded for "giving a tone and character to the war," and it was equally significant in bolstering American enthusiasm and in ultimately recognizing a series of celebrated American naval heroes.[13]

Hull, his officers, and crew were showered with celebrations and presentations from Boston to Charleston. Medals presented by Congress (with Latin inscriptions), engraved images of Hull on snuff boxes, and monumental pieces of silver were all part of the creation and commemoration of this new breed of popular American hero. By early September, subscriptions were being raised in the major cities for these presents. While there were precedents in eighteenth-century America for acknowledging valor and virtue with gifts of silver, there was a new and different motive now in these presentations. In Philadelphia, a committee of citizens selected the recently arrived and youthful Boston partners Thomas Fletcher and Sidney Gardiner to fashion "a piece of plate, of the most elegant workmanship, ornamented with appropriate emblems, devices and inscriptions."[14] The covered urn that they designed and executed is decidedly classical in form, with "emblems and devices" that echo French and English sources derived from ancient precedents (fig. 193). Though neither Fletcher nor Gardiner had traveled abroad by this time, their urn bore a striking similarity to one designed by Percier and Fontaine, which was executed by the Parisian silversmith Biennais and exhibited at l'Exposition de l'Industrie in 1806.[15] It was illustrated in *Recueil de Décorations intérieures* (Paris, 1801 and 1812), and it is difficult to ascertain whether or not the designers of Hull's urn had seen an image of the Percier and Fontaine piece; however, the possibility is strong that they saw something resembling it. Nevertheless, the message was clear to all who viewed this monumental, twenty-eight-inch silver urn. Though it celebrated a modern hero, it exuded classical taste and ornament, from the paw feet, anthemions, tridents, heads of Poseidon, acanthus leaves, ram's heads, entwined dolphins, and draped figures of Fame and Fortune to the crowning spread-winged eagle, symbol of Zeus as well as the new republic!

By early 1814, the great urn was finished, and Fletcher proudly wrote to his father: "Our great work the Urn for Capt Hull is at last completed. It weighs 502 ounces pure silver and has cost nearly 2300 dollars. I need not tell you how proud it makes us (we have had thousands to view it, and it is allowed to be the most elegant piece of workmanship in this Country)."[16] Given the exuberance and quality of Fletcher and Gardiner's first major piece of presentation silver, it is not surprising that by the time it was completed they already had commissions for five other significant pieces.[17] The "thousands" who came to view the urn (presumably in their shop) received major exposure to classical aesthetics, as well as superior design and craftsmanship. This urn was such a monumental success for the partnership, it is not surprising that Fletcher chose it as illustrative of his finest production when he had a trade advertisement engraved (fig. 194). Philip Hone was correct when he wrote about "Fletcher & Co," stating that "Nobody in this 'world' of ours hereabouts can compete with them in their kind of work."[18]

194

TRADE CARD: THOMAS
FLETCHER

c. 1822

James H. Young and George
Delleker, Philadelphia
Engraving on wove paper
6¹¹⁄₁₆ x 4⁵⁄₁₆ in. (plate)

The Athenaeum of Philadelphia

Hull's fame did not fade following this single victory, though for the duration of the war his duties were land-based. Gifts acknowledging his valorous act continued through the decade. In 1820, Governor Oliver Wolcott of Connecticut, Hull's native state, praised him for his "undaunted valor" and "distinguished exam-

ple of the union of heroic with civic virtues."[19] These remarks were occasioned by the presentation to Hull of a gold-hilted dress sword made by Nathan Starr, an eminent Middletown, Connecticut, armorer (fig. 195). An elaborately designed and finely wrought sword was a necessary accompaniment to the dress uniform of any American military or naval hero. Great expense and effort were spent on the creation of these symbols of virtuous martial character, and they often evoked classical themes and imagery. At the time that Starr was fashioning the sword for Hull, he was also making one "for Col. R. M. Johnson by order of the Genl. Government"; he further stated that his "blades are equal for beauty and service and cannot be distinguished from the celebrated Damascus blades."[20] The sword that he made for Col. Johnson cost $1200 and was embellished with images of Ceres, Minerva, Hercules, Fame, and an American Eagle. Both swords were presumably presented "in snug handsome cases, made of our native birdseye maple, & lined with velvet."[21] The accessories of a hero's uniform provided one more public expression of Americanized classical themes.

While Philip Hone thought no other silversmiths could compete with Fletcher and Gardiner, a committee of Baltimore citizens felt differently. They commissioned their own native silversmith, Andrew Ellicott Warner, to make the "rich and tasteful service of plate" that was presented to another War of 1812 naval hero, Stephen Decatur. Like Hull, Decatur distinguished himself within the first few months of the war and was responsible for the second major American triumph. On October 25, 1812, he and his crew on the *United States* shot away all three of the topmasts of the British frigate *Macedonia* near Madeira. Decatur was among those heroes of the War of 1812 of whom the city fathers of New York commissioned monumental portraits.[22] In addition to the large version now in New York's City Hall, Sully painted a smaller study while working on the main commission, presumably to assist in the drafting of such a large

canvas (fig. 196). Decatur, in full uniform replete with dress sword, evokes almost a Napoleonic image of heroic demeanor posed beside a fluted column.

Decatur's victories in the Mediterranean at the close of the war were presumably the reason for the Baltimore presentation service. Costing $6,000 and consisting of twelve pieces, the service was exhibited "for the gratification of the citizens for a few days at Mr. F. Lucas, No. 138 Market-Street."[23] The oval dishes, tureens, and ice pails that were shown to the public were spectacular but known forms. However, the candelabrum, weighing 350 ounces, was the most amazing piece in the service, perhaps unlike anything many of those who came to view the service had ever seen (fig. 197). With an overall form in imitation of a Roman tripod, the three double candle-holders were supported by winged caryatids with hoof feet. Great cast-silver garlands of fruit and flowers linked the three female figures, as, beneath them all, a cast figure of Poseidon posed triumphant holding a gold American flag. Massive paw feet with foliate brackets supported the triangular base on which was engraved, "The citizens of Baltimore to Commodore Stephen Decatur, *Rebus gestis insigni: Ob virtutes dilecto*." This appropriate Latin inscription proclaims, "Renowned for his valor, beloved for his virtues."

The overall design of this extraordinary candelabrum echoes antique precedents, but even more closely it suggests known French and English examples made in the first two decades

196

STEPHEN DECATUR

1814

Thomas Sully (1783–1872), Philadelphia

Oil on canvas

33¼ x 23½ in.

The Baltimore Museum of Art: Gift of John D. Schapiro, Baltimore (BMA 1976.83)

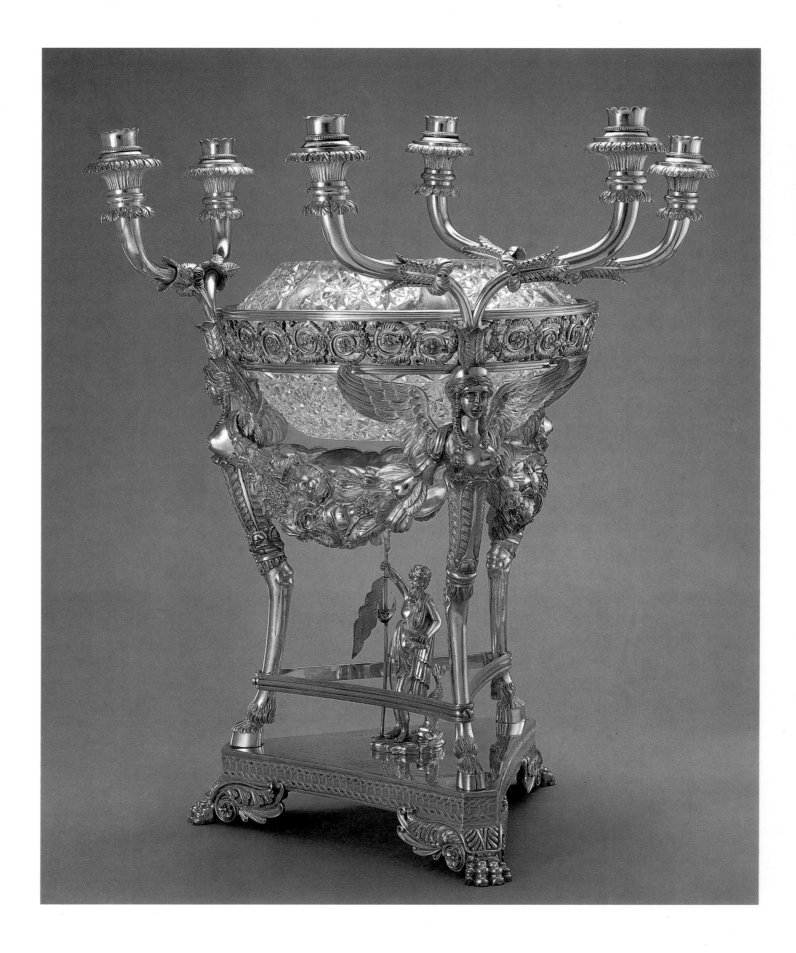

of the nineteenth century.[24] Fashioned almost entirely of cast elements bolted together, it suggests perhaps the hand of a foreign-trained journeyman working in Warner's shop. Did Warner actually design this piece himself? What might he have been looking at, or what firsthand experience or printed sources could he, or a member of his shop, have been inspired by? Was he familiar with similar imported examples owned in the Washington-Baltimore area at the time? Might he even have imported this piece?[25] Among the numerous pieces of classically styled American silver of the period, this candelabrum stands out as one of the most European in inspiration.[26]

With the recognition of numerous illustrious heroes in the early nineteenth century, a tradition was established, and rapidly developed, of recognizing and rewarding a wide spectrum of virtuous acts. People who worked with unselfish dedication for the good of a specific group, or the entire country, were likely to be saluted with a gift of a specially commissioned piece of silver. One need not have won a naval battle or promoted a major engineering feat like the Erie Canal. H. M. Dobbs, president of the New Orleans Mechanic Society, received a handsome silver urn, or wine cooler, in early 1831, marking his twenty-five years of "faithful services" as president of the Society (fig. 198). Stamped with the name "Harland" in a scroll, this classical urn is thought to have been made by Henry Harland, listed in an 1823–1824 New Orleans directory as a watchmaker. However, this rare American form, exhibiting a neatly cast band of grapes and vines and cast foliate handles, suggests the work of a master silversmith, not a watchmaker. Closely related to a wine cooler made and marked by Thomas Fletcher, this urn may have been fabricated elsewhere but purchased and marked by Harland.[27] Fletcher had well-established ties in New Orleans, since his brother James was a commission merchant in that city from 1809 until his death in 1820. Records indicate that Fletcher continued a merchandizing relationship with Louis Sesassier. In 1831 he made "a soup tureen and six covered dishes" for a client in New Orleans.[28] In 1830 New Orleans, the hub city for the vast amount of Mississippi River traffic, had a population of just over 46,000. Rich and growing rapidly, the city had already developed a taste for the classical style through its numerous French connections.

In 1832, the Friends of National Union in Charleston presented Reverend Samuel Gilman with a handsome silver vase made by John Ewan in the antique form so frequently copied by modern porcelain manufacturers (fig. 199). Gilman, a New Englander by birth with strong feelings about the strength of the Union, composed an ode for the Union Party of South Carolina. The ode was sung at a large meeting on July 4, 1831, and on April 19, 1832, Gilman was presented with the silver vase as a "testimony of the high sense which they entertain of the peculiar merits of the Ode." In addition to the presentation inscription on the front of the vase, four verses of the "National Ode," as it was called, were engraved on the reverse of the vase. Gilman's poetic talents as well as his essentially Federalist sympathies made him a political hero among this staunch group of South Carolinians who opposed the prevailing attitude favoring states' rights.

CANDELABRUM

1817

Presented to Stephen Decatur

Andrew Ellicott Warner

(1786–1870), Baltimore

Silver; cut glass

H. 20 in.

Private Collection

Through the 1830s, Americans continued to champion compatriots they perceived as having acted for the good of the whole. Daniel Webster was a well-known legal and political figure by 1830, already having demonstrated his talents many times as a strong constitutional lawyer and a brilliant orator. Like Gilman in Charleston, Webster was devoted to the strength and stability of the Federal union. As a New Englander with vested interests in textile manufacturing, he naturally became a champion of the region's new industrial enterprises that would contribute to the eventual supremacy of American manufacturing. Webster's most heroic speech came in January 1830 with his two-day defense of the constitutional union against South Carolina's advocacy of states' rights and nullification. This brilliant and convincing oration concluded with the inspiring proclamation, "Liberty and Union, now and forever, one and inseparable!" Hence, Webster became known as the "Defender of the Constitution" and was referred to by some as the "Godlike Daniel."

199

VASE

1832

Presented to Reverend Samuel
Gilman

John Ewan (1786–1852),
Charleston, South Carolina

Silver

H. 13 in.

*The Museum of Fine Arts, Houston;
The Bayou Bend Collection, museum
purchase with funds provided by
William James Hill and Miss Ima
Hogg, by exchange*

Even before his 1830 oration in the Senate, members of the Boston Athenaeum and personal friends commissioned artist Chester Harding to execute a full-length portrait of the statesman (fig. 200). Projected to cost $800, Harding spent $100 on a frame made by John Doggett, and in the end was only paid $600 for both painting and frame.[29] Harding's representation of Webster certainly reflected the latter's "Doric substantiality," which one admirer noted was "inimitable and unwasting."[30] Standing nobly beside a table, the great man is juxtaposed with a statue of Washington in classical drapery. The equation is obvious, Washington and Webster: two great statesmen, both humble men, lovers of liberty, and advocates of the Constitution.

The most significant public recognition of Webster came in 1835 when the citizens of Boston presented him with a monumental silver vase weighing 400 ounces and fashioned after the famed Warwick vase (fig. 201). This was not the first time this icon of antiquity had served as inspiration for modern silver, for in England it was reproduced numerous times in silver, bronze, and ceramic. When Thomas Fletcher visited London in 1815 and toured the shop of Rundell, Bridge and Rundell, he had seen a magnificent silver reproduction of the Warwick vase. Subsequently Fletcher modeled not only the presentation urns for DeWitt Clinton on this famous vase, but he also incorporated an adaptation of the vase into his 1829 presentation piece for Hugh Maxwell (fig. 99).[31] The Webster Vase, as it came to be known in Boston, though marked by the firm of Jones, Lows and Ball was actually fashioned by Samuel Ward and Obadiah Rich.[32] Exactly who determined that this should be the form used for Webster's present is unknown, but Ward and Rich may have been familiar with engravings of the original Warwick vase through its illustration in publications such as Henry Moses's *A Collection of Vases, Altars, Paterae* (London, 1814). Even if they did not have access to a correct delineation of the vase (and their interpretation indicates they may not

200

DANIEL WEBSTER

1828–1830; 1849–1851

Chester Harding (1792–1886), Boston. Frame by John Doggett (1780–1857), Roxbury, Massachusetts

Oil on canvas; original frame 93¼ x 58¹³⁄₁₆ in.

Boston Athenaeum; Gift of several subscribers, 1832

have), they certainly must have known the illustration, and brief account, on the frontispiece of *The Penny Magazine* for September 15, 1832.

This monumental, classically inspired vase was presented to Webster on October 12, 1835, at the Odeon in Boston. Prior to this occasion, the vase was on view at the retail store of Jones, Lows and Ball for the public to inspect. This assured any citizen the opportunity to see at least a copy of this magnificent relic of antiquity, regardless of the fact that the original was made of marble and weighed 8¼ tons. The vase was inscribed "To DANIEL WEBSTER, Defender of the CONSTITUTION of the United States; From the Citizens of BOSTON, October, 12th, 1835." Upon accepting this acknowledgment of his efforts on behalf of his countrymen, Webster gave an oration of over an hour, recognizing that the presentation was "to pay respect

to this Constitution . . . your sense of its value, your devotion to its true principles . . . not to pay an ostentatious personal compliment . . . not to manifest attachment to individuals."[33] While not a classical hero, in the eyes of his supporters in Boston Webster was a modern hero worthy of celebration and adulation by his peers.

The ancients acknowledged valor and virtuous behavior not only in government and military actions but also in competitive sporting events, as the remains of stadia all over the classical world attest. While some American citizens in the early nineteenth century might have argued against the morality and virtue of praising horse racing in particular, those involved in the activity found it imbued with classical overtones. Most obvious was their proclivity to give horses classical names such as Priam, Ariadne, Hermaphrodite, Cincinnatus, and Little Venus. More visually and materially suggestive of classical influence were the significant prizes, or silver presentation cups, awarded successful competitors. Often copies of ancient urn forms, some were made by American silversmiths, though occasionally they were the product of English shops.

During the first decade of the nineteenth century, between 1803 and 1806, the Philadelphia silversmith Samuel Williamson made one silver "punch urn" and three silver "Race Cups" for the Georgetown, D.C., firm of Burnett and Rigden, who in turn retailed them to the Washington Jockey Club.[34] Though it is unknown whether Williamson designed these himself, it is possible that they may have been designed by a journeyman working in his shop. Between 1803 and 1812, the English engraver William Carr worked for Williamson. Having come to Philadelphia in 1800, Carr may have been familiar with English racing cups and urns in the classical style. The "Race Cup" that Williamson billed Burnett and Rigden for on September 21, 1805, differed in design from the first two ordered (fig. 202). The account book entry distinctly noted this dramatic difference seen in the classically inspired "Snake Handles":

To One Race Cup	
wt 93 1/2 oz @ 13 pr oz	156.87
Engraving horse	10 "
Chasing of Snake Handles and Horse	4 "
Gilding of Ditto	19 "
Engraving of Ditto	5 "
Packing Box to Ditto	.62
	195.49[35]

Not only did this "Race Cup" have sinuous snake handles, similar to those on cups designed by Robert Adam and others,[36] but the handles may have been gilt. An interesting and practical feature of all three cups lay in the fact that the finials detach, and when the cover is removed it can be inverted and used as a punch bowl. Presumably the cup was filled with spirituous punch, which was then poured into the bowl and passed about in celebration.

On Friday, November 1, 1805, the *Alexandria Expositor* announced: "We have not heard the particulars of the 3rd days racing, but understand that Mr. Bradley Beans, Mare won the two mile heats for the City purse, and that the single four mile heat for the Subscription Cup, was won by Gen. Ridgeleys horse Post-Boy."[37] This was the second year in a row that Post-Boy won the cup, and the following year Ridgely's horse Maid of Oaks would win a third cup, all fashioned in Williamson's Philadelphia shop. The three silver race cups that Ridgely probably displayed at his Maryland mansion, "Hampton," contributed to the classical tradition and spirit that was embodied in many other aspects and furnishings at the lavish country house.

203

REGENCY COVERED
RACE CUP

1817/1818

Presented as a trophy in 1818 at
the Charleston Races, South
Carolina
Paul Storr (1771–1844), London
Silver-gilt (sterling standard)
H. 13 in.

*The Chrysler Museum, Norfolk,
Virginia; Gift of Walter P. Chrysler,
Jr., in honor of Roy B. Martin, Jr.*

Charleston, South Carolina, claimed to have had the first Jockey Club in England or America, having established one as early as 1734. With the eighteenth-century tradition of importing racing stock from England, it is not surprising that in the first quarter of the nineteenth century a number of the race cups presented for success in the Charleston races were produced by some of England's finest silversmiths in the classical style. Surviving today is a most remarkable example made for the 1818 Charleston races by Paul Storr, working for Rundell, Bridge and Rundell, Goldsmiths to the Crown. It ingeniously combines classical form and motifs with American symbolism (fig. **203**). Fishtailed centaurs holding tridents, laurel wreaths for victory, and grapevines for Bacchanalian celebration ornament the body of the cup. The motifs on the cover combine the stars and stripes with an American eagle grasping an olive branch and lightning bolts in its claws, and the entire piece has a gold wash.

By the early nineteenth century, for Americans the value of the classical concept of virtue began to wane, as they fashioned their own version of virtue, which "flowed from the citizen's participation in society, not in government."[38] This modern American virtue has been termed a "new domesticated virtue," and its importance to American culture has been cited as not only helping to "reconcile classical republicanism with modernity and commerce," but also in providing "the basis for all reform movements of the nineteenth century, and indeed for all subsequent modern liberal thinking."[39] With the new republic solidly entrenched, Americans not only replaced classical heroes with modern ones, but they replaced the concept of classical virtue with a more useful individual, family-oriented virtue. This important reshaping of the concept of virtue by Americans was evidenced in the title of a two-volume publication, *The Moral Monitor . . . Displaying the Importance and Enforcing the Observance of INDIVIDUAL AND SOCIAL VIRTUE* (Worcester, Massachusetts, 1801). This new domesticated virtue applied equally to upper-class men and women, and by the second decade of the nineteenth century the importance of women's virtues was growing in recognition.

Even by the late eighteenth century, Benjamin Rush, who was instrumental in founding the Young Ladies' Academy in Philadelphia, promoted the idea that "it is incumbent upon us to make ornamental accomplishments yield to principles and knowledge, in the education of our women."[40] Rush's statement foreshadowed the developments toward more serious academic education for upper- and middle-class women that would begin in the second quarter of the nineteenth century. Less than three decades later, in 1810, Joseph Hopkinson of Philadelphia expressed the enlightened perspective that "In the present state of society, woman is inseparably connected with everything that civilizes, refines, and sublimates man."[41] Increasingly upper-class women were recognized as "social beings," and their education was "calculated to unite, in the female character, cultivation of talents, and habits of economy and usefulness; particularly *domestic* habits . . . the important duties of her sex—of a *daughter*, a *wife*, a *mother*, or a *mistress of a family*."[42] In the previous century, women of upper-class families were sent to schools, or taught by tutors at home, to learn to read, do needlework, and play the piano, accomplishments that would "show" well, but these pursuits provided limited stimulation to their minds and failed to prepare them for broader conversation with their male counterparts. By the 1820s, this limited education was recognized as inadequate preparation for women "to fill the responsible character of wives and mothers," and eventually the nature of female education was expanded to prepare women "to educate their children . . . to make them enlightened as statesmen, valiant as soldiers, and virtuous as men."[43]

Upper- and middle-class women were not seen simply as mothers but as "the framer of their [children's] infant minds" and thus responsible for shaping "the character of the future man."[44]

There was a new emphasis on the worth of women and their responsibilities in raising children, presiding over the family, regulating the income, making the home a sweet refuge, and being an "enlightened associate and dear companion" to her husband.[45] Women were obliged to believe that their domestic employments would be "the source of unnumbered pleasures," and that "the sphere of woman's duty is to be looked for in private and domestic life." "To elevate, refine, and embellish all that comes within her circle" was the mandate for mothers, who would hopefully raise virtuous children possessing sentiments of duty and gratitude.[46]

A growing female academy movement by the end of the first decade of the nineteenth century led to more enlightened and advanced education for many upper-class women over the next two decades. Along with this growth in opportunities for female education came earnest efforts to introduce more academic studies, in addition to music, dancing, and drawing. Subjects such as ancient and modern languages, geography, history, mythology, natural science, chemistry, mineralogy, and philosophy were introduced in some academies and seminaries, as well as eventually in public schools for women. By 1839 in Boston, the innovative and educated Margaret Fuller held a series of "Conversations for Women" at the Boston Athenaeum, where "more Greek than Bostonian [was] spoken" as she met with friends to discuss Grecian mythology.[47] While these discussions represent an unusual type of education among upper-class women, they were nevertheless an indication of the desire and need that many women had for higher education and enlightened dialogue with others of their kind.

From Boston to Troy, New York, to Charleston, South Carolina, upper- (and some middle-) class young women found increasing opportunities to improve their minds and master "the cultivation of those graces which, in a greater or lesser degree, according to their respective stations in life, will recommend them to society."[48] The Troy Female Seminary was founded in 1821 by Emma Willard, who recognized that if "women were properly fitted by instruction, they would be likely to teach children better than the other sex," and hence might become teachers of children from other classes.[49] A large number of these schools were established by French émigrés like Madame Rivardi in Philadelphia, who modeled her avant-garde curriculum and dedication to serious female education on the well-known school of Madame Campan in Paris. In March 1823 Mrs. M. R. Meyniac of Charleston advertised in the *Courier* that she intended "to draw from similar European establishments those improvements in the System of Education which adorn or dignify female character."

Images depicting the activities that taught social accomplishments at these schools are rare, hence the identification of *The Crowning of Flora* as a painting by Jacob Marling of the May Day celebration at the Raleigh Academy in North Carolina represents an important visual document (fig. 204).[50] This annual event, reminiscent of ancient classical awards ceremonies where laurel wreaths were placed on the heads of the victors, was recorded in the Lynchburg, Virginia, *Echo* on July 10, 1816:

204

THE CROWNING OF FLORA

c. 1815

Jacob Marling (1774–1833),
Raleigh, North Carolina

Oil on canvas

30⅛ x 39⅛ in. (frame)

*The Chrysler Museum, Norfolk,
Virginia; gift of Edgar William and
Bernice Chrysler Garbisch, 80.181.20*

On the first day of May, the young ladies belonging to the Raleigh female academy assembled under the wide spreading trees which embosom their building, and proceeded to the election of a queen. . . . She was conducted to the rural throne [and] crowned with a chaplet of flowers. . . . [An] address to the queen was read, by Miss Anne W. Clark, of Georgia. . . . The echoes of the grove were awakened by the melody of music.[51]

The announcement ended with a brief advertisement for the exhibition of the "likeness of the May queen, as she appeared in her ensigns of royalty," which was sketched by Mr. Marling, who was "so well known for his skill and taste in painting." While Marling was an accomplished master who had taught students from Albany, New York, to Petersburg, Virginia, it was his wife, Louisa, who became the drawing and painting teacher at the academy in the spring of 1815. It has been suggested that the tall gentleman on the far right in the painting may be Marling himself, and the woman in the hat seated on the far left, Mrs. Marling.

Another evocative image of female students is seen in the sophisticated and detailed watercolor entitled *The Drawing Class*, by an unknown artist about 1815 (fig. 205). While nineteenth-century advertisements of drawing masters that offer "instruction in DRAWING, from nature by the rules of Perspective simplified . . . instruction in a new style of painting . . . applied to wood, glass, silk, and paper" are numerous, along with period manuals for drawing and painting, interior views of these schools are remarkably rare.[52] Drawing was deemed a most acceptable accomplishment for young ladies of means since it was "so conducive to refinement of [the] mind" and "at once useful and ornamental." Additionally, ladies were encouraged in this pursuit because it "gives new interest to the visible creation, and awakens in the mind new sources of enjoyment."[53]

The detail evidenced in this watercolor is particularly interesting for the furnishing of the room, with its long tables, benches, watercolor box, and other apparatus, as well as the manner in which the curtains are pulled back to allow for maximum light. Of special interest are the works, perhaps models, hanging on the walls; the large classical landscape on the right suggests a composition after Poussin or Claude, while the figural piece on the far left wall appears to be draped in classical garb or ceremonial robes. The views out of the windows indicate a city or townscape with brick buildings close together. It has been suggested that this scene may record a class at Robertson's Columbia Academy of Painting, a school in New York City between 1792 and 1821.[54]

In addition to drawing and painting on paper or canvas, ladies with leisure also applied their newly developed skills to more "useful and ornamental" productions such as small work boxes,

205

THE DRAWING CLASS

c. 1820

American

Watercolor on paper

14⅜ x 22 in.

Gift of Emily Crane Chadbourne, 1951.202, photograph © 1992, The Art Institute of Chicago, All Rights Reserved

as well as larger pieces of furniture like work tables and dressing tables. The colorful work box in figure 206 was owned and presumably painted by Alice Upson of Hartford County, Connecticut. As recommended in period publications, Miss Upson chose "the best shape . . . an octagon" for her box and ornamented each side "in striking and beautiful colours" with "pictorial embellishments . . . drawn and coloured from nature, or good copies."[55] The scene with which she ornamented the top of her box appears to be drawn from classical mythology, depicting a young maiden with her lyre awakening a sleeping old man. The overall composition and specificity of this painting suggest that the author was working from a print source, which she copied with truthfulness and proficiency.

206

WORKBOX

c. 1820–1830

New England

Inlaid maple with polychrome painting

W. 12 in.

From the collections of Henry Ford Museum & Greenfield Village, Dearborn, Michigan

Young ladies' lessons in ancient history, mythology, modern language and literature, and religion seem to have been integrally linked to their accomplishments in fine needlework and embroidery. Most of the pictorial needlework produced by young American students in the early nineteenth century was copied from engraved prints and drawings. Women like Susanna Rowson, of Boston, and Mrs. Saunders and Miss Beach, of Dorchester, Massachusetts, who ran female academies, usually maintained "collections of fine Drawings, English, and French Books, &c. provided for the use of pupils."[56] The academy run by Mrs. Saunders and Miss Beach could boast of a library of more than fifteen-hundred volumes, probably inherited by Clementina Beach from her father in 1797.[57] Hence, students might copy an illustration from a contemporary novel, a play by Shakespeare, the Bible, or classical mythology. The latter was especially favored by young ladies, perhaps for the heroic values and moral instruction that their teachers felt it might instill in them.

In 1807 Frances Mecia Campbell was attending Mrs. Saunders and Miss Beach's Academy when she wrought a needlework depicting "Telemachus and Mentor in the Island of Calipso" (fig. 207). Among the prints, perhaps drawn from books, available to students at the school must have been one engraved in 1786 by Francesco Bartolozzi after a painting by the English artist Angelica Kauffmann. The print that Frances Campbell copied depicts Telemachus, son of Odysseus, as he is searching for his father on the island of the nymph Calypso. Mentor, his tutor and an old friend of his father, is shown on the left, being led away as young ladies ply Telemachus with fruit, flowers, and drink. While Mentor (actually Athena in the guise of Mentor) is supposed to be giving Telemachus wise advice, the latter is being seduced by ladies who do not wish him to find

Odysseus. The story of Telemachus was a popular mythological theme in the material and cultural life of this period, as is evidenced by Andrew Jackson's choice in 1836 to decorate his stairhall at "The Hermitage" near Nashville, Tennessee, with French scenic wallpaper illustrating "*Les Paysages de Telemaque dans l'ile de Calypso*."[58]

As was the practice at Mrs. Saunders and Miss Beach's Academy, reverse-painted glasses inscribed with the student's name, the academy name, and the title of the picture, along with an appropriate gilt frame, were ordered from the looking glass manufactory of John Doggett in Roxbury, Massachusetts. Doggett's accounts record an entry on September 11, 1807, "To 1 Embroidery Frame & Glass for Miss Campbell . . . $11.00."[59] While there is no doubt that Miss Campbell did the embroidery, the superb quality of expression seen in the faces of the figures, as well as the background, suggest the hand of a more accomplished artist, possibly one of the mistresses of the school.

Young Sally Wheeler of Lynn, Massachusetts, portrayed another mythological theme in her needlework of "The Parting of Hector and Andromache" (fig. 208). Probably executed between

207

NEEDLEWORK PICTURE: TELEMACHUS AND MENTOR IN THE ISLAND OF CALIPSO

1807

Frances Mecia Campbell at Mrs. Saunders and Miss Beach's Academy, Dorchester, Massachusetts. Frame by John Doggett (1780–1857), Roxbury, Massachusetts

Silk embroidery and watercolor on silk; original gilded wood frame with églomisé mat

18 x 20½ in. (frame)

The Baltimore Museum of Art: Gift of Mr. and Mrs. James R. Herbert Boone; Gift of Maria Lovell Eaton and Mrs. Charles R. Weld; Gift of J. Gilman D'Arcy Paul; Bequest of John Henry Scarff; Gift of Florence Hendler Trupp, Baltimore; and Gift of the Women's Eastern Shore Society, by exchange (BMA 1989.352)

1810 and 1815, prior to Miss Wheeler's marriage in 1815, the exact print source has not been identified, though Angelica Kauffmann did paint this subject, albeit rather differently.[60] The parting of Hector from Andromache and his young son, Astyanax, was one of the most touching passages in the *Iliad*, as Andromache must have had a presentiment of her husband's impending death. Whether Miss Wheeler actually read this ancient epic poem thought to be by the Greek poet Homer is unknown. If she did, she might have drawn her source of inspiration from an illustration in the translation she had at hand. Although the school Miss Wheeler attended is not identified on the painted glass that covers her embroidery, as in the case with Frances Mecia Campbell's work, hers was also handsomely glazed and framed.

Ladies' work boxes and work tables were a necessary accoutrement for those who produced fine needlework, as most young women did at least prior to marriage and the more pressing needs of their domestic duties. Before the Revolution, women often kept their sewing, darning, and knitting in baskets, as suggested by contemporary prints, paintings, and watercolors. By the 1780s and 1790s though, a specialized form of furniture began to appear that was designed especially for use by ladies. Usually made with two narrow drawers, the top one often was divided into compartments to hold the various implements and threads necessary for sewing, while the lower one, having no bottom, held a fabric work bag attached to the inside of the drawer frame. Hence, once the drawer was pulled out, a lady could simply place her work in progress into this bag, or pouch, for safe keeping. Sometimes the top drawer was also fitted with a baize-covered writing surface that could be raised on an angle for reading or letter writing. In his 1803 *The Cabinet Dictionary*, Thomas Sheraton referred to this form as a "Pouch Table, or Table with a Bag, used by the ladies to work at, in which bag they deposit their fancy needle work."[61] Being relatively light, these pieces of furniture almost always had casters, making it easier to move them into place in front of a chair or sofa, as well as to locate them closer to the best source of light.

By the second decade of the nineteenth century, pouch or work tables were produced in America in a variety of forms with classical overtones, always with regional features that often related them to other forms of tables from the same geographic area. Tables with columns, lyre supports, and carved central pedestals were produced from Boston to Baltimore. In 1821, George Ticknor of Boston married Anna Eliot, daughter of the prosperous merchant Samuel Eliot. While well off, the Ticknors were not essentially extravagant, but the work table that George purchased for Anna, perhaps soon after their marriage, represents the finest Boston classical furniture of the 1820s (fig. 209). Related in overall form to French design sources of the period, as well as French dressing tables owned by Harriet Fulton (fig. 7) and Joseph Bonaparte, this table combines classical design, extraordinary materials, and superior workmanship.[62] The highly figured rosewood veneer and gilt-brass moldings that accent the overall form made this fashionable table quite costly. Designed to function both as a writing and a sewing table, its top drawer once had an adjustable surface with compartments to hold ink and other implements. The lower drawer still retains three neatly made mahogany trays for sewing notions, all surrounding a fabric-covered hinged lid that lifts to reveal the pouch, or work bag.[63]

209

WORK TABLE

c. 1815–1825

Boston

Rosewood veneer, mahogany; stamped and cast gilt brass

29 x 22 x 18 in.

Hood Museum, Dartmouth College, Hanover, New Hampshire; Gift of Mrs. William Dexter

While some work boxes were decorated by young ladies themselves, elegantly veneered work boxes were also made by cabinetmakers in imitation of more monumental, classically derived forms. The diminutive box made and labeled by the Newport upholsterer Simeon Hazard recalls contemporary cellarettes whose forms copied ancient sarcophagi (fig. 210). Hazard's label, affixed to the bottom of the box, is bounded by a bold Greek key motif and announces his "FURNITURE AND Upholstery Warehouse." The ogee-shaped top of the box lifts to reveal a removable upper tray fitted with compartments specifically for spools of thread and other sewing implements. Since this is the only known piece of furniture labeled by Hazard, a question arises whether the rest of his production as dramatically reflected classical influences.

210

WORK BOX

c. 1830–1847

Simeon Hazard (1817–1855), Newport, Rhode Island

Mahogany, mahogany veneer; ivory

12¼ x 13¾ x 11 in.

Museum of Art, Rhode Island School of Design, Providence; Gift of Mr. and Mrs. John S. Walton (76.198)

During the first half of the nineteenth century, music and dance became even more important in the cultivation of taste in young ladies and gentlemen than it had been in the eighteenth century. Furthermore, this attraction to the muse was transferred to a broader spectrum of the population as more and more families enjoyed informal, familial evenings centered around musical activities. Music was viewed as "a means of improving your taste, and giving refinement and delicacy to your emotions."[64] In addition young women were assured that "It will be a resource in adversity, will enable you to enliven domestic scenes, and should you be mothers, it will render you capable of instructing your children, or at least of knowing when they are well instructed."[65]

In 1806 Rosalie Stier Calvert of Maryland communicated to her sister her staunch belief that "music is an indispensable talent for a young lady. Dancing is even more essential. We start children dancing here at age five."[66] It was equally important for young gentlemen as well as ladies to learn to dance, since many social pleasures encompassed various celebrations and balls where it was essential to know the rudiments of dance. Occasionally there were classical allusions at these balls, as noted at a "fancy-ball" given by Mrs. Perez Morton of Boston in the early years of the nineteenth century. It seems that on this occasion

a *pas de deux*, arranged by Duport, a fashionable French dancing-master of the close of the last century, was danced by young [Lucius Manlius] Sargent and his friend [David] Sears in the characters of Cupid and Zephyr. Mr. Sargent does not particularize which was which; but to those of us who subsequently became familiar with the lives and lineaments of these two prominent citizens, either one of the winged mythological characters would seem better suited to the graceful figure and benignant countenance of Mr. Sears than to the stalwart form and rugged aspect of his partner.[67]

Young children were occasionally portrayed in classical roles, as has already been seen in the portrait of William Van Rensselaer as "Cupid" (fig. 123). In the charming portrait of Julia Eliza Montgomery Livingston, this winsome maiden appears as perhaps a muse, or possibly Psyche (fig. 211). Her pose and flowing diaphanous Greek dress recall figures depicted on ancient vases. There is also a similarity to several bas-reliefs executed by the noted Danish-born sculptor Bertel Thorvaldsen, who studied and worked in Italy from 1797 to 1819. The well-known "attitudes" portrayed by Lady Emma Hamilton, the second wife of Sir William Hamilton (and mistress of Lord Nelson), also seem to be evoked by this striking image.[68]

Julia Eliza Livingston was the daughter of Edward Livingston. However, since her mother died when she was only seven, leaving three young children, she was raised at "Massena," the home of her uncle, John Livingston. Attributed to John Vanderlyn and undated, it is possible that this may be a posthumous portrait. Miss Livingston died in 1814 at age twenty, and the symbolism of the butterfly seen in the upper right-hand corner could imply a state of resurrection.[69]

The image of young Julia Eliza Livingston visually echoes the verbal imagery of a popular book of poetry in the first half of the nineteenth century.

> With twenty chords my lyre is hung,
>   And while I wake them all for thee,
> Thou, O, virgin, wild and young,
>   Disport'st in airy levity.[70]

In 1800 the Irish poet Thomas Moore published *Odes of Anacreon*, a translation of poems presumed to be the work of that Greek poet. Traditionally Anacreon was thought of as a total voluptuary, and his songs sing of life filled with love, wine, and merriment. Hence, Moore's verse exhibits the same lightness and freedom, the same type of muselike levity embodied in the airy pose of Miss Livingston. Rosalie Calvert owned and read Moore's odes, and in 1805 she sent her brother, Charles, then living in Antwerp, "four books of poems by Thomas Moore," remarking that she had "often read them and with renewed pleasure each time."[71]

Thomas Crawford, the American sculptor living in Rome since 1835, must also have been familiar with Thomas Moore's Odes of Anacreon, for he chose Ode LXXII as inspiration for a simple yet impressive bas-relief sculpture (fig. 212). No doubt an echo of the work of the master Thorvaldsen, Crawford's interpretation comes close to the grace and expression of an ancient bas-relief. His handling of drapery in combination with symbols of music, merriment, and wine

(in the ewer and grapevines) heralded this as a work of "rare beauty" upon its arrival in Boston in June 1843.[72] When shown at the Boston Athenaeum's annual exhibition on June 20, its lyrical and poetic quality must have reinforced the contemporary notion that music was one of the most pleasant "interludes in the great drama of life's duties."[73]

Morality, virtue, refined taste, and a cultivated mind were all admired qualities for a woman, mother, and wife to possess in the early nineteenth century. When Philip Hone of New York met Mrs. Jared Sparks, a recent bride, he remarked upon her virtues: "She is one of the most interesting women I ever saw . . . not what would be called a perfect beauty, but with a face expressive as one of Raphael's Madonnas, and a form of Grecian mold. This lady writes well, paints beautifully, and excels in music. She is going to Boston, where they know how to appreciate such characters."[74] To excel in music was indeed desirable, for by the 1830s musical instruments were found in many prosperous upper- and middle-class homes, most likely a piano-forte, either square or cabinet. A fashionable practice, as advertised by painter Lewis Paduani in Charleston, in 1824, was for young women to have a likeness taken "in the act of performing on the Piano

Forte, the breadth of the Picture from 6 to 10 inches or large as life, executed upon the lowest terms."[75] In 1829, it was "estimated that twenty-five hundred Piano Fortes, of the aggregate value of $750,000, were made this year in the United States, of which nine hundred were made in Philadelphia, eight hundred in New York, seven hundred and seventeen in Boston, and a considerable number in Baltimore."[76]

George E. Blake's illustrated advertisement for his piano-forte manufactory on South 5th Street in Philadelphia graphically suggests that owning and playing a piano-forte elevates one to a state of refinement and taste (fig. 213). For many years Blake maintained a "music Library," also advertising that he rented pianos as well as selling quantities of bound sheet music, a large and lucrative trade given the popularity of music in the period. The classical allusions seen in the bust atop the piano, as well as the Grecian hairstyle, profile, and dress, amplify the inference that ladies accomplished on this instrument possessed classical taste as well as domestic virtue. Presumably excellence in music was appreciated in Philadelphia as well as Boston!

The elegant rosewood-veneered piano-forte labeled by Simon Sweitzer of Philadelphia (working 1829–1833) is testimony to the richness that was often lavished upon these important instruments (fig. 214). An upright, or cabinet, piano, its added ornament of gilt-stenciled decoration, brass candlearms, column mounts, and carved paw feet with *vert antique* and bronzed patina all combine to mark this as a superior product. The sophisticated case is closely related to pianos labeled by Charles Pommer and C.F.L. Albrecht, both German émigré craftsmen who came to Philadelphia in 1811–1813 and 1822 respectively.[77] Sweitzer's name suggests that he might also

212

ANACREON ODE LXXII

1842

Thomas Crawford (1813–1857), Rome

Marble bas-relief

Diam. 26⅛ in.

Boston Athenaeum; Gift of several subscribers, 1843

214 opposite

Musical evenings in the 1830s were an important part of American social and cultural life as is amply demonstrated by the large production of piano-fortes like the one shown here made by Simon Sweitzer in Philadelphia, c. 1829–1833. Other equipage necessary for a music salon were stools with seats that raised and lowered, stands (sometimes in the form of lyres) to hold books or sheets of music, and other elegant instruments such as imported harps. This ensemble is seen in a room from Waterloo Row, c. 1818, designed by Robert Mills and built in Baltimore.

George E. Blake, N°13 S° 5° S° Phil°

PIANO-FORTE MAKER, &°

have been of German (or Swiss) birth, or at least of that ancestry. The important stylistic and technical contributions made by German immigrants during this period have been well documented, although at present Sweitzer's background is unknown.[78]

Simon Sweitzer first appeared in Philadelphia directories (1828–1829) listed as a cabinetmaker, and later simply with the notation "manufactory" (1831–1833), suggesting that he operated a cabinetmaking establishment. Hence, he may have been supplying Albrecht, and possibly others, with piano-forte cases. The gilt-stenciled decoration, meant to imitate more expensive inlaid or cast-brass ornament, is related both in technique and pattern to the decoration on a rosewood-veneered bedroom suite made for William Wurtz of Philadelphia and attributed to Isaac Jones.[79] The indigo-dyed modern silk that conceals the works of the piano-forte is a replacement based on fragments of what was believed to be the original blue silk. While little else is known of Sweitzer's production, Albrecht's thriving business included exporting pianos to New Orleans, Richmond, New York, and Cincinnati.[80]

Whether playing a piano, harp, or other instrument, it was useful to have a specialized stool, the seat of which could swivel. These stools were made in a variety of forms, but most usually either a central pedestal with four paw feet or circular with four turned legs. By the 1820s and 1830s music stools with whimsical carved dolphins as the side seat rails were produced in the urban centers of New York and Philadelphia (fig. 215). The tails of the dolphins usually curved upward at the rear and terminated in a tight curl. The rear rail joining the dolphins' tails was usually turned and carved, echoing the carved pedestal and legs. An innovative American form, these dolphins echo those on other furniture and on all manner of useful objects from silverware to printing presses.

The harp is a very classical and most ancient instrument, and thus very appropriate for any accomplished young lady to master in the early nineteenth century. While having one's portrait painted "in the act of performing on the Piano Forte" might have been an indication of musical virtue, having one's portrait painted with a harp presented the ultimate image of a young woman of taste and accomplishment. Louisa Catherine Johnson Adams, Susan Gaston Donaldson, and Eliza Eichelberger Ridgely are but a few of the cultured women who were painted with harps.

During the first half of the nineteenth century most harps owned and used in America were made abroad. The one that Eliza Ridgely owned was purchased in London by her father in 1817. Made by the firm of Sebastian Erard, it is similar to others also owned by young Americans.[81] As a student at Miss Lyman's Institution in Philadelphia, Miss Ridgely became "a lady of learning as well as accomplishments," and evidence suggests that she was a serious student of music and a very competent harpist. Her additional courses of study at Miss Lyman's included natural history, botany, *Les Belles Lettres,* English grammar, Italian, and drawing.[82]

The harp shown in figure 214 was owned by Sophronia Pickerell when she was a student at Georgetown Academy in 1839–1845, and like Eliza Ridgely's harp it was made by a London firm, Schwieso, Grosjean and Company. Fine gilt harps were not only to be found in Eastern urban areas but in the Midwest as well. In 1832, young Clarissa Stoddart came to America from England with her family, bringing the Erard harp she had purchased in 1827. In her journal she described how they had sailed up the Hudson River and crossed New York State in sleighs and box sleds, all the while transporting her precious harp—and a piano-forte—securely crated.[83] Having traveled down the Allegheny and Ohio Rivers, the Stoddart family finally settled in Cincinnati, Ohio, where no doubt her London-made harp was much admired.

Eliza Ridgely was barely fifteen when Sully painted the striking portrait of her, clad in a Greek dress and tuning the strings of a harp that Sully had in his studio (fig. 216). Just ten years later she became the bride of John Ridgely, the third owner of "Hampton," a country house located in the lush rolling hills just beyond Baltimore. By then Mrs. Ridgely was a cultured and knowledgeable

CLASSICAL TASTE IN AMERICA

woman, whose taste for fashionable furnishings and fine art was quite cosmopolitan. In 1832, she and her husband gave a splendid entertainment at Hampton, which the *Baltimore American* described:

> Within the doors I found true hospitality where I am informed it has long presided; . . . good judgment and taste seem to have provided most amply: for neither the head nor the ear could devise nor desire any change. . . . The entertainments were all social and intellectual; presenting a fine opportunity to grow in knowledge and grace. . . . The repast was such as refinement alone could prepare . . . among the most hospitable, amiable, and refined.[84]

Like the Ridgelys, many Americans of varying social and economic levels strove to adorn their domestic lives with taste and refinement, as well as knowledge and grace. Nearly fifty years after the new republic was founded, the virtue and morality so highly admired in classical heroes was now centered in the American home. No longer did the people of this new nation have to look to the ancients for this inspiration, for they had transferred the concept of virtue to their own American heroes as well as their homes. While they had embraced the popular classical taste of European centers in their furnishings and fashions, it was more like a veneer covering an increasingly distinctive American psyche. Intellectual learning, knowledge of the ancients, their lives and habitats, had pervaded America. Classically inspired European goods had infiltrated the houses of the well to do. Yet when American patrons and artisans reinterpreted these sources, it was with an American accent—or classical taste American style.

CLASSICAL TASTE IN AMERICA

NOTES

PREFACE

1. Hugh Honour, "Neo-classicism," in *The Age of Neo-classicism* (London: Arts Council of Great Britain, 1972), p. xxiv.

2. Henry Moses, *A Collection of Vases, Altars, Paterae, Tripods, Candelabra, Sarcophagi, &c.* (London, 1814), n.p.

3. For a complete examination of the earliest visual evidence of classical motifs introduced into America on imported objects, see Graham Hood, "Early neoclassicism in America," *The Magazine Antiques* 140 (December 1991), pp. 978–985.

INTRODUCTION

1. Quoted in Myrtle A. Cline, *American Attitudes toward the Greek War of Independence, 1821–1828* (Atlanta, 1930), p. 28.

2. Other countries, such as India, were sometimes introduced into the sequence. *Massachusetts Magazine*, April 1795, p. 43; Hugh Honour, *Neo-classicism*, rev. ed. (Harmondsworth, England: Penguin Books, 1977), p. 50–51, 59; William Dunlap, *History of the Rise and Progress of the Arts of Design in the United States*, 1834, rev. ed., ed. Alexander Wyckoff, 3 vols. (New York: Benjamin Blom, 1965), 1, p. 4.

3. *Port Folio* 12 (1814), p. 559.

4. Dunlap, *Rise and Progress*, 1, p. 1–2.

5. Quoted in Linda K. Kerber, *Federalists in Dissent: imagery and Ideology in Jeffersonian America* (Ithaca, N.Y., Cornell University Press, 1970), p. 125; Robert C. Winthrop, A.M., "Memoir of the Hon. David Sears, A.M.," in *Massachusetts Historical Society Proceedings*, 2d ser., 2 (April 1886), p. 52.

6. One author who makes the connection between American and ancient democracy is William H. Pierson in *American Buildings and Their Architects* (Garden City, N.Y.: Doubleday and Company, 1970), p. 418.

7. Roman government troubled most Southern leaders, who were more attracted to the Greek city-states, whose small size was appealing in the South. Edwin A. Miles, "The Old South and the Classical World," *North Carolina Historical Review* 48 (July 1971), pp. 268–270.

8. Honour, *Neo-classicism*, p. 164.

9. For a select bibliography of early nineteenth-century writings on the arts, see Talbot Hamlin, *Greek Revival Architecture in America: Being an Account of Important Trends in American Architecture and American Life Prior to the War Between the States* (London: Oxford University Press, 1944), pp. 360–381.

10. Quoted in Sterling Boyd, *The Adam Style in America* (New York: Garland Publishing, 1985), p. 325.

11. Quoted in Hamlin, *Greek Revival Architecture*, p. 381.

12. Quoted in Pierson, *American Buildings and Their Architects*, p. 286.

13. Pierson, *American Buildings and Their Architects*, pp. 293–297.

14. For a similar destruction and recreation in Paris, see Priscilla Parkhurst Ferguson, "Reading Revolutionary Paris," in Phillipe Desan, Priscilla Parkhurst Ferguson, and Wendy Griswolk, eds., *Literature and Social Practice* (Chicago: University of Chicago Press, 1989), pp. 46–68.

15. Quoted in Henry-Russell Hitchcock and William Seale, *Temples of Democracy: The State Capitols of the U.S.A.* (New York: Harcourt Brace Jovanovich, 1976), pp. 112–113.

16. *Ibid.*, p. 47.

17. Quoted in *Ibid.*, p. 55.

18. *Ibid.*, pp. 55, 70–71, 104–105; Boyd, *Adam Style*, p. 327.

19. Hitchcock and Seale, *Temples of Democracy*, pp. 48, 63; Hamlin, *Greek Revival Architecture*, p. 276.

20. Hitchcock and Seale, *Temples of Democracy*, p. 48.

21. *Ibid.*, p. 84; see also pp. 56, 106, 115, 172.

22. *Ibid.*, pp. 104–105.

23. Quoted in Catherine W. Bishir, *North Carolina Architecture* (Chapel Hill: University of North Carolina Press, 1990), p. 163.

24. Bishir, *North Carolina Architecture*, p. 51 (quote), p. 177 (quote).

25. Robert J. Brink, ed., *Courthouses of the Commonwealth* (Amherst: University of Massachusetts Press, 1984), p. 94; *County Court Houses of the United States: The Seagram County Court House Archives and Other Photographic Collections in the Library of Congress*, 2 vols. (Essex, N.Y., n.d.); Paul Kenneth Goldner, "Temples of Justice: Nineteenth-Century County Courthouses in the Midwest and Texas" (Ph.D. diss., Columbia University, 1970), p. 122.

26. *Analectic Magazine* 6 (1815), p. 375.

27. Wayne Craven, *Sculpture in America,* rev. ed. (Newark: University of Delaware Press, 1984), p. 53.

28. Hitchcock and Seale, *Temples of Democracy*, p. 67.

29. Craven, *Sculpture in America*, pp. 51–52.

30. Hitchcock and Seale, *Temples of Democracy*, pp. 65–67.

31. After 1741, the president of the English Society of Dilettanti was required to wear a Roman toga when he presided, and after 1790 a Greek *chlamys*. The dress was justified by the Dilettanti's heavy involvement in the recovery of classical artifacts from Italy and Greece. John Buxton, *The Grecian Taste* (London and Basingstoke: The MacMillan Press Ltd., 1978), p. 1.

32. Garry Wills, *Cincinnatus: George Washington and the Enlightenment* (New York: Doubleday and Company, 1984), pp. 47–48.

33. Craven, *Sculpture in America*, pp. 106–108.

34. *Ibid.*, pp. 53–54, p. 62 (quote).

35. *Ibid.*, pp. 66, 69–70, 102, 112, 119.

36. Cline, *American Attitudes*, pp. 10–12, 22 (quote); Paul Constantine Pappas, *The United States and the Greek War for Independence, 1821–1828* (New York: Columbia University Press, 1985), describes the fund-raising efforts all across the United States.

37. Theodore Bozeman, *To Live Ancient Lives: The Primitivist Dimension in Puritanism* (Chapel Hill: University of North Carolina Press, 1988), pp. 35–38.

38. On Greek Revival churches, see Pierson, *American Buildings and Their Architects*, pp. 440–452; on the largely unstudied Greek Revival storefront, see Stuart M. Blumin, *The Emergence of the Middle Class: Social Experience in the American City, 1760–1900* (Cambridge, England: Cambridge University Press, 1989), pp. 95, 96, 99, 102–103.

39. Allan I. Ludwig, *Graven Images: New England Stonecarving and Its Symbols, 1650–1815* (Middletown, Conn.: Wesleyan University Press, 1966), pp. 68–69, 100–124, 334.

40. *Ibid.*, pp. 326, 337, 416. Classical influence was much slower to reach Southern burying grounds. In Davidson County, North Carolina, the first classical stones date from the 1840s. Ruth Little, "Folk Art in Stone," in Paul Baker Touart, *Building the Backcountry: An Architectural History of Davidson County, North Carolina* (Charlotte, N.C.: Davidson County Historical Society, 1987), p. 277.

41. Stuart Bruchey, *Enterprise: The Dynamic Economy of a Free People* (Cambridge, Mass.: Harvard University Press, 1990), p. 251.

42. Diane Lindstrom, *Economic Development in the Philadelphia Region, 1810–1850* (New York: Columbia University Press, 1978), pp. 11–12.

43. Bruchey, *Enterprise*, p. 150.

44. Hamlin, *Greek Revival Architecture*, pp. 178, 163–164; Pierson, *American Buildings and Their Architects*, pp. 432, 435–436, 450–451. After 1826 they got help from Asher Benjamin's widely circulated *The American Builder's Companion*, which gave details of the classical Greek orders.

45. For an analysis of the circumstances that brought about this democratization, see Gordon S. Wood, *The Radicalism of the American Revolution* (New York: Alfred A. Knopf, 1992), and Richard L. Bushman, *The Refinement of America: Persons, Houses, Cities* (New York: Alfred A. Knopf, 1992).

46. Classical forms were slower to reach the middle class in the South, indicating perhaps a longer continuance of traditional class structure.

CHAPTER 1

1. *The Diary of William Bentley, D.D.*, 4 vols. (1792–1819; reprint, Gloucester, Mass.: Peter Smith, 1962), 3, p. 55.

2. Anne Felicity Woodhouse, "Nicholas Biddle in Europe, 1804–1807," *Pennsylvania Magazine of History and Biography* 103 (January 1979), p. 6.

3. Foster Rhea Dulles, *Americans Abroad: Two Centuries of European Travel* (Ann Arbor: University of Michigan Press), p. 1.

4. Rembrandt Peale, *Notes on Italy Written during a Tour in the Year 1829 and 1830* (Philadelphia, 1831), p. 42.

5. William Howard Adams, ed., *The Eye of Thomas Jefferson* (Washington, D.C.: National Gallery of Art, 1976), p. 95.

6. Francis Boardman Crowninshield, ed., *Letters of Mary Boardman Crowninshield 1815–1816* (Cambridge, Mass.: Riverside Press, 1905), p. 52.

7. *Ibid.*, pp. 19–20.

8. Clement E. Conger and Betty C. Monkman, "President Monroe's Acquisitions," *Connoisseur* 192 (May 1976), pp. 56–63.

9. *Minutes of The New-York Historical Society*, December 10, 1867, p. 280. Archives of The New-York Historical Society. I wish to thank Timothy Anglin Burgard, Assistant Curator of Paintings at The New-York Historical Society, for calling this reference to my attention.

10. Bernard Chevallier, *Malmaison Château et domaine des origines à 1904* (Paris: Ministère de la Culture, de la Communication, du Bicentenaire et des Grands Travaux, 1989), p. 440, fig. 242.

11. A related French chamber table was originally owned by Joseph Bonaparte at "Point Breeze," and was possibly the "Dressing Bureau, with swing glass" listed in the "Toilet Room (Adjoining the Count's Bedroom)" and sold in the 1847 auction at "Point Breeze." The Burlington County Historical Society, Burlington, New Jersey, now owns this table.

12. Katell le Bourhis, ed., *The Age of Napoleon, Costume from Revolution to Empire: 1789–1815* (New York: Metropolitan Museum of Art; Harry N. Abrams, 1989), p. 122.

13. Letter from David Sears, Boston, to William H. Nevete, Esq., London, n.d. (probably December 1818), Sears Family Papers, on deposit to the Massachusetts Historical Society, Boston.

14. Clement E. Conger and Alexandra W. Rollins, eds., *Treasures of State: Fine and Decorative Art in the Diplomatic Reception Rooms of the U.S. Department of State* (New York: Harry N. Abrams, 1991), pp. 410–411.

15. le Bourhis, ed., *Age of Napoleon*, p. 223.

16. *Ibid.*, p. 234.

17. Margaret Law Callcott, ed., *Mistress of Riversdale: The Plantation Letters of Rosalie Stier Calvert 1795–1821* (Baltimore: Johns Hopkins University Press, 1991), pp. 34–35.

18. le Bourhis, ed., *Age of Napoleon*, p. 222.

19. Jane C. Nylander, "Henry Sargent's *Dinner Party* and *Tea Party*," *The Magazine Antiques* 121 (May 1982), pp. 1172–1183.

20. *Ibid.*, p. 1177.

21. Wendy C. Wick, "Stephen Girard: A Patron of the Philadelphia Furniture Trade" (Master's thesis, University of Delaware, 1977), p. 144.

22. Thomas Webster and Mrs. Parkes, *An Encyclopaedia of Domestic Economy* (New York, 1845), pp. 181–182.

23. Callcott, ed., *Mistress of Riversdale*, p. 152.

24. *Ibid.*, p. 174.

25. David Sears, Boston, to Messrs. Hottangues & Co., Paris, May 12, 1818. Letterbook, Box 1982–M29, Sears Family Papers.

26. David Sears, Boston, to S.V.S. Wilder, Esq., Paris, December 10, 1820. *Ibid.*

27. *Ibid.*

28. Edward S. Cooke, Jr., et al., *Upholstery in America and Europe from the Seventeenth Century to World War I* (New York: W. W. Norton & Company, 1987), pp. 254–256.

29. David Sears, Boston, to S.V.S. Wilder, Esq., Paris, December 10, 1820. Letterbook, Box 1982–M29, Sears Family Papers.

30. Quoted from the Will of Clara Endicott Sears, copy in Object Folder 1982.499 –.500, Department of European Decorative Arts, Museum of Fine Arts, Boston.

31. Winthrop, "Memoir of the Hon. David Sears," p. 411.

32. Stuart P. Feld, et al., *Neo-Classicism in America: Inspiration and Innovation, 1800–1840* (New York: Hirsch & Adler Galleries, 1991), no. 94. Though Mr. Clark's set of French porcelain is unmarked, Mr. Feld recently noted an almost identical set bearing the mark of Schoelcher (d. 1832) of Paris, who by that time was probably simply retailing high quality porcelains.

33. The 1836 estate inventory of New York art collector Luman Reed listed "1 harlequin teaset" in the "Tea room pantry." I want to thank Anne Harrell, University of Delaware Ph.D. candidate, for calling this reference to my attention as transcribed from the County of New York court record, Collection 61, The Joseph Downs Collection of Manuscripts and Printed Ephemera, Winterthur Library, Winterthur, Delaware.

34. Callcott, ed., *Mistress of Riversdale*, pp. 157–158.

35. Berry B. Tracy, *Federal Furniture and Decorative Arts at Boscobel* (New York: Boscobel Restoration; Harry N. Abrams, 1981), p.16.

36. Gaye Blake Roberts, introduction to *Wedgwood in London* (Staffordshire, England: Josiah Wedgwood & Sons, 1984), p. 12.

37. Norman Rice, *New York Furniture before 1840 in the Collection of the Albany Institute of History and Art* (Albany, N.Y.: Albany Institute of History and Art, 1962), p. 12.

38. David Sears, Boston, to Messrs. Grant Pillars & Co., Paris, November 16, 1819. Letterbook, Box 1982-M29 Sears Family Papers.

39. The mantel owned by Bruen was from his house at 156 Second Avenue, built between 1832 and 1838 (demolished 1916). It is now in the Museum of the City of New York (37.313) and was the gift of I. N. Phelps Stokes. I thank Dr. Deborah D. Waters, Curator of Decorative Arts at The Museum of the City of New York, for this information.

40. Will and Inventory of Edward Coleman, 1841, Philadelphia Probate Records, no. 113, Will Book 15:38.

41. Philipp Fehl, "The Account Book of Thomas Appleton of Livorno: A Document in the History of American Art, 1802–1825," *Winterthur Portfolio* 9 (1974), pp. 144–145.

42. Conger and Monkman, "President Monroe's Acquisitions," pp. 56–63.

43. Nathan Appleton of Boston owned a pair of faceted ormolu sticks with figural heads at the top, and human feet at the base, similar to the silver ones owned in New Orleans by Pierre Denis de La Ronde.

44. *Catalogue of Lighting Fixtures and Accessories* (England: O. & H. Smith, Printers, c. 1812), Rare Book Collection, Henry Francis du Pont Winterthur Museum, Winterthur, Delaware.

45. Memorandum dated October 6, 1978, in Object Folder 78.111, Registrar's Office, Winterthur Museum.

46. George Ticknor, *Life, Letters, and Journals of George Ticknor*, 2 vols., ed. George Hillard and Anna Ticknor (Boston: James Osgood and Company, 1876), 1, p. 63.

47. *The Picture of London* (London: Longman, Hurst, Rees, Orme & Brown, 1818), p. 122.

48. Peale, *Notes on Italy*, p. 327.

49. Peter Thornton and David Watkin, "New Light on the Hope Street Mansion in Duchess Street," *Apollo* 126 (September 1987), pp. 162–177.

50. *Ibid.*, p. 167.

51. Ian Jenkins, "Adam Buck and the Vogue for Greek Vases," *The Burlington Magazine* 130 (June 1988), pp. 448–457.

52. Callcott, ed., *Mistress of Riversdale*, p. 172.

53. Charles Merrill Mount, "Gilbert Stuart in Washington: With a Catalogue of His Portraits Painted between December 1803 and July 1805," in *Records of the Columbia County Historical Society*, 1971–1972 (Charlottesville: University Press of Virginia, 1973), pp. 81–127.

54. John Hervey, *Racing in America, 1665–1865*, 2 vols. (New York: Jockey Club, 1944), 2, p. 75.

55. Thomas Cook and Richard Parkin are listed in partnership in Philadelphia directories between 1820 and 1825. Precisely where they were born and trained is not known. In 1811 Richard Parkin was one of the committee of three cabinetmakers responsible for and listed in the front of the *Philadelphia Book of Prices*. In 1831–1833 Richard Parkin worked alone at 94 South Third Street, and by 1835–1840, he was located at Egyptian Hall, 134 South Second Street, a building that he appears to have leased from the cabinetmaker Joseph Barry. In 1835 a Thomas Cook was one of the two appraisers of upholsterer John Hancock's estate inventory. (I thank David Conradson for sharing this information regarding Hancock.) In 1840 a Thomas Cook died, presumably the cabinetmaker, as probate records indicate there were carpenter's tools worth $48.00 in his estate.

56. Thomas Hope, *Household Furniture and Interior Decoration* (London, 1807), p. 28.

57. Thornton and Watkin, "New Light," p. 171.

58. "Reminiscences of Eliza Leaycraft Smith," c. 1887, Manuscript Notebook in Box 12, Robinson Papers, Library of The New-York Historical Society.

59. Dulles, *Americans Abroad*, p. 31.

60. Peale, *Notes on Italy*, p. 75.

61. *Ibid.*, pp. 67–71

62. Meyer Reinhold, *Classica Americana: The Greek and Roman Heritage in the United States* (Detroit: Wayne State University Press, 1984), pp. 268–269.

63. This monumental canvas is now owned by The Fruitlands Museum, Harvard, Massachusetts.

64. For an extensive study of Americans who traveled to Italy, see Theodore E. Stebbins, Jr., et al., *The Lure of Italy: American Artists and the Italian Experience* (Boston: Museum of Fine Arts; New York: Harry N. Abrams, 1992).

65. Ticknor, *Journals*, 1, p. 169.

66. *Diary of William Bentley, D.D.*, 2, p. 349.

67. Will and Inventory of Edward Coleman, 1841, Philadelphia Probate Records, no. 113, Will Book 15:38.

68. Anita Delafield, "Montgomery Place, the home of Major and Mrs. John White Delafield," in *The Magazine Antiques* 91 (February 1967), p. 236. Attributed to Anthony G. Quervelle, but unmarked, this table was at Montgomery Place, at Annandale-on-the-Hudson, until the early 1980s, when it was sold by the Delafield family prior to the property being given to Historic Hudson, Inc. The table is now in a private collection.

69. For the definitive published examination of Quervelle's work, see Robert C. Smith, "The Furniture of Anthony Quervelle," pts. 1–5, in *The Magazine Antiques* 103 (May 1973), pp. 984–994; 104 (July, August 1973), pp. 90–99, 260–268; 105 (January, March 1974), pp. 180–193, 512–521.

70. The mate to this table retains the original gilt stenciled decoration on the stretcher and the skirt, as well as an original *vert antique* treatment on the acanthus leaves on the legs and the paw feet. Traces of gilt have been found on the table in figure 36, most especially on the acanthus leaves, though the evidence is not detailed enough to reconstruct the original surface treatment.

71. Robert C. Smith, "Philadelphia Empire Furniture by Antoine Gabriel Quervelle," *Antiques* 86 (September 1964), pp. 304–309. Today both center tables and one of the pier tables are still used in The White House.

72. The four mosaic butterflies that appear on the top of this table may be a trademark of the French manufactory that might have manufactured this top. See Denise Ledoux-Lebard, *Les Ebénistes Du xixe Siécle, 1795–1889* (Paris: Les Editions de l'Amateur, 1965), p. 175. Daniel Alcouffe, *Un âge d'or arts décoratifs 1814–1848* (Paris: Galleries Nationales du Grand Palais), p. 175. I want to thank Anthony A. P. Stuempfig for sharing his thoughts and research on this table with me.

73. Gervase Jackson-Stops, ed., *Treasure Houses of Great Britain* (Washington, D.C.: National Gallery of Art, 1985), p. 593.

74. A closely related pier table (accession number 1980.34) is in the collections of the Museum of Fine Arts, Boston. Having a plain marbletop, the front paw feet are similar, but lack the unusual carved drapery bracket on the inside front. Both tables have turned rear feet.

75. Winthrop, "Memoir," p. 413.

76. Box N-5, Sears Family Papers.

77. Winthrop, "Memoir," p. 413.

78. *The Classical Spirit in American Portraiture* (Providence, R.I.: Department of Art, Brown University, 1976), no. 24, p. 57.

79. From the Papers of Mann S. Valentine II, in the collection of the Valentine Museum, Richmond, Virginia.

80. *Travelers in Arcadia: American Artists in Italy, 1830–1875*, (Detroit: Detroit Institute of Arts, 1951), pp. 43–45.

81. Kathryn Greenthal, Paula M. Kozol, and Jan Seidler Ramirez, *American Figurative Sculpture in the Museum of Fine Arts, Boston* (Boston: Museum of Fine Arts, 1986), p. 21.

82. William L. Vance, *America's Rome*, vol. 1 (New Haven, Conn.: Yale University Press, 1989), pp. 369–370.

83. Peale, *Notes on Italy*, p. 246.

84. Vance, *America's Rome*, p. 204.

85. Biddle was actually the second American to reach Greece in the early nineteenth century, and Joseph Allen Smith of Charleston, South Carolina, was first. I am indebted to R. A. McNeal, of Lancaster, Pennsylvania, for this information. Dr. McNeal's forthcoming publication will be a welcome addition to the published primary source material on this topic. See: R. A. McNeal, ed., *Nicholas Biddle in Greece: Journals and Letters of 1806* (University Park, Penn.: Pennsylvania State University Press, 1993).

86. Christopher P. Monkhouse, "A Temple for Tomes: The Egyptian Elephant Folio Cabinet in The Providence Athenaeum," *Furniture History* (London) 26 (1990), pp. 157–167.

87. Nancy Scott Newhouse, "From Rome to Khartoum: Gleyre, Lowell, and the Evidence of the Boston Watercolors and Drawings," in *Charles Gleyre* (New York: Grey Art Gallery and Study Center, New York University, 1980), pp. 79–117.

88. Sarah Rogers Haight, *Letters from the Old World By a Lady of New York*, vol. 1 (New York: Harper & Brothers, 1840) p. 76.

89. *Ibid.*, p. 191.

90. *Ibid.*, p. 223.

91. *Ibid.*, p. 226.

92. Newspaper article dated Saturday, December 15, 1832, Special Collections, The Milton Eisenhower Library, Ms. 189, The Johns Hopkins University, Baltimore.

93. Much of the collection is now owned by The Johns Hopkins University where it is exhibited and still used in teaching.

94. Callcott, ed., *Mistress of Riversdale*, p. 80.

95. A selection of the fascinating series of letters between Stier and his daughter, Rosalie, who married George Calvert of Maryland, have recently been translated and published; in Callcott, ed., *Mistress of Riversdale*.

96. E. M. Woodward, *Bonaparte's Park and the Murats* (Trenton, N.J.: MacCrellish and Quigley, 1989), p. 82.

97. *Ibid.*, p. 42.

98. *Ibid.*

99. *Ibid.*, p. 43

100. There was a long tradition of Canova sculpting members of the Bonaparte family. The most renowned (and scandalous) sculpture was the one of Napoleon's beautiful sister, Pauline Borghese, reclining half-nude on a Grecian couch.

101. Woodward, *Bonaparte's Park*, p. 53.

102. *Ibid.*, p. 69.

103. Anthony J. Bleeker, *Catalogue of Rare, Original Paintings . . . Valuable Engravings, Elegant Sculpture, Household Furniture, . . . Belonging to the Estate of the Late Joseph Napoleon Bonaparte* (New York: P. Miller and Son, 1847), pp. 12–13. On microfilm in collection of New York Public Library.

104. Dunlap, *Rise and Progress*, 2, p. 88.

105. Ulysse Desportes, "Giuseppe Ceracchi in America and His Busts of George Washington," *Art Quarterly* 26 (Summer 1963), pp. 140–179.

106. *Catalogue of American Portraits in the New-York Historical Society*, 2 vols. (New Haven, Conn.: Yale University Press, 1974), pp. 149–150.

107. Dunlap, *Rise and Progress*, 3, pp. 287–288. In a letter of October 10, 1817, Latrobe wrote to Trumbull, "I will do for Carelli what I can, I fear it will be but little." See Talbot Hamlin, *Benjamin Henry Latrobe* (New York: Oxford University Press, 1955), p. 450.

CHAPTER 2

1. Joseph Hopkinson, *The Annual Discourse Delivered before the Pennsylvania Academy of Fine Arts* (Philadelphia: Bradford and Inskeep, 1810), p. 12.

2. When established in 1802, this institution was called the New York Academy of Arts; in 1808 Robert R. Livingston changed its name to the American Academy of Arts, and in 1817 John Trumbull changed it to the American Academy of the Fine Arts. I am grateful to Carrie Rebora, Assistant Curator, American Paintings and Sculpture, The Metropolitan Museum of Art, for clarifying these changes in name for me.

3. Gulian C. Verplank, *An Address Delivered at the Opening of the Tenth Exhibition of the American Academy of the Fine Arts* (New York: G. & C. Carvill, 1825), pp. 4–5.

4. *Ibid.*, pp. 46–47.

5. Benjamin Henry Latrobe, "Anniversary Oration, Pronounced before the Society of Artists of the United States," in *Port Folio* 5 (1811), pp. 4–5.

6. *Ibid.*, p. 6.

7. *Ibid.*, p. 11.

8. *Ibid.*, p. 17.

9. For an extensive examination of the history of "cabinets of curiosities," see Joy Kenseth, ed., *The Age of the Marvelous* (Hanover, N.H.: Hood Museum of Art, 1991); and Simon Welfare and John Fairley, *Cabinet of Curiosities* (New York: St. Martin's Press, 1992).

10. *Diary of William Bentley, D. D.*, 3, p. 52.

11. E. McSherry Fowble, "Without a Blush: The Movement toward Acceptance of the Nude as an Art Form in America, 1800–1825," *Winterthur Portfolio* 9 (1974), p. 105.

12. William B. Dinsmoor, "Early American Studies of Mediterranean Archaeology," *Proceedings of the American Philosophical Society* 87 (July 1943), p. 71.

13. *Ibid.*, p. 72.

14. In 1815, following the collapse of Napoleon's empire, these sculptures were returned to Italy.

15. Dinsmoor, "Early American Studies," p. 84.

16. Nancy E. Richards, "The American Academy of Arts, 1802–1818" (Master's thesis, University of Delaware, 1965), p. 48, and Fowble, "Without a Blush," p. 104.

17. Charles R. King, ed., *Life and Correspondence of Rufus King: Comprising His Letters, Private and Official, His Public Documents and His Speeches* (New York: G. P. Putnam's Sons, 1894–1900), 4, p. 449.

18. E. P. Richardson, "Allen Smith, Collector and Benefactor," *American Art Journal* 1 (Fall 1969), p. 10.

19. *Ibid.*, p. 10.

20. Woodhouse, "Nicholas Biddle in Europe," p. 16.

21. Richardson, "Allen Smith," p. 11.

22. Mabel Munson Swan, *The Athenaeum Gallery, 1827–1873* (Boston: Boston Athenaeum, 1940), p. 3.

23. *Ibid.*, p. 134.

24. *Ibid.*, p. 138.

25. *Ibid.*, p. 139.

26. Randall L. Skalsky has recently published an article which poses a creditable new theory about the meaning of the freize depicted on the Portland Vase. See William H. Honan, "For an Answer to a Roman Riddle, Find Pi," *The New York Times*, Thursday, March 26, 1992.

27. *The Boston Directory* (Boston: John H. Frost and Charles Stimson, Jr., 1821), n.p.

28. This sculpture is now in the collections of the Boston Athenaeum. See Jonathan P. Harding, *The Boston Athenaeum Collection: Pre-Twentieth Century American and European Painting & Sculpture* (Boston: Boston Athenaeum, 1984), p. 70.

29. Anna Wells Rutledge, *Artists in the Life of Charleston Through Colony and State from Restoration to Reconstruction*, Transactions of the American Philosophical Society, vol. 39, pt. 2 (Philadelphia: American Philosophical Society, 1949) p. 137.

30. *Index to American Art Exhibition Catalogues from the Beginning Through the 1876 Centennial Year*, compiled by James L. Yarnall and William H. Gerdts (Boston: G. K. Hall & Company, 1986).

31. *Catalogue of Peale's Italian Pictures . . .* (Philadelphia: Printed for the Publisher, 1831), microfiche Peale Family Papers, Winterthur Library, Winterthur, Delaware.

32. Dinsmoor, "Early American Studies," p. 89.

33. Franklin D. Scott, *Wertmuller: Artist and Immigrant Father* (Chicago: Swedish Pioneer Historical Society, 1963), p. 19.

34. Richard Koke, comp., *American Landscape and Genre Paintings in the New-York Historical Society: A Catalog of the Collection Including Historical, Narrative, and Maritime Art*, vol. 3, (New York: New-York Historical Society, 1982), p. 208.

35. Fowble, "Without a Blush," p. 120.

36. Wendy A. Cooper, *In Praise of America: American Decorative Arts, 1650–1830* (New York: Alfred A. Knopf, 1980), p. 249.

37. Vanderlyn's original canvas is now in the collection of The M. H. de Young Museum, San Francisco. See Marc Simpson, Sally Mills, and Jennifer Saville, *The American Canvas: Paintings from the Collection of the Fine Arts Museums of San Francisco* (New York: Hudson Hills Press; San Francisco: Fine Arts Museums of San Francisco, 1989), pp. 56–57.

38. Kenneth C. Lindsay, *The Works of John Vanderlyn: From Tammany to the Capitol* (Binghamton: University Art Gallery, State University of New York, 1970), p. 71.

39. *Ibid.*

40. Swan, *Athenaeum Gallery*, p. 121.

41. William H. Gerdts and Theodore E. Stebbins, Jr., *"A Man of Genius": The Art of Washington Allston* (Boston: Museum of Fine Arts, 1979), p. 39.

42. Louis Legrand Noble, *The Life and Works of Thomas Cole* (Cambridge, Mass.: Harvard University Press, 1964), p. 114.

43. Charles Russell Codman owned three other paintings, also by Fernando DeGalli Bibiena. The other views were of Venice, the Castle of St. Angelo, and the Falls at Tivoli. I am grateful to Richard Nylander for providing me with this information drawn from his research in the Codman Papers at the Society for the Preservation of New England Antiquities.

44. *An Exhibition of Paintings by Thomas Cole N.A. from the Artist's Studio, Catskill, New York* (New York: Kennedy Galleries, 1964), p. 8.

45. Elwood C. Parry III, *The Art of Thomas Cole: Ambition and Imagination* (Newark: University of Delaware Press, 1988), p. 126. In Dunlap, *Rise and Progress*, 3, p. 275, it is noted that "Miss Douglass of New York, has a well-selected collection of European and American pictures—the old masters are said to be good."

46. William Cullen Bryant. *A Funeral Oration occasioned by the death of Thomas Cole, delivered before the NATIONAL ACADEMY OF DESIGN, New-York, May 4, 1848* (New York: D. Appleton & Company, 1848).

47. Swan, *Athenaeum Gallery*, p. 7. Peale's *Court of Death* is currently in the collection of The Detroit Institute of Arts, Detroit.

48. Nylander, "Henry Sargent's *Dinner Party* and *Tea Party*," p. 1176.

49. *Francis Guy 1760–1720* (Baltimore: Museum and Library of Maryland History, Maryland Historical Society, 1981), p. 36.

50. *Diary of William Bentley D.D.*, 4, p. 129.

51. Corné's painting is also almost identical to Lorrain's depiction of *The Marriage of Isaac and Rebecca* (1648), which is in the collection of the National Gallery, London. *The Mill* is owned by the Galleria Doria-Pampilia, Rome, and was the painting that Ropes referred to. See H. Diane Russell, *Claude Lorrain 1600–1682* (Washington, D.C.: National Gallery of Art, 1982), pp. 164–165.

52. Fowble, "Without a Blush," p. 121.

53. Samuel F. B. Morse, *Academies of Arts. A Discourse, Delivered on Thursday, May 3, 1827, in the Chapel of Columbia College before the National Academy of Design on Its First Anniversary* (New York: G. and C. Carvill, 1827), pp. 52–56.

54. Henry Tudor, *Narrative of a Tour in North America* (London: James Duncan, 1834), 1, p. 380.

55. Box 13, Appleton Family Papers, Massachusetts Historical Society, Boston.

56. I want to thank Jane C. Nylander, Director, The Society for the Preservation of New England Antiquities, for first calling my attention to Barney Smith, and for sharing her research on him with me. Smith lived in the old Governor Hutchinson house on Milton Hill. I also thank J. Peter Spang for pointing out the following reference to the old Hutchinson House and Barney Smith's occupancy of it; for more information, see A. K. Teele, *The History of Milton, Mass., 1640–1887* (Boston: Rockwell and Churchill, 1887), pp. 134–140.

57. Norfolk County Probate Records (Docket no. 16798, Massachusetts State Archives, Boston, Mass.).

58. Sona K. Johnston, *American Paintings 1750–1900 from the Collection of The Baltimore Museum of Art* (Baltimore: Baltimore Museum of Art, 1983), pp. 148–150.

59. *The Columbian Sentinel* (Boston), November 2, 1825. I want to thank Richard Nylander for sharing this research with me.

60. This information and conjecture about Codman's acquisition of the *Three Graces* was shared with me by Richard Nylander.

61. See Charles A. Hammond and Stephen A. Wilbur, *Collecting Sculpture in America* (Waltham, Mass.: Gore Place, 1989).

62. Callcott, ed., *Mistress of Riversdale*, p. 166.

63. *Ibid.*, p. 309.

64. *Rendezvous for Taste*, (Baltimore: Peale Museum, 1956), p. 36.

65. The original letter, dated May 26, 1833, to General Thomas Cadwalader from Joseph Bonaparte, is in the possession of a descendant; a 1904 copy by Mary Henlen Cadwalader, Jr., is in the files of The Walters Art Gallery, Baltimore. I thank Julie Mirabito, an intern in the Department of Painting and Sculpture before 1900 during the summer of 1992, for her assistance in the translation of this letter.

66. Dinsmoor, "Early American Studies," p. 90. The Library Company of Philadelphia owns a copy of Lucien Bonaparte's *Musée Etrusque*, which was given to the Library in 1833 by the author.

67. Ella M. Foshay, *Mr. Luman Reed's Picture Gallery* (New York: Harry N. Abrams, 1990), pp. 40–41. I would like to thank Timothy Anglin Burgard, Assistant Curator of Paintings, Drawings and Sculpture, for calling this reference to my attention.

CHAPTER 3

1. Hope, *Household Furniture*, p. 3.

2. *Ibid.*, p. 14.

3. *Ibid.*, p. 9.

4. *Ibid.*, p. 17.

5. *Ibid.*, p. 51.

6. Thomas Sheraton, *The Cabinet Dictionary* 2 vols. (1803; reprint, New York: Praeger Publishers, 1970), 1, p. 146.

7. *Ibid.*, 2, p. 245.

8. Hopkinson, *Annual Discourse*, p. 31.

9. Michael K. Brown, "Duncan Phyfe" (Master's thesis, University of Delaware, 1978), p. 43.

10. George Smith, *Collection of Designs for Household Furniture and Interior Decoration* (1808; reprint, New York: Praeger Publishers, 1970), p. 9, pls. 39, 40A.

11. Charles F. Montgomery, *American Furniture: the Federal Period in the Henry Francis du Pont Winterthur Museum* (New York: Viking Press, 1966), pp. 118–119.

12. *The New-York Revised Prices for Manufacturing Cabinet and Chair Work* (New York: Southwick and Pelsse, 1810), p. 56.

13. Derek E. Ostergard, ed., *Bent Wood and Metal Furniture: 1850–1946* (New York: American Federation of the Arts, 1987), p. 22.

14. *Ibid.*, pp. 19–20.

15. Christopher P. Monkhouse and Thomas S. Michie, *American Furniture in the Pendleton House* (Providence, R.I.: Museum of Art, Rhode Island School of Design, 1986), pp. 184–186.

16. J. Michael Flanigan et al., *American Furniture from the Kaufman Collection* (Washington, D.C.: National Gallery of Art, 1986), pp. 138–139.

17. Conover Hunt-Jones, *Dolley and the "great little Madison"* (Washington, D.C.: American Institute of Architects Foundation, 1977), p. 38.

18. Page Talbott, "Seating Furniture in Boston," *The Magazine Antiques* 139 (May 1991), pp. 956–969.

19. See Beatrice B. Garvan, *Federal Philadelphia* (Philadelphia: Philadelphia Museum of Art, 1987); and Jack L. Lindsey, "An Early Latrobe Furniture Commission," *The Magazine Antiques* 139 (January 1991), pp. 208–219. While there is no direct link between this suite and the furniture Waln owned by Latrobe, the elegant suite of furniture consigned to Freeman's Auction House in Philadelphia in 1819(?) was consigned by the sheriff who was responsible for disposing of Waln's bankrupt estate. Two of the chairs from this set given to the Philadelphia Museum in the 1930s by the Rozet family by tradition were said to have been purchased by a Rozet at Freeman's.

20. George Smith, *A Collection of Ornamental Designs, after the Manner of the Antique, Compos'd for the Use of Architects, Ornamental Painters . . .* (London: J. Taylor, 1812), n.p.

21. Montgomery, *American Furniture*, pp. 126–127.

22. Flanigan et al., *American Furniture from the Kaufman Collection*, pp. 152–153.

23. Marshall B. Davidson and Elizabeth Stillinger, *The American Wing at The Metropolitan Museum of Art* (New York: Alfred A. Knopf, 1985), p. 71, fig. 87; Nancy McClelland, *Duncan Phyfe and the English Regency* (New York: William R. Scott, 1939), p. 292, pl. 280.

24. Transcription of Inventory of Luman Reed . . . taken July 16, 1836, from the County of New York court record, Collection 61, no.54.106.66, pp. 1, 5, Downs Collection, The Winterthur Library, Wilmington, Delaware.

25. Rodney Armstrong, "The Boston Athenaeum and Its Furnishings," *The Magazine Antiques* 136 (August 1989), p. 309.

26. Nylander, "Henry Sargent's *Dinner Party* and *Tea Party*," figs. 3, 4.

27. Berry B. Tracy et al., *Nineteenth-Century America, Furniture and Other Decorative Arts* (New York: Metropolitan Museum of Art, 1970), no. 79.

28. Talbott, "Seating Furniture in Boston," p. 969.

29. Pauline Agius, *Ackermann's Regency Furniture & Interiors* (Wiltshire, England: Crowood Press, 1984), p. 39.

30. Berry B. Tracy and William H. Gerdts, *Classical America, 1815–1845* (Newark, N.J.: Newark Museum, 1963), fig. 2. This object has been deaccessioned since its inclusion in the 1963 exhibition.

31. See Flanigan et al., *American Furniture from the Kaufman Collection*, pp. 156–157; Jonathan L. Fairbanks, *Collecting American Decorative Arts and Sculpture, 1971–1991* (Boston: Museum of Fine Arts, 1991), p. 42; and Montgomery, *American Furniture*, pp. 313–314. Two other closely related stools are in the collection at Hampton National Historic Site, Towson, Maryland. One is said to have been owned originally by Robert Gilmor, and the other originally by John Eager Howard, both of Baltimore. These are almost identical to each other, except they are not both the same size, one is slightly larger.

32. A recent cleaning and conservation of this remarkably well preserved piece of furniture revealed most of the original burnished gilt and *vert antique* surfaces. Originally the burnished gold leaf was coated with a tinted shellac, obviously meant to tone its brilliance. I want to thank Christine Thomson from the Society for the Preservation of New England Antiquities Conservation Center for her assistance and careful work on the frame of this sofa. I thank Betsy Lahikainen, who expertly completed the upholstery of the couch with her significant research and sensitive treatment. Thanks also go to Cynthia Moyer, who carefully treated the gilt stenciled decoration in the minor areas of abrasion.

33. Page Talbott, "Boston Empire Furniture," pts. 1, 2, The *Magazine Antiques* 107, 109 (May 1975, May 1976), pt. 1, pp. 878–888.

34. One of the large Grecian couches owned by Appleton is now in the collection of the High Museum of Art, Atlanta. According to information from Richard Nylander, Curator of the Society for the Preservation of New England Antiquities, its mate was destroyed in a fire in Santa Barbara in the 1920s.

35. *The Columbian Centinel* (Boston), April 12, 1823, n.p. I want to thank Page Talbott for calling this advertisement to my attention.

36. Agius, *Ackermann's Regency Furniture*, pp. 102–103.

37. Peter Nicholson and Michael Angelo Nicholson, *The Practical Cabinetmaker, Upholsterer, and Complete Decorator* (London, 1826), p. 11.

38. *Ibid.*

39. Feld et al., *Neo-Classicism in America*, p. 37, and Wendell Garrett, *Classic America: The Federal Style and Beyond* (New York: Rizzoli International Publications, 1992), pp. 72–73.

40. The myth of Mettius Curtius, 362 B.C., relates that a vast chasm from some unknown cause appeared in the Roman Forum, and the soothsayers declared it would never be filled up till Rome threw into it its best treasure. Mettius Curtius said, "Rome's best treasure is a self-sacrificing devoted patriot" and, mounting his charger, he leaped into the gulf, which immediately closed over him.

41. Rice, *New York Furniture before 1840*, p. 12.

42. *Ibid.*, pp. 31–36.

43. A four-post bedstead ordered in 1827 for the Black Mansion in Ellsworth, Maine, was called a "French bedstead," which referred to the manner in which it was hung.

44. In James Barron's *Modern and Elegant Designs of Cabinet and Upholstery Furniture* (London, 1814), he illustrates a page of six different fringes with a note that "the Stile of Fringes for this work is from Patterns Supply'd by Messrs David Yates and Sons." The French bedstead in the Black Mansion, Ellsworth, Maine, still retains its original white dimity hangings and the silk-wrapped mold fringe. An unused quantity of this fringe, retaining its original color, survives in almost pristine condition.

45. Richard G. Carrot, "The Egyptian Revival: Its Sources, Monuments, and Meaning" (Ph.D. diss., Yale University, 1961), p. 191.

46. Donald L. Fennimore, "Egyptian Influence in Early Nineteenth-Century American Furniture," *The Magazine Antiques* 137 (May 1990), pp. 1190–1201.

47. Josette Brédif, *Printed French Fabrics, Toiles de Jouy*, trans. Nina Bogin (New York: Rizzoli International Publications, 1989), pp. 150–151.

48. Fennimore, "Egyptian Influence," p. 1198.

49. Donald L. Fennimore, "Searching for Roots: The Genealogy of a Philadelphia Sideboard," *1990 Western Reserve Antiques Show Catalog*, 1990, pp. 14–15; and Fennimore, "Egyptian influence," p.1197.

50. An Egyptian-style sideboard (accession number 1972.235.1) labeled by Charles-Honoré Lannuier, and accompanying unlabeled knife boxes (accession numbers 1972.235.2–.3) are in the collection of The Metropolitan Museum of Art, New York.

51. Fennimore, "Egyptian Influence," figs. 12, 13.

52. Tracy and Gerdts, *Classical America*, fig. 38.

53. These armchairs are now in the collection of the Museum of the City of New York (accession numbers 36.110.1ab-.2ab). Another related set of side and armchairs is in a private collection in the Hudson River Valley. The latter set was owned by Mrs. Robert E. Livingston, nee Susan DePeyster, who inherited them from her parents. She then used them to furnish her house at 271 Fifth Avenue.

54. I want to thank Richard Flynt for sharing his extensive knowledge of this Egyptian phenomenon with me and for directing me to the following reference: *Padihershef: The Egyptian Mummy* (Springfield, Mass.: George Walter Vincent Smith Art Museum, 1984).

55. *Ibid.*, p. 31.

56. Edgar G. Miller, Jr., *American Antique Furniture*, 2 vols. (Baltimore: Lord Baltimore Press, 1937), 1, pp. 279–280; 2, pp. 833–834.

57. Feld et al., *Neo-Classicism in America*, p. 36.

58. Gerald W. R. Ward, *American Case Furniture in the Mabel Brady Garvan and Other Collections at Yale University* (New Haven, Conn.: Yale University Art Gallery, 1988), pp. 442–444.

59. The New-York Historical Society has in its collections the original handwritten vellum scroll also presented to Maxwell on August 22, 1929.

60. Donald L. Fennimore, "Elegant Patterns of Uncommon Good Taste: Domestic Silver by Thomas Fletcher and Sidney Gardiner" (Master's thesis, University of Delaware, 1971), p. 90.

61. David B. Warren, Katherine S. Howe, and Michael K. Brown, *Marks of Achievement: Four Centuries of American Presentation Silver* (Houston: Museum of Fine Arts; New York: Harry N. Abrams, 1987), p. 91.

62. Fennimore, "Elegant Patterns," p. 25.

63. Christie's, *Fine Silver and Objects of Vertu*, sale 7248, April 18, 1991, pp. 122–124.

64. Roger G. Kennedy, *Greek Revival America* (New York: Stewart, Tabori and Chang, 1990), pp. 314–316.

65. Deborah Ducoff-Barone, *The Early Industrialization of the Philadelphia Furniture Trade, 1800–1840* (Ann Arbor, Mich.: University Microfilms International, 1985), pp. 128–129.

66. Rudolph Ackerman, *The Repository of Arts*, v. 14 (August 1815), plate 9 opposite page 89. See also Richard D. Altick, *The Shows of London* (Cambridge, Mass.: The Belknap Press of Harvard University, 1978), pp. 234–252.

67. Monkhouse, "Temple for Tomes," p. 166, fig. 4.

68. *Ibid.*, p. 160.

69. Denise Ledoux-Lebard, *Les Ebénistes du XIX siècle, 1795–1889* (Paris: Editions de l'Amateur, 1965), p. 335.

70. Gregory R. Weidman, *Furniture in Maryland, 1740–1940*, (Baltimore: Maryland Historical Society), p. 77.

71. A careful recent examination of the frame of this sofa has indicated that the first covering was crimson silk. This information, combined with the "damask covering" notation on the bill, and several mid-twentieth century photographs of the sofa and chairs upholstered in a tattered damask, have led to the conclusion that the silk damask covering was probably a pattern very similar to the one illustrated in Mary Schoeser and Celia Ruffey, *English and American Textiles from 1790 to the Present* (New York: Thames and Hudson, 1989), p. 21, fig. 10.

72. On Finlay's 1832 bill the fourteen chairs were described as "Hollow back framed chairs without Damask for seats."

73. Sotheby's, *Fine American Furniture . . .*, sale 5736, June 23, 1988, lot 487. A virtual mate to this table was found in England in the 1970s, and is currently in a private collection. Two other related examples are known and also privately owned, though none of these exceptional swan-lyre pier tables were documented by their makers.

74. Tracy et al., *Nineteenth-Century America*, fig. 70.

75. Warren et al., *Marks of Achievement*, pp. 112–113.

76. Tracy and Gerdts, *Classical America*, fig. 115; and Jennifer F. Goldsborough, *Silver in Maryland* (Baltimore: Maryland Historical Society), p. 143.

77. I want to thank Jennifer F. Goldsborough, Chief Curator of The Maryland Historical Society, for sharing with me this important discovery that she made.

78. For more detailed information on Veron, see Waters, "'The Workmanship of an American Artist': Philadelphia's Precious Metals Trade and Craftsmen, 1788–1832" (Ph.D. diss., University of Delaware, 1981), pp. 84–85.

79. For a concise, detailed account of the principle on which these lamps functioned, see Webster and Parkes, *Encyclopaedia of Domestic Economy*, p. 179.

80. Sotheby's, *Warhol Sale*, sale 6000, vol. 5, April 29–30, 1988, lot 3231.

81. Michael Flanigan of Baltimore and Robert Mussey of Milton, Massachusetts, collaborated on the restoration of this pier table. With extensive research into cabinetmaker's and finisher's manuals of the period, the materials and techniques used by Mussey attempted to approximate those originally employed in Quervelle's shop.

82. Wick, *Stephen Girard*, p. 52. For another similar table see advertisement for "Thomas & Karen Schwenke," *The Magazine Antiques* 113 (May 1978), p. 1011.

83. David L. Barquist, "American Looking Glasses in the Neoclassical Style, 1780–1815," *The Magazine Antiques* 141 (February 1992), pp. 320–331.

84. Robert C. Smith, "Architecture and Sculpture in Nineteenth-Century Mirror Frames," *The Magazine Antiques* 109 (February 1976), pp. 350–359.

85. Smith, *Designs for Household Furniture*, p. 25.

86. A fish slice with dolphin motif by Simon Chaudron (accession number 1970.2) of Philadelphia is owned by The Art Institute of Chicago, and one by John W. Forbes (accession number 1983.238) of New York is in The Wadsworth Atheneum, Hartford, Connecticut.

87. Fennimore, "Elegant Patterns," p. 25.

88. *Ibid.*, pp. 55–56.

89. Herbert Hoffman, "Rhyta and Kanthaoi in Greek Ritual," *Greek Vases in the J. Paul Getty Museum* 4, Occasional Papers on Antiques, 5 (1989), p. 144.

90. Sheraton, *The Cabinet Dictionary*, 1, p. 154.

91. *Ibid.*, 2, p. 285.

92. Monkhouse and Michie, *American Furniture in Pendleton House*, p. 112.

93. Davidson and Stillinger, *American Wing*, pp. 71–72. And Sotheby's, *Fine American Furniture, Folk Art, Folk Paintings and Silver*, sale 5473, June 26, 1986, lot 149.

94. Baldwin Gardiner (1791–1869) was the younger brother of Sidney Gardiner (1787–1827), and in 1815 married Louise-Leroy Veron, sister of Lewis Veron and of the wives of Sidney Gardiner and Thomas Fletcher. From 1814 until 1826 he was in business as a retailer in Philadelphia, and from 1817 until 1826 part of Gardiner, Veron & Company. In 1827 he moved to New York and opened a furnishings warehouse at 149 Broadway. He also produced silver items from his own manufactory, though he also purchased special items from Thomas Fletcher and other Philadelphia silversmiths. He was located in New York City (39 Nassau Street after the fall of 1836) until 1848, when he moved to California. I want to thank Deborah D. Waters for sharing with me this information from her forthcoming publication of the collection of American silver in The Museum of the City of New York.

95. Webster and Parkes, *Encyclopaedia of Domestic Economy*, p. 183.

96. Vitruvius, the Roman architect and engineer, in the first century B.C. recounted the myth of the caryatid's origin. The Caryae were a group of the Greek people living in the Peloponnese; during battle between the Greeks and Persians they became allies of the Persians. Following a Greek victory, the Caryae women were enslaved and forced to carry burdens on their heads as penance for their disloyalty.

97. I am grateful to Tammis Groft, Chief Curator of The Albany Institute of History and Art for calling this painting to my attention, and to Mary Alice Mackay, Researcher, for research about the sitter and its history.

98. An almost identical lamp, with unmarked font, is in the Black Mansion, Ellsworth, Maine, and is believed to have been ordered in 1827–1828 when the house was initially furnished through Boston merchandisers.

99. Webster and Parkes, *Encyclopaedia of Domestic Economy*, p. 182.

100. Feld et al., *Neo-Classicism in America*, pp. 32–33; and Christie's, *Fine American Furniture, Silver, Folk Art and Historical Prints*, sale 7214, January 26, 1991, lot 310, pp. 190–191. Two other related, but not identical, pier tables were offered for sale by Sotheby's, sale 6350, October 25, 1992, lots 454, 455. While these are said to have the same provenance as the table discussed in Feld, their history does not match that of the table sold by Christie's in 1991 and illustrated in figure 125. Perhaps future research will clarify the original ownership of all of these related tables by Lannuier. .

101. Cooper, *In Praise of America*, pp. 249–250, fig. 286.

102. Weidman, *Furniture in Maryland*, pp. 113–114, 186–187, 200.

103. *Ibid*., pp. 113–114.

104. Travis C. McDonald, Jr., the architectural historian who researched the construction and decoration of the Wickham House, is preparing an article for future publication, "On the Edge of Fashion: The Wickham House and Early Nineteenth-Century Neoclassicism in Richmond."

105. Richmond City Hustings Court, December 21, 1839, Book 8, p. 24.

106. I am indebted to Barbara Batson of the Valentine Museum, Richmond, Virginia, for sharing with me research compiled by herself and Jane Webb Smith, also of the Valentine Museum staff.

107. Alice Cooney Frelinghuysen, *American Porcelain 1770–1820* (New York: Metropolitan Museum of Art, 1989), p. 12.

108. *Ibid*., pp. 78–79.

109. *Ibid*., pp. 96–97.

110. Feld et. al., *Neo-Classicism in America*, p. 126.

111. Frelinghuysen, *American Porcelain*, p. 100.

112. Cooper, *In Praise of America*, pp. 42–43, 45.

113. Moses, *Vases, Altars*, pls. 29–32, 34.

114. Tracy et al., *Nineteenth-Century America*, no. 31.

115. *Ibid*., no. 29.

116. Philippa Lewis and Gillian Darley, *Dictionary of Ornament* (New York: Pantheon Books, 1986), p. 20.

117. *Ibid*., p. 32.

118. Feld et al., *Neo-Classicism in America*, p. 100.

119. Douglas R. Kent, "History in Houses: Hyde Hall, Otsego County, New York," *Antiques* 92 (August 1967), pp. 187–193.

120. A portrait of George Hyde Clarke, painted by Samuel F. B. Morse in 1833, is in the collection of The Saint Louis Art Museum.

121. Feld et al., *Neo-Classicism in America*, p. 125.

122. For more information about Baldwin Gardiner's retailing career, see Waters, "Workmanship," pp. 82–85.

123. I want to thank Stuart P. Feld for sharing with me a photocopy of this bill from Baldwin Gardiner, the original of which is in the Cornell University Archives.

124. A related Marquand cake basket with identical cast feet, but more ornate cast grapevine ornament was sold at Christie's, sale 6622, June 4, 1988, lot 62. The same cast feet appear on a basket marked by New York retailer Baldwin Gardiner.

125. Waters, "Workmanship," p. 164.

126. Feld et al., *Neo-Classicism in America*, p. 91.

127. *Ibid*., p. 164.

128. The Pierces of Portsmouth also owned a cake basket and salver by Thomas Fletcher.

129. These pattern books are now in the Rare Book Collection of the Library of The Philadelphia Museum of Art. The Philadelphia Museum of Art is undertaking a two-volume reprint of these important books, with an introduction and essays by Jack L. Lindsey, Curator of American Decorative Arts, to be published in 1993.

130. Phillip H. Curtis, "The Production of Tucker Porcelain, 1826–1828: A Reevaluation," in Ian M. G. Quimby, ed., *Ceramics in America* (Charlottesville: University Press of Virginia, 1973), pp. 362, 366.

131. Frelinghuysen, *American Porcelain*, p. 17.

132. J. Leander Bishop, *A History of American Manufactures from 1608 to 1860*, 3 vols. (Philadelphia: Edward Young and Company, 1866), 2, p. 362.

133. Frelinghuysen, *American Porcelain*, p. 16.

134. I want to thank Alice C. Frelinghuysen for calling my attention to these vases and for sharing her knowledge and insights with me regarding the difference in their bodies. When viewed under both short-wave and long-wave ultraviolet light, as well as transmitted light, one of the vases bears no relationship to the fluorescence observed in any known Tucker porcelain.

135. Rebecca J. Beal, *Jacob Eichholtz 1776–1842* (Philadelphia: Historical Society of Pennsylvania, 1969), pp. 137–138, 331.

136. Donald L. Fennimore, "Brass Hardware on American Furniture, Part II," *The Magazine Antiques* 140 (July 1991), pp. 80–91.

137. Page Talbott, "The Furniture Trade in Boston, 1810–1835," *The Magazine Antiques* 141 (May 1992), p. 850.

138. Marilyn Johnson, then Assistant Curator in The American Wing, The Metropolitan Museum of Art, New York, discovered this material in 1968. I want to thank her for sharing with me her recollections of this important body of imported cast and stamped brasses.

139. Catherine Lynn, *Wallpaper in America from the Seventeenth Century to World War I* (New York: W. W. Norton and Company, 1980), p. 44.

140. I want to thank C. Ford Peatross, Curator of Architectural Drawings, Library of Congress, Washington, D.C., for calling this fascinating resource of American wallpapers to my attention.

141. This printed "legend" describing the wallpaper accompanies it and is in the Prints and Photographs Division, Library of Congress, Washington, D.C.

CHAPTER 4

1. *The Penny Magazine*, March 4, 1837, p. 85.

2. Russell Lynes, *The Tastemakers* (New York: Harper and Row, 1954), p. 10.

3. Advertisement of "Fancy Chair Store, William Brown, Jun." in *New York Annual Advertiser*, 1810, p. 10.

4. Walter Nugent, *Structures of American Social History* (Bloomington: Indiana University Press, 1981), pp. 26, 30.

5. *Philadelphia: Three Centuries of American Art, Selections from the Bicentennial Exhibition Held at the Philadelphia Museum of Art*. (Philadelphia: Philadelphia Museum of Art, 1976) p. 244.

6. For an excellent and extensive study on this topic in rural New England see William J. Gilmore, *Reading Becomes a Necessity, Material and Cultural Life in Rural New England, 1780–1835* (Knoxville: University of Tennessee Press, 1989).

7. Joseph Hopkinson, *Annual Discourse Delivered before the Pennsylvania Academy of Fine Arts* (Philadelphia: Bradford and Inskeep, 1810), p. 15.

8. For an extensive study of magazines in America, see Frank Luther Mott, *A History of American Magazines 1741–1850* (Cambridge, Mass.: Harvard University Press, Belknap Press, 1957).

9. *Cincinnati Literary Gazette*, February 28, 1824, p. 72.

10. Thomas Mackellar, *The American Printer: A Manual of Typography* (Philadelphia: Mackellar, Smith's & Jordan, 1872), p. 211.

11. Abraham Rees, *The Cyclopaedia; or, Universal Dictionary of Arts, Sciences, and Literature* (Philadelphia: Samuel F. Bradford; Murray, Fairman and Co., 1810–1824), 24, p. 402.

12. *The Oxford English Dictionary*, vol. 10 (Oxford, England: Clarendon Press, 1933), p. 310.

13. I want to thank Jane Nylander, Director of the Society for the Preservation of New England Antiquities, for first calling my attention to this fascinating object. John K. Palmer advertised as a druggist and chemist in Boston directories beginning in 1833. In 1835 he was listed separately as a chemist, as well as in partnership with W. H. Jones and George Blake, Jr., "Agents for the Tremont Laboratory Warehouse . . . Wholesale and Retail Dealers in Drugs and Medicines, and Manufacturers of Chemicals, Perfumery, Patent Medicines. . ." By 1848 Palmer was listed as an eclectic physician, and by 1849 as a physician.

14. Cornelius Vermule, *Numismatic Art in America* (Cambridge, Mass.: Harvard University Press, Belknap Press, 1971), p. 30.

15. William H. Guthman, "Decorated American Militia Equipment," *The Magazine Antiques* 126 (August 1984), p. 125.

16. For a fuller discussion of bandboxes, see Lynn, *Wallpaper in America*, pp. 292–300.

17. Lilian Baker Carlisle, *Hat Boxes and Bandboxes at The Shelburne Museum*, vol. 4 (Shelburne, Vt.: Shelburne Museum, 1960), pp. 146–147.

18. J. Jefferson Miller, *English Yellow-Glazed Earthenware* (Washington, D.C.: Smithsonian Institution Press, 1974), pp. 74, 84.

19. George L. Miller, "George M. Coates, Pottery Merchant of Philadelphia, 1817–1831," *Winterthur Portfolio* 19 (Spring 1984), p. 41.

20. Neil M. D. Ewins, *Staffordshire Ceramic Trade with North America, c. 1780–1880* (unpublished thesis for B.A. [Hons] History of Design and the Visual Arts, Staffordshire Polytechnic, 1990), p. 7.

21. *Ibid.*, p. 7.

22. *Ibid.*, p. 8.

23. William Darby and Theodore Dwight, Jr., *A New Gazetteer of the United States of America* (Hartford, Conn.: Edward Hopkins, 1833), p. 418–419.

24. Lura Woodside Watkins, "Henderson of Jersey City and His Pitchers," *The Magazine Antiques* 50 (December 1946), p. 389.

25. "Dealer Notes," *The Magazine Antiques* 26 (September 1934), p. 109.

26. Geoffrey A. Godden, *The Illustrated Guide to Ridgway Porcelains* (London: Barrie & Jenkins, 1972), pp. 35–37.

27. I want to thank Diana Stradling for her generous help in locating this particular pitcher, and providing invaluable research data on it. It is her current belief that possibly this pitcher may even have been made in the very same mold as that used by Ridgway, since molds were sold in England and brought to this country for use by American potteries.

28. Kenneth M. Wilson, *New England Glass and Glassmaking* (New York: Thomas Y. Crowell Company, 1972), p. 260–261.

29. Downs Collection, 86 x 75.

30. Rees, *Cyclopaedia*, 32, n.p., s.v. "Salt."

31. Wilson, *New England Glass and Glassmaking*, p. 230.

32. *Ibid.*, p. 127.

33. An illuminating illustration in James Mease and Thomas Porter, *Picture of Philadelphia from 1811 to 1831* (Philadelphia: R. Desilver, 1831), 2, p. 59, shows a view of "Dr. Dyott's Philadelphia Cheap Drug, Medicine, Chemical, Colour and Glass Warehouse" with barrels and boxes being loaded into a wagon marked "Jacob Slouch/Pitsburgh [*sic*]."

34. Wilson, *New England Glass and Glassmaking*, p. 127

35. Tudor, 1, p. 81.

36. In 1842 Catharine Beecher estimated that it took one ton of coal to fire one stove through the winter. I thank Gail Caskey Winkler for this interesting insight.

37. Tammis Kane Groft, *Cast with Style: Nineteenth-Century Cast-Iron Stoves from the Albany Area* (Albany, N.Y.: Albany Institute of History and Art, 1981), p. 73.

38. J. Leander Bishop, *A History of American Manufactures from 1608 to 1860*, 3 vols. (Philadelphia: Edward Young and Company, 1866), 2, p. 248.

39. *Address of the American Society for the Encouragement of Domestic Manufactures, to the People of the United States* (New York: Van Winkle, Wiley & Company, 1817), p. 7.

40. Bishop, 2, p. 301.

41. *Address of the American Society for the Encouragement of Domestic Manufactures*, p. 30.

42. Ed Polk Douglas, "Rococo Roses, Part III: Blessed Are the Meek(s)," *New York-Pennsylvania Collector*, August 1979.

43. For more information on the immigration of German cabinetmakers to Philadelphia, see Charles L. Venable, "Philadelphia Biedermeier, Germanic Craftsmen and Design in Philadelphia, 1820–1850" (Master's thesis, University of Delaware, 1986).

44. *The American Advertising Directory, for Manufacturers and Dealers in American Goods for the Year 1832* (New York: Jocelyn, Darling & Company, 1832).

45. George J. Henkels, *Household Economy* (Philadelphia: King & Baird, 1867), p. 21. I want to thank Robert Mussey of Milton, Massachusetts, for calling this reference to my attention.

46. I want to thank Zane Z. Studenroth, Jr., for first calling to my attention the fact that this desk and bookcase might be by Meads and Alvord. The work of Jeane Newbold Miller on Meads and Alvord has also provided valuable information (see *Checklist for an Exhibition of Furniture by John Meads (1777–1859): An Albany Cabinetmaker Furnishes Hyde Hall* [Springfield, N.Y.: Hyde Hall, 1989]). Gilbert Tapley Vincent has also contributed helpful insights into the work of Meads at Hyde Hall and its relationship to this desk and bookcase.

47. Sandra L. Tatman and Roger W. Moss, *Biographical Dictionary of Philadelphia Architects: 1700–1930* (Boston: G. K. Hall & Company, 1985), pp. 331–332. I want to thank Gail Caskey Winkler for calling my attention to this reference.

48. While this table no longer bears the Meeks label, when Mimi Miller, of Historic Natchez, Inc., first examined it at "Melrose," it still retained its original Meeks label.

49. Davidson and Stillinger, *American Wing*, pp. 164–165.

50. *American Advertising Directory*, p. 214.

51. *Ibid.*, p. 165.

52. *The Columbian Centinel* (Boston), April 12, 1823. I would like to thank Page Talbott, of Philadelphia, for calling my attention to this reference.

53. A bill in the Tradecard Collection of The American Antiquarian Society, Worcester, Massachusetts, from the furniture and upholstery warehouse of William Hancock is dated May 19, 1829, and lists the upholstery warehouse at nos. 39, 41, 45, and 49 Market Street. Page Talbott notes ("Furniture Trade," p. 850), that in 1829 William Hancock was listed in directories at 37–53 Cornhill (also called Market), and in 1831 at 37–45 Cornhill. By 1833 he was at 45 Cornhill only.

54. I want to thank Jessica Nicoll for sharing with me the paper she presented at the 1988 "Culture and Comfort" symposium at the Strong Museum, Rochester, New York. The paper was titled "'Elegance and Ease': William Hancock's 'Patent Elastic Spring Seat' Rocking Chairs" (revised, 1989).

55. Tracy et al., *Nineteenth-Century America*, no. 65; and Talbott, "Seating Furniture in Boston," p. 959, pl. 4.

56. Tradecard Collection.

57. I want to thank David H. Conradson for sharing with me the following information on Hancock which was drawn from his research for "Chairs of Every Description Constantly on Hand: John Hancock and Company, 1830–1840," his master's thesis for the University of Delaware, 1992.

58. While a mahogany rocking chair upholstered in haircloth cost $17, this was the least expensive upholstery fabric. In 1832 one of Hancock's clients, R. Farquharson, paid $30 for a mahogany rocking chair upholstered in crimson plush, and the boxing. This chair may also have had some carved elements. I thank David H. Conradson for calling my attention to this information.

59. The inventory of John Hancock was discovered by David H. Conradson in the Philadelphia Probate Records. His full transcription and brief analysis of it, titled "The Stock-in-Trade of John Hancock and Company," will appear in the May 1993 issue of *Furniture History*, published by The Chipstone Foundation.

60. Bishop, 2, p. 396.

61. Kenneth D. Roberts, *Some Observations Concerning Connecticut Clockmaking, 1790–1850*, Bulletin, Supplement no.6 (Columbia, Penn.: National Association of Watch and Clock Collectors, 1970), p. 20.

62. *Ibid.*, p. 31.

63. *Cincinnati Annual Advertiser* (Cincinnati, 1829), advertisement of L. Watson, n.p.

64. *The Cincinnati Directory for the Year 1829* (Cincinnati: Robinson and Fairbank, 1829), advertisement of Isaac M. Lee, n.p.

65. For a comprehensive examination of this material, see Skemer, "David Alling's Chair Manufactory: Craft Industrialization in Newark, New Jersey, 1801–1854," *Winterthur Portfolio* 22 (Spring 1987), pp. 1–21.

66. *Ibid.*, p. 7.

67. *Ibid.*, p. 11.

68. Deborah Chotner, *American Naive Paintings* (Washington, D.C.: National Gallery of Art, 1992), pp. 565–566. I want to thank Ms. Chotner, Assistant Curator of American and British Paintings at the National Gallery of Art, for sharing with me her research on this painting prior to her recent publication.

69. *Klink's Albany Directory, for the Year 1822* (Albany, N.Y.: E. and E. Hosford, 1822), n.p.

70. William Voss Elder III, *Baltimore Painted Furniture, 1800–1840* (Baltimore: Baltimore Museum of Art, 1972), pp. 20–27.

71. This chair has recently undergone careful analysis with regard to its original upholstery technique, and the original (1823) foundation and stuffing in the seat and back were found to be intact. The current fabric on it is a modern reproduction based on the description in the original Constantine bill. The legs of the chair were reduced due to damage sustained from the 1831 State House fire, and they have been restored based on their similarity to the 1818 Constantine chairs for the U.S. Senate.

72. I want to thank Raymond L. Beck, Historical Researcher and Curator of the North Carolina State Capitol for the extensive research in state archives that he has done on the documentation of this chair and its accompanying furnishings. He has willingly shared his research in the historical accounts of the State House, and made important observations about the influence of this particular chair upon the taste of the North Carolina gentry. I wish also to acknowledge his unflagging efforts and attention to the restoration of both the chair and its proper reupholstery by Leroy Graves of Colonial Williamsburg. The chair's restoration was made possible through a grant from The Women's Club of Raleigh in 1991. Box 2, Treasurer's and Comptroller's Papers, North Carolina Archives, Capitol Buildings, Raleigh, North Carolina.

73. McClelland, *Duncan Phyfe*, p. 301, pl. 290.

74. John Bivins, *Furniture of Coastal North Carolina* (Winston-Salem, N.C.: Museum of Early Decorative Arts, 1989), pp. 507–508.

75. *Diary of Thomas Wilson*, (1797–1876), [Surveyor, Native of Huntington Tyrone Township, Penna., written on trip South to visit relatives—November 1825—March 1827.] The original is on loan from the Wilson Family to the Southern Historical Collection, University of North Carolina, Chapel Hill. I want to thank Raymond L. Beck for calling my attention to this reference.

76. Darby and Dwight, *New Gazetteer*, p. 463.

77. Elizabeth R. Murray, *Wake: Capital County of North Carolina* (Raleigh, N.C.: Capital County Publishing Company, 1983), p. 210.

78. Tradition relates that during the State House fire the Speaker's chair was thrown from a second floor window in an effort to save it; amazingly, only the legs and crest appear to have suffered damage in this heroic act. For more information about the history of this chair, see Raymond L. Beck, "Thomas Constantine's 1823 Senate Speaker's Chair for the North Carolina State House: Its History and Preservation," *Carolina Comments* 41 (January 1993), pp. 25–30.

79. See "Collectors' Notes," *The Magazine Antiques* 107 (May 1975), pp. 953–954; 113 (May 1978), p. 1129; and 123 (May 1983), pp. 1074–1075.

80. Darby and Dwight, *New Gazetteer*, p. 332.

CHAPTER 5

1. Reinhold, *Classica Americana*, p. 143. For a more complete discussion of this American quest for virtue, see "The Classics and the Quest for Virtue in Eighteenth-Century America," in *ibid.*, pp. 142–173.

2. *Ibid.*, p. 150.

3. Gordon S. Wood, intro. and ed., *The Rising Glory of America, 1760–1820* (New York: George Braziller, 1971), p. 56.

4. Unpublished paper, Gordon S. Wood, "The Legacy of Rome in the American Revolution" (p. 31), given at conference "America's Italy: Classic, Romantic, and Modern Italian Cultural Traditions and the Making of America," September 17–19, 1992, Washington, D.C.

5. Reinhold, *Classica Americana*, p. 145.

6. *Ibid.*, p. 161.

7. E. McClung Fleming, "From Indian Princess to Greek Goddess: The American Image, 1783–1815," *Winterthur Portfolio* 9 (1974), pp. 37–66.

8. Wills, *Cincinnatus*, p. 110–111.

9. Hopkinson, *Annual Discourse*, p. 23.

10. For a complete discussion of Mills and the competition and construction of this monument, see John M. Bryan, ed., *Robert Mills, Architect* (Washington, D.C.: American Institute of Architects Press, 1989), pp. 146–154.

11. Stanley J. Idzerda, Anne C. Loveland, and Marc H. Miller, *Lafayette, Hero of Two Worlds: The Art and Pageantry of His Farewell Tour of America, 1824–1825* (Hanover, N.H.: Queens Museum, 1989), p. 126.

12. *Three Centuries of Art in Philadelphia* (Philadelphia: Philadelphia Museum of Art, 1976), p. 262.

13. Leslie J. Anderson "Isaac Hull Memorabilia at the USS *Constitution* Museum," *The Magazine Antiques* 126 (July 1984), pp. 119–123. It has been claimed by historians that Hull defeated the *Guerriere* in under thirty minutes. The source for this misinformation is apparently a ballad in which Hull tells the crew of the *Constitution* that he will give them double shots of brandy if they can defeat Dacres' *Guerriere* in under thirty minutes. Though this ballad had enormous contemporary popularity, the fact was that naval battles of that time period would take several hours. Indeed it could often take forty-five minutes for the warships just to position for a single volley, as the ships passed each other. I am indebted to Robb Goldstein, of Chatham, New York, for the above information.

14. Elizabeth Ingerman Wood, "Thomas Fletcher: A Philadelphia Entrepreneur of Presentation Silver," *Winterthur Portfolio* 3 (1967), p. 143.

15. *Ibid.*, p. 144, fig. 3.

16. Fennimore, "Elegant Patterns," p. 87.

17. The five other commissions were for Bainbridge, Jones, Morriss, Biddle, and the immortal Perry. See Wood, "Thomas Fletcher," for more details on the other commissions.

18. Warren, Howe, and Brown, *Marks of Achievement*, pp. 122–124.

19. *The Hartford Courant*, November 21, 1820, p. 1.

20. Major James E. Hicks, *Nathan Starr, U.S. Sword and Arms Maker* (Mount Vernon, N.Y.: James E. Hicks, 1940), p. 104.

21. *Ibid.*, p. 106.

22. Johnston, *American Paintings*, pp. 150–151.

23. Warren, Howe, and Brown, *Marks of Achievement*, pp. 109–110.

24. See Charles H. Tatham, *Designs for Ornamental Plate* (London, 1806), pls. 3, 4, 27. Also, Timothy B. Schroder, *The Gilbert Collection of Gold and Silver* (New York: Thames and Hudson, 1988), pp. 382–384. *Carlton House: The Past Glories of George IV's Palace* (London: Her Majesty Queen Elizabeth II, 1991), p. 130.

25. An energy dispersive X-ray fluorescence analysis of the silver content in five places on the candelabrum revealed an average content of 95.6%. This is higher than is usually seen in American silver of the period, including presentation silver. This high content is consistent with the pre-Revolutionary French standard of 95.8%, and the post-Revolutionary standard of 95.0%. While this evidence does not provide any conclusive information about the origin of the candelabrum, it does suggest the possibility that this piece of silver may be of French manufacture, or made from an earlier piece of French silver that Warner may have taken in trade and used to fashion a later piece.

26. The cut-glass bowl which now rests within the circular, scroll ornamented ring at the top is not thought to be original to the piece, but probably late nineteenth or early twentieth century. European precedents suggest that the original "liner" might have been cut glass, or perhaps blown blue glass. By the 1830s Susan Wheeler Decatur was in desperate financial straits and was forced to sell much of the silver which had been presented to her husband during his brief career. It was probably at this time that the candelabrum was sold, presumably directly to Philadelphia entrepreneur William Swaim, owner of the Philadelphia Baths and discoverer of an early patent medicine, Swaim's Panacea, "for the cure of Scrofula or King's Evil."

27. Feld et al., *Neo-Classicism in America*, p. 106.

28. Waters, " The Workmanship of an American Artist," pp. 92–93.

29. Harding, *Boston Athenaeum Collection*, pp. 38–39.

30. Frederick Voss, *John Frazee 1790–1852, Sculptor* (Boston and Washington: National Portrait Gallery, Smithsonian Institution and the Boston Athenaeum, 1986), p. 86.

31. Wood, "Thomas Fletcher," pp. 159–165.

32. Martha Gandy Fales, "Obadiah Rich, Boston Silversmith," *Antiques* 94 (October 1968), pp. 565–569.

33. From *The Works of Daniel Webster*, vol. 1 (Boston: Chas. C. Little, and James Brown, 1851), pp. 326–327.

34. I am indebted to Rachel E. C. Layton for sharing her research on Williamson and these four racing cups. For more information, see Rachel E. C. Layton, "Samuel Williamson's Presentation Silver: Important New Discoveries," *Silver* 25 (January–February 1992), pp. 8–13. The cup at Hampton is the only one of the four marked by Williamson; the 1803 cup is marked by Burnett and Rigden and the 1804 cup is unmarked. For more information on Williamson see Rachel E. C. Layton, "Trading and Silversmithing: The Mercantile Activities of Samuel Williamson, 1794–1813" (Masters thesis, University of Delaware, 1992).

35. Layton, "Samuel Williamson's Presentation Silver," p. 10.

36. In the collection of the Colonial Williamsburg Foundation is a silver-gilt racing trophy, the Richmond Cup (a prize for the Richmond races, Richmond, England), made in London, 1776–77, by Daniel Smith and Robert Sharp. See Philip Kopper, *Colonial Williamsburg* (New York: Harry N. Abrams, 1986), pp. 244–245.

37. *Alexandria Expositor*, November 1, 1805. I would like to thank Rachel Layton for sharing this newspaper entry with me.

38. Wood, intro. and ed., *Rising Glory*, p. 31.

39. *Ibid.*, p.32.

40. Thomas Woody, *A History of Woman's Education in the United States*, vol. 1 (New York: Science Press, 1929), p. 303. I want to thank Gail Caskey Winkler for sharing with me her work on women's education between 1790 and 1850, and bringing this material to my attention.

41. Hopkinson, *Annual Discourse*, p. 34.

42. *The Female Instructor; or, Young Woman's Friend and Companion: Being a Guide to all the Accomplishments Which Adorn the Female Character, Either as a Useful Member of Society—A Pleasing Companion, or, a Respectable Mother of a Family* (London: Henry Fisher, Son, and P. Jackson, 1836), preface, n.p.

43. "Female Education, by Miss Susan Barry . . . July, 1822," in *School Exercises of the Lafayette Female Academy* (Lexington, Ky., 1826), pp. 44–45.

44. *The Lady's Book* (Philadelphia: L.A. Godey & Company, 1830), 1–2, p. 97.

45. *Female Instructor*, preface, n.p.

46. Mrs. Phelps, *The Female Student; or, Lectures to Young Ladies on Female Education* (New York: Leavitt, Lord & Company, 1836), p. 394.

47. Caroline W. Healy, *Margaret and Her Friends* (Boston: Roberts Brothers, 1895), p. 6.

48. *Lady's Book*, 1–2, p. 97.

49. Woody, *Women's Education*, p. 311.

50. Davida Deutsch of New York made this discovery and it was first published in *The Luminary,* Summer 1988, pp. 3–4.

51. *Ibid.*

52. Rutledge, *Artists*, p. 185.

53. Phelps, *Female Student*, p. 380–381.

54. Linda Grant DePauw and Conover Hunt, *Remember the Ladies* (New York: Viking Press, 1976), pp. 108–109.

55. *Lady's Book*, 4, p. 40.

56. Nylander, "Some Print Sources of New England Schoolgirl Art," *The Magazine Antiques* 110 (August 1976), pp. 292–301.

57. Betty Ring, "Mrs. Saunders' and Miss Beach's Academy, Dorchester," *The Magazine Antiques* 110 (August 1976), p. 307.

58. Lynn, *Wallpaper in America*, pp. 218–219, figs. 9–24.

59. John Doggett Account Books, 1802–7, September 11, 1807, p. 177, Downs Collection.

60. Betty Ring suggests that the source may be the engraving "The Parting of Hector and Andromache," published by W. Durrell in New York in 1808. For an illustration of Durrell's engraving and another version of this needlework, see Betty Ring, *Let Virtue Be Guide to Thee* (Providence, R.I.: Rhode Island Historical Society, 1983), pp. 198–199. Another needlework example of this same subject is in The Connecticut Historical Society, worked by Maria Bissell at Lydia Rose's school in 1810. See also Sotheby's, sale 5282, February 1, 1985, lot 370.

61. Sheraton, *Cabinet Dictionary*, 2, p. 292.

62. A French dressing table now in the Burlington County Historical Society has a history of ownership at "Point Breeze," Bordentown, New Jersey. It may be the "mahogany Washstand, with white marble top" or "Dressing Bureau, with swing glass" in the "Toilet Room (Adjoining the Count's Bedroom)" in the 1847 "Point Breeze" auction catalogue. These French tables relate to documented Boston examples and suggest a strong French influence on some Boston classical furniture of this period.

63. I want to thank Harold Sack, Deanne Levison, and Robert Fileti, all of Israel Sack Inc., and Sack Conservation, for their generosity and astute research in the cleaning and restoration of this table.

64. Phelps, *Female Student*, p. 375.

65. *Ibid.*, p. 376.

66. Callcott, ed., *Mistress of Riversdale*, p. 150.

67. Winthrop, "Memoir of the Hon. David Sears," pp. 408–409.

68. For more information on Mrs. Hamilton and her "attitudes," see Frederick Rehberg, *Emma Hamilton's Attitudes*, (Cambridge, Mass.: Houghton Library, Harvard University, 1990).

69. Carolyn J. Weekley et al., *Joshua Johnson, Freeman and Early American Portrait Painter* (Baltimore: Maryland Historical Society; Williamsburg, Va.: Abby Aldrich Rockefeller Folk Art Center, 1987), p. 120.

70. Thomas Moore, *Odes of Anacreon* (London, 1800), Ode 72.

71. Callcott, ed., *Mistress of Riversdale*, p. 158.

72. Sylvia E. Crane, *White Silence: Greenough, Powers, and Crawford, American Sculptors in Nineteenth-Century Italy* (Coral Gables, Fla.: University of Miami Press, 1972), p. 307.

73. Phelps, *Female Student*, p. 368.

74. Allan Nevins, ed., *The Diary of Philip Hone, 1828–1851* (New York: Kraus Reprint Company, 1969), p. 80.

75. Rutledge, *Artists*, p. 213.

76. Bishop, *American Manufacturers*, 2, p. 339.

77. Venable, *Philadelphia Biedermeier*, p. 238, 332.

78. *Ibid.*

79. Sotheby's, *Important Americana*, sale 5810, January 26–28, 1989, lot 1463. This suite is now in the collection of the Winterthur Museum.

80. Venable, *Philadelphia Biedermeier*, p. 239.

81. Eliza Ridgely's Sebastian Erard harp is owned by Hampton National Historic Site, Towson, Maryland.

82. Hastings, *A Guidebook to Hampton National Historic Site*, p. 13.

83. Julia S. Berrall, "The Israel Crane House in Montclair, New Jersey," *The Magazine Antiques* 104 (December 1973), p. 1059–1060.

84. Lynne Dakin Hastings, *A Guidebook to Hampton National Historic Site* (Towson, Md.: Historic Hampton, 1986), p. 15.

ACKNOWLEDGMENTS

It has been thirty years since the first major exhibition focusing on this subject, *Classical America*, was presented by Berry B. Tracy and William H. Gerdts at The Newark Museum in 1963. Again in 1970, Mr. Tracy featured this period of taste in his centennial exhibition *19th-Century America* at The Metropolitan Museum of Art. To these two significant, groundbreaking exhibitions I owe my first debt of gratitude. Now, nearly a quarter of a century later, renewed interest in this topic has generated a fresh and introspective look at this period.

An extraordinary number of friends, colleagues, and collectors have contributed unfailingly to this publication and the exhibition that it accompanies. That so many gave so willingly of their time and talent makes the fruition of both the book and the exhibition truly heartwarming. *Classical Taste in America, 1800–1840* came into being over five years ago when Arnold Lehman, Director of The Baltimore Museum of Art, gave his enthusiastic endorsement to my ambitious proposal, thus committing the full support of the Museum. From that time through the implementation of the project, he and Brenda Richardson, Deputy Director for Art, exercised prudent administrative guidance, always extending wise counsel.

The funding of *Classical Taste* was especially demanding, as it came at a time of nearly universal economic constraints. With Arnold Lehman spearheading this effort, former Director of Development Joy Peterson Heyrman and former Development Associate Elizabeth Smith played pivotal roles in securing initial funding. Elspeth Udvarhelyi, Deputy Director for Development, and Cecilia Meisner, Development Associate, have continued this effective campaign.

In the fall of 1988, a team of colleagues met to discuss and define the primary concepts and directions the project would take. Michael K. Brown, Stuart P. Feld, Donald L. Fennimore, Jane C. Nylander, Richard Nylander, and the late Oswaldo Rodriguez-Roque together gave the project its focus and impetus. Throughout its evolution, they continued to consult, review, and enhance its ultimate presentation. In addition, other friends and colleagues listened faithfully, looked at objects, discussed concepts, and read drafts, always adding that essential refinement; for this invaluable and generous collaboration, I heartily thank Dean F. Failey, Wendy Kaplan, Mark Leithauser, Christopher P. Monkhouse, Jan Seidler Ramirez, Gaillard Ravenel, Frances P. Smyth, Page Talbott, William L. Vance, Charles L. Venable, Gordon S. Wood, and Gail Kaskey Winkler. I also want to acknowledge the initial contribution in the early stages of the project made by former project Research Assistant Deborah A. Federhen.

Perhaps the largest debt of gratitude goes to the numerous lenders to the exhibition—individuals and institutions, public and private—who have generously shared both objects and information. To all of those individuals and institutions on the accompanying "Lenders to the Exhibition" list I extend my deepest thanks. In addition, there are other individuals who have assisted with numerous kindnesses and contributions, and I would like to extend special thanks to the following colleagues: Phyllis Abrams, Martha Aikens, Ellenor M. Alcorn, Louise Todd Ambler, Cathy Anderson, David Anderson, Mark Anderson, Diana Arecco, Rodney Armstrong, Linda Bantel, Georgia B. Barnhill, Deborah Barone, David L. Barquist, James Barter, Judith Barter, Barbara Batson, Raymond L. Beck, Diane Berger, David J. Berman, Ada Bortoluzzi, Leslie Greene Bowman, Michael Brophy, Susan Buck, Timothy Anglin Burgard, Gene Canton, Nancy Carlisle, John A. Cherol, Deborah Chotner, Nicholai Cikovsky, Jr., H. Nichols B. Clark,

Stiles T. Colwill, David Conradson, Suzanne C. Crilly, Mary Butler Davies, Nancy Davis, Bert Denker, Katherine K. Dibble, Anne M. Donaghy, Murray B. Douglas, Melanie Ennis, Jonathan L. Fairbanks, Jeannine Falino, Susan Faxon, Robert Fileti, Sue Finkel, Oscar P. Fitzgerald, J. Michael Flanigan, Steve Florey, Richard Flynt, Kathy Francis, Alice C. Frelinghuysen, Richard Gallerani, Wendell D. Garrett, Jennifer F. Goldsborough, Anne Golovin, Betsy Gordon, Tammis K. Groft, Kellen Haak, Lynne Dakin Hastings, Ike Hay, Kathy Healy, Morrison H. Heckscher, Carrie Hastings Hedrick, Kathryn B. Hiesinger, Erica Hirschler, Judith Hollander, Holly Hotchner, Melissa B. Houghton, Charles F. Hummel, Anthony Jansen, Will Jeffers, B. Frank Jewell, Brock W. Jobe, Denise J. H. Johnson, Kathleen E. Johnson, Phillip M. Johnston, Jay Jordan, Patricia E. Kane, Anizia Karmazyn, Peter M. Kenny, Douglas Kent, Susan Kleckner, Anna Gruber Koester, Dean Lahikainen, Elizabeth Lahikainen, Amanda Lange, Lee Langston-Harrison, Priscilla Lawrence, Rachel E. C. Layton, Robert Leath, Henry Lei, Deanne Levison, Jack L. Lindsey, James I. McDaniel, Dr. and Mrs. William C. McGehee, Mary Alice Mackay, Caitlin McQuade, Ann Smart Martin, Eileen A. Mason, Thomas S. Michie, George Miller, Mimi and Ron Miller, Kathleen Catalano Milley, Robert Moeller, Betty C. Monkman, Mark P. O. Morford, Cynthia Moyer, Charles W. Newhall III, Jessica F. Nicoll, Sarah Nicols, Patrick Noon, John Pearce, C. Ford Peatross, Martha Pike, Anne L. Poulet, Walter E. Raynes, Jr., Carrie Rebora, Sue Reed, Ellen R. Reeder, Wayne Reynolds, Lynn Springer Roberts, Catherine Rogers, Tom Rosenblum, Rodris Roth, Bill Samaha, J. Thomas Savage, Jr., John Scherer, Karol A. Schmiegel, Julie Schwan, Arlene and Bill Schwind, Sam Shogren, Earl Shuttleworth, Jeanne Sloane, Mary L. Sluskonis, Elizabeth Smith, Jane Webb Smith, Janice Sorkow, J. Peter Spang III, Jane S. Spillman, Frederick W. Stayner, Theodore E. Stebbins, Damie Stillman, Diana and Gary Stradling, Jill Thomas-Clark, D. Dodge Thompson, Neville Thompson, Christine Thomson, Robert F. Trent, Nadia Tscherny, Gary Vikan, Gilbert T. Vincent, Joann Warner, David B. Warren, Deborah Dependahl Waters, Gregory R. Weidman, Michael Wentworth, Dr. Donald White, and Elise Wright.

The presentation and quality of images are paramount in any publication, but are especially important when illustrating objects of quality and splendor. I am indebted to many individuals for the superior photography provided for this publication, but I would especially like to thank Alex Jamison for his excellence and patience in much of the new photography for this publication. Additionally, I want to recognize the work of Mark Gulezian, who often collaborated with Alex Jamison, as well as the special efforts of photographers David Bohl, John Chew, George J. Fistrovich, Jim Frank, Eric Kvalsvik, Duane Suter, and Arthur Vitols.

The staff of The Baltimore Museum of Art offered tireless support at every level. In implementing *Classical Taste,* the staff of Registration, Exhibitions, Installations, Conservation, Library, Rights and Reproductions, and Public Relations all worked in the most dedicated fashion to assure that the highest professional standards would be met. While every staff member involved gave generously of his or her time and talents, I am eager to acknowledge, in particular, the critical contributions of Frances Klapthor, Associate Registrar; Marge Lee, Director, Public Relations; Karen Nielsen, Director, Design and Installation; and David Penney, Exhibitions Manager, all of whom were essential to the project's realization. The design of the exhibition was developed in cooperation with Quenroe Associates, and I would like to thank Elroy Quenroe, Charles Mack, Allyson Smith, and David Hamill for their creative and sensitive installation plan.

The Baltimore Museum of Art's Friends of the American Wing, and Young Friends of the American Wing, were always encouraging and generously funded the purchase of several important classical objects now featured in the exhibition. For this continuing support I offer a particular salute of thanks.

Many people have contributed to this effort in infinite ways, and many have been cited above. But a few remain whose support and contributions deserve particular mention and appreciation. Meyer Reinhold of Boston University has been an inspiration from the start for his pioneering research and publication of *Classica Americana*. Richard L. Bushman, whose insightful scholarship of this period has contributed a brilliant introductory essay, has been a willing and encouraging influence, adding a cultural balance to the aesthetic focus. George and Linda Kaufman, collectors and dear friends, have contributed in more ways than perhaps they are even aware, and for this I am extremely grateful. Eric Martin Wunsch, Harold Sack, and Elaine Wilde have all been immensely supportive and encouraging, and have my most sincere thanks. From the Museum's earliest discussions with Abbeville Press, former Senior Editor Walton Rawls was warmly enthusiastic, with sage suggestions for both the intellectual and visual content of the book. His sensitive editing of the manuscript enhanced it greatly. The creative design of the book came from Monika Keano, whose delight with the subject and patience with the author's revisions must be gratefully acknowledged.

Finally, I owe my deepest appreciation to a most tolerant, supportive, and hard-working staff in the Department of Decorative Arts. As project Research Assistant, Jeannine A. Disviscour has contributed beyond all expectations to the overall accomplishment of this effort, managing everything from loan requests to photography, along with research, a detailed review of the manuscript, and the final compilation of picture captions, checklist, and bibliography. Associate curator M. B. Munford has enthusiastically and tirelessly tackled seemingly endless tasks of conservation, research, and photography management, as well as a much appreciated, meticulous reading of the manuscript. Consultant curator William Voss Elder III has strengthened the project with specific insights, details, and knowledge of particular objects; Bill has added balance and breadth to the exhibition and publication. Sona Johnston, Curator of Painting and Sculpture before 1900, has provided a review of both the object selection and the manuscript, always with thoughtful and valued suggestions. Anita Jones, Associate Curator in Charge of Textiles, has also given generously of her time. Our faithful department volunteer, Janet W. Flagle, spent countless hours assisting with numerous preparatory tasks. Viola Holmes, Departmental Secretary, cheerfully and willingly provided all manner of support, including the primary compilation of the selected bibliography. And finally, while I could not have accomplished this without the contributions of all of those cited above, a most special debt of gratitude goes to Mark M. Haller, whose immeasurable support and tireless good spirits were ever present.

Wendy A. Cooper
Curator, Decorative Arts
The Baltimore Museum of Art

LENDERS TO THE EXHIBITION

Adams National Historic Site, National Park Service, Quincy, Massachusetts
Addison Gallery of American Art, Phillips Academy, Andover, Massachusetts
Albany Institute of History and Art, Albany, New York
American Antiquarian Society, Worcester, Massachusetts
The American Numismatic Society, New York, New York
The Andalusia Foundation, Andalusia, Pennsylvania
Anonymous Lenders
The Art Institute of Chicago, Chicago, Illinois
The Athenaeum of Philadelphia, Philadelphia, Pennsylvania
The Baltimore Museum of Art, Baltimore, Maryland
Bartow-Pell Mansion Museum, Bronx, New York
James Biddle
Boston Athenaeum, Boston, Massachusetts
The Carnegie Museum of Art, Pittsburgh, Pennsylvania
The Charleston Museum, Charleston, South Carolina
Cheekwood, Tennessee Botanical Gardens and Fine Arts Center, Inc., Nashville, Tennessee
Chester County Historical Society, West Chester, Pennsylvania
The Chrysler Museum, Norfolk, Virginia
Cooper-Hewitt Museum, National Museum of Design, Smithsonian Institution, New York, New York
The Corning Museum of Glass, Corning, New York
Mr. and Mrs. Richard C. Dabrowski
Dallas Museum of Art, Dallas, Texas
Allan L. Daniel
Diplomatic Reception Rooms, Department of State, Washington, D.C.
Dyckman House Museum, New York, New York, on permanent loan to Boscobel Restoration Inc., Garrison, New York

Charles Everett
Elizabeth Feld
Peter A. Feld
Mr. and Mrs. Stuart P. Feld
Dr. Milton E. Flower
The Fogg Art Museum, Harvard University, Cambridge, Massachusetts
Hull P. Fulweiler
The Gibbes Museum of Art/Carolina Art Association, Charleston, South Carolina
Cora Ginsburg
Hampton National Historic Site, National Park Service, Towson, Maryland
Henry Ford Museum & Greenfield Village, Dearborn, Michigan
The Henry Francis du Pont Winterthur Museum, Winterthur, Delaware
David Conrad Hislop
Historic Hudson Valley, Tarrytown, New York
The Historic New Orleans Collection, New Orleans, Louisiana
The Hitchcock Museum, Riverton, Connecticut
Hood Museum, Dartmouth College, Hanover, New Hampshire
Friends of Hyde Hall, Inc., Otsego County, New York
Independence National Historical Park, National Park Service, Philadelphia, Pennsylvania
James Monroe Museum and Memorial Library, Fredericksburg, Virginia
Richard H. Jenrette
Mr. and Mrs. George M. Kaufman
Kaufman Americana Foundation, Norfolk, Virginia
The Library of Congress, Washington, D.C.
Los Angeles County Museum of Art, Los Angeles, California
Milly B. McGehee

State of Maryland, Department of General Services, on extended loan to The Baltimore Museum of Art
Maryland Historical Society, Baltimore, Maryland
Joseph O. Matthews
Melrose, Natchez National Historical Park, National Park Service, Natchez, Mississippi
The Metropolitan Museum of Art, New York, New York
Mint Museum of Art, Charlotte, North Carolina
Christopher P. Monkhouse
Munson-Williams-Proctor Institute, Museum of Art, Utica, New York
Museum of Art, Rhode Island School of Design, Providence, Rhode Island
Museum of Fine Arts, Boston, Massachusetts
The Museum of Fine Arts, Houston, Texas
Museum of the City of New York, New York
National Museum of American History, Smithsonian Institution, Washington, D.C.
National Gallery of Art, Washington, D.C.
The Newark Museum, Newark, New Jersey
The New Jersey Historical Society, Newark, New Jersey
New Jersey State Museum, Trenton, New Jersey
The New-York Historical Society, New York, New York
New York State Museum, Albany, New York
New York State Historical Association, Cooperstown, New York
North Carolina Museum of Art, Raleigh, North Carolina
North Carolina Division of Archives and History, Raleigh, North Carolina

The Octagon Museum, The American Architectural Foundation, Washington, D.C.
Old Sturbridge Village, Sturbridge, Massachusetts
Peabody and Essex Museum, Salem, Massachusetts
Pennsylvania Academy of the Fine Arts, Philadelphia, Pennsylvania
The Penobscot Marine Museum, Searsport, Maine
Philadelphia Museum of Art, Philadelphia, Pennsylvania
Public Library of the City of Boston, Massachusetts
Betty Ring
The Saint Louis Art Museum, Saint Louis, Missouri
Walter and Kathryn Sandel
Dorothy McIlvain Scott
Sears Family
Society for the Preservation of New England Antiquities, Boston, Massachusetts
Stephen Girard Collection, Girard College, Philadelphia, Pennsylvania
Anthony A. P. Stuempfig
Peter G. Terian
The University Museum of Archaeology and Anthropology, University of Pennsylvania, Philadelphia, Pennsylvania
Valentine Museum, Richmond, Virginia
The Walters Art Gallery, Baltimore, Maryland
Westmoreland Museum of Art, Greensburg, Pennsylvania
Yale Center for British Art, New Haven, Connecticut
Yale University Art Gallery, New Haven, Connecticut

PHOTOGRAPHY CREDITS

BIBLIOGRAPHY

Ackermann, Rudolph. *The Repository of Arts, Literature, Commerce, Manufactures, Fashions and Politics*. London: R. Ackermann, 1809–1828.

Adair, William. *The Frame in America, 1700–1900: A Survey of Fabrication Techniques and Styles*. Washington, D.C.: American Institute of Architects Foundation, 1983.

Adams, William Howard, ed. *The Eye of Thomas Jefferson*. Washington, D.C.: National Gallery of Art, 1976.

Agius, Pauline. *Ackermann's Regency Furniture & Interiors*. Wiltshire, England: Crowood Press, 1984.

Albany Institute Annual Report 1968. Albany, N.Y.: Albany Institute of History and Art, 1968.

American Antiques from Israel Sack Collection. Vol. 6. Washington, D.C.: Highland House Publishers, 1979.

American Art at Harvard. Cambridge, Mass.: Fogg Art Museum, Harvard University, 1972.

American Paintings in the Museum of Fine Arts, Boston. 2 vols. Boston: Museum of Fine Arts; Greenwich, Conn.: New York Graphic Society, 1969.

Armstrong, Rodney. "The Boston Athenaeum and its furnishings." *The Magazine Antiques* 136 (August 1989), pp. 302–315.

Baigell, Matthew. *Thomas Cole*. New York: Watson-Guptill, 1981.

Barquist, David L. "American looking glasses in the neoclassical style, 1780–1815." *The Magazine Antiques* 141 (February 1992), pp. 320–331.

Barron, James. *Modern and Elegant Designs of Cabinet and Upholstery Furniture*. London, 1814.

Bartlett, Jean Smith, and Mary Means Huber. "The Bartow-Pell Mansion in New York City." *The Magazine Antiques* 115 (May 1979), pp. 1032–1041.

Beal, Rebecca J. *Jacob Eichholtz 1776–1842*. Philadelphia: Historical Society of Pennsylvania, 1969.

Beck, Raymond L. "Thomas Constantine's 1823 Senate Speaker's Chair for the North Carolina State House: Its History and Preservation." *Carolina Comments* 41 (January 1993), pp. 25–30.

Belden, Louise Conway. *Marks of American Silversmiths in the Ineson-Bissell Collection*. Charlottesville: University Press of Virginia; Winterthur, Del.: Henry Francis du Pont Winterthur Museum, 1980.

Biddle, James. "Nicholas Biddle's Andalusia, a nineteenth-century country seat today." *Antiques* 86 (September 1964), pp. 286–290.

———. "Andalusia." *The Magazine Antiques* 130 (December 1986), pp. 1220–1227.

Birch, Thomas, Jr. *Catalogue of Valuable Paintings & Statuary, The Collection of the Late Joseph Bonaparte, Count de Survilliers*, 1845. Library, Baltimore Museum of Art.

Bleeker, Anthony J. *Catalogue of Rare, Original Paintings, . . . Valuable Engravings, Elegant Sculpture, Household Furniture . . . Belonging to the Estate of the Late Joseph Napoleon Bonaparte*. New York: P. Miller and Son, 1847. New York Public Library. Microfilm.

Brédif, Josette. *Printed French Fabrics, Toiles de Jouy*. Translated by Nina Bogin. New York: Rizzoli International Publications, 1989.

Bridges, Daisy Wade. "Carolina gold and the U.S. Branch Mint in Charlotte." *The Magazine Antiques* 106 (December 1974), pp. 1041–1046.

Brown, Joan Sayers. "Silver and gold owned by Stephen Decatur Jr." *The Magazine Antiques* 123 (February 1983), pp. 399–405.

Brown, Michael K. "Duncan Phyfe." Master's thesis, University of Delaware, 1978.

Bryan, John M., ed. *Robert Mills, Architect*. Washington, D.C.: American Institute of Architects Press, 1989.

Buhler, Kathryn C. *American Silver 1655–1825 in the Museum of Fine Arts, Boston*. 2 vols. Boston: Museum of Fine Arts, 1972.

Butler, Joseph T. "Montgomery Place revisited." *The Magazine Antiques* 134 (August 1988), pp. 294–303.

Callcott, Margaret Law, ed., *Mistress of Riversdale: The Plantation Letters of Rosalie Stier Calvert 1795–1821*. Baltimore: Johns Hopkins University Press, 1991.

Carlisle, Lilian Baker. *Hat Boxes and Bandboxes at The Shelburne Museum*. Vol. 4. Shelburne, Vt.: Shelburne Museum, 1960.

Carrot, Richard G. "The Egyptian Revival: Its Sources, Monuments, and Meaning." Ph.D. diss., Yale University, 1961.

Carson, Barbara. *Ambitious Appetites, Dining, Behavior and Patterns of Consumption in Federal Washington*. Washington, D.C.: American Institute of Architects Press, 1990.

Catalogue of American Portraits in the New-York Historical Society. 2 vols. New Haven, Conn.: Yale University Press, 1974.

Chevallier, Bernard. *Malmaison Château et domaine des origines à 1904*. Paris: Ministère de la Culture, de la Communication, du Bicentenaire et des Grands Travaux, 1989.

Chew, Paul A., ed. *The Permanent Collection*. Greensburg, Pa.: Westmoreland Museum of Art, 1978.

Cicognara, Count. *The Works of Antonio Canova in Sculpture and Modelling*. Boston: James Osgood and Company, 1876.

The Classical Spirit in American Portraiture. Providence, R.I.: Department of Art, Brown University, 1976.

Conger, Clement E., and Betty C. Monkman. "President Monroe's Acquisitions." *Connoisseur* 192 (May 1976), pp. 56–63.

Conger, Clement E., and Alexandra W. Rollins, eds. *Treasures of State: Fine and Decorative Art in the Diplomatic Reception Rooms of the U.S. Department of State*. New York: Harry N. Abrams, 1991.

Cooke, Edward S., Jr., et al. *Upholstery in America and Europe from the Seventeenth Century to World War I*. New York: W. W. Norton & Company, 1987.

Cooper, Wendy A. *In Praise of America: American Decorative Arts, 1650–1830*. New York: Alfred A. Knopf, 1980.

Crane, Sylvia E. *White Silence: Greenough, Powers, and Crawford, American Sculptors in Nineteenth-Century Italy*. Coral Gables, Fla.: University of Miami Press, 1972.

Crescent City Silver: An Exhibition of Nineteenth-Century New Orleans Silver. New Orleans: Historic New Orleans Collection, 1980.

Cullity, Brian. *Arts of the Federal Period*. Sandwich, Mass.: Trustees of Heritage Plantation of Sandwich, 1989.

"D. & J. Henderson Price List." *The Magazine Antiques* 26 (September 1934), pp. 108–109.

Davidson, Marshall B., and Elizabeth Stillinger. *The American Wing at The Metropolitan Museum of Art*. New York: Alfred A. Knopf, 1985.

de Guillebon, Regine de Plinval. *Porcelains of Paris 1770–1850*. Translated by Robin R. Charleston. New York: Walker and Company, 1972.

Deutsch, Davida. "The Crowning of Flora: Mr. Marling and Ladies Identified." *The Luminary* (Winston-Salem, N.C.: Museum of Early Southern Decorative Arts), Summer 1988, pp. 3–4.

The Diary of William Bentley, D. D. 4 vols. 1792–1819. Reprint. Gloucester, Mass.: Peter Smith, 1962.

Dietz, Ulysses. *Century of Revivals*. Newark, N.J.: The Newark Museum, 1983.

Dinsmoor, William B. "Early American Studies of Mediterranean Archaeology." *Proceedings of the American Philosophical Society* 87 (July 1943), pp. 70–104.

Druesedow, Jean L. "In Style: Celebrating Fifty Years of the Costume Institute." *The Metropolitan Museum of Art Bulletin* 45 (Fall 1987).

Ducoff-Barone, Deborah. *The Early Industrialization of the Philadelphia Furniture Trade, 1800–1840*. Ann Arbor, Mich.: University Microfilms International, 1985.

Dulles, Foster Rhea. *Americans Abroad: Two Centuries of European Travel*. Ann Arbor: University of Michigan Press, 1964.

Dunlap, William. *A History of the Rise and Progress of The Arts of Design in the United States*. (1834) Vol. 2. Edited by Frank W. Bayley and Charles E. Goodspeed. Boston: Goodspeed & Co., 1918. Revised edition edited by Alexander Wyckoff. 3 vols. New York: Benjamin Blom, 1965.

Elder, William Voss, III. *Baltimore Painted Furniture, 1800–1840*. Baltimore: Baltimore Museum of Art, 1972.

Elder, William Voss, III, and Jayne E. Stokes. *American Furniture, 1680–1880, from the Collection of The Baltimore Museum of Art*. Baltimore: Baltimore Museum of Art, 1987.

Ennès, Pierre. "Les amis du Louvre." *la revue du Louvre et des Musées de France* 3 (1990), pp. I–II.

Erffa, Helmut von, and Allen Staley. *The Paintings of Benjamin West*. New Haven, Conn.: Yale University Press, 1986.

An Exhibition of Paintings by Thomas Cole N.A. from the Artist's Studio, Catskill, New York. New York: Kennedy Galleries, 1964.

Fairbanks, Jonathan L. *Collecting American Decorative Arts and Sculpture, 1971–1991*. Boston: Museum of Fine Arts, 1991.

Fairbanks, Jonathan L., and Elizabeth Bidwell Bates. *American Furniture, 1620 to the Present*. New York: Richard Marek Publishers, 1981.

Fales, Dean A., Jr. *American Painted Furniture 1660–1880*. New York: E. P. Dutton & Company, 1972.

Fales, Martha Gandy. "Obadiah Rich, Boston silversmith." *Antiques* 94 (October 1968), pp. 565–569.

———. "Jewelry in Charleston." *The Magazine Antiques* 138 (December 1990), pp. 1216–1227.

Fehl, Philipp. "The Account Book of Thomas Appleton of Livorno: A Document in the History of American Art, 1802–1825." *Winterthur Portfolio* 9 (1974), pp. 123–151.

Feld, Stuart P., et al. *Neo-Classicism in America: Inspiration and Innovation, 1800–1840*. New York: Hirschl & Adler Galleries, 1991.

Fennimore, Donald L. "Elegant Patterns of Uncommon Good Taste: Domestic Silver by Thomas Fletcher and Sidney Gardiner." Master's thesis, University of Delaware, 1971.

———. "American Neoclassical Furniture and its European Antecedents." *The American Art Journal* 13 (Autumn 1981), pp. 49–65.

———. "Searching for Roots: The Genealogy of a Philadelphia Sideboard." *1990 Western Reserve Antiques Show Catalog*, 1990, pp. 14–15.

———. "Egyptian influence in early nineteenth century American furniture." *The Magazine Antiques* 137 (May 1990), pp. 1190–1201.

———. "Brass Hardware on American Furniture." *The Magazine Antiques* 140 (July 1991), pp. 80–91.

Fennimore, Donald L., and Robert T. Trump. "Joseph B. Barry, Philadelphia cabinetmaker." *The Magazine Antiques* 135 (May 1989), pp. 1212–1225.

Flanigan, J. Michael, et al. *American Furniture from the Kaufman Collection*. Washington, D.C.: National Gallery of Art, 1986.

Fleming, E. McClung. "From Indian Princess to Greek Goddess: The American Image, 1783–1815." *Winterthur Portfolio* 3 (1967), pp. 37–66.

Foshay, Ella M. *Mr. Luman Reed's Picture Gallery*. New York: Harry N. Abrams, 1990.

Fowble, E. McSherry. "Without a Blush: The Movement toward Acceptance of the Nude as an Art Form in America, 1800–1825." *Winterthur Portfolio* 9 (1974), pp. 103–121.

Frelinghuysen, Alice Cooney. *American Porcelain 1770–1820*. New York: The Metropolitan Museum of Art, 1989.

Garrett, Elizabeth Donaghy. *At Home: The American Family 1750–1870*. New York: Harry N. Abrams, 1990.

Garrett, Wendell. *Classic America: The Federal Style and Beyond*. New York: Rizzoli International Publications, 1992.

Garvan, Beatrice B. *Federal Philadelphia*. Philadelphia: Philadelphia Museum of Art, 1987.

Gerdts, William H., and Theodore E. Stebbins, Jr. *"A Man of Genius": The Art of Washington Allston*. Boston: Museum of Fine Arts, 1979.

Gilmore, William J. *Reading Becomes a Necessity of Life: Material and Cultural Life in Rural New England, 1780–1835*. Knoxville: University of Tennessee Press, 1989.

Goldsborough, Jennifer F. *Silver in Maryland*. Baltimore: Maryland Historical Society, 1983.

Greenthal, Kathryn, Paula M. Kozol, and Jan Seidler Ramirez. *American Figurative Sculpture in the Museum of Fine Arts, Boston*. Boston: Museum of Fine Arts, 1986.

Groce, George C., and David H. Wallace. *The New-York Historical Society's Dictionary of Artists in America, 1564–1860*. New Haven, Conn.: Yale University Press, 1957.

Groft, Tammis Kane. *Cast with Style: Nineteenth-Century Cast-Iron Stoves from the Albany Area*. Albany, N.Y.: Albany Institute of History and Art, 1981.

Guthman, William H. "Decorated American militia equipment." *The Magazine Antiques* 126 (August 1984), pp. 124–133.

Hamlin, Talbot. *Benjamin Henry Latrobe*. New York: Oxford University Press, 1955.

Harding, Jonathan P. *The Boston Athenaeum Collection: Pre–Twentieth Century American and European Painting & Sculpture*. Boston: Boston Athenaeum, 1984.

Haskell, Francis, and Nicholas Penny. *Taste and the Antique: The Lore of Classical Sculpture, 1500–1900*. New Haven, Conn.: Yale University Press, 1981.

Hastings, Lynne Dakin. *A Guidebook to Hampton National Historic Site*. Towson, Md.: Historic Hampton, 1986.

Hawley, Henry. *Neo-Classicism, Style and Motif*. Cleveland: Cleveland Museum of Art; New York: Harry N. Abrams, 1964.

Hill, Dorothy Kent. "A Handsome Greek Amphora." *Walters Bulletin* 9:1 (October 1956), pp. 1–3.

Hipkiss, Edward J. *Eighteenth-Century American Arts, The M. and M. Karolik Collection*. Cambridge, Mass.: Harvard University Press, 1941.

Hoffmann, Herbert. "Rhyta and Kanthaoi in Greek Ritual." *Greek Vases in the J. Paul Getty Museum* Vol. 4. Malibu, California: Occasional Papers on Antiquities, 5 (1989), pp. 131–166.

Hood, Graham. *American Silver: A History of Style, 1650–1900*. New York: Praeger Publishers, 1971.

———. "Early neoclassicism in America." *The Magazine Antiques* 140 (December 1991), pp. 978–985.

Hope, Thomas. *Household Furniture and Interior Decoration*. London, 1807.

Howard, Seymour. "Thomas Jefferson's Art Gallery for Monticello." *Art Bulletin* 59 (December 1977), pp. 583–600.

Howat, John K. *Nineteenth Century America: Paintings and Sculpture*. New York: Metropolitan Museum of Art, 1970.

Hunt-Jones, Conover. *Dolley and the "great little Madison."* Washington, D.C.: American Institute of Architects Foundation, 1977.

Idzerda, Stanley J., Anne C. Loveland, and Marc H. Miller. *Lafayette, Hero of Two Worlds: The Art and Pageantry of His Farewell Tour of America, 1824–1825*. Hanover, N.H.: Queens Museum, 1989.

In the Most Fashionable Style: Making a Home in the Federal City. Washington, D.C.: Octagon, 1991.

Jenkins, Ian. "Adam Buck and the vogue for Greek vases." *The Burlington Magazine* 130 (June 1988), pp. 448–457.

Jobe, Brock, et al. *Portsmouth Furniture: Masterworks from the New Hampshire Seacoast*. Boston, Mass.: Society for the Preservation of New England Antiquities, 1993.

Johnson, John. *Typographia*. London, 1824.

Johnston, Sona K. *American Paintings 1750–1900 from the Collection of The Baltimore Museum of Art*. Baltimore: Baltimore Museum of Art, 1983.

Jones, Anita. *Patterns in a Revolution: French Printed Textiles, 1759–1821*. Cincinnati: Taft Museum, 1990.

Jones, Karen M., ed. "Collector's notes." *The Magazine Antiques* 123 (May 1983), pp. 1074–1075.

Kane, Patricia E. "Samuel Gragg: His Bentwood Fancy Chairs." *Yale University Art Gallery Bulletin* 33 (Autumn 1971), pp. 26–37.

————. *300 Years of American Seating Furniture: Chairs and Beds from the Mabel Brady and Other Collections at Yale University*. Boston: New York Graphic Society, 1976.

Kennedy, Roger G. *Greek Revival America*. New York: Stewart, Tabori and Chang, 1990.

Kenney, John Tarrant. *The Hitchcock Chair*. New York: Clarkson N. Potter, Inc., 1971.

Kent, Douglas R. "History in houses: Hyde Hall, Otsego County, New York." *Antiques* 92 (August 1967), pp. 187–193.

Koke, Richard, comp. *American Landscape and Genre Paintings in The New-York Historical Society: A Catalog of the Collection including Historical, Narrative, and Maritime Art*. Vol. 3. New York: New-York Historical Society, 1982.

Larsen, Ellouise Baker. *American Historical Views on Staffordshire China*. 3d ed. New York: Dover Publications, 1975.

Layton, Rachel E. C. "Samuel Williamson's Presentation Silver: Important New Discoveries." *Silver* 25 (January–February 1992), pp. 8–13.

le Bourhis, Katell, ed. *The Age of Napoleon, Costume from Revolution to Empire: 1789–1815*. New York: Metropolitan Museum of Art; Harry N. Abrams, 1989.

Ledoux-Lebard, Denise. *Les Ebénistes du XIX siècle, 1795–1889*. Paris: Editions de l'Amateur, 1965.

Levy, Bernard, and S. Dean Levy. *The New York Chair*. New York: Bernard and S. Dean Levy, 1984.

Lindsay, Kenneth C. *The Works of John Vanderlyn: From Tammany to the Capitol*. Binghamton: University Art Gallery, State University of New York, 1970.

Lindsey, Jack L. "An early Latrobe furniture commission." *The Magazine Antiques* 139 (January 1991), pp. 208–219.

Lipman, Jean, and Alice Winchester. *The Flowering of American Folk Art 1776–1876*. New York: Viking Press, 1974.

Lynn, Catherine. *Wallpaper in America from the Seventeenth Century to World War I*. New York: W. W. Norton and Company, 1980.

McClelland, Nancy. *Duncan Phyfe and the English Regency*. New York: William R. Scott, 1939.

McFadden, David Revere, and Mark A. Clark. *Treasures for the Table: Silver from the Chrysler Museum*. New York: Hudson Hills Press; American Federation of Arts, 1989.

McKearin, George S., and Helen McKearin. *American Glass*. New York: Crown Publishers, 1948.

Made in Ohio: Furniture 1788–1888. Columbus, Ohio: Columbus Museum of Art, 1984.

Mahey, John A. "The Studio of Rembrandt Peale." *American Art Journal* 1 (Fall 1969), pp. 20–40.

M. and M. Karolik Collection of American Watercolors and Drawings 1800–1875. Vol 1. Boston: Museum of Fine Arts, 1962.

Metcalf, Pauline C. *Ogden Codman and the Decoration of Houses*. Boston: David R. Godine; The Boston Athenaeum, 1988.

Michie, Thomas S., and Christopher P. Monkhouse. "Pattern books in the Redwood Library and Athenaeum, Newport, Rhode Island." *The Magazine Antiques* 137 (January 1990), pp. 286–299.

Miller, George L. "George M. Coates, Pottery Merchant of Philadelphia, 1817–1831." *Winterthur Portfolio* 19 (Spring 1984), pp. 37–49.

Miller, J. Jefferson II. *English Yellow-Glazed Earthenware*. Washington, D.C.: Smithsonian Institution Press, 1974.

Monkhouse, Christopher P. "A Temple for Tomes: The Egyptian Elephant Folio Cabinet in The Providence Athenaeum." *Furniture History* (London) 26 (1990), pp. 157–167.

Monkhouse, Christopher P., and Thomas S. Michie. *American Furniture in the Pendleton House*. Providence, R.I.: Museum of Art, Rhode Island School of Design, 1986.

Montgomery, Charles F. *American Furniture: The Federal Period, in The Henry Francis du Pont Winterthur Museum*. New York: Viking Press, 1966.

Montgomery, Florence. *Printed Textiles: English and American Cottons and Linens 1700–1850*. New York: Viking Press, 1970.

Moody, Margaret. "American furniture at Dartmouth College." *The Magazine Antiques* 120 (August 1981), pp. 326–333.

Moses, Henry. *A Collection of Vases, Altars, Paterae, Tripods, Candelabra, Sarcophagi, &c.* London, 1814.

Mount, Charles Merrill. "Gilbert Stuart in Washington: With a Catalogue of His Portraits Painted Between December 1803 and July 1805." In *Records of the Columbia County Historical Society, 1971–1972*, pp. 81–127. Charlottesville: University of Virginia Press, 1973.

Naeve, Milo M., and Lynn Springer Roberts. *A Decade of Decorative Arts: The Antiquarian Society of The Art Institute of Chicago*. Chicago: Art Institute of Chicago, 1986.

Nicholson, Peter, and Michael Angelo Nicholson. *The Practical Cabinetmaker, Upholsterer, and Complete Decorator*. London, 1826.

Nicoll, Jessica F. "'Elegance and Ease': William Hancock's 'Patent Elastic Spring Seat' Rocking Chairs." Paper presented at the "Culture and Comfort" symposium, Strong Museum, Rochester, N.Y., 1988, revised 1989.

Nygren, Edward J. *Views and Visions, American Landscape before 1830*. Washington, D.C.: Corcoran Gallery of Art, 1986.

Nylander, Jane C. "Vose and Coates, Cabinetmakers." *Old Time New England* 64 (Winter–Spring 1974), pp. 87–91.

————. "Some print sources of New England schoolgirl art." *The Magazine Antiques* 110 (August 1976), pp. 292–301.

————. "Henry Sargent's *Dinner Party* and *Tea Party*." *The Magazine Antiques* 121 (May 1982), pp. 1172–1183.

Ostergard, Derek E., ed. *Bent Wood and Metal Furniture: 1850–1946*. New York: American Federation of Arts, 1987.

Owsley, David T. "The American Furniture Collection." *Carnegie Magazine* 50 (June 1976), pp. 261–280.

Padihershef: The Egyptian Mummy. Springfield, Mass.: George Walter Vincent Smith Art Museum, 1984.

Parry, Ellwood C. III. *The Art of Thomas Cole: Ambition and Imagination*. Newark: University of Delaware Press, 1988.

Peale, Rembrandt. *Notes on Italy Written during a Tour in the Year 1829 and 1830*. Philadelphia, 1831.

Pearce, John N., Lorraine W. Pearce, and Robert C. Smith. "The Meeks family of cabinetmakers," *Antiques* 85 (April 1964), pp. 414–420.

Perkins, Robert F., Jr., William J. Garvin III, and Mary M. Shaughnessy, eds. *The Boston Athenaeum Art Exhibition Index, 1827–1874*. Cambridge, Mass.: MIT Press, 1980.

Pictorial Dictionary of British 19th Century Furniture Design. Woodbridge, Suffolk, England: Antique Collectors' Club, 1977.

Poesch, Jessie. *The Art of the Old South: Painting, Sculpture, Architecture & the Products of Craftsmen 1550–1860*. New York: Alfred A. Knopf, 1983.

Reilly, Robin. *Wedgwood*. 2 vols. London: Macmillan London Limited, 1989.

Reilly, Robin, and George Savage. *The Dictionary of Wedgwood*. Woodbridge, Suffolk, England: Antique Collectors' Club, 1980.

Reinhold, Meyer. *Classica Americana: The Greek and Roman Heritage in the United States*. Detroit: Wayne State University Press, 1984.

Rhode Island School of Design Museum Notes 70 (October 1983), p. 20.

Rice, Norman. *New York Furniture before 1840 in the Collection of the Albany Institute of History and Art*. Albany, N.Y.: Albany Institute of History and Art, 1962.

Richards, Nancy E. "The American Academy of Arts, 1802–1818." Master's thesis, University of Delaware, 1965.

Richmond, Helen. *Isaac Hull: A Forgotten American Hero*. Boston: USS Constitution Museum, 1983.

Ring, Betty. "Mrs. Saunders' and Miss Beach's Academy, Dorchester." *The Magazine Antiques* 110 (August 1976), pp. 302–312.

Roth, Rodris. "The Interior Decoration of City Houses in Baltimore, 1783–1812." Master's thesis, University of Delaware, 1956.

Rutledge, Anna Wells. *Artists in the Life of Charleston Through Colony and State from Restoration to Reconstruction*. Transactions of the American Philosophical Society, vol. 39, pt. 2. Philadelphia: American Philosophical Society, 1949.

Sander, Penny J. "Collections of the Society." *The Magazine Antiques* 129 (March 1986), pp. 596–605.

Scherer, John L. *New York Furniture: The Federal Period 1788–1825*. Albany, N.Y.: State University of New York, 1988.

Schwartz, Robert D. *The Stephen Girard Collection: A Selective Catalog*. Philadelphia: Girard College, 1980.

Schweizer, Paul D., ed. *Masterworks of American Art from the Munson-Williams-Proctor Institute*. New York: Harry N. Abrams, 1989.

Scott, Franklin D. *Wertmuller: Artist and Immigrant Father*. Chicago: Swedish Pioneer Historical Society, 1963.

Selections from the Collection of the Carolina Art Association. Charleston, S.C.: Carolina Art Association, 1977.

Sheraton, Thomas. *The Cabinet Dictionary*. 2 vols. 1803. Reprint. New York: Praeger Publishers, 1970.

Simpson, Marc, Sally Mills, and Jennifer Saville. *The American Canvas: Paintings from the Collection of The Fine Arts Museums of San Francisco*. New York: Hudson Hills Press; San Francisco: The Fine Arts Museums of San Francisco, 1989.

Skemer, Don C. "David Alling's Chair Manufactory: Craft Industrialization in Newark, New Jersey, 1801–1854." *Winterthur Portfolio* 22 (Spring 1987), pp. 1–21.

Smith, George. *Collection of Designs for Household Furniture and Interior Decoration*. 1808. Reprint. New York: Praeger Publishers, 1970.

———. *A Collection of Ornamental Designs, after the Manner of the Antique, Compos'd for the Use of Architects, Ornamental Painters. . . .* London: J. Taylor, 1812.

Smith, Philip Chadwick Foster, and Nina Fletcher Little. *Michele Felice Corné, 1752–1845, Versatile Neapolitan Painter of Salem, Boston, and Newport*. Salem, Mass.: Peabody Museum of Salem, 1972.

Smith, Robert C. "Late classical furniture in the United States, 1820–1850." *Antiques* 74 (December 1958), pp. 519–523.

———. "Philadelphia Empire Furniture by Antoine Gabriel Quervelle." *Antiques* 86 (September 1964), pp. 304–309.

———. "The furniture of Anthony G. Quervelle, Part I: The pier table." *The Magazine Antiques* 103 (May 1973), pp. 984–994.

———. "The furniture of Anthony G. Quervelle, Part II: The pedestal tables." *The Magazine Antiques* 104 (July 1973), pp. 90–99.

———. "The furniture of Anthony G. Quervelle, Part III: The worktables." *The Magazine Antiques* 104 (August 1973), pp. 260–268.

———. "The furniture of Anthony G. Quervelle, Part IV: Some case pieces." *The Magazine Antiques* 105 (January 1974), pp. 180–193.

———. "The furniture of Anthony G. Quervelle, Part V: Sofas, chairs, and beds." *The Magazine Antiques* 105 (March 1974), pp. 512–521.

———. "Architecture and sculpture in nineteenth-century mirror frames." *The Magazine Antiques* 109 (February 1976), pp. 314–315, 350–359.

Spillman, Jane Shadel. *American and European Pressed Glass*. Corning, N.Y.: Corning Museum of Glass, 1981.

Springer, Lynn E. "American furniture in the Saint Louis Art Museum." *The Magazine Antiques* 121 (May 1982), pp. 1184–1194.

Staiti, Paul J. *Samuel F. B. Morse*. Cambridge, England: Cambridge University Press, 1989.

Stebbins, Theodore, Jr., et al. *The Lure of Italy: American Artists and the Italian Experience*. Boston: Museum of Fine Arts; New York: Harry N. Abrams, 1992.

Stewart, Patrick L. "The American Empire Style: Its Historical Background." *American Art Journal* 10 (November 1978), pp. 97–105.

Swan, Mabel Munson. *The Athenaeum Gallery 1827–1873*. Boston: Boston Athenaeum, 1940.

Talbott, Page. "The Furniture Industry in Boston, 1810–1835." Master's thesis, University of Delaware, 1974.

———. "Boston Empire furniture." Pts. 1, 2. *The Magazine Antiques* 107, 109 (May 1975, May 1976), pp. 878–887, 1004–1013.

———. "Seating furniture in Boston." *The Magazine Antiques* 139 (May 1991), pp. 956–969.

———. "The Furniture trade in Boston, 1810–1835." *The Magazine Antiques* 141 (May 1992), pp. 842–855.

Tatman, Sandra L., and Roger W. Moss. *Biographical Dictionary of Philadelphia Architects: 1700–1930*. Boston: G. K. Hall & Company, 1985.

Thornton, Peter, and David Watkin. "New Light on the Hope Street Mansion in Duchess Street." *Apollo* 126 (September 1987), pp. 162–177.

Ticknor, George. *Life, Letters, and Journals of George Ticknor*. 2 vols. Edited by George S. Hillard and Anna Ticknor. Boston: James Osgood and Company, 1876.

Tracy, Berry B. *Federal Furniture and Decorative Arts at Boscobel*. Garrison, N.Y.: Boscobel Restoration; New York: Harry N. Abrams, 1981.

Tracy, Berry B., and William H. Gerdts. *Classical America, 1815–1845*. Newark, N.J.: Newark Museum, 1963.

Tracy, Berry B., et al. *Nineteenth-Century America, Furniture and Other Decorative Arts*. New York: Metropolitan Museum of Art, 1970.

Tucker Pattern Books. 2 vols. Rare Books Collection, Library, Philadelphia Museum of Art.

Vance, William L. *America's Rome*. Vol 1. New Haven, Conn.: Yale University Press, 1989.

Venable, Charles L. "Philadelphia Biedermeier, Germanic Craftsmen and Design in Philadelphia, 1820–1850." Master's thesis, University of Delaware, 1986.

———. *American Furniture in the Bybee Collection*. Austin: University of Texas Press; Dallas: The Dallas Museum of Art, 1989.

Vermule, Cornelius. *Numismatic Art in America*. Cambridge, Mass.: Harvard University Press, Belknap Press, 1971.

Wainwright, Clive, et al. *George Bullock, Cabinet-maker*. London: John Murray, 1988.

Ward, Gerald W. R. *American Case Furniture in the Mabel Brady Garvan and Other Collections at Yale University*. New Haven, Conn.: Yale University Art Gallery, 1988.

Warren, David B., Katherine S. Howe, and Michael K. Brown. *Marks of Achievement: Four Centuries of American Presentation Silver*. Houston: Museum of Fine Arts; New York: Harry N. Abrams, 1987.

Waters, Deborah D. "'The Workmanship of an American Artist': Philadelphia's Precious Metals Trades and Craftsmen 1788–1832." Ph.D. diss., University of Delaware, 1981.

Watkin, David. *Thomas Hope and the Neo-Classical Idea*. London: William Clowes and Sons, 1968.

Watkins, Lura Woodside. "Henderson of Jersey City and his pitchers." *The Magazine Antiques* 50 (December 1946), pp. 388–392.

Webster, Thomas, and Mrs. Parkes. *An Encyclopaedia of Domestic Economy*. New York, 1845.

Weidman, Gregory R. *Furniture in Maryland, 1740–1940*. Baltimore: Maryland Historical Society, 1984.

Weis, Frederick L. *Checklist of the Portraits in the Library of the American Antiquarian Society*. Worcester, Mass.: Proceedings of The American Antiquarian Society, 1947.

Wells-Cole, Anthony, et al. *Country House Lighting 1660–1890*. Temple Newsam Country House Studies 4. Leeds, England: Leeds City Art Galleries, 1992.

The White House: An Historic Guide. Washington, D.C.: The White House Historical Association, 1962.

Wick, Wendy C. "Stephen Girard: A Patron of the Philadelphia Furniture Trade." Master's thesis, University of Delaware, 1977.

Wills, Garry. *Cincinnatus: George Washington and the Enlightenment*. New York: Doubleday and Company, 1984.

Wilson, Kenneth M. *New England Glass and Glassmaking*. New York: Thomas Y. Crowell Company, 1972.

Wilton-Ely, John. *The Mind and Art of Giovanni Battista Piranesi*. London: Thames & Hudson, 1978.

Winchester, Alice. "Living with Antiques: The home of Mr. and Mrs. Mitchel Taradash." *Antiques* 63 (January 1953), pp. 44–47.

Wolcott, Cora Codman. *A History of the Codman Collection of Pictures*. Brookline, Mass.: Twin Pines Farm, 1935.

Wood, Elizabeth Ingerman. "Thomas Fletcher: A Philadelphia Entrepreneur of Presentation Silver." *Winterthur Portfolio* 3 (1967), pp. 136–171.

Woodward, E. M. *Bonaparte's Park and the Murats*. Trenton, N.J.: MacCrellish and Quigley, 1989.

Woodward, Roland H., Gainor B. Davis, and Wayne Craven. *Bass Otis, Painter, Portraitist and Engraver*. Wilmington, Del.: Historical Society of Delaware, 1976.

Wright, Nathalia. *Horatio Greenough, the First American Sculptor*. Philadelphia: University of Pennsylvania Press, 1963.

———. "Horatio Greenough's Roman Sketchbook." *Art Quarterly* 26 (Autumn 1963), pp. 323–332.

EXHIBITION CHECKLIST

Key to Checklist

Objects without a number are included in the exhibition but are not illustrated in this book. Numbered objects reference picture caption numbers.

● Baltimore venue only
◆ Houston venue only
∗ Mint venue only
■ Baltimore and Mint venues only
▼ Mint and Houston venues only

1 *Ewer* 1834
Marked by Baldwin Gardiner (1791–1869; working in New York 1827–1848)
Stamped on underside "B•GARDINER" and "NEW•YORK" in serrated rectangles and with three pseudo hallmarks: a head, letter "G," and a lion in clipped rectangles on both sides of mark; inscribed on front below spout "Presented to/Capt. George Maxwell/By/John Hagan/Wm. Oliver/Charles Brugier Jr./in behalf of the Passengers on a Voyage/on board the Ship Europe/Sailed from Liverpool on the/16th March and arrived at/New York on the 8th April 1834"
Silver
H. $16\frac{3}{16}$ in. (41.1 cm.)
Collection Charles Everett

2 *Thomas Jefferson* 1821
Thomas Sully (1783–1872), Philadelphia
Inscribed on back "Painted by T. Sully/1821TS"
Oil on canvas
29 x 18 in. (73.7 x 45.7 cm.)
Diplomatic Reception Rooms, Department of State
Ref.: Conger and Rollins, eds., *Treasures of State*, pp. 415–416.

3 *Armchair* (c. 1800–1810), one of four
French
Mahogany
36½ x 23 x 21¼ in. (92.7 x 58.4 x 54 cm.)
James Monroe Museum, Fredericksburg, Virginia
Ref.: *In the Most Fashionable Style*, p. 10.

4 *Armchair* (c. 1800)
France
Painted and gilded wood
38 x 26¾ x 28 in. (96.6 x 68 x 71.1 cm.)
Courtesy The New-York Historical Society, New York; Gift of Louis Borg, 1867.438
Ref.: Chevallier, *Malmaison*, pp. 158–159, 304, 308, 329, 440.

5 *Armchair* (c. 1800), one of ten
France
Stamped on underside "MEYNARD"
Mahogany, beech
35½ x 23¼ x 23½ in. (90.2 x 59.1 x 59.1 cm.)
Historic Hudson Valley, Tarrytown, New York; Gift of J. Dennis Delafield
Ref.: Butler, "Montgomery Place revisited," pp. 294–303.

Old Age/Winter (c. 1830)
Probably Europe after Albert Bertel Thorwaldsen (1770–1844)
Plaster bas-relief; painted wood
Diam. 35¼ in. (89.6 cm.)
Historic Hudson Valley, Tarrytown, New York; Gift of J. Dennis Delafield

6 *Side Chair* (c. 1820–1830), one of six
New York
Grained and stenciled mahogany veneer, mahogany, ash
32 x 19 x 17½ in. (81.3 x 48.3 x 44.5 cm.)
The Newark Museum; Gift of Mrs. Van Horn Ely, 1965. 65.211
Ref.: Dietz, *Century of Revivals*, p. 16.

8 *Court Train* (c. 1809–1812)
France
Silk velvet embroidered in flat and embossed silver strips and thread
L. 95 in. (241.4 cm.)
The Metropolitan Museum of Art, New York; Gift of Geraldine Shields and Dr. Ida Russel Shields, 1948 (CI 48.41.1)
Ref.: le Bourhis, ed., *Age of Napoleon*, p. 89.

9 *Demi-Parure* (c. 1820)
France or Germany
Iron and cut steel with japanned and gilt decoration
Tiara: 3¾ x 7¼ in. (9.5 x 18.5 cm.); Necklace: L. 18⅞ in. (48 cm.); Earrings: L. 1⅜ in. (3.5 cm.)
Courtesy The Charleston Museum, Charleston, South Carolina
Ref.: Fales, "Jewelry in Charleston," pp. 1224–1225.

10 *Mrs. John Quincy Adams* (Louisa Catherine Johnson Adams) 1816
Charles Robert Leslie (1794–1859), London
Unsigned
Oil on canvas
36½ x 29 in. (92.7 x 73.7 cm.)
Diplomatic Reception Rooms, Department of State
Ref.: Conger and Rollins, eds., *Treasures of State*, pp. 410–411.

11 *Elizabeth Patterson Bonaparte* 1817
François-Joseph Kinson (or Kensoen) (1771–1839), Paris
Inscribed on back "Madame Jerome Bonaparte née Patterson peint à Paris année 1817 par Kinson"
Oil on canvas
$25\frac{9}{16}$ x 21⅜ in. (65 x 54.3 cm.)
Maryland Historical Society, Baltimore; Gift of Mrs. Charles Joseph Bonaparte
Ref.: le Bourhis, ed., *Age of Napoleon*, pp. 232–234.

12 *Dress with Train* (c. 1803–1806)
France
White cotton mull with white cotton embroidery
L. 96¾ in. (245.8 cm.)
The Metropolitan Museum of Art, New York; Purchase, Gifts in memory of Elizabeth N. Lawrence, 1983 (1983.6.1)
Ref.: le Bourhis, ed., *Age of Napoleon*, p. 105; Druesedow, "In Style," pp. 26–27.

13 *Mrs. Robert Gilmor, Jr.* (Sarah Reeve Ladson Gilmor) 1823
Thomas Sully (1783–1872), Baltimore
Signed in lower left "TS 1823"
Oil on canvas; original frame
36¼ x 28 in. (92.1 x 71.1 cm.)
The Gibbes Museum of Art/Carolina Art Association, Charleston, South Carolina
Ref.: *Selections from the Collection of the Carolina Art Association*, p. 88.

14 *Robert Gilmor, Jr.* 1823
Thomas Sully (1783–1872), Philadelphia
Inscribed on back "[ ]/[ ]rence/182[ ]"
Oil on canvas
29⅜ x 24¾ in. (74.6 x 62.9 cm.)
The Baltimore Museum of Art: Gift of Albert Hendler, Bernard R. Hendler, Bernice Hendler Kolodny, and Florence Hendler Trupp, by exchange (BMA 1960.43)
Ref.: Johnston, *American Paintings*, pp. 153–155.

16 *Center Table* (c. 1810–1820)
Probably France
Mahogany, mahogany veneer, elm, *Populus* sp. (poplar/aspen/cottonwood); marble; ormolu
30 x 38 in. (76.2 x 96.6 cm.)
The Walters Art Gallery, Baltimore
Ref.: Nylander, "*Dinner Party* and *Tea Party*," p. 1176

17 *Annular Lamp* (c. 1790), one of a pair
France
Cut glass; ormolu
H. 32 in. (81.3 cm.)
Stephen Girard Collection, Girard College, Philadelphia
Ref.: Schwartz, *Stephen Girard Collection*, no. 67.

● 18 *Pair of Candelabra* (c. 1804–1815)
Rabiat, France
Marked on cast base "Rabiat" in script
Gilt bronze
H. 35¾ in. (90.8 cm.)
The Saint Louis Art Museum: Friends purchase with funds donated by the Measuregraph Company in honor of Henry B. Pflager
Ref.: Springer, "American Furniture," p. 1191.

● 18 *Pair of Pedestals* (c. 1820)
Baltimore
White pine with painted and gilded decoration
H. 36 in. (91.5 cm.)
The Saint Louis Art Museum: Friends purchase with funds donated by the Measuregraph Company in honor of Henry B. Pflager
Ref.: Springer, "American Furniture," p. 1191.

19 *Curtain* (1824), border fragment
France
Silk
7¼ x 29⅜ in. (18.4 x 74.6 cm.)
Society for the Preservation of New England Antiquities, Boston; Gift of Dorothy S.F.M. Codman
Ref.: Cooke et al., *Upholstery in America*,

pp. 254–256.

19 *Curtain Valence* (1824)
France
Silk with wooden mold fringe
19½ x 76 in. (49.5 x 193.1 cm.)
Society for the Preservation of New England Antiquities, Boston; Gift of Dorothy S.F.M. Codman
Ref.: Cooke et al., *Upholstery in America*, pp. 254–256.

Curtain (c. 1805), fragment
Dudding & Co., England
Glazed chintz
17⅜ x 24¼ in. (44.1 x 61.6 cm.)
Collection Cora Ginsburg
Ref.: Cooke et al., *Upholstery in America*, p. 211.

20 *Pair of Vases* (c. 1820)
France, probably Paris
Hard-paste porcelain with polychrome and gilt decoration
H. 28⅞ in. (73.4 cm.); 28¾ in. (73 cm.)
Courtesy Museum of Fine Arts, Boston; Bequest of Miss Clara Endicott Sears
Ref.: Ennès, "Louvre," pp. I–II.

21 *Pair of Vases* (c. 1810–1820)
Marc Schoelcher (1766–1832), Paris
Marked on underside in overglaze black "Schoelcher" and incised "S"
Hard-paste porcelain with polychrome and gilt decoration
H. 13⅜ in. (34 cm.)
Collection Anthony A. P. Stuempfig
Ref.: de Guillebon, *Porcelains of Paris*, pp. 31–35, 174–182.

22 *Tea Service* (c. 1800)
Dihl and Guérhard, Paris
Marked on underside, teapot: "Mf de Guérhard & Dihl [ ] Paris" in overglaze red and "S" in overglaze gold; sugar vase: "Dihl" in underglaze blue; cream pitcher: "Mfre de Dihl et Guérhard à Paris" in overglaze gold; cup and saucer G-C-6a,b: "Mf de Dihl et Guérhard [ ]" in overglaze red
Hard-paste porcelain with marbleized glazes
Teapot H. 5¾ in. (14.6 cm.); Sugar vase H. 6¾ in. (17.2 cm.); Cream pitcher H. 8½ in. (21.6 cm.); 4 cups and saucers H. 2½ in. (6.4 cm.)
Stephen Girard Collection, Girard College, Philadelphia
Ref.: Schwartz, *Stephen Girard Collection*, no. 63.

23 *Teapot, Coffee Cup, and Saucer* (1803)
Wedgwood Manufactory, Staffordshire, England
Incised on underside of each "WEDGWOOD"
Jasperware
Teapot and cover H. 5⅛ in. (13 cm.); Coffee cup and saucer H. 2¹³⁄₁₆ in. (7.1 cm.)
Dyckman House Collection, New York, New York; On permanent loan to Boscobel Restoration Inc., Garrison, New York
Ref.: Tracy, *Boscobel*, pp. 15–17, 130–131.

24 *Fireplace Mantel* (c. 1815)
France
Marble
49 x 70 x 12¾ in. (124.5 x 177.9 x 32.4 cm.)
Museum of Art, Rhode Island School of Design, Providence, Rhode Island; Gift of the Viscountess Rothermore, 82.285
Ref.: *Rhode Island School of Design Museum Notes*, p. 20.

24 *Mantel Clock* (c. 1800–1810)
France
Marble; bronze, ormolu
23¼ x 16⅛ x 7⅝ in. (59.1 x 41 x 19.4 cm.)
Albany Institute of History and Art, Albany, New York; Gift of Mr. and Mrs. Arnold Cogswell, 1967.37
Ref.: *Albany Institute Annual Report 1968*.

24 *Fireboard* (c. 1805)
France
Wove paper, wood
34 x 37⅜ x 1 in. (86.4 x 95 x 2.5 cm.)
Historic Hudson Valley, Tarrytown, New York; Gift of J. Dennis Delafield

25 *Pair of Candlesticks* (1803–1819)
Paris
Stamped on base, shaft, and nozzle of each with silver assay marks for Paris, first standard; maker's mark underside of base unidentified "JGAB" in lozenge; inscribed on flat upper surface of base with an eagle, bow, quiver with arrows, small pond with bird and shield inscribed "PDL"
Silver
H. 11¼ in. (28.6 cm.)
The Historic New Orleans Collection; Gift of Mr. James A. Stouse, 1977.308.6.1–2
Ref.: *Crescent City Silver*, pp. 64–65.

25 *Pair of Candlesticks* (1809–1812), two of at least eight
Jean Simon Chaudron (American, born in France 1758–1846) and Anthony Rasch (American, born in Bavaria 1778–1859), working together 1809–1812, Philadelphia
Stamped on outside edge of base "CHAUDRON'S & RASCH" in curved banner on matted ground and "STER.AMERI.MAN" in banner of similar form; upper surface of base inscribed "UTL" in script; base of shaft adjacent to screw and top of base adjacent to screw socket incised "VII" on 74.3.1 and shaft "IIII" and base "VI" on 74.3.2
Silver
H. 12⅛ in. (30.8 cm.)
Courtesy Winterthur Museum, Winterthur, Delaware
Ref.: Cooper, *In Praise of America*, pp. 258, 261.

25 *Pair of Candlesticks* (1785), from a set of four
Marie-Joseph Gabriel Genu, Paris
Stamped on candlestick and bobèche with silver assay marks for Paris, first standard, 1785; maker's mark "JCMG" in lozenge; inscribed on shaft "SG" in script
Silver
H. 8½ in. (21.9 cm.)
Stephen Girard Collection, Girard College, Philadelphia
Ref.: Schwartz, *Stephen Girard Collection*, no. 79.

26 *Covered Urn* (1819–1838)
Marc Augustin(?) Le Brun, Paris
Stamped with silver assay marks for Paris, first standard; on side of lid, on rim near mouth, and on side of base with laureled head in circle facing left, on outside of base with bearded head in clipped rectangle, maker's mark "ML" in lozenge; inscribed on lid and body "LEH" in script beneath a seated stag crest
Silver
H. 12¾ in. (32.4 cm.)
The Baltimore Museum of Art: Anonymous Gift in Memory of Lydia Howard DeFord (BMA 1969.24a–b)

26 *Ewer* (1819–1838)
Maker's mark "J_CA" not identified, Paris
Stamped with silver assay marks for Paris, first standard: under rim with bearded head in clipped rectangle, on foot rim with laureled head in circle facing left, marker's mark "J_CA" in lozenge on foot rim
Silver
H. 14 in. (35.6 cm.)
Hampton National Historic Site, National Park Service, Towson, Maryland
Ref.: Hastings, *Hampton*, p. 41.

27 *Covered Bowl in Stand* (1817–1834)
Bowl: Edward Lownes (1792–1834), Philadelphia; stand: probably France
Bowl: stamped on underside "E. LOWNES" in a rectangle with a fleur-de-lys above it; stand: unmarked
Silver
H. 7⁹⁄₁₆ in. (19.2 cm.)
Courtesy Winterthur Museum, Winterthur, Delaware

● 28 *The Artist and His Family* 1813
Adam Buck (1759–1833), London
Signed on base of statue at right "ADAM•BUCK•1813•"
Watercolor and graphite on card
17½ x 16½ in. (44.5 x 41.9 cm.)
Yale Center for British Art, Yale University, New Haven, Connecticut; Paul Mellon Collection
Ref.: Jenkins, "Adam Buck."

29 *Shelf Clock* (1817)
Works: Aaron Willard (1757–1844), Boston
Mahogany, pine; églomisé panels; brass
36 x 13½ x 5⅞ in. (91.5 x 34.3 x 14.9 cm.)
Courtesy Museum of Fine Arts, Boston. Gift of Mrs. Charles Wilson, Gift of Mary D. B. Wilson in memory of Charles H. Wilson of Hingham, Massachusetts
Ref.: Fales, *American Painted Furniture*, p. 172.

31 *Side Chair* (c. 1800)
England or Continental Europe
Beech; cane
32½ x 21½ x 24 in. (82.6 x 54.6 x 61 cm.)
The Octagon Museum, The American Architecture Foundation, Washington, D.C.
Ref.: *In the Most Fashionable Style*, pp. 4–5.

32 *John Randolph* (c. 1803–1805)
Gilbert Stuart (1755–1828), Washington, D.C.
Unsigned
Oil on canvas
29⅛ x 24⅛ in. (74 x 61 cm.)
National Gallery of Art, Washington, D.C.; Andrew W. Mellon Collection
Ref.: Mount, "Gilbert Stuart," pp. 81–127.

33 *Sideboard* (1820–1825)
Thomas Cook and Richard Parkin, Philadelphia
Paper label nailed to the backboard of the lower left pedestal end: "COOK & PARKIN/Cabinet and Chair Makers/No. 58/Walnut Street/Between Park & Third Streets/South Side/Philada."
Mahogany, mahogany veneers, white pine, tulip poplar
63¼ x 98½ x 24¾ in. (160.7 x 250.3 x 62.9 cm.)
The Baltimore Museum of Art: Gift from the Estate of Margaret Anna Abell; Gift of Mr. and Mrs. Warren Wilmer Brown; Gift of Jill and M. Austin Fine, Baltimore; Bequest of Ethel Epstein Jacobs, Baltimore; Gift of Mrs. Clark McIllwaine; Gift of William M. Miller and Norville E. Miller II; Bequest of Leonce Rabillon; and Gift of Mr. and Mrs. Louis E. Schecter, by exchange (BMA 1989.26)

33 *Cellarette* (c. 1820)
Baltimore
Mahogany veneer, mahogany
28½ x 21 x 21 in. (72.4 x 53.4 x 53.4 cm.)
Hampton National Historic Site, National Park Service, Towson, Maryland
Ref.: Hastings, *Hampton*, p. 47.

33 *Musidora* (c. 1813)
Thomas Sully (1783–1872)
Signed in lower left "TS" and "B.West."
Oil on panel
22¾ x 18¼ in. (57.8 x 46.4 cm.)
Private Collection, Washington, D.C., on extended loan to The Baltimore Museum of Art (BMA R.9029)

Ref.: von Erffa and Staley, *Benjamin West*, p. 229.

34 *Household Furniture and Interior Decoration* 1807
Thomas Hope (1769–1831), London
Half-leather with marble boards; paper
18½ x 11¹³⁄₁₆ in. (47 x 30 cm.)
Boston Athenaeum; Gift of James Lloyd, 1819

35 *Erinna, A Greek Poetess* 1845
Rembrandt Peale (1778–1860), Philadelphia
Signed in lower right "R.Peale./1845"
Oil on canvas
18½ x 15½ in. (47 x 39.4 cm.)
Collection Dorothy McIlvain Scott, Baltimore: Promised Gift to The Baltimore Museum of Art (BMA R.13178)
Ref.: Mahey, "Rembrandt Peale."

Head of a Roman Woman, from Nature (1832)
Thomas Cole (1801–1848), Rome
Unsigned
Oil on canvas
24½ x 20 in. (62.2 x 50.8 cm.)
The Baltimore Museum of Art: Purchased as the gift of Stiles Tuttle Colwill, Lutherville, Maryland, in Memory of his Mother, Marion Tuttle Colwill (BMA 1992.219)

● 36 *Center Table* (c. 1827–1830)
Anthony Gabriel Quervelle (1789–1856), Philadelphia
Table stamped three times with stenciled label "Anthony Quervelle/Cabinet and Sofa Manufactory/126 So. 2nd Street/PHILAD"; top of brass bun feet stamped "Yates & Hamper" with crown and "G" ("Cabinet brass founders" at 44 Leicester Square L.S., London in 1826–1827); marble top imported from Rome or Florence
Mahogany, mahogany veneer; various marbles; brass top
30⅛ x 46¾ in. (76.6 x 118.8 cm.) (diam. of top)
The Baltimore Museum of Art: Friends of the American Wing Fund, Decorative Arts Fund, and Purchase with exchange funds from: Gift of Mrs. Edwin O. Anderson, Maplewood, New Jersey; Gift of Elizabeth Baer; Gift of Ellen Howard Bayard; Gift of Harrison T. Beacham; Gift of Col. Louis Beck, Baltimore; Gift of Harry C. Black; Gift of David K. E. Bruce, in Memory of Mrs. Dwight F. Davis, Washington, D.C.; Gift of Mrs. W. W. Crocker; Gift of Mr. and Mrs. Johnson Garrett, Washington, D.C.; Gift of Howard M. Greenbaum, Annapolis, Maryland, in Memory of His Father, Harry Greenbaum; Nelson and Juanita Greif Gutman Collection; Gift of Mr. and Mrs. J. Benjamin Katzner, Baltimore; Gift of Mrs. Albert Lowenthal; Gift of Dr. John L. Peck; Gift of Mr. and Mrs. David Stockwell; Gift of Dr. Richard W. TeLinde, Baltimore; Gift of Mr. and Mrs. Bernard Trupp, Baltimore; Gift of William C. Whitridge, Stevenson, Maryland (BMA 1990.73)
Ref.: Smith, "Anthony G. Quervelle, Part I," pp. 992–993; Feld et al., *Neo-Classicism in America*, p. 107, no. 79.

37 *Pier Table* (c. 1810–1825)
Boston
Mahogany veneer; marble mosaic; brass
34¼ x 44½ x 20½ in.
Collection Anthony A. P. Stuempfig
Ref.: Talbott, "The Furniture Industry," p. 144, fig. 10.

38 *"The Travellers," David Sears and Sons* (1833–1834)
Rome
Unsigned
Oil on canvas; original frame
68¾ x 49½ in. (174.7 x 125.8 cm.)
The Penobscot Marine Museum, Searsport, Maine

39 *Horatio Greenough* (c. 1839)
William James Hubard (1807–1862), Florence
Unsigned
Oil on canvas; original frame
36 x 29⅜ in. (91.5 x 74.6 cm.)
Valentine Museum, Richmond, Virginia
Ref.: Greenthal, Kozol, and Ramirez, *American Figurative Sculpture*, pp. 4–7; Wright, *Horatio Greenough*, pp. 201–203.

40 *Inkstand* (c. 1838–1847)
Obadiah Rich (1809–1888), Boston
Stamped on underside of base "O.RICH." in rectangle and incised "fine/BOSTON"
Silver; colorless glass
H. 5⅝ in. (14.3 cm.)
The Fogg Art Museum, Harvard University, Cambridge, Massachusetts; Bequest of Mrs. William Norton Bullard
Ref.: *American Art at Harvard*, no. 176; Fales, "Obadiah Rich," pp. 565–569.

41 *Chafing Dish* (c. 1838–1847)
Attributed to Obadiah Rich (1809–1888), Boston; Retailed by Jones, Ball and Poor, Boston (c. 1838–1847)
Stamped on underside of tray "JONES, BALL & POOR."; "BOSTON"; and "PURE COIN"; each in a rectangle. Engraved on stand top with coat of arms of the Warren Family of Boston.
Silver
3¼ x 6½ in. (8.2 x 16.5 cm.)
Courtesy Winterthur Museum, Winterthur, Delaware
Ref.: Buhler, *American Silver*, p. 437; Fales, "Obadiah Rich," pp. 565–569.

42 *Mrs. John Jones Schermerhorn* (Mary S. Hone) 1837
Thomas Crawford (1811/1813?–1857), Rome
Signed on back "T.Crawford Fec^t-Rome 1837"
Marble
H. 25¼ in. (64.1 cm.)
Courtesy The New-York Historical Society, New York; Gift of Mrs. Mary Schermerhorn Fuller and Robert G. Hone, 1918.28
Ref.: *Catalogue of American Portraits*, p. 697.

43 *Point Breeze, the Estate of Joseph Napoleon Bonaparte at Bordentown, New Jersey* (c. 1817–1820)
Attributed to C. B. Lawrence (c. 1790–c. 1864), Philadelphia
Unsigned
Oil on canvas
27 x 36½ in. (68.6 x 92.7 cm.)
The Art Institute of Chicago; Through prior acquisition of the Friends of American Art Collection, 1987.170
Ref.: Nygren, *Views and Visions*, pp. 272–273.

44 *Pier Table* (c. 1800–1810)
France
Mahogany, mahogany veneer, oak; marble; mirror; ormolu
39 x 72 x 23 in. (99.1 x 182.9 x 58.4 cm.)
Philadelphia Museum of Art; Gift of Edward Hopkinson
Ref.: *The White House*, p. 67.

Joseph Bonaparte 1813
C. S. Pradier, France, after F. Gerard
Inscribed on front "F. Gerard pinx^t" and "C. S. Pradier Sculp^t 1813"
Engraving on paper
22½ x 16 in. (57.1 x 40.7 cm.)
Stephen Girard Collection, Girard College, Philadelphia
Ref.: Schwartz, *Stephen Girard Collection*, no. 87.

45 *Tea Service* (1824–1827)
Louis Decasse and Nicolas Louis Edouard Chanou, New York
Stamped on the underside within a circle "DECASSE & CHANOU." and "New York" separated by large eagle with shield (stamped in red, except for teapot and large plate); incised on underside of large plate "EC No 3/x"
Porcelain with gilt decoration
Teapot H. 6½ in. (16.5 cm.); Stand L. 7⅞ in. (20 cm.); Sugar bowl H. 5⁵⁄₁₆ in. (13.5 cm.); Cream pitcher H. 4¼ in. (10.8 cm.); Cup and saucer H. 2⅜ in. (6 cm.); Plate Diam. 8⁵⁄₁₆ in. (21.1 cm.); Plate Diam. 7⅜ in. (18.7 cm.)
Kaufman Americana Foundation, Norfolk, Virginia
Ref.: Frelinghuysen, *American Porcelain*, pp. 80–82.

46 *George Clinton* 1792
Giuseppe Ceracchi (1751–1801), New York
Unsigned
Terracotta
H. 27½ in. (69.9 cm.)
Courtesy The New-York Historical Society, New York; X.42
Ref.: *Catalogue of American Portraits*, pp. 149–150.

47 *Maria Hester Monroe* 1820
Pietro Cardelli (d. 1822), Washington
Signed "Pr Cardelli f 1820"
Plaster bas-relief
19¾ x 15 in. (50.2 x 38.1 cm.)
James Monroe Museum, Fredericksburg, Virginia

48 *Apollino* (c. 1800–1830)
Probably Italy
Marble
H. 32 in. (81.3 cm.)
The Andalusia Foundation, Andalusia, Pennsylvania
Ref.: Biddle, "Andalusia," p. 1221.

49 *Chancellor Robert R. Livingston* 1804
John Vanderlyn (1775–1852), Paris
Unsigned
Oil on canvas
46¼ x 35¼ in. (117.5 x 89.6 cm.)
Courtesy The New-York Historical Society, New York; Gift of Mrs. Thomson Livingston, 1876.1
Ref.: *Catalogue of American Portraits*, pp. 480–481.

Veduti de Roma (c. 1748–1778)
Giovanni Battista Piranesi (1720–1778), Rome
21⅛ x 17 in. (53.7 x 43.1 cm.)
Private Collection

50 *39 Impressions of Antique Intaglios* (c. 1800–1811), one tray from a set of 24 forming three cases
Probably the Paoletti brothers, Rome
Plaster impressions set with gilt paper mounts, fitted into a wooden tray lined with blue paper
Tray: 13 x 8⅛ in. (33 x 20.6 cm.)
Boston Athenaeum; Gift of Samuel Elam, Newport, Rhode Island, and the Hon. Richard Sullivan, Boston, 1811

48 Impressions of Antique Intaglios (c. 1800–1811), one tray from a set of 24 forming three cases
Probably the Paoletti brothers, Rome
Plaster impressions set with gilt paper mounts, fitted into a wooden tray lined with blue paper
Tray: 13 x 8⅛ in. (33 x 20.6 cm.)
Boston Athenaeum; Gift of Samuel Elam, Newport, Rhode Island, and the Hon. Richard Sullivan, Boston, 1811

51 *Cast of the Portland Vase* (c. 1782)
Cast by James Tassie (1735–1799) from the mold made by Giovanni Pichler, England
Plaster
H. 9¾ in. (24.8 cm.)
Boston Athenaeum; Gift of Francis Calley

Gray, 1830
Ref.: Reilly, *Wedgwood*, vol. 1, pp. 664–665.

52 *Venus* (nineteenth century)
After Antonio Canova (1757–1822), Italy or England
Marble
68 x 21 x 21 in. (172.8 x 53.4 x 53.4 cm.)
Courtesy the Trustees of the Public Library of the City of Boston
Ref.: Cicognara, *Antonio Canova*, pls. 21, 22.

53 *Ceres* 1809
Adolph Ulrich Wertmüller (1751–1811), Philadelphia
Signed in lower right "A. Wertmuller S./Philad. 1809"
Oil on canvas
18 x 14⅞ in. (45.7 x 37.8 cm.)
Westmoreland Museum of Art, Greensburg, Pennsylvania; Gift of William A. Coulter Fund, 74.221
Ref.: Chew, ed., *Permanent Collection*, pp. 141–142.

54 *Ceres* (c. 1808)
François-Joseph Bosio (1768–1845), Paris
Unsigned
Marble
42¹¹⁄₁₆ x 16¼ x 12¹³⁄₁₆ in. (108.5 x 41.3 x 32.6 cm.)
Boston Athenaeum; Bequest of Edmund W. Dana
Ref.: Harding, *Boston Athenaeum Collection*, p. 75; Birch, *Collection of the Late Joseph Bonaparte*, p. 7.

55 *Ariadne Asleep on the Island of Naxos* (1811–1831)
John Vanderlyn (1775–1852), France or United States
Unsigned
Oil on canvas
70 x 87½ in. (177.9 x 222.3 cm.)
Courtesy The New-York Historical Society, New York; Gift of Mrs. Lucy Maria Durand Woodman, 1907.28
Ref.: Koke, comp., *American Landscape and Genre Paintings in the New-York Historical Society*, pp. 208–210.

56 *Caius Marius Amid the Ruins of Carthage* 1832
John Vanderlyn (1775–1852), New York
Signed in lower right "J. Vanderlyn/pinxt.1832/New York."
Oil on panel
32 x 25⅜ in. (81.3 x 64.5 cm.)
Albany Institute of History and Art, Albany, New York
Ref.: Lindsay, *John Vanderlyn*, p. 71; Simpson, Mills, and Saville, *American Canvas*, pp. 56–57.

57 *Italian Landscape* (c. 1805)
Washington Allston (1779–1843), Rome
Signed in lower left "W Allston"
Oil on canvas
40 x 50¾ in. (101.6 x 129 cm.)
Addison Gallery of American Art, Phillips Academy, Andover, Massachusetts
Ref.: Gerdts and Stebbins, *"A Man of Genius,"* p. 47.

Classical Landscape 1804
Germany, after Claude Lorrain (1600–1682)
Engraved "GEMALT von Claude Lorrain, gezeichnet und gestochen in Rom von W.F. Gmelin 1804./SEINER KURFURSTLEICHEN DURCHLAUCHET ZA BRADEN./CARL FREDERICH /Nach dem original- GEMALDE, GENANNT IL MOLINO DI CLAUDIO, IM PALLASE Doria zu Rom. LANGE 9 palm, HOHE 6p: 9z:/Zu finden in Rom begm verfasser und in Mannheim bex Doni Artaria./Unterthangist gewidmet/von W.F. Gmelin."
Engraving on paper
30½ x 36½ in. (77.5 x 92.7 cm.) (sight)
Society for the Preservation of New England Antiquities, Boston. Gift of Dorothy S.F.M. Codman

58 *Dido and Aeneas Going to the Hunt* (c. 1831)
Joshua Shaw (1776–1860), Philadelphia
Oil on canvas
26⅛ x 38½ in. (66.4 x 97.8 cm.)
Munson-Williams-Proctor Institute, Museum of Art, Utica, New York
Ref.: Schweizer, ed., *Masterworks of American Art*, pp. 34–35.

59 *View of the Colosseum* 1723
Fernando Degalli (1657–1743) or a follower of Gaspar Von Wittel (1653–1736)
Illegible signature in lower right
Oil on canvas
27⅞ x 52⅜ in. (70.8 x 133.1 cm.)
Society for the Preservation of New England Antiquities, Boston. Codman House, Lincoln, Massachusetts. Gift of Dorothy S.F.M. Codman
Ref.: Wolcott, *Codman Collection*, p. 62.

60 *Ruins of the Temples at Paestum* 1832
Thomas Cole (1801–1848), New York or Florence
Inscribed on back "T Cole/Florence/1832"
Oil on canvas
16 x 24 in. (40.7 x 61 cm.)
Collection Anthony A. P. Stuempfig
Ref.: Parry, *Thomas Cole*, pp. 126–127; *Exhibition of Paintings by Thomas Cole*, p. 8.

61 *The Tea Party* (c. 1823)
Henry Sargent (1770–1845), Boston
Unsigned
Oil on canvas
64¼ x 52¼ in. (163.3 x 132.8 cm.)
Courtesy Museum of Fine Arts, Boston. Gift of Mrs. Horatio A. Lamb in memory of Mr. and Mrs. Winthrop Sargent
Ref.: Nylander, "*Dinner Party* and *Tea Party*," pp. 1172–1183; *American Paintings in the Museum of Fine Arts, Boston*, no. 852, pl. 154.

62 *The School of Athens* (1780–1800)
Giovanni Joannes Volpato (1733–1803) after Raphael (1483–1520), Rome
Inscribed in bottom margin "PIO SEXTO PONT. MAX"; beneath bottom edge of engraving, on left "Bernardinus Nocchi delineavit" and on right "Joannes Volpato sculptsit, et vendit Roma"
Engraving on paper; original frame
22¾ x 30¼ in. (57.8 x 76.9 cm.) (sight)
Society for the Preservation of New England Antiquities, Boston. Harrison Gray Otis House, Boston. Gift of the children of Arthur and Susan Cabot Lyman

63 *Italian Classical Landscape* 1805
Michel Felice Corné (1752-1832), possibly Boston
Signed "M. Corné.pinxit/1805"
Oil on canvas
35¼ x 59⅜ in. (89.5 x 150.8 cm.) (sight)
Society for the Preservation of New England Antiquities, Boston. Harrison Gray Otis House, Boston. Gift of Sumner Appleton Weld
Ref.: Smith and Little, *Michele Felice Corné*, p. 38.

64 *Fielding Lucas, Jr.* (1808)
Thomas Sully (1783–1872), Philadelphia
Unsigned
Oil on canvas
29 x 24 in. (73.7 x 61 cm.)
The Baltimore Museum of Art: Group of Friends Purchase Fund (BMA 1935.29.1)
Ref.: Johnston, *American Paintings*, pp. 148–150.

65 *Ganymede* (c. 1835)
Possibly Italy
Unsigned
Marble
21 x 12½ x 10⅛ in. (53.4 x 31.8 x 25.7 cm.)
Courtesy Museum of Fine Arts, Boston. Gift of Mrs. Henry Lyman
Ref.: Greenthal, Kozol, and Ramirez, *American Figurative Sculpture*, p. 472.

Mercury (c. 1835)
Possibly Italy
Unsigned
Marble
18 x 13½ x 14⅛ in. (45.7 x 34.3 x 35.9 cm.)
Courtesy Museum of Fine Arts, Boston. Gift of Mrs. Henry Lyman
Ref.: Greenthal, Kozol, and Ramirez, *American Figurative Sculpture*, pp. 472–473.

● 66 *Robert Gilmor, Jr.* (1830–1832)
William James Hubard (1808–1862), Baltimore
Unsigned (suggestion of a signature in lower right on papers near portfolio)
Oil on panel
20 x 14¾ in. (50.8 x 37.5 cm.)
The Baltimore Museum of Art: Charlotte Abbott Gilman Paul Bequest Fund (BMA 1956.287)
Ref.: Johnston, *American Paintings*, pp. 84–85.

67 *Attic Black-Figure Neck-Amphora* (c. 530 B.C.)
Possibly the Antimenes Painter, Athens
Reddish-brown earthenware
H. 21¼ in. (54 cm.)
Private Collection, on loan to The Walters Art Gallery, Baltimore
Ref.: Hill, "A Handsome Greek Amphora," pp. 1–3.

● *Attic Red-Figure Kylix* (c. 470 B.C.), replacement stem and foot
Attributed to the Penthesilea Painter
Foot signed on underside "Nikosthenes" (in ancient Greek); underside of foot with paper label "Fouilles de Canino 1831. Marche triumphale douze fig. jaunes, nom d'Auteur inscrite."
Reddish-brown earthenware
H. 3¾ in. (9.5 cm.)
The University Museum of Archaeology and Anthropology, University of Pennsylvania, Philadelphia; Gift of American Philosophical Society
Ref.: Dinsmoor, "Mediterranean Archaeology," pp. 90–91, fig. 13.

68 *Richard K. Haight Family* (c. 1848)
Attributed to Nicolino Calyo (1799–1884), New York
Unsigned
Gouache on paper
15 x 20 in. (38.1 x 50.8 cm.)
Museum of the City of New York; Bequest of Elizabeth Cushing Iselin, 74.97.2

69 *Center Table* (c. 1820–1830)
Baltimore
Wood grained to simulate rosewood with polychrome, stenciled and freehand gilt decoration; painted composition top; brass
29¾ x 32⅝ in. (75.6 x 82.9 cm.)
The Baltimore Museum of Art: Friends of the American Wing Fund (BMA 1992.214)
Ref.: Elder, *Baltimore Painted Furniture*, p. 54, no. 30.

69 *Lamp Stand* (c. 1820–1830)
Baltimore
Wood grained to simulate rosewood with polychrome, stenciled and freehand gilt decoration; brass
H. 62⅜ in. (158.5 cm.)
The Baltimore Museum of Art: Young Friends of the American Wing Fund (BMA 1992.215)
Ref.: Elder, *Baltimore Painted Furniture*, p. 54, no. 31.

70 *Side Chair* (1810–1820)
Attributed to Duncan Phyfe (1768–1856),

New York
Mahogany, mahogany veneer
32½ x 18½ x 18¾ in. (82.6 x 47 x 47.6 cm.)
Collection Mr. and Mrs. George M. Kaufman
Ref.: Winchester, "Living with Antiques," pp. 44–45.

71 *Side Chair* (1810–1820)
New York
Mahogany
33 3/16 x 18¼ x 15 in. (84.3 x 46.4 x 38.1 cm.)
Museum of the City of New York; Bequest of Mrs. Miles Whiting, 71.120.12a
Ref.: McClelland, *Duncan Phyfe*, pp. 262–263, pl. 248.

72 *Armchair* (1810–1820)
Attributed to Duncan Phyfe (1768–1856), New York
Mahogany
33⅛ x 20⅜ x 16¾ in. (84.1 x 51.8 x 42.6 cm.)
Private Collection
Ref.: Hipkiss, *Eighteenth-Century American Arts*, pp. 180–181, pl. 117.

73 *Side Chair* (1808–1820)
Samuel Gragg (1772–1855), Boston
Stamped on underside of seat rail "S. Gragg/Boston/Patent"
Painted ash and hickory
34⅛ x 18 x 20 in. (86.7 x 45.7 x 50.8 cm.)
Courtesy Museum of Fine Arts, Boston. Charles Hitchcock Tyler Residuary Fund
Ref.: Kane, "Samuel Gragg," pp. 26–37.

74 *Side Chair* (c. 1815–1825), one of a pair
Philadelphia
Mahogany, rosewood, ebony, ash, white pine; brass
33¼ x 19 x 23⅛ in. (84.5 x 48.3 x 58.8 cm.)
Collection Mr. and Mrs. George M. Kaufman
Ref.: Flanigan et al., *Kaufman Collection*, pp. 138–139, no. 50.

76 *Dolley Madison* (c. 1817)
Bass Otis (1764–1861), Washington, D.C.
Unsigned
Oil on canvas
29 x 24 in. (73.7 x 61 cm.) (frame)
Courtesy The New-York Historical Society, New York; Gift of Thomas J. Bryan, 1867.308
Ref: Hunt-Jones, *Dolley*, pp. 32–34.

77 *Side Chair* (c. 1815–1825), one of a pair
Boston
Inscribed on slip seat frame "Formerly belonged to Greenville Temple Winthrop"
Mahogany, birch
33⅛ x 19 x 22⅜ in. (84.2 x 48.3 x 56.9 cm.)
Courtesy Winterthur Museum, Winterthur, Delaware
Ref.: Flanigan et al., *Kaufman Collection*, pp. 140–141, no. 51.

78 *Side Chair* (c. 1808–1810)
Philadelphia
Painted white oak, yellow poplar, white pine; cane
34¼ x 17 11/16 x 20 11/16 in. (87 x 44.9 x 52.6 cm.)
Kaufman Americana Foundation, Norfolk, Virginia
Ref.: Lindsey, "Latrobe furniture commission," pp. 208–219.

78 *Side Chair* (c. 1820–1830), one of original set of twelve
Baltimore
Painted maple and cherry with stenciled and freehand gilt decoration; cane
33⅞ x 20⅜ x 24 3/16 in. (86.1 x 51.8 x 61.5 cm.)
The Baltimore Museum of Art: The George C. Jenkins and Decorative Arts Funds (BMA 1972.46.1)
Ref.: Elder, *Baltimore Painted Furniture*, p. 61.

79 *Side Chair* (c. 1805–1815)
Attributed to Duncan Phyfe (1768–1854), New York
Mahogany
31 x 17½ x 16 in. (78.8 x 44.5 x 40.7 cm.)
Collection Mr. and Mrs. George M. Kaufman
Ref.: Levy, *New York Chair*, p. 43.

79 *Settee* (c. 1800–1810)
New York
Mahogany, ash, cane
34⅝ x 57⅞ x 24¾ in. (88 x 147.1 x 62.9 cm.)
Collection Mr. and Mrs. George M. Kaufman
Ref.: Flanigan et al., *Kaufman Collection*, pp. 152–153, no. 57; Kane, *American Seating Furniture*, pp. 246–247.

80 *Foot Stool* (c. 1810–1815)
New York
Mahogany, ash
17¾ x 19 x 16 in. (45.1 x 48.3 x 40.7 cm.)
Collection Peter G. Terian
Ref.: McClelland, *Duncan Phyfe*, p. 94, pl. 85; Kane, *American Seating Furniture*, p. 216.

81 *Foot Stool* (1836–1837)
Hancock, Holden & Adams, Boston
Paper label on underside
"FURNITURE/AND/UPHOLSTERY WARE-HOUSE./HANCOCK, HOLDEN & ADAMS, UPHOLSTERERS,/No. 37 CORNHILL . . . late [of Ma]rket Street,/boston,/Have on hand, and are constantly manufacturing, every article in the /CABINET AND CHAIR LINE./Orders gratefully received and faithfully executed./Upholstery Goods/of all kinds, and the business as usual attended to in all of its branches./FEATHERS of every description. BEDS, MATRESSES, & c."
Mahogany veneer, white pine
15½ x 20 3/16 x 15¾ in. (39.4 x 51.3 x 40 cm.)
Collection Mr. and Mrs. Stuart P. Feld
Ref: Talbott, "Boston Empire furniture," pt. 2, pp. 1005, 1007.

82 *Portrait of a Seated Boy* 1825
Bass Otis (1764–1861), probably Philadelphia
Signed in lower left "B. Otis 1825"
Oil on canvas
20¾ x 14¾ in. (52.7 x 37.5 cm.)
Westmoreland Museum of Art, Greensburg, Pennsylvania; Gift of William A. Coulter Fund, 60.91
Ref.: Woodward, Davis, and Craven, *Bass Otis*, p. 75.

83 *"Stool"* (c. 1820–1840), or window bench
Attributed to John Finlay (1777–1851) and/or Hugh Finlay (1781–1831), Baltimore
Cherry and walnut painted to simulate rosewood
24 x 72 x 21 in. (61 x 183 x 53.4 cm.)
Collection Mr. and Mrs. George M. Kaufman
Ref.: Montgomery, *American Furniture*, pp. 313–315; Elder, *Baltimore Painted Furniture*, p. 49.

84 *Window Bench* (c. 1808–1810)
Philadelphia or Baltimore
Painted and gilded wood; brass; cane
20⅞ x 52 7/16 x 16 11/16 in. (53 x 133.2 x 42.4 cm.)
Collection Mr. and Mrs. George M. Kaufman
Ref.: Lindsey, "Latrobe furniture commission," pp. 208–219.

85 *Grecian Couch* (c. 1815–1825)
New York
Ebonized wood with stenciled, gilded, and *vert antique* decoration
33⅞ x 89½ x 25¼ in. (78.5 x 227.4 x 64.2 cm.)
The Baltimore Museum of Art: Gift of Cornelia Machen Geddes, Sacramento, California (BMA 1991.147)

86 *Grecian Couch* (c. 1818–1830), one of a pair
Boston
Rosewood with rosewood graining, birch, maple; brass
34⅞ x 70¼ x 23¾ in. (88.6 x 178.5 x 60.3 cm.)
Courtesy Museum of Fine Arts, Boston. Gift of a Friend of the Department, the William N. Banks Foundation, Gift of the Seminarians, Dr. and Mrs. J. W. McMeel, and Anonymous Gift
Ref.: Bates and Fairbanks, *American Furniture*, pp. 278–279. Talbott, "Boston Empire furniture," pt. 1, pp. 881, 885, 887.

87 *Slipcover for Grecian Couch* (1815–1825)
Boston, fabric made by Richard Ovey, London
Glazed chintz
46½ x 27 in. (118.2 x 68.6 cm.)
Society for the Preservation of New England Antiquities, Boston; Gift of William Sumner Appleton
Ref.: Cooke et al., *Upholstery in America*, pp. 254–255.

Upholstery Textile (1815–1825), fragment
Boston, fabric made by Richard Ovey, London
Glazed chintz
38 x 26 in. (96.6 x 66.1 cm.)
Society for the Preservation of New England Antiquities, Boston; Gift of William Sumner Appleton
Ref.: Cooke et al., *Upholstery in America*, pp. 254–255.

88 *Center Table* (c. 1825)
New York
Rosewood veneer with gilt and verte decoration, tulip poplar; scagliola; brass
29 x 36 in. (73.7 x 91.5 cm.)
Museum of the City of New York; Gift of Mrs. Egerton L. Winthrop, 36.160
Ref.: Feld et al., *Neo-Classicism in America*, p. 37.

89 *Bedstead* (c. 1817)
Charles-Honoré Lannuier (1779–1819), New York
Paper labels at the inside of headboard and footboard "H^{re}. Lannuier./Cabinet Maker from Paris/Kips is Whare house of/new fashion fourniture/Broad Street, N°. 60,/New-York./H^{re}. Lannuier/Ebéniste de Paris/Tient Fabrique &/Magasin de Meubles/les plus à la Mode,/New-York."
Mahogany, satinwood, and ash with painted and gilded decoration; ormolu
45½ x 85½ x 60 in. (115.6 x 217.3 x 152.5 cm.)
Albany Institute of History and Art, Albany, New York; Gift of Constance Van Rensselaer Thayer Dexter
Ref: Rice, *New York Furniture*, pp. 12–13, 31–36; Tracy et al., *Nineteenth-Century America*, no. 39.

90 *Crown and Stretcher Supports from a Bedstead* (c. 1810–1815)
Attributed to Charles-Honoré Lannuier (1779–1819), New York
Paper label inside front right rail of bedstead "H^{re}. Lannuier./Cabinet Maker from Paris/Kips is Whare house of/new fashion fourniture/Broad Street, N°. 60,/New-York./H^{re}. Lannuier/Ebéniste de Paris/Tient Fabrique &/Magasin de Meubles/les plus à la Mode,/New-York."

Mahogany; ormolu
Crown: 45 x 7⅞ x 24 in. (114.3 x 20 x 61 cm.)
Bartow-Pell Mansion Museum, Bronx, New York; Gift of Mary Ellis Nevius and Henry S. Peltz
Ref.: Bartlett and Huber, "Bartow-Pell Mansion," p. 1040.

91 *Toile Fragment: "Les Monuments de l'Egypte"* (c. 1808)
Designed by Jean-Baptiste Huet (1745–1811), Jouy, France
Roller-printed cotton
57¼ x 72 in. (146.1 x 183 cm.)
The Baltimore Museum of Art: Gift of Dena S. Katzenberg, Baltimore (BMA 1984.158)
Ref.: Jones, *Patterns in a Revolution*, pp. 18, 30; Brédif, *Printed French Fabrics*, pp. 150–151.

▼ 92 *Sideboard* 1813
Joseph B. Barry (c. 1760–1838, working 1810–1822), Philadelphia
Signed in pencil on underside of bottle carousel "J.B. Barry/1813"
Mahogany, tulip poplar; brass
51¼ x 82¼ x 24¾ in. (130.2 x 209 x 62.9 cm.)
Private Collection
Ref.: Fennimore and Trump, "Joseph B. Barry," p. 1214.

● 93 *Sideboard* (1810–1815)
Attributed to Joseph B. Barry (c. 1760–1838, working 1810–1822), Philadelphia
Mahogany; brass
50⅞ x 87⅝ x 25¾ in. (170.9 x 222.7 x 65.4 cm.)
Courtesy Winterthur Museum, Winterthur, Delaware
Ref.: Fennimore, "Searching for Roots"; Fennimore, "Egyptian influence," pp. 1195, 1198.

93 *Knife Boxes* (1810–1815)
Attributed to Joseph B. Barry (c. 1760–1838, working 1810–1822), Philadelphia
Mahogany; brass
17⅝ x 13½ x 12¾ in. (44.8 x 34.3 x 32.4 cm.)
Courtesy Winterthur Museum, Winterthur, Delaware
Ref.: Fennimore, "Searching for Roots"; Fennimore, "Egyptian influence," pp. 1195, 1198.

● 94 *Card Table* (1819–1824)
Isaac Vose (1767–1823) and Isaac Vose, Jr. (1794–1872), Boston
Stenciled label on bottom of card compartment "ISAAC VOSE & SON/CABINET, Chair &/Furniture Warehouse/ Washington St./BOSTON"
Mahogany, mahogany veneer, oak
29⅛ x 32½ x 18 in. (74 x 82.6 x 45.7 cm.)
The Saint Louis Art Museum; Gift of Mrs. Daniel K. Catlin
Ref.: Springer, "American Furniture," p. 1189; Nylander, "Vose and Coates," pp. 87–91, figs. 1, 2.

95 *Partial Dessert Service* (c. 1800–1825)
Derby Porcelain Works (1756–1848), Derby, England
Marked on underside in underglaze red enamel with crown over crossed batons with six dots and script "D"
Soft-paste porcelain with polychrome and gilt decoration
Covered glacière on stand H. 11⅞ in. (30.2 cm.); Covered tureen on stand H. 6¼ in. (15.9 cm.)
Courtesy Museum of Fine Arts, Boston. Gift of Miss Rosamond Lamb in memory of Mr. and Mrs. Winthrop Sargent
Platter L. 16 in. (40.7 cm.)
Courtesy Museum of Fine Arts, Boston. Gift of the Misses Aimee and Rosamond Lamb

96 *Sugar Tongs* (1825–1828)
Maltby Pelletreau, John Bennett & D. C. Cooke, New York (working together 1825–1828)
Stamped on outside of arm "P.B&C." in a curved-end rectangle and "13" in a circle
Silver
L. 6 in. (15.2 cm.)
Courtesy Winterthur Museum, Winterthur, Delaware; Gift of Sewell C. Biggs

97 *Armchair* (c. 1815–1825)
New York
Ebonized and gilded maple
38 x 26½ x 27¾ in. (96.6 x 67.3 x 70.5 cm.)
Courtesy Winterthur Museum, Winterthur, Delaware
Ref.: Fennimore, "Egyptian influence," pp. 1198, 1201.

98 *Cellarette* (c. 1810–1820)
New York
Rosewood and mahogany veneer, eastern white pine, soft maple, alder, probably ebony, ebonized and gilt decoration; brass
30³⁄₁₆ x 34⁷⁄₁₆ x 21⁷⁄₁₆ in. (76.7 x 87.5 x 54.5 cm.)
The Mabel Brady Garvan Collection, Yale University Art Gallery, New Haven, Connecticut
Ref.: Ward, *American Case Furniture*, pp. 442–444.

99 *Vase* 1829
Marked by Baldwin Gardiner (1791–1869; working in New York 1827–1848), made by Thomas Fletcher (1787–1866), Philadelphia
Stamped on bottom of the upper section and top and bottom of the lower section "B.GARDINER" within a curved band and "NEW YORK" within a curved band; inscribed on front of base "Presented to Hugh Maxwell Esqr. by the Merchants of the City of New York in testimony of/their high opinion of the ABILITY, FIRMNESS, INDUSTRY, PERSEVERANCE & PUBLIC-SPIRIT,/ exhibited by him in the discharge of his duties as District Attorney, A.D. 1829"; on side of base "EXTRACT FROM THE LAST/WILL AND TESTAMENT/ OF/HUGH MAXWELL/WHO DIED/March 31, 1873."; on back side of base "I give to the President of the Law Institute of the City of New York and to his successors in office my silver/vase given as a mark of regard for professional services as District Attorney by the Merchants of the City of/New York while acting as such under the appointment of Governors Tomkins and Clinton. I also/give to the said Institute the portraits of Kent and Emmett, my honored friends."
Silver
24 x 20¹⁄₁₆ x 17¼ in. (61 x 51 x 43.8 cm.)
Courtesy The New-York Historical Society, New York; on permanent loan from the New York Law Institute, L.1959.5
Ref.: Hood, *American Silver*, pp. 197, 200–201.

100 *Side Chair* (c. 1805–1825)
New York
Painted, grained, and stenciled wood, rush; ormolu
32⅛ x 16⅞ x 19¾ in. (81.6 x 42.9 x 50.2 cm.)
The Carnegie Museum of Art, Pittsburgh; Bequest of Mary E. Schenley, 1931
Ref.: Owsley, "American Furniture Collection," pp. 274, 276, 278.

● 101 *Sofa* (1832)
John Finlay (1777–1851), Baltimore
Ebonized and gilded wood, tulip poplar
39 x 82 x 24 in. (99.1 x 208.3 x 61 cm.)
Hampton National Historic Site, National Park Service, Towson, Maryland
Ref.: Hastings, *Hampton*, pp. 40–43.

101 *Side Chair* (1832), one of six
John Finlay (1777–1851), Baltimore
Maple and sweet gum with ebonized and gilt decoration, white pine
33⅜ x 18¾ x 17 in. (84.8 x 47.6 x 43.2 cm.)
Hampton National Historic Site, National Park Service, Towson, Maryland
Ref.: Hastings, *Hampton*, pp. 40–43.

102 *Pier Table* (c. 1830–1840)
New York
Ebonized, gilt, and stenciled wood; marble; mirror
38 x 44 x 18 in. (96.6 x 111.8 x 45.7 cm.)
Kaufman Americana Foundation, Norfolk, Virginia
Ref.: Sotheby's, *Fine American Furniture*, sale 5736, June 23, 1988, lot 487.

103 *Tea and Coffee Service* 1818–1819
Anthony Rasch and Company (working 1807–1809, 1813–1819, 1820), Philadelphia
Stamped on underside of sugar bowl "A. RASCH" in rectangle and unidentified marks on underside of waste bowl consisting of spread eagle flanked by pseudo hallmarks, inscribed on central portion of body of each "In grateful remembrance of the gallantry of Captain Johnston Blakely late of the U.S. Navy who during a short cruise in the sloop of war *Wasp* in the year 1814 captured the two British sloops of war *Reindeer* and *Avon* and was afterwards lost at sea. This plate is presented to his daughter Udney Maria Blakely by the State of North Carolina."
Silver; ebonized wood
Coffee pot H. 11⅛ in. (28.3 cm.); Teapot H. 9⅞ in. (25.1 cm.); Sugar bowl H. 8⅛ in. (20.6 cm.); Cream pitcher H. 9¼ in. (23.5 cm.); Waste bowl H. 6¼ in. (15.9 cm.)
North Carolina Museum of Art, Raleigh; Gift of Mr. and Mrs. Charles Lee Smith, Jr., in honor of Dr. Robert Lee Hunter
Ref.: Warren, Howe, and Brown, *Marks of Achievement*, p. 112.

104 *Tea and Coffee Service* (1841)
Samuel Kirk (1793–1872), Baltimore
Stamped on outside rim of foot "SAM•KIRK" in curved-end rectangle and "11OZ" "S•K" in rectangle; oval Maryland shield and "F" inscribed on lid with McKim crest and "HM^{C}K"
Silver, parcel gilt; ivory or bone
Coffee pot H. 14⅜ in. (36.5 cm.); Teapot H. 9⅜ in. (23.8 cm.) (upper right); Sugar bowl H. 7 in. (17.8 cm.)
National Museum of American History, Smithsonian Institution, Washington, D.C.; Gift of Mrs. William Duncan McKim
Teapot H. 9½ in. (24.1 cm.) (upper left); Cream pitcher H. 8¾ in. (22.2 cm.); Waste bowl H. 6⅛ in. (15.6 cm.)
Maryland Historical Society, Baltimore; Gift of Mrs. William Duncan McKim
Ref.: Goldsborough, *Silver in Maryland*, p. 143; Tracy and Gerdts, *Classical America*, no. 115.

105 *Argand Lamp* (c. 1810–1815)
Probably England, labeled and retailed by Lewis Veron (1793–1853), Philadelphia
Stamped rectangular brass label on argand burner tube "LEWIS VERON/& CO./PHILADELPHIA"
Brass, bronze; glass; marble
H. 24⅜ in. (61.9 cm.)
The Faith P. and Charles L. Bybee Collection, Dallas Museum of Art; Gift of Faith P. Bybee

106 *Wall Clock* (c. 1825–1835)
Works: Aaron Willard (1757–1844),

Boston
Inscribed on dial "Aaron Willard./BOSTON"
Gilt wood; brass; églomisé panels
H. 38½ in. (97.8 cm.)
Private Collection
Ref.: *American Antiques from Israel Sack Collection*, p. 1459.

▼ 107 *Pier Table* (c. 1825–1830)
Attributed to Anthony Gabriel Quervelle (1789–1856), Philadelphia
Mahogany and mahogany veneer with gilt and *vert* decoration; mirror
44 x 50 x 24 in. (111.8 x 127 x 61 cm.)
Private Collection
Ref.: Smith, "Anthony G. Quervelle, Part I," pp. 992–993.

● 108 *Pier Table* (c. 1825–1830)
Attributed to Anthony Gabriel Quervelle (1789–1856), Philadelphia
Mahogany, mahogany veneer with gilt and *vert* decoration; mirror
43¹⁵⁄₁₆ x 50⅛ x 23¹⁵⁄₁₆ in. (111.6 x 127.3 x 60.8 cm.)
Courtesy Winterthur Museum, Winterthur, Delaware
Ref.: Smith, "Anthony G. Quervelle, Part I," pp. 992–993.

109 *Card Table* (1817)
Henry Connelly (1770–1826), Philadelphia
Mahogany, eastern white pine
30 x 36⅜ x 19½ in. (76.2 x 92.4 x 49.5 cm.)
Stephen Girard Collection, Girard College, Philadelphia
Ref.: Schwartz, *Stephen Girard Collection*, no. 23.

110 *Looking Glass* (c. 1835–1845)
New York
Gilt pine; mirror
42 x 37½ in. (106.7 x 95.2 cm.)
Private Collection
Ref.: Smith, "Architecture and sculpture," pp. 314–315, 353.

111 *Girandole Mirror* (c. 1808–1815), one of a pair
Probably London
Gilded pine; mirror; glass; brass
41 x 25¼ x 3⅛ in. (104.2 x 64.2 x 7.9 cm.)
Society for the Preservation of New England Antiquities, Boston. Rundlet-May House, Portsmouth, New Hampshire. Gift of Ralph May
Ref.: Jobe et al., *Portsmouth Furniture*, 1993.

112 *Fish Slice* (1813–1845)
Lewis Quandale (working 1813–1845), Philadelphia
Stamped on back of blade near base "L.QUANDALE" in a rectangle, flanked at each end by a spread eagle within a circle, inscribed "THS/to/MMS" adjacent to mark
Silver; mother-of-pearl
L. 14½ in. (36.8 cm.)
Courtesy Winterthur Museum, Winterthur, Delaware

113 *Pair of Sauceboats* (c. 1817)
Anthony Rasch and Company (working 1807–1809, 1813–1819, 1820), Philadelphia
Stamped "A.RASCH & CO." in a rectangle and "PHILADELPHIA" in a rectangle on 59.152.1, engraved with the crest and arms of the Milligan family of Maryland
Silver
H. 8³⁄₁₆; 8¾ in. (21.3; 22.2 cm.)
The Metropolitan Museum of Art, New York; Sansbury-Mills Fund, 1959 (59.152.1,.2)
Ref.: Tracy and Gerdts, *Classical America*, no. 93; Tracy et al., *Nineteenth-Century America*, no. 37.

114 *Covered Ewer* (1807–1811)
Jean Simon Chaudron (1758–1846), Philadelphia
Stamped under base twice "CHAUDRON" in rectangle and "STER AMER MAN" in ribbon
Silver
H. 16¼ in. (41.3 cm.)
Collection Peter A. Feld

115 *Covered Ewer* (1812–1820)
Thomas Fletcher (1787–1866) and Sidney Gardiner (d. 1827), Philadelphia
Stamped on underside of plinth "FLETCHER & GARDINER" in rectangle and in opposite corner "PHILAD^{a}." in rectangle
Silver
H. 16 in. (40.7 cm.)
Courtesy Winterthur Museum, Winterthur, Delaware

116 *Set of Three Argand Lamps* (c. 1827–1848)
Messenger and Son, Birmingham, England, retailed by Baldwin Gardiner (1791–1869; working in New York 1827–1848)
Stamped on underside "Messenger and Son"; stamped rectangular brass label on argand burner tube "B.GARDINER/N.YORK."
Parcel-gilt bronze; glass
25 x 18½ x 9¾ in. (63.5 x 47 x 24.8 cm.); 21¾ x 13 x 9¾ in. (55.3 x 33 x 24.8 cm.)
The Baltimore Museum of Art: Bequest of Ellen Howard Bayard (BMA 1939.203a–c)

117 *Pair of Argand Lamps* (c. 1830–1840)
Possibly Thomas Messenger (and Sons), Birmingham, England
Bronze; glass
11⅛ x 13 x 6¼ (28.3 x 33 x 15.9 cm.)
Adams National Historic Site, National Park Service, Quincy, Massachusetts
Ref.: Wells-Cole et al., *Country House Lighting*, pp. 145–146.

118 *Pier Table* (1818)
Boston
Rosewood; marble; brass, ormolu; mirror
34¹⁵⁄₁₆ x 50¹¹⁄₁₆ x 23½ in. (88.8 x 128.8 x 59.7 cm.)
Society for the Preservation of New England Antiquities, Boston. Harrison Gray Otis House, Boston. Gift of Miss Edith Standen and Mr. Anthony Standen
Ref.: Sander, "Collections of the Society," p. 601.

118
Pedestal (1818), one of a pair
Boston
Rosewood; gilt brass
H. 47 in. (119.4 cm.)
Society for the Preservation of New England Antiquities, Boston. Harrison Gray Otis House, Boston. Gift of Sumner Appleton Weld
Ref.: Sander, "Collections of the Society," p. 601.

118
The Three Graces (c. 1810–1840)
Possibly Italy
Alabaster
H. 18½ in. (47 cm.)
Society for the Preservation of New England Antiquities, Boston. Harrison Gray Otis House, Boston. Gift of Dorothy S.F.M. Codman
Ref.: Metcalf, *Ogden Codman*, p. 17, pl. 1.

119 *Card Table* (c. 1805–1820)
Attributed to Duncan Phyfe (1768–1856), New York
Stamped "Thomas Cornell Pearsall. Made for him by Duncan Phyfe."
Mahogany, satinwood; brass
31 x 37⅜ x 20 in. (78.8 x 95 x 50.8 cm.)
Collection Peter G. Terian
Ref.: McClelland, *Duncan Phyfe*, p. 290, pl. 278.

120 *Secrétaire à Abattant* (c. 1820–1825)
Boston
Mahogany, mahogany veneer, white pine, tulip poplar; marble; ormolu, brass
57¾ x 52⅜ x 19¹⁄₁₆ in. (146.6 x 133 x 48.3 cm.)
The Art Institute of Chicago; Gift of the Antiquarian Society through Lena Turnbull Gilbert Fund, 1983.30
Ref.: Naeve and Roberts, *Decade of Decorative Arts*, pp. 68–70; Talbott, "Boston Empire Furniture," pt. 2, pp. 1006, 1010, 1012.

121 *Sinumbra Lamp* (1827–1848)
Thomas Messenger and Sons, Birmingham, England, retailed by Baldwin Gardiner (1791–1869; working in New York 1827–1848), New York
Stamped on underside of base "MESSENGER & SONS/BIRMINGHA[M]//[PU]BLISHED AS THE/ACT DIRECTS"; stamped rectangular brass label on argand burner tube "B.GARDINER/N.YORK."
Brass, iron; glass
H. 27¾ in. (70.5 cm.)
Courtesy Winterthur Museum, Winterthur, Delaware

▼ 122 *Pier Table* (1805–1819)
Charles-Honoré Lannuier (1779–1819), New York
Stamped four times on front corner blocks "H. LANNUIER/NEW-YORK"
Rosewood veneer, mahogany, white pine, poplar, ash; ormolu, cast and gilt lead caryatid figures; marble
36 x 50¼ x 22½ in. (91.5 x 127.7 x 57.2 cm.)
The Metropolitan Museum of Art, New York; Rogers Fund, 1953 (1953.181.a,b)

123 *"Portrait of a Child, as Cupid," William Paterson Van Rensselaer, Jr.* (c. 1837)
Francesco Anelli (c. 1805–c. 1878), Albany, New York; frame manufactured by B. G. Whitman, New York, 1837
Portrait, unsigned; frame inscribed "Made by B. G. Whitman, New York 1837 [ ] to 20 Nº 3535 Suffook [ ]"
Oil on canvas; original frame
40¼ x 50¼ in. (102.3 x 127.7 cm.)
Albany Institute of History and Art, Albany, New York; Gift of Justine Bayard Erving

124
Solar Lamp (1843–1849)
Cornelius and Co. (working c. 1840–1851), Philadelphia
Stamped oval label on font "CORNELIUS & CO./PHILAD./PATENT/APRIL 1ST, 1843."
Brass; marble; glass
H. 30½ in. (77.5 cm.)
Private Collection

● 125 *Pier Table* (1816–1819)
Charles-Honoré Lannuier (1779–1819), New York
Stamped twice at the top of each front leg "H.LANNUIER/NEW-YORK"
Mahogany and secondary woods with *vert antique* and gilt decoration; marble; ormolu, brass; mirror
35 x 47¾ x 19⁹⁄₁₆ in. (88.9 x 121.3 x 49.7 cm.)
Collection Peter G. Terian
Ref.: Feld et al., *Neo-Classicism in America*, p. 16; Christie's, *Fine American Furniture*, sale 7214, January 26, 1991, lot 310.

126 *Armchair* (1810–1819), one of a pair
Attributed to Charles-Honoré Lannuier (1779–1819), New York
On the inside of the front seat rail of one of the chairs "Bosley" in chalk
Mahogany with gilt decoration, maple; ormolu
35½ x 22 x 20½ in. (90.2 x 55.9 x 52.1 cm.)
Maryland Historical Society, Baltimore; Bequest of J. B. Noel Wyatt
Ref.: Weidman, *Furniture in Maryland*, pp. 113–114.

127 *Card Table* (c. 1815)

Charles-Honoré Lannuier (1779–1819), New York
Paper label under well "H^{re}. Lannuier./ Cabinet Maker from Paris/Kips is Whare house of/new fashion fourniture/Broad Street, N°. 60,/New-York./H^{re}. Lannuier/Ebéniste de Paris/Tient Fabrique &/Magasin de Meubles/les plus à la Mode,/New-York."
Mahogany veneer, mahogany, rosewood, satinwood, poplar; ormolu, brass
29⅞ x 36 x 21 in. (75.7 x 91.5 x 52.4 cm.)
Valentine Museum, Richmond, Virginia; Bequest of Captain Williams Carter Wickham

128 *Vase* (1816)
Dr. Henry Mead, New York
Soft-paste porcelain
H. 13¹⁄₁₆ in. (35.1 cm.)
Philadelphia Museum of Art: Exchanged with Franklin Institute
Ref.: Frelinghuysen, *American Porcelain*, pp. 78–79.

● 129 *Pair of Vases* (1833–1838)
Tucker and Hemphill or Joseph Hemphill, Philadelphia
Porcelain with painted and gilded decoration; ormolu
H. 22 in. (55.9 cm.)
Philadelphia Museum of Art: Purchased: The Baugh-Barber Fund, the Thomas Skelton Harrison Fund, the Elizabeth Wandell Smith Fund, Funds given in memory of Sophie E. Pennebaker, and Funds contributed by the Barra Foundation, Mrs. Henry W. Breyer, Mr. and Mrs. M. Todd Cooke, the Dietrich Americana Foundation, Mr. and Mrs. Anthony N. B. Garvan, the Philadelphia Savings Fund Society, and Andrew M. Rouse (1984-160-1,2)
Ref.: Frelinghuysen, *American Porcelain*, pp. 98–100.

130 *Two-Handled Vase* (1834–1840)
Attributed to Phoenix Glass Works (1819/1820–1870), South Boston, Massachusetts
Quarter engraved with gilded initials "M.B."
Colorless free-blown glass; 1834–1840 silver eagle quarter
H. 11¾ in. (29.9 cm.)
Los Angeles County Museum of Art; Purchased with Funds provided by the Michael J. Connell Foundation

131 *Covered Vase with Presentation Box* 1816
Jesse Churchill (1773–1819) and Daniel Treadwell (working 1805–1816), Boston
Vase: stamped on underside of base in a corner "Churchill &/Treadwell" in a rectangle, inscribed on front "GRAND LODGE OF MASSACHUSETTS/to/THE REVEREND and RIGHT WORSHIPFUL BROTHER/THADDEUS MASON HARRIS. D. D./PAST GRAND CHAPLAIN and CORRESPONDING SECRETARY./A. L. [*Anno Lucia*, or Year of Light] 5816 [1816]./MEMORIA tenemus quae non rumunerare possumus.
Vase: silver; box: mahogany, chestnut, ebony; ormolu; blue paper lining
Vase H. 14½ in. (36.8 cm.); Box H. 17¾ in. (45.1 cm.)
Collection Mr. and Mrs. Stuart P. Feld
Ref.: Feld et al., *Neo-Classicism in America*, p. 68.

132 *Covered Tureen and Four Matching Covered Sauce Tureens* (c. 1820)
Anthony Rasch and Company (working 1807–1809, 1813–1819, 1820), Philadelphia
Stamped on bottom of each "A. RASCH & CO." and "PHILADELPHIA" in rectangles, the covers and bases of each of the sauce tureens are etched "1," "1"; "2," "2"; "3," "3"; "4," "4"; engraved on lid of each "D.M.S." with crest
Silver
Covered tureen: H. 12 in. (30.5 cm.)
Collection of the Sears Family
4 Covered Sauce tureens: H. 9¾ in. (24.8 cm.)
Collection Mr. and Mrs. Stuart P. Feld
Ref.: Sotheby's, sale 5809, January 27, 1989, lot 892.

133 *Flatware* (1830–1840)
Thomas Fletcher (1787–1866), Philadelphia
Variously stamped on back "T.FLETCHER" and "PHILA." in two rectangles and "T" "F" "P" each on diagonally lined ground in cartouches with head in a circle and eagle within shield in circle; all inscribed on back "B" except fish slice which is inscribed "B" on front
Silver
Fish slice L. 14⅜ in. (36.5 cm.); Serving spoon L. 14⅜ in. (36.5 cm.); Soup spoon L. 8¹⁵⁄₁₆ in. (22.7 cm.); Fork L. 7¾ in. (19.7 cm.); Dessert spoon L. 7⅜ in. (18.7 cm.); Fork L. 6⅞ in. (17.5 cm.); Teaspoon L. 6¹⁄₁₆ in. (15.4 cm.)
Collection Mr. James Biddle

134 *Mrs. George Hyde Clarke* (Ann Low Cary, widow of Richard Fenimore Cooper) (1838)
Charles C. Ingham (1796–1863), New York
Unsigned
Oil on canvas
36 x 29 in. (91.5 x 73.7 cm.)
New York State Historical Association, Cooperstown, New York

135 *Curtain Rod* (1833)
Retailed by Peter Morange, Albany, New York
Gilt pine
L. 139¾ in. (355.1 cm.)
Friends of Hyde Hall, Inc., Otsego County, New York
Ref.: Kent, "History in houses," p. 190.

136 *Chandelier* (1833)
Probably England, retailed by Baldwin Gardiner (1791–1869; working in New York 1827–1848), New York
Stamped brass label on alcohol burner "B.GARDINER/N.YORK."
Cast brass with resin coating; glass
H. 64 in. (162.6 cm.); Diam. 40 in. (101.6 cm.)
Friends of Hyde Hall, Inc., Otsego County, New York

137 *Cake Basket* (1830–1838)
Frederick Marquand and Company (working 1830–1838), New York
Stamped on underside "MARQUAND" and "&C°." in curved rectangles and "NEW•YORK" in curved serrated rectangle
Silver
W. 16½ in. (41.9 cm.)
The Baltimore Museum of Art: Decorative Arts Fund (BMA 1988.6)

138 *Cake Basket* (1813–1825)
Harvey Lewis (working 1813–1825), Philadelphia
Stamped twice on underside "H.LEWIS" in rectangle with serrated ends, engraved label on handle "MSR" in script
Silver
Diam. 10⅛ in. (25.7 cm.)
Private Collection

Cake Basket (c. 1825)
Thomas Fletcher (1787–1866) and Sidney Gardiner (d. 1827), Philadelphia
Stamped on underside "FLETCHER & GARDINER./PHILA" in a circle, exterior of one side of base engraved "R. F. Stockton." in script
Silver
W. 17 in. (43.2 cm.)
The Baltimore Museum of Art: Middendorf Foundation Fund; and Purchase with exchange funds from Gift of Mrs. Daniel Baker, Jr.; Gift of Alberta and Henry G. Burke, Baltimore; Gift of Mrs. W. W. Crocker; Gift of Maria Lovell Eaton and Mrs. Charles R. Weld, from the Estate of Mary M. Eaton; The Mary Frick Jacobs Collection; Gift of Mr. and Mrs. Benjamin Katzner, Baltimore; Bequest of Philip B. Perlman; and Gift of Florence Hendler Trupp, Baltimore (BMA 1993.2)

139 *Pair of Sauceboats on Stands* (c. 1825–1830), from a set of four
Thomas Fletcher (1787–1866), Philadelphia
Stamped on bottom of sauceboat "T. FLETCHER,/PHILAD." in oval; on the bottom of stand "T. FLETCHER" and "PHILA." in rectangles; engraved under mouth of each sauceboat and on top of each stand with the crest from the Pierce family coat of arms; one sauceboat and stand with additional engraving: sauceboat "S. C. P./ to/A. B. P./1895"; stand engraved on the top "S. C. P./1877/TO/A. B. P./1895" and on bottom "Anne R. P. Burroughs.-1855./Sarah C. Kennard.-1877./Anne B. Peirce.-1895."
Silver
Sauceboat H. 8¾ in. (22.2 cm.); Stand L. 10¹⁵⁄₁₆ in. (27.8 cm.)
Collection Elizabeth Feld

140 *"Grecian Shape" Pitcher* (1827–1838)
Tucker Factory (1827–1838), Philadelphia
Porcelain with gilt and polychrome decoration
H. 8½ in. (21.6 cm.)
The Baltimore Museum of Art: Purchase with exchange funds from The Mary Frick Jacobs Collection (BMA 1992.121)
Ref.: Frelinghuysen, *American Porcelain*, pp. 14–20; *Tucker Pattern Books*, vol. 2 n.p.

140 *"Vase Shape" Pitcher* (1827–1838)
Tucker Factory (1827–1838), Philadelphia
Porcelain with gilt and blue decoration
H. 9 in. (22.9 cm.)
The Baltimore Museum of Art: Purchase with exchange funds from Bequest of Elizabeth Arens and Adelaide Arens Morawetz, from the Estate of Henry Arens; Bequest of Ellen Howard Bayard; Nelson and Juanita Greif Gutman Collection; and The Mary Frick Jacobs Collection (BMA 1992.120)
Ref.: Frelinghuysen, *American Porcelain*, pp. 14–20; *Tucker Pattern Books*, vol. 2, n.p.

141 *Spill Vase* (c. 1827–1838)
Paris, decorated at the Tucker Factory (1827–1838), Philadelphia
Porcelain with gilt and green decoration
H. 6¾ in. (17.2 cm.)
The Metropolitan Museum of Art, New York; The Horace W. Goldsmith Foundation Gift, 1991 (1991.325.1,.2)
Ref.: Frelinghuysen, *American Porcelain*, pp. 16–17.

141 *Spill Vase* (1827–1838)
Tucker Factory (1827–1838), Philadelphia
Porcelain with gilt and green decoration
H. 6¾ in. (17.2 cm.)
The Metropolitan Museum of Art; The Horace W. Goldsmith Foundation Gift, 1991 (1991.325.1,.2)
Ref.: Frelinghuysen, *American Porcelain*, pp. 16–17.

142 *Mrs. John Frederick Lewis* (Eliza Mower Lewis) 1827
Jacob Eichholtz (1776–1842), Philadelphia
Inscribed on back, not in artist's hand "Mrs. Eliza Lewis wife of Jno. F. Lewis painted in A.D. 1827 by J. Eichholtz."
Oil on canvas
36 x 28½ in. (91.5 x 72.4 cm.)
Courtesy Pennsylvania Academy of the Fine Arts, Philadelphia; Gift of Mrs. John Frederick Lewis (The John Frederick Lewis Memorial Collection)
Ref.: Beal, *Jacob Eichholtz*, pp. 137–138, 331.

143 *Trade Catalog: Designs for Curtain Pins, Curtain Poles, Drawer Handles, Knob Cupboard Turns, Bed Caps, Cloak Pins, Doorknobs, etc.* (1829–1833)
Thomas Potts (working 1829–1833), Birmingham, England
Paper; leather; brass
6½ x 10 in. (16.5 x 25.4 cm.)
Museum of Art, Rhode Island School of Design, Providence, Rhode Island; Gift of Samuel H. Tingley, 49.088
Ref.: Michie and Monkhouse, "Pattern books," pp. 295, 297.

144 *Pair of Curtain-Rod Ornaments* (c. 1825–1835), from a set of four
England
Stamped brass
H. 11¼ in. (28.6 cm.)
The Faith P. and Charles L. Bybee Collection, Dallas Museum of Art
Ref.: Venable, *American Furniture*, pp. 137–138.

145 *Cap and Collar for Column* (c. 1820–1830)
England or France
Ormolu
H. 2¼ in. (5.7 cm.)
The Metropolitan Museum of Art, New York; Gift of Mrs. Edward Hunting Smith, 1968 (Inst. 68.8.3a,b)

145 *Candle Arm with Cup and Bobèche* (c. 1820–1830)
France
Brass
L. 11½ in. (29.2 cm.)
The Metropolitan Museum of Art, New York; Gift of Mrs. Edward Hunting Smith, 1968 (Inst. 68.8.10a,b)

145 *Backplate with Ring Pull* (c. 1820–1830)
England or France
Brass
L. 4⅞ in. (12.4 cm.)
The Metropolitan Museum of Art, New York; Gift of Mrs. Edward Hunting Smith, 1968 (Inst. 68.8.31a,b)

145 *Decorative Mount* (c. 1820–1830)
England or France
Brass
Diam. 2⅝ in. (6.7 cm)
The Metropolitan Museum of Art, New York; Gift of Mrs. Edward Hunting Smith, 1968 (Inst. 68.8.48)

145 *Mount* (c. 1820–1830)
France
Cast onto backside "TR"
Brass
L. 9½ in. (24.1 cm.)
The Metropolitan Museum of Art, New York; Gift of Mrs. Edward Hunting Smith, 1968 (Inst. 68.8.67)

145 *Pair of Side Mounts* (c. 1820–1830)
France
Brass
L. 2½ in. (6.4 cm.)
The Metropolitan Museum of Art, New York; Gift of Mrs. Edward Hunting Smith, 1968 (Inst. 68.8.76,.77)

146 *"Paper Hanging 42"* 1814
Virchaux and Company, Philadelphia
Inscribed on back "No. 709/Title of "Paper Hanging 42", Number Forty two/ Deposited 7 Dec 1814/by Virchaux & Co as Proprietors"; associated separate sheet of paper inscribed "Number Forty-Two top border for number forty one. Composed of a horizontal garland of green leaves, with a red althea flower in the center and bud, on the top an arch ornamented with pearls, palms, and rosettes, and an eagle with extended wings in gold colour on a purple ground work. The same star as those on the paper number forty one, are repeated between the arch and the garland.// Messrs. Virchaux & Co. intend to execute this design of their own invention on every different ground with correspondent colors, at their Manufactory of Paper Hangings."
Polychrome printed wallpaper
11½ x 28½ in. (29.2 x 72.4 cm.)
Prints and Photographs Division, Library of Congress, Washington, D.C.

"Paper Hanging 66" (1812–1816)
Virchaux and Company, Philadelphia
Associated separate sheet of paper inscribed "Number Sixty Six Ground imitating a garden gate, of open ornamental iron work, gilt, on one side a pilaster forming the intervals./Messrs. Virchaux & Co, by right obtained from Joseph Ramee, intend to execute this design of his invention, on every different ground, with correspondent colours, at their Manufactory of Paper Hangings."
Polychrome printed wallpaper
22¾ x 25 in. (57.8 x 63.5 cm.)
Prints and Photographs Division, Library of Congress, Washington, D.C.

"Paper Hanging 67" (1812–1816)
Virchaux and Company, Philadelphia
Associated separate sheet of paper inscribed "Number Sixty Seven Border for number Sixty Six, forming spears to surmount the columns of the Paper, with a wreath Crowning the pillaster./Ground imitating a garden gate, of open ornamental iron work, gilt, on one side a pilaster forming the intervals./Messrs. Virchaux & Co, by right obtained from Joseph Ramee, intend to execute this design of his invention, on every different ground, with correspondent colours, at their Manufactory of Paper Hangings."
Polychrome printed wallpaper
12¼ x 18¼ in. (31.1 x 46.4 cm.); 24¼ x 18¼ in. (61.6 x 46.4 cm.)
Prints and Photographs Division, Library of Congress, Washinton, D.C.

● *Wallpaper Dado* (c. 1805)
Dufour et Compagnie, France
Block-printed paper
22½ x 63 in. (57.2 x 160.1 cm.)
Cooper-Hewitt Museum, National Museum of Design, Smithsonian Institution, New York; Gift of John Judkyn in memory of his mother, Florence Judkins (1953-213-1)
Ref.: Lynn, *Wallpaper in America*, pp. 140–141, 148, 214, 229, 241.

148 *Counterpoise Lever from a Columbian Printing Press* (c. 1813)
Probably Philadelphia
Cast iron
20 x 50¾ in. (50.8 x 128.9 cm.)
Collection Allan L. Daniel
Ref.: Johnson, *Typographia*, pp. 547–552.

149 *"Palmer's Odoriferous Compound or American Sweet Bag"* (c. 1835–1840)
Massachusetts
Silk
2¾ x 3½ in. (7 x 8.9 cm.)
Courtesy Essex Institute, Salem, Massachusetts
Ref.: *The Oxford English Dictionary*, s.v. "sweet."

150 *United States Currency*
1795 dollar, silver Diam. 1⁹⁄₁₆ in. (4 cm.); 1795 dollar, silver Diam. 1⁹⁄₁₆ in. (4 cm.); 1809 half dollar, silver Diam. 1¼ in. (3.2 cm.); 1809 half dollar, silver Diam. 1¼ in. (3.2 cm.); 1817 cent, copper Diam. 1⅛ in. (2.9 cm.); 1817 cent, copper Diam. 1⅛ in. (2.9 cm.); 1840 dollar, silver Diam. 1⁹⁄₁₆ in. (4 cm.); 1841 dollar, silver Diam. 1⁹⁄₁₆ in. (4 cm.)
Collection The American Numismatic Society, New York
Ref.: Vermule, *Numismatic Art*, pp. 28–36.

United States Currency
Charlotte, North Carolina
1838 $2.50, gold Diam. ¹¹⁄₁₆ in. (1.7 cm.); 1839 $2.50, gold Diam. ¹¹⁄₁₆ in. (1.7 cm.); 1840 $5.00, gold Diam. ¹³⁄₁₆ in. (2.1 cm.); 1841 $5.00, gold Diam. ¹³⁄₁₆ in. (2.1 cm.)
Mint Museum of Art, Charlotte, North Carolina
Ref.: Bridges, "Carolina gold," pp. 1041–1046.

151 *Militia Helmet* (c. 1820–1840)
Donald Fairchild, New Milford, Connecticut
Paper label on interior of cap "DONALD FAIRCHILD,/[ ] LE,/[ ], CAP,/[&],/TRUNK MAKER,/New-Milford, Conn."
Leather; tin; paper
H. 11 in. (28 cm.)
Courtesy Winterthur Museum, Winterthur, Delaware; Gift of Mrs. Alfred C. Harrison
Ref.: Guthman, "Militia equipment," pp. 128–130.

152 *Short Sword and Scabbard* (c. 1833)
N. P. Ames, Springfield, Massachusetts
Blade hilt inscribed "N. [P. AMES] SPRINGFIELD" on one side and "UNITE[D STATES] 183[ ]" on the other, knuckle guard is stamped with inspector's proof marks "ORD." and "HKC." in an oblong cartouche
Steel; brass; leather scabbard
L. 25 in. (63.5 cm.)
Old Sturbridge Village, Sturbridge, Massachusetts

153 *Covered Bandbox* (c. 1830)
United States
Block-printed paper on cardboard; newspaper lining
13 x 17¾ x 14 in. (33 x 45 x 35.6 cm.)
Cooper-Hewitt Museum, National Museum of Design, Smithsonian Institution, New York; Gift of Eleanor and Sarah Hewitt, 1913-17-8a,b
Ref.: Carlisle, *Hat Boxes*, pp. 146–147.

Watch Stand and Watch (c. 1820–1835)
Pennsylvania
Box: rosewood; watch case: silver
11⅝ x 10¾ x 8 in. (29.5 x 23.6 x 20.3 cm.)
Chester County Historical Society, West Chester, Pennsylvania

154 *Pillar Print*, fragment (c. 1830–1835)
England
Cotton chintz
82 x 50 in. (208.4 x 127.5 cm.)
Old Sturbridge Village, Sturbridge, Massachusetts
Ref.: Montgomery, *Printed Textiles*, pp. 324–326.

155 *Tea Service* (c. 1790–1810)
England
Transfer-printed earthenware
Teapot H. 5⅞ in. (14.9 cm.); Sugar bowl H. 5⅞ in. (14.9 cm.); Cream pot H. 6 in. (15.2 cm.); 4 Tea bowls and saucers H. 2½ in. (6.4 cm.)
Old Sturbridge Village, Sturbridge, Massachusetts
Ref.: Miller, *English Yellow-Glazed Earthenware*, p. 36.

156 *Plate* (c. 1820–1840)
Ralph Stevenson (working 1805–1840) and Williams, Cobridge, England
Marked on back in underglaze blue "WATER WORKS/[PHI]LADELPHIA" in two scrolls with "R.S.W." between scrolls
Transfer-printed earthenware
Diam. 10 in. (25.4 cm.)
The Baltimore Museum of Art: Bequest of George C. Jenkins (BMA 1930.65.51)
Ref.: Larsen, *Views on Staffordshire China*, p. 129.

156 *Covered Sauce Tureen, Stand, and Ladle* (1814–1830)
J. and W. Ridgway (working 1814–1830), Hanley, England
Sauce tureen marked on underside in

underglaze blue "BANK SAVANNAH/EXCHANGE CHARLESTON" around a rectangle, tureen lid marked similarly "INSANE HOSPITAL/BOSTON" and stand marked similarly "BANK SAVANNAH"
Transfer-printed earthenware
H. 7¼ in. (18.4 cm.)
The Baltimore Museum of Art: Bequest of George C. Jenkins (BMA 1930.65.199a–b,.200)
Ref.: Larsen, *Views on Staffordshire China*, pp. 88, 90.

157 *Platter* (1829–1836)
James and Ralph Clews (working c. 1819–1836), Cobridge, England
Marked on back in underglaze mulberry "Picturesque Views/Pittsburgh, Pa." and at underside center stamped with mark of Clews factory
Transfer-printed earthenware
L. 19⅞ in. (50.5 cm.)
The Carnegie Museum of Art; AODA Discretionary Fund, 82.49
Ref.: Larsen, *Views on Staffordshire China*, pp. 68–69.

158 *Pitcher* (c. 1830)
David Henderson (working 1828–1845), Jersey City, New Jersey
Marked on underside in raised script "Henderson/a"
Glazed stoneware
H. 10⁵⁄₁₆ in. (26.2 cm.)
New Jersey State Museum; Gift of Rudolph V. Kuser (CH 1991.22.4)
Ref.: "D. & J. Henderson Price List," pp. 108–109; Watkins, "Henderson of Jersey City," pp. 389–390.

Salt Dish (c. 1830–1840)
Probably Boston and Sandwich Glass Company (1825–1888), Massachusetts
Dark amber pressed glass
H. 2 in. (5.1 cm.)
The Corning Museum of Glass, Corning, New York
Ref.: Spillman, *Pressed Glass*, no. 670.

Salt Dish (c. 1830–1840)
Probably New England
Pale green pressed glass
H. 1¾ in. (4.4 cm.)
The Corning Museum of Glass, Corning, New York
Ref.: Spillman, *Pressed Glass*, no. 760.

Salt Dish (c. 1830–1840)
New England
Colorless and silver-stain yellow pressed glass
H. 2 in. (5.1 cm.)
The Corning Museum of Glass, Corning, New York
Ref.: Spillman, *Pressed Glass*, no. 731.

160 *Salt Dish* (c. 1830–1840)
Boston and Sandwich Glass Company (1825–1888), Massachusetts, or New England Glass Company (1818–1888), Cambridge, Massachusetts
Opaque powder-blue pressed glass
H. 1¾ in. (4.4 cm.)
The Baltimore Museum of Art: Purchase with exchange funds from Bequest of C. Edward Snyder (BMA 1993.1)
Ref.: Spillman, *Pressed Glass*, no. 660.

161 *Covered Salt Dish* (c. 1820–1830)
Probably Boston and Sandwich Glass Company (1825–1888), Massachusetts
Colorless pressed glass
H. 3⅛ in. (7.9 cm.)
The Baltimore Museum of Art: Decorative Arts Fund (BMA 1989.333)

162 *Candlestick* (c. 1830–1835)
New England
Colorless pressed glass
H. 8¹³⁄₁₆ in. (22.4 cm.)
The Corning Museum of Glass, Corning, New York; Gift of Louise S. Esterly
Ref.: Spillman, *Pressed Glass*, no. 798.

162 *Covered Casket with Tray* (c. 1830–1840)
Midwest
Colorless pressed glass
H. 5 in. (12.7 cm.)
The Corning Museum of Glass, Corning, New York
Ref.: Spillman, *Pressed Glass*, no. 157.

162 *Compote* (c. 1835–1850)
New England
Colorless pressed glass
H. 5⅝ in. (14.3 cm.)
The Corning Museum of Glass, Corning, New York; Gift of Louise S. Esterly
Ref.: Spillman, *Pressed Glass*, no. 137.

163 *Pair of Lamps* (c. 1830–1840)
New England Glass Company (1818–1888), Cambridge, Massachusetts
Opaque white pressed glass
H. 11⅛ in. (28.3 cm.)
The Corning Museum of Glass, Corning, New York
Ref.: Spillman, *Pressed Glass*, no. 789.

164 *Astral Lamp* (c. 1825–1850)
New England Glass Company (1818–1888), Cambridge, Massachusetts
Amethyst and clear glass; brass; steel
H. 17½ in. (44.5 cm.)
Courtesy Winterthur Museum, Winterthur, Delaware

165 *Two-handled Vase* (c. 1820–1840)
Probably New England
Colorless free-blown glass
H. 5 in. (12.7 cm.)
Old Sturbridge Village, Sturbridge, Massachusetts
Ref.: Wilson, *New England Glass*, pp. 215, 217.

166 *Flask* (c. 1825–1840)
Baltimore Glass Works (1800–1890), Baltimore
Molded into bottle in semicircle above portrait bust of Washington "WASHINGTON" and on reverse in semicircle around Battle Monument of Baltimore "BALTIMORE GLASS WORKS"
Light green blown-molded glass
H. 7⅜ in. (18.7 cm.)
The Corning Museum of Glass, Corning, New York
Ref.: McKearin and McKearin, *American Glass*, p. 517.

167 *Base-burning Stove* (c. 1832)
H. Nott and Company, Albany, New York
Cast into center front panel "NOTT'S PATENT."
Cast iron; isinglass
59 x 29 x 19 in. (149.9 x 73.7 x 48.3 cm.)
New York State Museum, Albany
Ref.: Groft, *Cast with Style*, pp. 21–22, 74.

168 *Trade Advertisement: Joseph Meeks and Sons* 1833
George Endicott and Moses Swett, New York
Hand-colored lithograph on paper
21½ x 17 in. (54.6 x 43 cm.)
The Metropolitan Museum of Art, New York; Gift of Mrs. R. W. Hyde, 1943 (43.15.8)
Ref.: Pearce, Pearce, and Smith, "Meeks family of cabinetmakers," pp. 414–420.

169 *Desk and Bookcase* (c. 1825–1835)
Attributed to John Meads (1777–1859) and William Alvord, Albany, New York (working together c. 1824–1835, partners 1827–1835)
Stamped once at top left rear of upper case and once at top left of lower case with the brand of the Vanderpoel family "J V P" cojoined
Mahogany, mahogany and rosewood veneers, tulip poplar, white pine, maple; brass, ormolu; glass
89¾ x 50½ x 27½ in. (228.1 x 128.3 x 69.9 cm.)
The Baltimore Museum of Art: Young Friends of the American Wing Fund (BMA 1989.616)
Ref.: Christie's, sale 6922, October 21, 1989, lot 291.

170 *The Cabinet Maker's Assistant* (1840)
John Hall, Baltimore. Printed by J. Murphy
5½ x 9¼ in. (14 x 23.5 cm.)
Courtesy The Winterthur Library: Printed Book and Periodical Collection, Winterthur, Delaware

◆ 171 *Man Seated, "Mr. Wing"* (c. 1840)
New England
Unsigned
Watercolor and gouache on paper
17¹⁄₁₆ x 14½ in. (43.4 x 36.8 cm.)
Courtesy M. and M. Karolik Collection of American Watercolors and Drawings, Museum of Fine Arts, Boston .
Ref.: *M. and M. Karolik Collection*, pp. 52–53.

172 *Center Table* (1830–1845)
Joseph W. Meeks and Sons, New York
Original fragmentary paper label on wooden support beneath top now missing
Mahogany veneer, white pine; "Egyptian" marble
29⅛ x 36½ in. (74 x 92.7 cm.)
Melrose, Natchez National Historical Park, National Park Service, Natchez, Mississippi
Ref.: Pearce, Pearce, and Smith, "Meeks family of cabinetmakers," pp. 414–420.

173 *Pier Table* (c. 1840)
John and Joseph W. Meeks (1836–1856), New York
Fragmentary paper label on front face of top rear rail "[ ] & J.W. MEEKS,/ CABINET MAKERS,/[ ]EET, second door bel[ ]/[ ] HOUSE/[ ]W YORK/[ ] STREET,"
Mahogany veneer, white pine; "Egyptian" marble
41¼ x 40 x 21 in. (104.8 x 101.6 x 53.4 cm.)
Collection Milly B. McGehee
Ref.: Scherer, *New York Furniture*, p. 75.

● 174 *Boy with Sinumbra Lamp* (c. 1840)
John Bradley, New York (working 1837–1845)
Oil on canvas
34¼ x 27 in. (87 x 68.6 cm.)
Private Collection
Ref.: Garrett, *At Home*, p. 144.

● 175 *Mrs. Henry Knox Newcomb* (Mary MacCarty Stiles Newcomb) (c. 1835)
Elizabeth (Eliza) Goodridge (1798–1882), Massachusetts
Unsigned
Watercolor on ivory
3⅜ x 2¹¹⁄₁₆ in. (8.8 x 6.8 cm.)
American Antiquarian Society, Worcester, Massachusetts;
Bequest of Miss Harriet E. Clarke, 1944
Ref.: Weis, *Portraits*, no. 87.

175 *Mrs. Henry Knox Newcomb* (Mary MacCarty Stiles Newcomb) (c. 1835)
Elizabeth (Eliza) Goodridge (1798–1882), Massachusetts
Unsigned
Watercolor on ivory
3¾ x 2⅞ in. (9.6 x 7.3 cm.)
American Antiquarian Society, Worcester, Massachusetts;
Bequest of Dwight Foster Dunn, 1937
Ref.: Weis, *Portraits*, no. 88.

176 *Young Man on Scroll Sofa* (c. 1840)
Attributed to Joseph Whiting Stock (1815–1855), New England
Unsigned
Oil on canvas
54 x 40 in. (137.2 x 101.6 cm.)
Private Collection
Ref.: Fairbanks and Bates, *American Furniture*, p. 375.

177 *Chest of Drawers with Looking Glass* 1823
Alexander P. W. Kinnan and States M. Mead, New York
Paper label on reverse of mirror "[FUR]NITURE./KINNAN & MEAD/Have at their Cabinet, Chair, and/Upholstery Ware Houses, 93 and/94 Broad-street, between Pearl and/Stone Streets, a superior and com-/plete assortment of eleg[ant] and high-/ly finished Furnit[ure. So]uthern gentlemen and other[s ar]e respect-/fully invited to call and examine for/themselves./N. B. The above comprises an assortment of elegant Rose-/Wood Furniture and Gentlemen's Portable Writing Desks, of/exquisite workmanship./ New-York, October, 1823."
Mahogany with gilt stenciling; mirror
63 x 36 x 25 in. (170 x 92.5 x 63.5 cm.)
Collection Joseph O. Matthews

178 *Pier Glass* (c. 1825)
John H. Williams, New York
Partially legible paper label affixed to backboard
Pine with gilt decoration; mirror
54 x 28 in. (137.2 x 71.1 cm.)
Museum of the City of New York; Anonymous Gift in memory of Margaret D. Stearns, 89.89
Ref.: Smith,"Architecture and sculpture," p. 355, fig. 11.

179 *Trade Advertisement: T. Palmer & Co., No. 108 Baltimore Street, Baltimore* 1835
John Penniman, Baltimore
Lithograph on paper
12$^{9}/_{16}$ x 16$^{1}/_{16}$ in. (31.9 x 40.8 cm.)
Library of Congress, Washington, D.C.

180 *Rocking Chair* (1829–1835)
William Hancock, Boston, retailed by John Hancock and Company, Philadelphia
Paper label under seat plank "UPHOLSTERY/Furnishing Rooms./John Hancock & Co./UPHOLSTERS,/Southwest Corner of Walnut and Third Streets,/PHILADELPHIA,/Keep all Kinds of Upholstery Goods, and attend/personally to every branch of the business./ALSO, A GREAT VARIETY OF SPLENDID/SPRING SEAT ROCKING CHAIRS,/Which, for ease and comfort, cannot be surpassed./LIKEWISE, THOSE HIGHLY APPROVED/PATENT SWELLED BEAM WINDLASS BEDSTEADS,/ which have so justly acquired a reputation in New York and elsewhere."
Maple and pine with gilt decoration
41 x 24 x 27 in. (104.2 x 61 x 68.6 cm.)
Courtesy Winterthur Museum, Winterthur, Delaware
Ref.: Talbott, "Boston Empire furniture," pt. 2, pp. 1006–1007, 1013; Nicoll, "Elegance and Ease."

181 *Shelf Clock* (c. 1820)
Phineas Deming (c. 1755–), Vienna, Ohio
Paper label inside case "Improved Patent Clocks Made and Sold by Phineas Deming, Vienna, Ohio . . ."
Tiger maple, tulip poplar; painted and gilded wooden dial; églomisé panel
30¼ x 17½ x 5 in. (78.1 x 44.5 x 12.7 cm.)
Collection Walter and Kathryn Sandel
Ref.: *Made in Ohio*, p. 65.

182 *Side Chair* (c. 1820–1830), one of six
Baltimore
Ebonized wood with gilt stencil decoration; ormolu
33¾ x 18 x 23 in. (85.6 x 45.7 x 58.4 cm.)
The Baltimore Museum of Art: Gift of Florence Hendler Trupp, Baltimore (BMA 1977.33.5)

182 *Side Chair* (c. 1820–1840)
Pennsylvania
Ebonized tulip poplar and hickory with painted and gilded decoration
35⅛ x 18$^{7}/_{16}$ x 22 in. (89.3 x 46.8 x 55.9 cm.)
Collection Milton E. Flower

183 *Side Chair* (c. 1832–1843)
Hitchcock, Alford & Co., Hitchcocksville, Connecticut
Stenciled label on back seat rail "Hitchcock, Alford & Co, Hitchcocksville, Conn. Warrented."
Painted and stenciled maple; cane
34½ x 17 x 15½ in. (87.7 x 43.2 x 39.4 cm.)
The Hitchcock Museum, Riverton, Connecticut
Ref.: Kenney, *Hitchcock Chair*, p. 180.

184 *The House and Shop of David Alling, Newark, New Jersey* (c. 1835)
United States
Unsigned
Oil on canvas
18¼ x 26½ in. (47 x 67.3 cm.)
The New Jersey Historical Society; Gift of Mrs. Clarence W. Alling (1928.5)
Ref.: Skemer, "David Alling's Chair Manufactory," pp. 1–21.

185 *Martha Eliza Stevens Edgar Paschall* (c. 1823)
United States
Unsigned
Oil on canvas
52¼ x 40⅜ in. (132.8 x 102.6 cm.) (frame)
National Gallery of Art, Washington, D.C.; Gift of Mary Paschall Young Doty and Katharine Campbell Young Keck
Ref.: Lipman and Winchester, *Flowering of American Folk Art*, pp. 26–27.

186 *Speaker's Armchair* 1823
John and Thomas Constantine, New York
Mahogany; replacement brass casters
35 x 25 x 24 in. (88.9 x 63.5 x 61 cm.)
North Carolina Division of Archives and History, Raleigh, North Carolina
Ref.: Beck, "Senate Speaker's Chair," pp. 25–30.

187 *Sideboard* (1837–1844)
William Alexander, Sharpsburg, Pennsylvania
Stamped four times: on inside bottom of both carved drawers and on the frame directly behind these drawers "W^{M} ALEXANDER"
Mahogany, mahogany veneer, pine; marble; mirror
57¼ x 75¼ x 26¼ in. (146.7 x 191.2 x 66.7 cm.)
Collection David Conrad Hislop
Ref.: Jones, "Collector's notes," pp. 1074–1075.

188 *Ephraim Hubbard Foster Family* (c. 1825)
Ralph E. W. Earl (1788–1838), Tennessee
Unsigned
Oil on mattress ticking; original frame
53$^{3}/_{16}$ x 70$^{1}/_{16}$ in. (135.1 x 178 cm.)
Cheekwood, Tennessee Botanical Gardens and Fine Arts Center, Inc., Nashville; Gift of Mrs. Josephus Daniels (69.2)
Ref.: Poesch, *The Art of the Old South*, pp. 171–172.

189 *Toile Fragment: The Apotheosis of Washington and Franklin* (c. 1785)
England
Inscribed on banderole "WHERE LIBERTY DWELLS THERE IS MY COUNTRY"; on a shield held by the figure of America "AMERICAN/INDEPEND/ANCE/1766"; on a tree "STAMP/ACT/LIBERTY/TREE"; and on the circular building "TEMPLE OF FAME"
Copperplate-printed cotton
95 x 56⅝ in. (241.4 x 143.9 cm.)
Private Collection; on extended loan to The Baltimore Museum of Art (BMA R.12393)
Ref.: Montgomery, *Printed Textiles*, pp. 279–282.

190 *Lafayette and Miss Haywood Viewing Canova's Statue of General George Washington* (c. 1831–1841)
Albert Newsam (1809–1864), Philadelphia, after Joseph Weisman and Emanuel Gottlieb Leutze (1816–1868), published by Peter S. Duval (1831–1879). Lithograph inscribed at bottom "J. Weisman & Leutze, pinx^{t}...P.S. Duval, Lith, Phil^{a}...Drawn on Stone by A. Newsam/CANOVA'S STATUE/OF/GENERAL GEORGE WASHINGTON,/As it appeared on the Pedestal, in the State House Rotunda, at Raleigh, North Carolina./A beautiful light falling from the Dome Window, upon the slab of marble, illuminates the whole Statue. Lafayette is represented viewing this masterly representation of his beloved General./Entered according to Act of Congress in the Year 1840, by J. Weisman, in the Clerk's Office of the District of the Eastern District of P.^{a}" Lithograph on paper
30 x 24 in. (76.2 x 61 cm.)
North Carolina Division of Archives and History, Raleigh, North Carolina
Ref.: *Classical Spirit*, p. 52.

191 *William Strickland* 1829
John Neagle (1796–1865), Philadelphia
Signed in lower center "J. Neagle 1829"
Oil on canvas
30 x 25 in. (76.2 x 63.5 cm.)
Yale University Art Gallery, New Haven, Connecticut; The Mabel Brady Garvan Collection
Ref.: Tracy and Gerdts, *Classical America*, no. 268.

192 *Triumphal Arch in Honor of Lafayette* 1824
Samuel Honeyman Kneass (1806–1858), Philadelphia
Signed in lower left "Samuel H. Kneass"
Watercolor and ink on paper
21¾ x 30⅝ in. (55.3 x 77.8 cm.)
Courtesy Independence National Historical Park Collection, Philadelphia
Ref.: Idzerda, Loveland, and Miller, *Lafayette*, pp. 127–128.

193 *Covered Urn* (1812–1813)
Thomas Fletcher (1787–1866) and Sidney Gardiner (d. 1827), Philadelphia
Inscribed at front lower right face "FLETCHER & GARDINER FECER.^{T} PHILAD.^{A}" and at back center of urn "THE CITIZENS OF PHILADELPHIA, at a meeting convened on the 5th of Sept'r 1812, voted/this Urn, to be presented in their name to CAPTAIN ISAAC HULL, Commander of the/UNITED STATES FRIGATE CONSTITUTION, as a testimonial of their sense of his distinguished/gallantry and conduct, in bringing to action, and subduing the BRITISH FRIGATE GUERRIERE,/on the 19th day of August 1812, and of the eminent service he has rendered to his/Country, by achieving, in the first naval conflict of the war, a most signal and decisive/victory, over a foe that had till then challenged an unrivalled superiority on the/ocean, and thus establishing the claim of our Navy to the affection and confidence/of the Nation./Engraved by W^{m}. Hooker"
Silver
28¼ x 21 x 12½ in. (71.8 x 53.4 x 31.8 cm.)
Collection Hull P. Fulweiler
Ref.: Wood, "Thomas Fletcher," pp. 143–147.

194 *Trade Card: Thomas Fletcher* (c. 1822)
James H. Young and George Delleker, Philadelphia
Inscribed at bottom center "Young & Delleker, sc."
Engraving on wove paper
6$^{11}/_{16}$ x 4$^{5}/_{16}$ in. (17 x 11 cm.) (plate)
The Athenaeum of Philadelphia
Ref.: Wood, "Thomas Fletcher," p. 145.

195 *Dress Sword and Scabbard* 1819
Nathan Starr, Middletown, Connecticut

Engraved on back of hilt "Oui Trans Sust" in banner below three staffs twined with a grapevine; on front of scabbard on oval plaque "Voted by the General Assembly of the State/of Connecticut to their fellow citizen Captain/Isaac Hull in testimony of their sense of his/virtues, gallantry, and naval skill."; on back of scabbard "Made at N.STARRS Man.^{Y}/
Middletown, Conn."; blade etched "N.Starr/Middletown, Conn."
Gilt handle; Damascus steel blade
L. 33½ in. (85.1 cm.)
Collection Hull P. Fulweiler
Ref.: Richmond, *Isaac Hull*, pp. 30–31.

196 *Stephen Decatur* (1814)
Thomas Sully (1783–1872), Philadelphia
Unsigned
Oil on canvas
33¼ x 23½ in. (84.5 x 59.7 cm.)
The Baltimore Museum of Art: Gift of John D. Schapiro (BMA 1976.83)
Ref.: Johnston, *American Paintings*, pp. 150–151.

197 *Candelabrum* 1817
Andrew Ellicott Warner (1786–1870), Baltimore
Stamped on underside "AND^{W}.E.WARNER" in a rectangle followed by "BAL^{T}" and three pseudo hallmarks; engraved on top of pedestal "The Citizens of Baltimore to/Commodore Stephen Decatur/Rebus gestis insigni Obvirtutes dilecto." and on underside of pedestal "Presented by/William Swaim,/To/Mrs. E. Swaim,/And by her, to her daughter,/Mrs. Oliver Hopkinson."
Silver; cut glass
H. 20 in. (50.8 cm.)
Private Collection
Ref.: Brown, "Stephen Decatur Jr."; Cooper, *In Praise of America*, p. 107.

198 *Urn* (c. 1831)
Henry Harland, New Orleans
Stamped on bottom of urn "HARLAND" in a scroll with a star in a circle and "D" in a rectangle at each end and three pseudo hallmarks; engraved on front of urn "To H. M. Dobbs president/of the/New-Orleans Mechanic Society"; on back of urn "Presented by the members in testimony of respect/for 25 years faithful services/Jany 22d 1831"
Silver
H. 9 15/16 in. (25.2 cm.)
Yale University Art Gallery, New Haven, Connecticut; The Mabel Brady Garvan Collection
Ref.: Warren, Howe, and Brown, *Marks of Achievement*, p. 122–124.

199 *Vase* 1832
John Ewan (1786–1852), Charleston, South Carolina
Stamped "J.EWAN" on each of the four sides of the plinth; engraved on front of vase "To the author/of the National Ode written for the 4th of July 1831,/The Rev^{d}. Samuel Gilman/and as a tribute of affectionate respect/for the Patriot the Scholar/the friends of National Union/have presented/THIS VASE./Charleston So. Ca."; on the back of the vase are four stanzas of the Ode written for the Union meeting of July 4, 1831.
Silver
H. 13 in. (33 cm.)
The Museum of Fine Arts, Houston; The Bayou Bend Collection, museum purchase with funds provided by William James Hill and Miss Ima Hogg, by exchange

● 200 *Daniel Webster* (1828–1830; 1849–1851)
Chester Harding (1792–1886), Boston. Frame by John Doggett (1780–1857), Roxbury, Massachusetts
Signed in lower right "C. HARDING 1849"
Oil on canvas; original frame
93¾ x 58 11/16 in. (238.2 x 149.3 cm.)
Boston Athenaeum; Gift of several subscribers, 1832
Ref.: Harding, *Boston Athenaeum Collection*, p. 39.

201 *Vase* 1835
Obadiah Rich (1809–1888) and Samuel L. Ward, Boston (working 1832–1835)
Stamped on left side of plinth "JONES, LOWS & BALL"; "Boston"; "Pure Silver Coin" in italics, and "1835" all in rectangles; engraved on front face of plinth "To DANIEL WEBSTER,/Defender of/the CONSTITUTION of the United States;/From Citizens of BOSTON, October 12th 1835."; inscribed underneath, where body joins the base, beneath a flange of leafage "Made by Ward & Rich Boston, 1835."
Silver
H. 13¾ in. (34.9 cm.)
Courtesy the Trustees of the Public Library of the City of Boston
Ref.: Fales, "Obadiah Rich," pp. 565–569.

202 *Covered Race Cup* 1805
Samuel Williamson (1772–1843), Philadelphia
Stamped four times under the base in each corner and once under the punch bowl "WILLIAMSON"; engraving of horse and rider signed "Francis Shallus, fecit."
Silver, gilt interior
H. 20⅜ in. (51.8 cm.)
Hampton National Historic Site, National Park Service, Towson, Maryland
Ref.: Layton, "Samuel Williamson's Presentation Silver," pp. 8–13.

203 *Regency Covered Race Cup* 1817/1818
Paul Storr (1771–1844), London
Stamped with full hallmarks on side of cup near handle; partial marks on inside of cover and on bottom of finial "PS" (maker's mark); Lion passant (sterling standard); Leopard head crowned (London assay); Roman "b" (Date letter for 1817–1818); engraved around foot "RUNDELL BRIDGE ET RUNDELL AURIFICES REGIS ET PRINCIPIS WALLIAE REGENTIS BRITANNIAS FECERUNT LONDINI" [Made in London by Rundell Bridge and Rundell, Goldsmiths to the King and to the Prince of Wales, Regent of Britain]; engraved on cup within a wreath "Charleston Races/South Carolina/February 1818" and on lid with the directional signs "E S W"
Silver-gilt (sterling standard)
H. 13 in. (33 cm.)
The Chrysler Museum, Norfolk, Virginia; Gift of Walter P. Chrysler, Jr., in honor of Roy B. Martin, Jr.
Ref.: McFadden and Clark, *Treasures for the Table*, p. 20, no. 44.

204 *The Crowning of Flora* (c. 1815)
Jacob Marling (1774–1833), Raleigh, North Carolina
Unsigned
Oil on canvas
30⅛ x 39⅛ in. (76.5 x 99.4 cm.) (frame)
The Chrysler Museum, Norfolk, Virginia; Gift of Edgar William and Bernice Chrysler Garbisch, 80.181.20
Ref.: Deutsch, "Crowning of Flora," pp. 3–4.

206 *Workbox* (c. 1820–1830)
New England
Inlaid maple with polychrome painting
W. 12 in. (30.5 cm.)
From the collections of Henry Ford Museum & Greenfield Village, Dearborn, Michigan
Ref.: Fales, *American Painted Furniture*, p. 181.

● 207 *Needlework Picture: "Telemachus and Mentor in the Island of Calipso"* (1807)
Frances Mecia Campbell at Mrs. Saunders' and Miss Beach's Academy, Dorchester, Massachusetts. Frame by John Doggett (1780–1857), Roxbury, Massachusetts
Painted in gilt on églomisé mat "Wrought by Frances Mecia Campbell...at Mrs. Saunders and Miss Beach's Academy./TELEMACHUS and MENTOR in the ISLAND of CALIPSO"
Silk embroidery and watercolor on silk; original gilt wood frame with églomisé mat
18 x 20½ in. (45.7 x 52.1 cm.) (frame)
The Baltimore Museum of Art: Gift of Mr. and Mrs. James R. Herbert Boone; Gift of Maria Lovell Eaton and Mrs. Charles R. Weld; Gift of J. Gilman D'Arcy Paul; Bequest of John Henry Scarff; Gift of Florence Hendler Trupp, Baltimore; and Gift of the Women's Eastern Shore Society, by exchange (BMA 1989.352)
Ref.: Ring, "Mrs. Saunders' and Miss Beach's Academy," pp. 302–312.

● *Telemachus and Mentor in the Island of Calypso* 1786
Engraved by Francesco Bartolozzi (1727–1815) after a painting by Angelica Kauffmann (1741–1807)
Inscribed on front "Angelica Kauffmann Pinx^{t}...F Bartolozzi Sculpt./TELEMACHUS and MENTOR in the ISLAND of CALYPSO./Calypso takes Mentor aside to speak with him while she employed her most beautiful Nymphs to entertain and amuse/Telemachus, in hopes by their artful address to be able to detain him in her Island./ Telemachus book 7th/From the Original Picture in the Collection of GEORGE BOWLES Esq$^{r.}$ to Whom this Plate is respectfully Dedicated, by his most Obliged Obedient Servant,/Mary Ryland./LONDON, publish'd June 7: 1786 by M.RYLAND, N° 55 the corner of Berner Street, Oxford Street.
Stipple engraving on paper
15⅞ x 18½ in. (40.3 x 47 cm.)
Collection Mr. and Mrs. Richard C. Dabrowski

208 *Needlework Picture: "The Parting of Hector and Andromache"* (c. 1810)
Sally Wheeler, New England
Painted in gilt on églomisé mat "The Parting of Hector and Andromache/by Sally Wheeler"
Silk embroidery and watercolor on silk; original gilt wood frame with églomisé mat
22 x 24 in. (55.9 x 61 cm.) (frame)
Old Sturbridge Village, Sturbridge, Massachusetts; Gift of Dr. Lloyd Hawes, 1972
Ref.: Nylander, "Some print sources," p. 297.

◆ *Needlework Picture: "Disinterestedness of Phocion"* (c. 1815)
Sarah Battelle, at Mrs. Saunders' and Miss Beach's Academy, Dorchester, Massachusetts
Painted in gilt on églomisé mat "Disinterestedness of Phocion./Wrought by Sarah Battelle./At Mrs Saunders and Miss Beach's Academy, Dorchester."
Silk embroidery and watercolor on silk; original gilt wood frame with églomisé mat
12 x 15½ in. (30.5 x 39.4 cm.)
Collection Betty Ring
Ref.: Ring, "Mrs. Saunders' and Miss Beach's Academy," p. 307.

209 *Work Table* (c. 1815–1825)
Boston
Rosewood veneer, mahogany, chestnut; stamped and cast gilt brass
29 x 22 x 18 in. (73.7 x 55.9 x 45.7 cm.)
Hood Museum, Dartmouth College, Hanover, New Hampshire; Gift of Mrs. William Dexter
Ref.: Moody, "American Furniture at Dartmouth College," pp. 326–333.

210 *Work Box* (c. 1830–1847)
Simeon Hazard (1817–1855), Newport,

Rhode Island
Paper label on bottom of box "FURNI-
TURE/AND/Upholstery Warehouse,/SIME-
ON HAZARD,/UPHOLSTERER,/NO. 1 Church
Street, NEWPORT, R.I./Has on hand and is
constantly manufacturing every article in
the/Cabinet and Chair line./Upholstery
Goods/of all kinds, and the business as
usual attended to in all its
branches/Orders thankfully received and
faithfully executed."
Mahogany, mahogany veneer, chestnut,
pine, cedar; ivory
12¼ x 13¾ x 11 in. (31.1 x 34.9 x 28 cm.)
Museum of Art, Rhode Island School of
Design, Providence; Gift of Mr. and Mrs.
John S. Walton (76.198)
Ref.: Monkhouse and Michie, *Pendleton
House*, pp. 74–75.

* 211 *Julia Eliza Montgomery Livingston* (c.
1801–1803 or c. 1815)
John Vanderlyn (1775–1852), New York
Unsigned
Oil on canvas; original frame
27¼ x 22 in. (70.5 x 55.9 cm.)
Collection Richard H. Jenrette

212 *Anacreon Ode LXXII* 1842
Thomas Crawford (1813–1857), Rome
Signed at flattened bottom edge "ANACRE-
ON, ODE LXXII/T. CRAWFORD, FECᵀ ROMA.

1842."
Marble bas-relief
Diam. 26⅜ in. (67 cm.)
Boston Athenaeum; Gift of several sub-
scribers, 1843
Ref.: Harding, *Boston Athenaeum Collection*,
p. 24.

213 *Trade Advertisement: George E. Blake*
(1817–1824)
William Woodruff, Philadelphia
Inscribed on front "W. Woodruff Sᵒ.
Philᵃ./George E. Blake Nᵒ. 13. Sᵒ. 5ᵗʰ. Sᵗ.
Philᵃ./Pianos to Hire…Music
Bound./PIANO-FORTE MAKER. ᶜtᶜ."
Engraving on paper
11½ x 8½ in. (29.2 x 21.6 cm.)
Collection Christopher P. Monkhouse

Sheet Music: "Come Honor the Brave!" (c.
1824)
Published by George E. Blake,
Philadelphia
Inscribed on front "Entered according to
act of Congress the sixth day of September
1824_By G.E. Blake of the State of
Pennsylvania./COME HONOR THE
BRAVE!/Written by Mᴿ. W. STRICKLAND,/
in commemoration of/THE ARRIVAL/OF/
Genˡ. LaFayette,/arranged to a popular
air/BY A. B./Grand civic Arch erecting in
Chestnut street opposite the State House."

Engraving on paper
20¼ x 9¾ in. (51.5 x 24.8 cm.)
Collection Christopher P. Monkhouse

214 *Single-action Harp* (1825–1830)
Schwieso, Grosjean & Co., England
Brass harmonic curve engraved "Schwieso,
Grosjean & Cᵒ #125,/Nᵒ 11 Soho Square
London."
Ebonized and gilded wood; brass, iron
66½ x 17 x 35½ in. (169 x 43.2 x 90.2
cm.)
The Baltimore Museum of Art: Gift of
Wallace Todd (BMA 1972.30)

214 *Cabinet Piano* (1829–1833)
Simon Sweitzer, Philadelphia (working
1829–1833)
Brass plaque above keyboard engraved "S.
SWEITZER/Philadelphia."
Rosewood veneer with gilt stenciling,
pine, tulip poplar, maple; ormolu, brass;
modern silk
76½ x 45½ x 26½ in. (194.4 x 115.6 x
67.4 cm.)
The Baltimore Museum of Art: Young
Friends of the American Wing Fund (BMA
1991.97)

214 *Music Stand* (1830–1840)
United States, possibly Baltimore
Mahogany, mahogany veneer, white pine
37 x 23½ x 15 in. (94 x 59.7 x 38.1 cm.)

The Baltimore Museum of Art: Decorative
Arts Fund (BMA 1988.76)

215 *Piano Stool* (c. 1825–1835)
New York
Mahogany; brass
35 x 16½ x 16½ in. (88.9 x 41.9 x 41.9
cm.)
Collection David Conrad Hislop

216 *Lady with a Harp: Eliza Eichelberger
Ridgely* 1818
Thomas Sully (1783–1872), Philadelphia
Inscribed in lower left on harp pedestal
"TS1818"
Oil on canvas
84⅜ x 56⅛ in. (214.4 x 142.6 cm.)
National Gallery of Art, Washington,
D.C.; Gift of Maude Monell Vetlesen
Ref.: Hastings, *Hampton*, p. 50.

● *Two Ionic Column Capitals from the
Baltimore Exchange* (c. 1816)
United States
Italian marble
17⅝ x 31¼ x 19½ in. (44.8 x 80.7 x 49.5
cm.)
Collection Department of General
Services, State of Maryland, on extended
loan to The Baltimore Museum of Art
(BMA R.10888.1–2)

INDEX